THE NEW CAMBRIDGE COMPANION TO
CHRISTIAN DOCTRINE

What is Christian doctrine? This Companion guides students and scholars through the key issues in the contemporary practice of Christian theology. Including twenty-one essays, specially commissioned from an international team of leading theologians, the volume outlines the central features of Christian doctrinal claims and examines leading methods and theological movements. The first part of the book explores the ten most important topics in Christian doctrine, offering a nuanced historical analysis, as well as charting pathways for further development. In the second part, essays address the most significant movements that are reshaping approaches to multiple topics across disciplinary, as well as denominational and ecclesiastical, borders. Incorporating cutting-edge biblical and historical scholarship in theological argument, this Companion serves as an accessible and engaging introduction to the main themes of Christian doctrine. It will also guide theologians through a growing literature that is increasingly diverse and pluriform.

Michael Allen is the John Dyer Trimble Professor of Systematic Theology and Academic Dean at Reformed Theological Seminary. He is the author, most recently, of *The Fear of the Lord: Essays on Theological Method* and *The Knowledge of God: Essays on God, Christ, and Church.*

T0384594

(continued after the index)

THE NEW CAMBRIDGE COMPANION TO

CHRISTIAN DOCTRINE

Edited by

Michael Allen
Reformed Theological Seminary

CAMBRIDGE
UNIVERSITY PRESS

Shaftesbury Road, Cambridge CB2 8EA, United Kingdom

One Liberty Plaza, 20th Floor, New York, NY 10006, USA

477 Williamstown Road, Port Melbourne, VIC 3207, Australia

314–321, 3rd Floor, Plot 3, Splendor Forum, Jasola District Centre,
New Delhi – 110025, India

103 Penang Road, #05–06/07, Visioncrest Commercial, Singapore 238467

Cambridge University Press is part of Cambridge University Press & Assessment,
a department of the University of Cambridge.

We share the University's mission to contribute to society through the pursuit of
education, learning and research at the highest international levels of excellence.

www.cambridge.org
Information on this title: www.cambridge.org/9781108840446

DOI: 10.1017/9781108885959

First published 2023

A catalogue record for this publication is available from the British Library.

Library of Congress Cataloging-in-Publication Data
NAMES: Allen, Michael, 1981– editor.
TITLE: The New Cambridge companion to Christian doctrine / edited by Michael Allen,
   Reformed Theological Seminary, Florida.
DESCRIPTION: Cambridge, United Kingdom ; New York, NY, USA : Cambridge University
   Press, 2023. | Series: Cambridge companions to religion | Includes bibliographical
   references and index.
IDENTIFIERS: LCCN 2022030201 (print) | LCCN 2022030202 (ebook) | ISBN 9781108840446
   (hardback) | ISBN 9781108794640 (paperback) | ISBN 9781108885959 (epub)
SUBJECTS: LCSH: Theology. | Theology, Doctrinal.
CLASSIFICATION: LCC BR118 .N4835 2023 (print) | LCC BR118 (ebook) | DDC 230–dc23/eng/
   20220715
LC record available at https://lccn.loc.gov/2022030201
LC ebook record available at https://lccn.loc.gov/2022030202

ISBN 978-1-108-84044-6 Hardback
ISBN 978-1-108-79464-0 Paperback

Contents

Contributors

Michael Allen
Reformed Theological Seminary

John Behr
University of Aberdeen

J. Todd Billings
Western Theological Seminary

Daniel Castelo
Duke Divinity School

Oliver Crisp
University of St. Andrews

Tom Greggs
University of Aberdeen

Wesley Hill
Western Theological Seminary

Willie James Jennings
Yale Divinity School

Adam Johnson
Biola University

Kristen Deede Johnson
Western Theological Seminary

Harvey Kwiyani
Global Connections

Matthew Levering
Mundelein Seminary

Ian A. McFarland
Candler School of Theology

Simon Oliver
Durham University

Catherine Pickstock
University of Cambridge

Shelli M. Poe
Iliff School of Theology

Andrea Saner
Eastern Mennonite University

Katherine Sonderegger
Virginia Theological Seminary

John Swinton
University of Aberdeen

Kevin Vanhoozer
Trinity Evangelical Divinity School

Thomas Joseph White
The Angelicum

Preface

The study of Christian doctrine continues into this third millennium without any signs of ceasing. Its practitioners have multiplied and diversified. Its resources – translations and editions of texts produced throughout the centuries and publication of new essays and books from theologians around the globe – expand year by year. Various movements and approaches have arisen in recent years, whether to introduce new concerns or to summon a revival of some older concerns in a fresh way. Significant things are afoot in the world of Christian divinity.

In 1997, Colin Gunton edited the first iteration of this companion. It marked a significant revival of interest in the discipline on the far side of mid-century skepticism about its possibilities, whether in the guise of Bultmannian demythologization or of doctrinal criticism. Its chapters from many mid-career and a few senior voices oriented the student to the passion and principles of the theological task. Twenty-five years have passed, and this *New Cambridge Companion to Christian Doctrine* seeks to serve as a fresh resource that might aid the reader in a like manner for the years ahead. The task of theology is no less important and the need for illuminating initiation into its practice even more necessary today.

Part I focuses upon topics (*loci*) of Christian theological interest. They seek to outline where recent work has turned and to explore its relationship to deeper streams of Christian theological reflection. Entries here turn to scripture, to elements of the historic Christian tradition, and to a range of pertinent conversation partners. They also evince a range of methodological approaches, as contributors to Part I represent a snapshot of ecclesiastical traditions (including Orthodoxy in various Eastern churches, Roman Catholicism, and a spate of Protestant traditions). This new companion seeks to manifest the diversity of ecclesiastical contexts more fully than the first edition.

Part II considers major theological movements or conversations. Some constitute a sensibility or concern though they do not exactly involve a school with a particularly homogenous or unified coherence. Some constitute something with significantly greater commonality, while still other conversations are by their very nature far more diverse. Several of these conversations wind up involving many, if not all, major Christian doctrines. Analytic theology, for instance, has been turned to consider doctrines ranging from theology proper to Christology to anthropology and human moral psychology. Similarly wide-ranging spectrums of attention can be identified for several other movements or disciplinary sensibilities explored in Part II. Attentive readers will observe overlap between Parts I and II at many points, where either topical analysis takes in one or more such movements and their contribution to that theme or where exposition of a given movement unfurls its relevance to particular doctrinal topics.

The companion guides and equips the new practitioner about the old ways and some new opportunities, for Jesus did say that "every scribe who has been trained for the kingdom of heaven is like a master of a house, who brings out of his treasure what is new and what is old" (Matt. 13:52). The chapters that follow span many of the topics that constitute the content of Christian doctrine, though they are not comprehensive in scope. Selections have been made regarding topics and later trajectories or movements to help initiate and equip the reader to engage later with other matters that are not discussed at any length herein. For instance, analogies or parallels between feminist theology and liberation theology, suggest that the chapter on the former will help prepare (though not render moot) later engagement of the latter project in a way that has been prepared by engagement of the former. Each chapter also concludes with a list of further recommended reading, signaling the goal of this companion to help the theologian in training to journey further along the path and to introduce them to a capable host of other texts.

It remains to thank those who have contributed significantly to the production of this companion. It has been a pleasure to work with Beatrice Rehl of Cambridge University Press as well as her capable team. The contributors have all worked diligently to meet deadlines and to fine-tune writing. The value of this volume surely depends on their insight and clarity more than anything else. It goes without saying that while the contributors might agree on a number of things, they also surely diverge from one another (and from the editor) in a range of judgments, both great and small. The companion introduces the student to compelling versions of varied perspectives to Christian doctrine, and it makes no effort to avoid or downplay divergences. It is hoped that engaging each of these chapters will help guide the theological student along a pedagogical path that is marked by skill and good cheer, by real seriousness and abiding hope. Thinking well about God demands no less and, thankfully, continues to promise so much more.

Part I

Doctrines

1 The Triune God

MICHAEL ALLEN

Christian doctrine focuses upon God and the way in which God grants not just life but also meaning to all other things. To turn to the doctrine of God, therefore, is to consider both a particular item of concern (namely, God or *theos*) and a specific way of considering all things (a theological view of all reality). Here we must remember that Christian theology should have both a contemplative and an active element. Contemplative reason considers God for his own sake, seeking to know and to intelligently perceive God as fully and faithfully as possible. This one is worthy of praise and honor and, no less, of our intellectual efforts. Active reason also looks to God, now not simply as a discrete object of study but as the horizon of all studies, casting light on our study of topics ranging from nature itself to human being in particular.

This chapter will introduce Christian thinking about God by addressing four concerns. First, the insistent necessity to attend to the living and true God will be explored, along with its consequent fixation on fleeing idolatry of every sort. Second, the triune nature of the Godhead – Father, Son, and Spirit, equal in honor and glory – will be explored. Third, the self-presentation of this living, triune God as being perfect and transcendent as well as present and near invites reflections on how eternity and history should be related. Fourth, these more specific reflections on this particular God revealed in these specific ways will return us to the exercise of both contemplative and active reasoning in seeking to develop not only a theology of the triune God but also a trinitarian theology of all things.

THE LIVING AND TRUE GOD

First, we begin where Scripture begins: differentiating the living and true God from all rivals and possible peers.[1]

The Bible begins with a creation account that says much about the created order but speaks just as emphatically of the Creator. "In the beginning God" marks out the fundamental reality upon which all else will be said. Some interpreters will interpret that prepositional phrase "in the beginning" not so much to speak as the first moment or the beginning of time itself but as the ongoing fundament and ground of all times and spaces. Whether or not that is the most appropriate rendering of the phrase, the structure of the text does differentiate and prioritize God with respect to all other reality. God's speech ushers created reality into being and order (signaled by the subjunctive "let ..." repeated seven times and followed by the eighth "let us make [hu]man[ity] in our image, after our likeness"). The cosmological account does not itemize everything that might be named, though its span is surely global (taking in the heavens and the earth, every quadrant and category of occupant). Ancient Near Eastern study helps show that the specific references in Genesis 1 refer to created beings that were representative of the deities of that time. Israel's peers might worship the sun, moon, and stars; Genesis 1 clarifies that the Creator God of Israel made them of nothing but by his own Word. There is a whole panoply of gods on offer in the ancient Near East, yet only one God stands as the beginning and the creator of all.

Not only creation but also redemption serves to mark out God's singularity. Significant acts of deliverance occur earlier in Genesis (i.e., the rescue of Israel from famine in the Joseph narrative told in Gen. 37–50) and are later alluded to in the prophets (Amos 9:7). The Exodus account serves, however, as the great paradigm of redemption in the Old Testament and the Bible more broadly. God has heard the cries of the Hebrew slaves and remembered his covenant promises to their ancestors (Exod. 2:23–25). These liberated slaves flee polytheistic Egypt and journey toward pagan Canaan. The polyphony of gods swarms all round them, so it is not surprising that God's instruction will convey his divine jealousy and his legislation will summon them to single-minded devotion. This pedagogical purpose can be seen in two moments, two texts, by peering at Exodus and then at Deuteronomy.

---

[1] For the argument that one must begin with the one true God prior to reflection on either three persons or the incarnation of the Son of God, see especially Katherine Sonderegger, *Systematic Theology, Volume 1: The Doctrine of God* (Minneapolis: Fortress, 2015).

First, the Exodus was intended from its first plotting not only to deliver slaves from Pharaoh's clutches but also to lead them to the worship or service of the LORD (Exod. 3:12 *et passim*). The deliverance comes slowly, surprising for an act of the Almighty Creator. He slowly presses the point through the cycle of ten plagues. What we glean from reading this narrative over against its Egyptian setting, however, shows that this patience plays a pedagogical role. The Lord's slow defeat of Pharaoh takes in ten signs whereby his mastery of the religious icons of Egypt proves potent; whereas Egyptians look to the frog as an insignia of Pharaoh's divine rule, Israel's God shows that he can fashion thousands upon thousands of those beings by a mere word. In so working plague by plague, God shows his "outstretched hand" and "strong arm," terms that had been regularly used to speak of Pharaoh's own might. The Exodus has given not only freedom to Israel but witness to God's singularity as King of Kings and Lord of Lords. Not surprisingly, then, the First Commandment offered atop Sinai to God's people says: "I am the LORD your God, who brought you out of the land of Egypt, out of the house of slavery. You shall have no other gods before me" (Exod. 20:2–3).

Second, the subsequent giving of the law in the book of Deuteronomy will serve as an enduring foundation for Israel's religious devotion and a basis for the ministry of Israel's prophets and kings. Deuteronomy 5 recites the Decalogue as an abiding canon of her ethical pattern. Deuteronomy 6–11 reflects more fully upon that First Commandment. The famous and oft-recited lines of Deut. 6:4–5 offer perhaps the single most significant statement of the oneness of God in the entire Bible: "Hear, O Israel: The LORD our God, the LORD is one. You shall love the LORD your God with all your heart and with all your soul and with all your might." The Exodus puts to death fealty to an exploitative poser in Egypt and brings to life total devotion to the one true God, whose service alone is perfect freedom. Israel is called to hear (Hebrew *shema*) that her LORD is one or singular. While some have argued that this is merely a statement of her monogamous piety, lexical comparison with over 300 parallel constructions leads to reading verse 4 as a metaphysical statement of reality.[2] It speaks not only of Israel having one God but of her God being one or unique.

---

[2] R. W. L. Moberly, "'YHWH Is One': The Translation of the Shema," in *From Eden to Golgotha: Essays in Biblical Theology* (South Florida Studies in the History of Judaism 52; Atlanta: Scholars, 1992), 75–82.

Deut. 6:5 follows and extends this metaphysical point into an ethical corollary: because Israel's God is uniquely divine, all of her life ought to be given unto him – and him alone – in loving devotion. Here too stands a contrast with the ways of Egypt and Canaan alike. In those societies, gods were service providers (over the harvest or fertility or war), and so one's devotion had to be spread widely to cover all the varied needs of one's life. Israel shall not deal with such middlemen but must bow lovingly before the God of all. Jesus will take up this command repeatedly in addressing the rabbinic question regarding the greatest commandment (Mt. 22:38; Lk. 10:27).

This primary theological teaching regarding divine singularity expresses itself methodologically in the divine insistence that the great spiritual error is not atheism but idolatry. Even the Christian – like the non-Christian – continues to flirt with the tendency to remake God in one's own image for, as John Calvin said, our "nature, so to speak, is a perpetual factory of idols."[3] Theology bears a purgative and ascetical task, then, in fixing its sights upon the self-revelation on the one true God, alert and intent to have its own prejudiced presumptions challenged.

THE TRIUNITY OF GOD

Second: the living and true God reveals himself as Father, Son, and Holy Spirit, without in the least qualifying or compromising this one's singularity and oneness, therefore prompting us to reflect on what it would mean for God to be triune.

Father, Son, and Spirit are revealed in varied ways in Scripture from the beginning (God, divine speech or *logos*, and Spirit or wind are all present in the creation account of Genesis). Yet clarity about personal distinctions comes later when the incarnational mission of the Son offers occasion for extensive reflection on his relationship with and to the Father. "The Word became flesh and dwelt among us, and we have seen his glory, glory as of the only Son from the Father, full of grace and truth" (Jn. 1:14). Here and elsewhere, the incarnate Son is shown to be fully God ("full of grace and truth" applies the divine attributes to him that were acclaimed of YHWH in the Greek translation of Exod. 34:6–7) while also referring to him as Son from the Father. That chapter also

[3] John Calvin, *Institutes of the Christian Religion* (Library of Christian Classics; ed. John T. McNeill; trans. Ford Lewis Battles; Louisville: Westminster John Knox, 2006), 1:108 (I.xi.8).

illustrates the way in which New Testament reflection on that Father–
Son relationship provides occasion for viewing earlier revelations as
being personal. "In the beginning was the Word, and the Word was with
God, and the Word was God. He was in the beginning with God. All
things were made through him" (Jn. 1:1–3). Riffing on Genesis 1, one
can no longer read "and God said" in that creation account without
seeing God's speech or *logos* as personal and distinct, divine, and a
perfect image of Son from the Father.[4]

Language of trinity or triunity will be developed to honor both
concerns – the common divinity of Father, Son, and Spirit and also,
simultaneously, the differentiated and ordered life of the one true God
of Israel. Thomas Aquinas would speak of how this means we attend to
both what is "common" to the whole Godhead and what is "proper" to
each particular person therein. The challenge is that these categories
operate in a qualitatively distinct way: proper distinctions in no
way diminishing or modifying common life and being and common
existence in no wise undercutting the similarly basic differentiation of
persons by means of what is proper to each of them. Temptation
frequently arises to try to somehow modify one claim to alleviate a
perceived tension with the other, but that logic falsely assumes that
they exist within the same plane or category (as if more commonality
involves less proper distinction).

Arians in the fourth century have been the paradigmatic offshoot
with respect to modifying a claim (in this case common eternality and
full divinity of Father and Son) for the sake of making space for another
tenet (the personal distinction of Son alongside or beneath Father). They
stand in for what could be called a subordinationist or adoptionist
approach to the Son, who they viewed as a latecomer to the divine
family, firstborn among creatures, to be sure, but nonetheless lacking
in God's eternity. Athanasius and others argued that an Arian Christ
could not be worshiped, indeed could not show forth the Father, restore
life in God, or grant immortality to anyone. The Nicene-
Constantinopolitan Creed of 381 would respond philosophically by
saying that the Son is *homoousios* ("of one being") with the Father.
Further, the Son is begotten, not created; in so doing, the Creed did not

[4] On the two-testament witness of Scripture as ingredient to the development of the
doctrine of the Trinity, see David Yeago, "The New Testament and the Nicene
Dogma: A Contribution to the Recovery of Theological Exegesis," *Pro Ecclesia* 3,
no. 2 (1994), 152–164; and C. Kavin Rowe, "Biblical Pressure and Trinitarian
Hermeneutics," *Pro Ecclesia* 11, no. 3 (2002), 295–312.

define begetting, but it emphatically differentiated it from the term used to describe the making of all creatures. The Creed also underscored those concerns poetically: "God from God, Light from Light, True God from True God." The Son is from the Father, to be sure, but the Son is God, Light, and True or Fully God just as much as the Father is those glorious things. The philosophical and poetic language of that Creed serves both polemical and positive purposes: ruling out subordinationist approaches like Arianism but also exemplifying ways of keeping alert to the divine oneness without missing their distinctness either.

In the same era, theologians were busy working on the exegetical imagination incumbent in trinitarian thinking. Many texts speak of the Son in a humble manner, ranging from speaking of his birth to his thirst to his very death. Other texts acclaim him in divine fashion, as one able to forgive sins or as one who created all things. Gregory of Nazianzus offered an exegetical rule that the former sort of text applies to the Son in his incarnate state and according to his humanity, while the latter text speaks of the Son in his divine person and nature.[5] The route to an orthodox consensus regarding trinitarian confessions was overlain with the development of alert exegetical categories to tend to the breadth of scriptural teaching. A generation later, Augustine of Hippo would also highlight a third category: texts not only spoke of the Son in the form of God (forma dei) or the form of incarnate Servant (forma servi) but sometimes also in his eternal, personal differentiation from Father and Spirit.[6] "For as the Father has life in himself, so he has granted the Son also to have life in himself" (Jn. 5:26) attests full divinity (the Son's "life in himself"), to be sure, but also conveys an ordered distinction vis à vis the Father (who grants him that life in himself). That granting of self-existent life is neither an incarnational reality of his servant form, nor is it something to be overlooked. In that and other verses, the Scriptures show us not only that he is one with God the Father but that he is Son to that Father and personally distinct.[7]

The Nicene Creed uses the language of eternal processions to gesture toward or prompt reflection on those personal distinctions. The Son is "eternally begotten of the Father"; this eternal generation is unlike the later making or creation of all other beings and is instead

[5] Gregory Nazianzus, "Oration 30: On the Son."
[6] Augustine, The Trinity (Works of St. Augustine I/5; ed. John E. Rotelle; trans. Edmund Hill; Brooklyn, NY: New City, 1991), 98–99 (II.i).
[7] On the need not only for a high (that is, divine) Christology but also for right mapping of the personal relations of origin in the triune life, see Wesley Hill, Paul and the Trinity: Persons, Relations, and the Pauline Letters (Grand Rapids: Eerdmans, 2015).

"before all time." The Spirit proceeds from the Father in eternity as well. In the Western Church, the Spirit has been confessed to proceed also from the Son (filioque). That creedal addition occurred later (at the Council of Toledo in 589) without input from the Eastern Church, and both its procedural roots and its principled claims have been a matter of perennial dispute. Whether in Eastern or Western form, the language of the Spirit's eternal procession serves to differentiate his own divine life. These divine processions are eternal, which stands against another perennial threat to trinitarian theology: modalism. In the mid-fourth century, opposition to Arius was widespread, but it soon became apparent that his opponents were not necessarily united in their positive affirmations of God. Many believed the Son to be truly God albeit for a season in time. They thought God was first Father to Israel, then Son in the incarnational sojourn, and now was known to be Spirit after Pentecost. Divine persons in this approach were really modes of the divine life, true and fully divine but temporary and changing; hence, these approaches were termed "modalist." Yet Scripture reveals the three persons engaged interpersonally at simultaneous moments: Father and Son engaged in prayer repeatedly, or Father, Son, and Spirit each involved in the event of Jesus's baptism in the Jordan River. As one historian described the exegetical and doctrinal challenge involved in refining the Nicene approach to the Trinity, then, "fourth-century Trinitarian orthodoxy was the net product of rejecting modalism's claim as the necessary cost for defeating subordinationism."[8]

This second theological teaching manifests another methodological principle, namely, that God is to be known not only over against his created beings but also in his own self-differentiated and triunely ordered perfect existence. A Christian doctrine of God cannot be satisfied with a high (divine) view of Christ and the Spirit but also must tend to their personal relations within the life of the one true God.

THE ETERNAL AND HISTORICAL

Third: we learn of God from God's works, and yet those works include revelation of the divine life beyond history; this self-revelatory illumination of eternity helps us to perceive God in himself and also history in him.

---

[8] Michel Rene Barnes, "The Fourth Century as Trinitarian Canon," in *Christian Origins: Theology, Rhetoric and Community* (ed. Lewis Ayres and Gareth Jones; Christian Origins; London: Routledge, 1998), 62 (47–67).

In the last section, God's eternal processions (Son from Father, Spirit from Father [and also from the Son, in the Western expansion of the original Nicene-Constantinopolitan Creed]) were explored. Each of these personal processions comes to manifestation (and becomes a matter for our knowledge) in that they extend into divine missions in what we call the divine economy: the work of Son and Spirit in creation and redemption as they are sent by the Father. The way God acts here in nature and grace manifests something – analogically, not univocally – of who God is in himself eternally. The eternal processions of the persons are the root of the divine missions in creaturely history. The divine missions in this history reveal to us something of that glorious life of divine procession.[9] Thinking well of this God, then, demands we explore the relationship of these missions and those processions, of this history and that eternity.

The challenge can be framed in various ways. Eternity and temporal existence. Infinity and finite reality. Changelessness and flux. These pairings are jarring and may seem to posit a gulf that cannot be traversed. Theologians wrestle with the challenge in thinking about God's relation to all that is not divine. Guidance can be found, however, in Scripture's own metaphysical and covenantal teaching and in thinking along the way that Christian theologians have sought to unpack its further entailments. No text functions as significantly as does Exodus 3.[10] Israel's God has heard her cries, seen her plight, and remembered his covenant. God summons Moses to the burning bush and commissions him to approach Pharaoh with a message of deliverance. Amid Moses's varied words of hesitant pushback comes the following question and divine answer:

> If I come to the people of Israel and say to them, "The God of your fathers has sent me to you," and they ask me, "What is his name?" what shall I say to them? God said to Moses, "I AM who I AM." And he said, "Say this to the people of Israel, 'I AM has sent me to you.'" God also said to Moses, "Say this to the people

[9] On the Thomistic language of processions and missions, see Gilles Emery, *The Trinitarian Theology of St. Thomas Aquinas* (Oxford: Oxford University Press, 2004), 51–77 and 360–412.

[10] See Michael Allen, "Exodus 3 after the Hellenization Thesis," *Journal of Theological Interpretation* 3, no. 2 (2009): 179–196; repr. in *The Knowledge of God: Essays on God, Christ, and Church* (London: T&T Clark, 2022); and Andrea Saner, *"Too Much to Grasp": Exodus 3:13–15 and the Reality of God* (Journal of Theological Interpretation Supplement 11; Winona Lake, IN: Eisenbrauns, 2015).

of Israel, 'The LORD, the God of your fathers, the God of Abraham, the God of Isaac, and the God of Jacob, has sent me to you.' This is my name forever, and thus I am to be remembered throughout all generations." (Exod. 3:13–15)

Moses needs proof that his mission is not the result simply of too much time in the sun, so God offers a new name. Augustine of Hippo identified two names given here: a "name of mystery" and then a "name of mercy." First, God names himself YHWH or I AM. In fact, God names himself first with a longer line: 'I AM who I AM' (YHWH and I AM abbreviate this fuller language). This initial name could be rendered in the past ("I have been whom I have been") or future tense ("I will be who I will be"). The Apocalypse will later attest each of these as well as the present tense: "I AM the first and the last and the living one" (Rev. 1:17–18). What is most significant depends not on the tense, however, but on the syntactical construction of the line. "I AM who I AM" identifies this God tautologously, showing that, strictly speaking, God cannot be compared to anyone or anything else. God exists in his own class or category, not ultimately like unto any other point of comparison. By contrast, reflect on how often we identify others relative to their and our peers: "so-and-so is someone's sibling or neighbor or coworker." Uniquely, God cannot be likened to anyone else. Kathryn Tanner speaks here of what could be called "qualitative divine transcendence," wherein God's distinction from all else is not merely quantitatively greater but actually qualitatively other.[11] This name YHWH accents the distinctive transcendence of the living and true God. Not surprisingly, Augustine says that this name denotes mystery.

This holy and high God does not leave Moses with mere caution, however, but goes further and offers a second divine name. This triune God is also "the LORD, the God of your fathers, the God of Abraham, the God of Isaac, and the God of Jacob." Here the very same God identifies himself quite differently. As transcendent, he is also known amid the family history of Israel. He was present and thus manifest in the tales of the patriarchs. While distinct, he truly disclosed himself through his address of, provision for, and covenant with those early "fathers" of Israel. God's perfection does not foreclose his presence. Divine transcendence – at least of this radically qualitative sort – actually makes immanence possible. Augustine, therefore, identifies this second

---

[11] Kathryn Tanner, *God and Creation in Christian Theology: Tyranny or Empowerment?* (Minneapolis: Fortress, 1988).

name as a "name of mercy," wherein the lofty one who alone inhabits eternity also comes to bring his glory near.

Whether in creating a world (Gen. 1:1–2) or in becoming incarnate (Jn. 1:14), the question of how the eternal God can be holy and also engaged in such historical and temporal action has captivated theological attention through the ages. Augustine wrestled with the question of creation and God's changelessness. Didn't a creative act demand admission that God changes in bringing other things into existence? Augustine argued that the difference between a creation "in time" and a creation "of time" was fundamental to speaking well of that admittedly mysterious event: the beginning of all creaturely things by God's singular agency (*ex nihilo*).[12] The incarnational example cannot be addressed in exactly the same way, for assumption of humanity occurs at a given point in history and, further, it speaks of the assumption of a new nature by a triune person (the eternal Son of God assuming a human nature). The same principle, however, and a commitment to that radical divine transcendence do provide a means of explaining the character of this scandal, which isn't to alleviate but to accent its wondrous and surpassing mystery.[13] In recent decades, however, Robert Jenson and other theologians have opted for another approach wherein God too experiences narrative change in the flow of this elected history; the gospel does not simply reveal God but also involves God's unfolding self-constitution.[14] Such an approach might be called "evangelical historicism," arguing that a Christocentric method is the only means of staving off a purportedly pagan notion of God's life that isn't rightly revised by the flux of gospel history.[15] Suffice it to say here that while such approaches may lay claim to reform the Christian doctrine of God by means of the revelation of the God of the gospel in that gospel narrative, it might be asked whether – ironically – such approaches have actually pulled up limp in following through the purgative exegetical and doctrinal work performed by early Christian theologians in prior centuries.[16]

---

[12] Augustine, *The City of God*, bk. 11. See also Augustine, *The Trinity*, bk. 5, ch. 4.

[13] Kathryn Tanner, *Jesus, Humanity, and the Trinity: A Brief Systematic Theology* (Minneapolis: Fortress, 2001), 1–35; Rowan Williams, *Christ the Heart of Creation* (London: T&T Clark, 2018); and Aaron Riches, *Ecce Homo: On the Divine Unity of Christ* (Interventions; Grand Rapids: Eerdmans, 2016).

[14] Robert W. Jenson, *Systematic Theology*, Volume One: *The Triune God* (New York: Oxford University Press, 1997).

[15] See further Katherine Sonderegger's chapter on Christ in the present volume (Chapter 5).

[16] One such example would be the way in which they transformed the doctrine of divine simplicity, on which, see Andrew Radde-Gallwitz, *Basil of Caesarea, Gregory of*

The perfection and presence of God, however, also shape the way in which human language of God may be spoken and heard.[17] A radically transcendent God – qualitatively distinct – cannot be directly identified with anything, for he is ultimately only identified with himself ("I AM who I AM"). And yet he is spoken and revealed unto humans through the medium of language, giving hope that the miracle of divine knowledge does occur by his grace. God sees fit to employ language (however incapable it may seem of itself, as is also true of flesh or of the burning bush) to communicate his being, works, and ways to his creatures. In this vein, theologian have felt compelled to articulate an understanding of theological language as analogous in nature, marked by similarity and also by ever greater dissimilarity when using earthly words to speak of the heavenly Lord. The doctrine of analogy communicates a metaphysical claim that has consequences for all theological language in whatever genre; matters of metaphor or imagery go above and beyond it as further literary variations of divine self-presentation.

This third divine instruction gestures toward the significance of analogical reasoning in all theological speech. The Fourth Lateran Council declared that "between Creator and creature there can be remarked no similarity so great that a greater dissimilarity between them cannot be seen."[18] Creaturely knowledge and naming of the creative and redemptive God of the gospel involves the mysterious provision of theological language that apprehends his truth without comprehending him and that wholly depends on the gracious self-presentation of this Holy One of Israel, the transcendent and true triune God.

THEOLOGY AND PERCEPTION

Fourth: the perception of God and practice of doctrine must be defined ultimately by the one whom we seek to perceive and know; the living, triune God of the covenant summons forth singular contemplation wherein we perceive his beauty and goodness as well as all-inclusive reasoning wherein we begin to perceive his connection to all things.

Nyssa, and the Transformation of Divine Simplicity (Oxford Early Christian Studies; Oxford: Oxford University Press, 2009).
[17] On knowledge, see Michael S. Horton, *Covenant and Eschatology: The Divine Drama* (Louisville: Westminster John Knox, 2002); on language, see D. Stephen Long, *Speaking of God: Theology, Language, and Truth* (Grand Rapids: Eerdmans, 2009).
[18] "Canon 2," in *English Historical Documents*, Volume III: *1189–1327* (ed. H. Rothwell; London: n.p., 1975), iii.644–645.

Early Christian theologians found this ordering of contemplative and active reasoning to be of fundamental concern. Origen began his master-work, *On First Principles*, by wrestling with the use of anthropomorphic and, more broadly, creaturely language applied unto the Creator him-self.[19] And Augustine would later say: "So then it is difficult to contemplate and have full knowledge of God's substance, which without any change in itself makes things that change, and without any passage of time in itself creates things that exist in time. That is why it is necessary for our minds to be purified before that inexpressible reality can be inexpressibly seen by them; and in order to make us fit and capable of grasping it, we are led along more endurable routes, nurtured on faith as long as we have not yet been endowed with that necessary purification."[20] Contemplative pursuit of knowledge of the Trinity serves a spiritually significant preparation for active or practical knowledge of other things, lest idolatrous and disordered perceptions of them remain undisturbed.

Contemporary theology flirts with various modes of practical reasoning, the most widespread approach trading under the name "social trinitarianism." Here the doctrine of the Trinity serves as exemplar of social or communal relations. More often than not, the connection between divine relationality and human politics or community comes through a reading of the creation of humanity in the "image of God" involving sociality as its core (Gen. 1:26–27). Theologians as diverse as Karl Barth and Pope John Paul II have argued in such a direction, suggesting that either sexual differentiation or more generic relational distinctiveness form the core of this divine image. Metropolitan John Zizioulas has written most influentially of "being as communion" with the divine life construed in a personalist manner.[21] Most social trinitarians have argued that the equal glory and honor of the three divine persons forms a model for human egalitarianism, by which all social hierarchies are undercut.[22] Some have argued contrariwise that the functional obedience of Son to Father sets a pattern for at least certain social relations of submission and authority.[23]

---

[19] Origen, *On First Principles*, Volume 1 (Oxford Early Christian Texts; ed. and trans. John Behr; Oxford: Oxford University Press, 2017), 24–39 (I.1)

[20] Augustine, *The Trinity*, 66.

[21] John D. Zizioulas, *Being as Communion: Studies in Personhood and the Church* (Crestwood, NJ: St. Vladimir's Seminary Press, 1985).

[22] See Jürgen Moltmann, *The Trinity and the Kingdom: The Doctrine of God* (trans. Margaret Kohl; London: SCM, 1981; repr. Minneapolis: Fortress, 1993); and Miroslav Volf, *After Our Likeness: The Church as the Image of the Trinity* (Sacra Doctrina; Grand Rapids: Eerdmans, 1997).

[23] For example, see Bruce Ware, *Father, Son, and Holy Spirit: Relationships, Roles, and Relevance* (Wheaton: Crossway, 2005).

Many patristic scholars and constructive theologians have argued that social trinitarianism promises what it does not deliver, namely, legitimately divine and trinitarian grounds for human social visions. Social trinitarians have often sought to present purportedly "Eastern" approaches that are more personalist and relational than so-called "Western" or "Latin" trinitarianisms that apparently veer into abstractions and an essentialism. Yet wider study of even those Eastern theologians, such as Gregory Nyssa and Gregory Nazianzus, shows that they share many of the same concerns as their purported alternatives such as Hilary of Poitiers or Augustine of Hippo. That disjunctive history doesn't stand under scrutiny.[24] What of the social utility? In both iterations, whether egalitarian or hierarchical, social trinitarianism runs the risk of misperceiving the analogical and mysterious character of divine life relative to all human lives.[25] In each mode – whether egalitarian or functionally hierarchical – social trinitarianism runs the risk of projecting political and relational prejudices into key terms of trinitarian theology such as "order" or "person."

While the criticisms of social trinitarianism help to restore the place of divine incomprehensibility and radically qualitative transcendence, there remains the danger of overreaction. Knowing God involves contemplating him and perceiving all his works rightly. Therefore, knowing God cannot be completely severed from perceiving God vis à vis the self and world. "From him and through him and to him" are all things (Rom. 11:36), so appropriately knowing creaturely reality will invariably involve reading it as related to God in multiple ways. Divine ineffability marks any claims we make about vestiges of God (*vestigia trinitatis*) in this world, but that cannot simply nullify the task of so tracing his handprints. Augustine's masterwork *De Trinitate* was not complete until biblical and creedal language had been not only explored but put to use in pondering self and world in its second half.[26] Whether or not Augustine's exact modalities for tracing reality's triune shape are most promising, the mission remains pertinent and the journey itself is productive.

[24] Lewis Ayres, *Nicaea and Its Legacy: An Approach to Fourth Century Trinitarian Theology* (New York: Oxford University Press, 2004).
[25] See especially the critique offered in Kathryn Tanner, *Christ the Key* (Current Issues in Theology; Cambridge: Cambridge University Press, 2010), 222–224.
[26] On reading *De Trinitate*, see Luigi Gioia, *The Theological Epistemology of Augustine's* De Trinitate (Oxford: Oxford University Press, 2005).

Medieval theologians would introduce the concept of "reduction" (*reductio*) to trinitarian theology.[27] When studying the biological world or psychological processes, the explorer needs not only to consider their immanent, creaturely shape but also to "reduce" them to their ultimate divine source in various ways. Oddly, this mode of reflection sounds to modern ears inverted; for most of our contemporaries, reductive thinking is narrow and superficial in some respect, whereas medieval theologians like Bonaventure and Bernard intend to explore the metaphysical and gracious depths of reality by talking of "reducing" or tracing them to their primary cause. Modern intellectual work perhaps functions more reductively by naturalizing and thereby limiting its inquiry, refusing to pursue the summons to relate all such studies to a deeper unity.[28] Social trinitarianism may drift toward a false confidence that triune perception related to self and world can be practiced apart from the metaphysical turbulence wrought by radical divine transcendence, but modern naturalized intellect refuses to recognize the very need to perceive more than what Charles Taylor calls the "immanent frame."[29] Even when opposing the too pacific posture of the former, it would be disastrous to fall unknowingly into the latter malady.

In this regard, John Webster spoke regularly of the need to practice a "theological theology," over time showing that such a commitment would always require one to trace a moral quandary or a contemporary debate back to its roots in the divine life and the divine works, whether of nature or of grace.[30] Doing so slows the process of theological judgment, alerting the theologian to begin always with God as a means of expressing the "fear of the Lord [which] is the beginning of wisdom" (Ps. 111:10; 112:1). Locating a creaturely being or action as participating graciously in God's creative and redemptive work, as mired by sin or regenerated in Christ, helps better identify that creaturely reality as it

---

[27] Bonaventure, *The Reduction of Arts to Theology* (ed. Z. Hayes; St. Bonaventure: Franciscan Institute, 1996); on which see John Webster, '*Regina artium*: Theology and the humanities', in *The Domain of the Word: Scripture and Theological Reason* (London: T&T Clark, 2012), 171–192.

[28] John Milbank, 'The Conflict of the Faculties: Theology and the Economy of the Sciences', in *Faithfulness and Fortitude: In Conversation with the Theological Ethics of Stanley Hauerwas* (ed. Mark Nation and Samuel Wells; Edinburgh: T&T Clark, 2000), 39–57.

[29] Charles Taylor, *A Secular Age* (Cambridge, MA: Harvard University Press, 2007), 542 *et passim*.

[30] The most mature statement of his project is John Webster, 'What Makes Theology Theological'? in *God without Measure*, volume one: *God and the Works of God* (London: T&T Clark, 2015), 213–224.

actually is. To perceive that finite being, though, demands reduction or tracing back to the infinite being of God (not as an abstract principle but according to scriptural categories such as creation, election, covenant, and sin).

Such trinitarian contemplation generates practical wisdom. "To know the divine persons was necessary for us for two reasons," said Thomas Aquinas as he concluded his discussion of the Trinity. "One, in order to have a right view of the creation of things." A grave error is thereby avoided: "For by maintaining that God made everything through his Word we avoid the error of those who held that God's nature compelled him to create things." Rather, a new way of viewing all of created reality will control the Christian imagination: "By affirming that there is in him the procession of Love we show that he made creatures, not because he needed them nor because of any reason outside himself, but from love of his own goodness."[31]

Trinitarian contemplation will also prompt practical reasoning regarding the order of grace. Thomas went on to say that "the other and more important reason is so that we may have the right view of the salvation of mankind, accomplished by the Son who became flesh, and by the gifts of the Holy Spirit."[32] The objective work of the incarnate Son involves nothing less than the humble presence of the high and holy God, at the Father's will and by the Spirit's power. Then the life-giving agency of that glorious Holy Spirit, sent by Father and Son to testify to that Son's resurrection of his body unto the heavenly Father, also manifests a divine commitment to ensure the appropriation of those redemptive works such that the kingdom and its citizens actually receive those evangelical blessings.[33] The trustworthiness of the gospel promise stems from that triune agency that is not only necessary but sufficient in the order of grace, ensuring not only its possibility but also its actuality in human life.

The fourth theological focus also brings with it a methodological demand: "the fear of the Lord is the beginning of wisdom" or, otherwise put, awe-struck attentiveness always and everywhere to God must serve as the basis of further reflection if we are to think adequately of

---

[31] Thomas Aquinas, *Summa theologiae*, Volume 6: *The Trinity (1a.27–32)* (ed. Ceslaus Velecky; Oxford: Blackfriars, 1965), 109.

[32] Thomas Aquinas, *Summa theologiae*, 109.

[33] Sarah Coakley provides analysis of how trinitarian perception necessarily trades in reflection on love and desire, all of which is expressed more broadly in her argument for a *théologie totale*: *God, Sexuality, and the Self: An Essay "On the Trinity"* (Cambridge: Cambridge University Press, 2013).

God – who wills not to exist alone but to give, share, renew, and eventually fulfill other lives with his own – and also to ponder all things truly as they live, move, and have their being only in him.

Further Reading

Allen, Michael (2022), "Exodus 3 after the Hellenization Thesis," *Journal of Theological Interpretation* 3, no. 2 (2009): 179–196; repr. in *The Knowledge of God: Essays on God, Christ, and Church* (London: T&T Clark), 17–34.

Augustine (1991), *The Trinity* (Works of St. Augustine I/5; ed. John E. Rotelle; trans. Edmund Hill; Brooklyn, NY: New City).

Coakley, Sarah (2013), *God, Sexuality and the Self: An Essay "On the Trinity"* (Cambridge: Cambridge University Press).

Emery, Gilles (2011), *The Trinity: An Introduction to Catholic Doctrine on the Triune God* (trans. Matthew Levering; Washington, DC: Catholic University of America Press).

Hill, Wesley (2015), *Paul and the Trinity: Persons, Relations, and the Pauline Letters* (Grand Rapids: Eerdmans).

Levering, Matthew (2004), *Scripture and Metaphysics: Aquinas and the Renewal of Trinitarian Theology* (Challenges in Contemporary Theology; Oxford: Blackwell).

Sanders, Matthew (2017), *The Triune God* (New Studies in Dogmatics; Grand Rapids: Zondervan).

Sonderegger, Katherine (2015 and 2020), *Systematic Theology*, Volumes 1 and 2 (Minneapolis: Fortress).

Swain, Scott R. (2020), *The Trinity: An Introduction* (Short Studies in Systematic Theology; Wheaton: Crossway).

Tanner, Kathryn (1988), *God and Creation in Christian Theology: Tyranny or Empowerment?* (Minneapolis: Fortress).

Vanhoozer, Kevin J. (2010), *Remythologizing Theology: Divine Action, Passion, and Authorship* (Cambridge Studies in Christian Doctrine; Cambridge: Cambridge University Press).

Webster, John (2015), *God Without Measure, Volume 1: God and the Works of God* (London: T&T Clark).

Williams, Rowan (2016), "*Sapientia* and the Trinity: Reflections on *De Trinitate*," *Augustiniana* 40, no. 1 (1990): 317–332; repr. as "*Sapientia*: Wisdom and Trinitarian Relations," in *On Augustine* (London: Bloomsbury), 171–190.

2 Creation and Providence

SIMON OLIVER

According to scripture and the historic Christian creeds, God is almighty and the creator of all things, visible and invisible. This entails that the world is neither a brute fact nor without origin, meaning, and purpose. Rather, it is the work of a divine agency that creates and provides for creatures and orders them to their proper ends. That divine agency is not part of the world but is the transcendent yet immanent and continual source of the world's existence. These claims arise from wonder and reflection on the contingency, fragility, beauty, and rational order of the world, contemplation of scripture, and the discernment of God's revelation in and through creation. The Christian theology of creation and providence, having its roots in the Hebrew scriptures and ancient philosophy, was developed in relation to the Trinitarian doctrine of God, the incarnation of Christ, and the hope of redemption. It has been articulated in creative and critical conversation with many other traditions of enquiry into the origin, workings, and purpose of the cosmos, from ancient pagan creation myths to the modern natural sciences.

This chapter will begin with an exploration of the saga of creation found in Genesis and its relation to wider scriptural accounts of God's creative act. Whilst the Christian theology of creation begins with Genesis, it is also influenced by another aspect of ancient Jewish thought, namely, the teaching that, if we are to speak intelligibly of God's act of creation, we must speak of God creating 'out of nothing' or *ex nihilo*. The meaning and implications of creation *ex nihilo* will therefore be the second focus of this chapter. We will see that the distinctively Christian theology of creation *ex nihilo* arises particularly in relation to the Trinitarian doctrine of God and to Christology. This raises important questions concerning divine providence, namely, how God provides for, orders, and directs creation toward its proper ends. Finally, this chapter will examine challenges confronted by the Christian doctrine of creation and providence, including the modern ecological crisis.

THE BEGINNING: GENESIS

Scripture's first book, Genesis, features two accounts of creation in its opening chapters. The first is the familiar seven-day account, beginning with God calling light into existence and culminating in the creation of man and woman in God's image on the sixth day. The seventh day, when God completed creation, is hallowed as a day of rest. This is the origin of the Sabbath gifted to the people of Israel at the exodus from Egypt (Exod. 16:29; 20:8–11), around which turns the weekly pattern of Jewish worship. The second account of creation, in the second and third chapters of Genesis, includes the formation of the first man from the dust of the earth and woman from the man's rib. It describes their life in the Garden of Eden, the tragic sin of the first man and woman, and their expulsion from the Garden in what became known as the Fall.

The history and composition of the account of creation in Genesis is complex. The text is frequently ascribed to two authors, the 'P' or priestly writer (Gen. 1:1–2.4a) who is concerned with the cosmic order which structures the ritual life of the Temple in Jerusalem, and the 'J' or Yahwist writer (Gen. 2:4b–3) who refers to God by the personal name 'Yahweh' revealed to Moses on Mount Horeb (Exodus 3). Whilst the first account is particularly concerned with the order, abundance, and goodness of creation, and the provision of food to sustain life (Gen. 1:29–30), the second account is concerned with God's intimacy with creation (God directly addresses the man and woman and walks in the garden) and creation's interconnectedness and yearning for fulfilment. God uses one part of the cosmic order to meet the need of another part. For example, the earth needs to be tilled (Gen. 2.5; 2.15), the vegetation needs water (2.5), the man needs the breath of life (2.7), the man needs food that is pleasant and good (2.9), and the man needs a companion and helper (2.18). There is a providential order to creation in which one part supplies the needs of another.

The accounts of creation in Genesis were placed together during the exile of the elite of Judah in Babylon in the early sixth century BC, or soon after their return to Jerusalem in the early 530s BC. They are influenced by creation myths in the ancient Near East such as the Akkadian epics *Atrahasis* (the title being the name of the protagonist, meaning 'exceedingly wise') and *Enuma Elish* ('The Epic of Creation'), which may date from as early as the eighteenth-century BC. It is the unique features of Genesis, however, which are more significant for the later development of the Christian doctrine of creation. First is the peaceable character of God's act of creation. Whereas other ancient creation myths depict the formation of the world and humanity as the outcome of a conflict between the gods or the overcoming of violent chaos, in Genesis, there is no sense of God the creator battling against an opposing force or primeval chaos. Whilst the theme of struggle against chaos is ubiquitous in ancient Near Eastern myths and present elsewhere in the Old Testament, God's act of creation depicted in Genesis is one of peaceful ordering. Secondly, God's creation is announced as 'good' on six occasions in the opening chapter of Genesis, and 'very good' on the sixth day when God sees the whole. This implies that the created order is not morally indifferent or devoid of intrinsic value. Creation is rational and intelligible, being open to classification and naming (Gen. 2:19–20), precisely because it is good and providentially ordered to certain ends and not simply because it follows predictable patterns. Thirdly, the opening chapters of Genesis also imply that evil and suffering are not an original and intrinsic part of creation but an alien intrusion. This gives rise to an important aspect of the doctrine of creation that is also inspired by Platonic philosophy, namely, the view that evil does not have an existence of its own but is the absence or privation of the good (*privatio boni*) in the same way that darkness is the absence of light. In the context of the good and intelligible order of creation, evil is that which is dark and unintelligible. Finally, creation is announced as 'finished' on the sixth day (Gen. 2:1) and we read that, on the seventh day, God finished the work that he had done and rested (Gen. 2:2). Does this imply that creation, being finished, is fixed with no further creaturely development? Does God simply allow creation to run its course? Augustine of Hippo, in his *Literal Commentary on Genesis*, writes, 'it is not, you see, like a mason building houses; when he has finished he goes away, and his work goes on standing when he has stopped working on it and gone away. No, the world will not be able to go on standing for a single moment, if God withdraws from it his controlling hand'.[1] For Augustine and many theologians of early Christianity, creation is always contingent and never self-standing; it does not exist in its own right but only by the sustaining and guiding power of God. It is not the case, therefore, that God creates and stands back as we might stand back from the things we make; as we will see below with respect to the doctrine of creation out of nothing, God sustains creation in existence at every moment. For Augustine, creation is 'finished' in the sense that it contains within

---

[1] Augustine, 'De Genesi ad litteram'('On the Literal Meaning of Genesis'), IV.12.22 in *On Genesis*, trans. Edmund Hill, O.P. (New York: New City Press, 2002), 253.

itself the potential to become what God wills it to be. Realising that potential in an unfolding cosmic drama and the continual development and flourishing of creatures towards the perfection of creation is the work of God's providence and creatures' self-fulfilment.

The account of creation in Genesis has been the source of great controversy, particularly since the development of evolutionary biology and natural scientific accounts of the origins of the cosmos in the nineteenth and twentieth centuries. For the most part, we have come to understand that the universe and the earth's abundant life are not the result of a seven-day creation but of billions of years of cosmic development and millions of years of evolution. Yet Genesis is not a work of natural history that can be measured against Darwin's *On the Origin of Species* or modern cosmology. It is not centrally concerned with how God did or did not assemble the universe, nor with empirically derivable facts concerning how the universe functions. Rather, it is concerned with the unity, meaning, and purpose of creation. It begins with the same realisation upon which the edifice of modern science is built, namely, that the cosmos is ordered in such a way that we can make sense of it, explore it, and delight in it according to a variety of rational procedures. Genesis perhaps makes a significant additional claim concerning creation that is shared by many ancient cosmologies: it is rational and ordered precisely because it is good and purposive. The meaning and beauty of the cosmos – not simply its predictable or manipulable functions – are open to exploration in myriad ways, including metaphysical and theological enquiry.

Whilst the drama of Genesis is fundamental, the Christian doctrine of creation also developed from other scriptural teachings and in response to the wider intellectual culture of the ancient Mediterranean. Of some importance were a set of religious movements collectively known as 'Gnosticism', from the Greek *gnosis* meaning 'knowledge'. Some Gnostics regarded themselves as Christians and the possessors of a secret salvific knowledge delivered through Christ and the Apostles; although by the second century, they had developed into varied sects and were increasingly separate from the Church and proto-orthodox Christianity. Whilst it is difficult to define Gnosticism, its various teachings were rejected by Christian theologians because the Gnostics often regarded the material world as radically separate from a higher spiritual realm and not the intentional creation of a benevolent and omnipotent God. Gnosticism drew a distinction between the supreme and unknowable Divine Being and the lesser 'craftsman god' who formed the material cosmos. The material realm was the result of a 'fall' and therefore something to be escaped. The Jewish and Christian scriptures, however, teach that God's creation, material and spiritual, is good. The New Testament consistently refers to God as the source of all things (Rom. 11:36; 1 Cor. 8:6; Eph. 3:9; Rev. 4:11). Moreover, according to the Gospel of John, the eternal Word of God was incarnate within creation, assuming material human nature to bring salvation from sin and life in all its fulness.

Far from being the result of a fall and fundamentally sundered from God, early Christian theologians came to the view that the material creation was of divine origin, sustained and providentially ordered at every moment by God and sanctified by Christ. This understanding of creation was expressed in a treatise written around AD 160 by Tatian, an Assyrian convert to Christianity. In his 'Oration to the Greeks' he stated: 'For matter is not, like God, without beginning, nor, as having no beginning, is of equal power with God; it is begotten, and not produced by any other being, but brought into existence by the Framer of all things alone.'[2] Around two decades later, Theophilus of Antioch, writing to an educated pagan named Autolycus in defence of Christianity, claimed that 'all things God has made out of things that were not into things that are, in order that through His works His greatness may be known and understood'.[3] Around the same time, Irenaeus, Bishop of Lyons, was expounding the same teaching in a treatise against the heresies of the Gnostic schools.[4] These texts express the development of the doctrine of creation *ex nihilo* (out of nothing), expounded not simply in opposition to Gnosticism but positively from the scriptural witness, earlier Jewish teaching, and aspects of Platonism. Through the second century and beyond, the doctrine of creation *ex nihilo* achieved ever greater metaphysical precision.

CREATION *EX NIHILO*

According to the doctrine of creation *ex nihilo* as it is classically expounded, creation is not the mere fabrication of the cosmos out of

---

[2] Tatian, 'Address of Tatian to the Greeks', in *Ante-Nicene Fathers, Volume 2*, ed. Alexander Roberts and James Donaldson, trans. J. E. Ryland (Peabody, MA: Hendrickson, 1995), V, 67.

[3] Theophilus of Antioch, "To Autolycus', in *Ante-Nicene Fathers, Volume 2*, ed. Alexander Roberts and James Donaldson, trans. Marcus Dods (Peabody, MA: Hendrickson, 1995), I.iv, 90.

[4] Irenaeus of Lyons, 'Against Heresies', in *Ante-Nicene Fathers, Volume 1*, ed. Alexander Roberts and James Donalsdon, trans. Alexander Roberts (Peabody, MA: Hendrickson, 1994), II.x, 369–370.

some already-existent matter. Neither is the universe of everlasting time, as Aristotle thought. Rather, creation is the fundamental coming-to-be of that which is not God, and we must therefore speak of God creating out of nothing. This 'nothing' is not a mysterious something – a great vacuum, for example – from which, or within which, God creates. We might say that there is no *thing* out of which God creates; all things, including matter, time, and space, come from God in an act of sovereign freedom. Because God does not work with some pre-existent matter, this immediately distinguishes God's act of creation from our acts of making. When we fabricate something, we turn one thing – some clay, for example – into something else – a pot. As Thomas Aquinas would put it, creation is not a change; it is not one thing becoming another but rather the ground of all change within creation. It is the instantiation of that which is not God – not just the being of particular things but created being in its most universal aspect. This is why, for a thinker such as Aquinas, only God can truly create, because 'to create' means to cause the very existence of things from nothing, and this requires an absolute power.[5] All our creative acts presuppose something already in existence – something with which to work – and so they also presuppose God's act of creation *ex nihilo*.

The claim that there is no material cause in creation – no stuff out of which God fabricates the cosmos – draws our attention to another important distinction between our acts of making and God's act of creation. When we make something – a pot, for example – we are constrained by the material with which we work. The material resists and challenges us as we re-form it into something else. The material also limits us; there are things we can make out of a given material, but there are other things for which that material is quite unsuitable. Unlike our acts of making, however, God is not limited or resisted in his creation by pre-existent material. God does not have to overcome a violent chaos or coax the cosmos into being. There is no limit to God's creativity because God is the absolute cause of created being itself. This aspect of creation *ex nihilo* is consonant with a distinctive feature of the drama of Genesis discussed earlier, namely, the peaceable nature of creation. In other ancient Near Eastern accounts, a deity was challenged

---

[5] Thomas Aquinas, *Summa Theologiae* (Volume 13 Latin/English Edition of the Works of St. Thomas Aquinas) trans. Laurence Shapcote (Lander, WY: The Aquinas Institute for the Study of Sacred Doctrine, 2012), 1a.45.2 ad 2 and 1a.45.5.c. Thomas Aquinas, *Summa Contra Gentiles Book Two: Creation*, trans. James F. Anderson (Notre Dame, IN: University of Notre Dame Press, 1975), II.6.1.

by a primordial chaos that had to be overcome and that constantly threatened creation's integrity, whereas in Genesis there is no such overcoming or challenge; God is simply the source of creation's existence, order, and goodness. This is a peaceable act, not an act of coercion or overcoming. Creation *ex nihilo* is a metaphysical exposition of this scriptural teaching. God is not challenged or limited in the creative act; it is an expression of gratuitous and peaceable freedom.

Does the account of creation in the first verse of Genesis, however, suggest that God creates at a moment in time from a pre-existent material chaos rather than *ex nihilo*? In the New Revised Standard Version, we read that 'in the beginning when God created the heavens and the earth ... darkness covered the face of the deep'. It is important to stress that providing a precise metaphysical account of the origins of the cosmos was not the principal aim of the priestly writer of the first chapter of Genesis. Nevertheless, much depends on what the text means by 'beginning'. In the Greek translation of the Old Testament known as the Septuagint, dating from the third century BC, and also in some modern translations of the Hebrew text, we find a particular understanding of the beginning of creation: 'In the beginning (*en archē*) God created the heavens and the earth.' The 'when' of some translations is not included in the Greek Septuagint version. Some translators also point out that the Hebrew text does not require the inclusion of 'when'. This is important because there are two senses of 'beginning'. We might think of a temporal beginning in statements such as 'at the beginning of the meal' or 'when I begin to study'. This sense of beginning refers to a moment in time in which there is a 'before' and an 'after'. Some modern translations of the first verse of Genesis imply this temporal sense of beginning because they refer to *when* God created – at this moment rather than that moment. On this view, it seems that God created within a temporal flow and there was something already in existence in addition to God before God began to create. Another sense of beginning, however, refers to something's principle or foundation. For example, 'the beginning of wisdom is the fear of the Lord' or 'charity is the beginning of virtue'. This kind of beginning is not temporal but metaphysical: 'beginning' refers to the foundation or principle of something. If this is the kind of beginning that the Septuagint translators had in mind, not to mention some renderings of the Hebrew, it is more consistent with the beginning proposed by creation *ex nihilo*: an absolute origin or principle of all things including time and matter, rather than a beginning within time. On this view, whilst creation has an absolute origin or *archē*, it is not a moment within time; strictly speaking, we should not speak of a 'before' and 'after' to God's creation. Rather, God's act of creation is also the creation of time, so it does not happen within time. Whilst time is not endless but an aspect of God's creation, creation nevertheless has a fundamental beginning.

Perhaps the most radical implication of creation *ex nihilo* is that it entails not only an absolute beginning to creation but also a radical asymmetry between God and creation. We can see this by following a line of thought proposed by the thirteenth-century theologian Thomas Aquinas, but one that has very strong precedent in the theology of the early Church. One of Aquinas's principal concerns, shared with his theological predecessors, is to make a clear and precise distinction between God and creation. This is important lest we conceive of God idolatrously as a very big creature. If God is creator, the characteristics that belong to creatures as contingent and dependent beings, such as temporality and finitude, must be denied of God. For this reason, Aquinas insists that, if we are to speak of God, we must speak of God as existing essentially. God's existence is not dependent upon anything else; if it were, God would be created, not the creator. Aquinas insists that God exists in himself through his essence. It is of God's essence to exist; hence, we say that in God, essence (what God is) is perfectly continuous with existence (that God is). As Aquinas would put it, God is *ipsum esse per se subsistens*, or 'self-subsistent being itself'.[6] God does not receive his existence as an addition to his essence. As a long tradition of theological reflection would put it, God is simple, meaning that God is not composed or structured of essence plus existence; in God, essence and existence are one. On the other hand, creation's existence is contingent; creation might not exist. For example, it is not of a horse's essence that it exist, so its existence (that it is) is an addition to its essence (what it is). Creaturely existence is composed or structured of essence plus existence. So creatures, in not being self-explanatory, point beyond themselves; their existence invites further explanation. This means that existence is not proper to creatures; it is received as a gift. As Aquinas puts it, whereas God exists essentially, creation exists by participation in God's being. In itself, strictly speaking, creation is nothing. It exists by sharing in, receiving, or participating in God who exists essentially.

There are two important corollaries of this view. First, when we speak of God's act of creation, we are not to think of there being some

---

[6] Aquinas, *Summa Theologiae*, 1a.4.2.c.

entity called 'God' to which we add another entity alongside God that we call 'creation'. For Aquinas, it is not a matter of there being 'God' and then suddenly, at the moment of creation, 'God plus the universe'. There is only one focus of existence, namely, God. Everything else exists by sharing in God's existence just as terrestrial things are warm or visible not in their own right, but because they participate in the light of the sun. Secondly, creation is in continual receipt of its being from God. It is held in existence at every moment by God's gracious donation of being; at no moment does creation exist outside a fundamental relation to God the creator. This brings us to a vital aspect of creation *ex nihilo*: as well as creating without any pre-existent material, God sustains creation in existence 'out of nothing' at every moment. Creation hovers over nothingness at every instant, held in existence by God's sustaining power. Every moment, not just the first moment, is *ex nihilo*. The radical asymmetry between God and creation expressed in creation *ex nihilo* means that the difference between God and creation is not like the difference between one thing and another. It is not a difference of degree or a difference of kind; it is a sheer difference in which God is wholly transcendent. At the same time, God's radical transcendence, God's absolute otherness, means that God can be immanent or infinitely close to creation without collapsing into creation, as it were, or being confused for a very big creature.

A final implication of creation *ex nihilo* and the classical doctrine of God is that creation is a free and gratuitous gift. If God is replete and eternally fulfilled – 'pure act', to use the medieval scholastic terminology – God does not gain from creation. Whereas I might fulfil my potential in being creative – in writing this chapter, for example – and thereby gain or realise something for myself, God does not fulfil anything in himself by creating because God is eternally fulfilled. If we were to speak of God as having potential that is yet to be fulfilled or characteristics yet to be realised, we would be speaking of a being not yet perfected and therefore subject to processes and time; we would be speaking of a creature. According to the ancient and medieval Christian tradition, God is all that God could ever be, which means that God is eternally creator. God does not need to create to fulfil himself, so God's act of creation has no 'ulterior motive'. Creation is the expression of an absolute and gratuitous love that is in no way motivated by need or compulsion. It is the absolutely free gift of being – the expression of God's eternal joy and bliss in the coming-to-be of creation, *ex nihilo*.

THE TRINITY AND CREATION

This presents Christian theology with an important question concerning creation: why does God create if there is no need for creation? If
there is no inchoate or chaotic material awaiting the perfecting work of
God, and if God does not fulfil himself by creating, there seems to be no
reason to create. Is creation therefore the act of God's inscrutable will?
Is it a random or capricious act – something that God just decides to do –
which is impenetrable to reason and further theological enquiry? Does
the act of creation and the difference between God and creation have
any basis or ground in God himself?

    To address these questions, we can return to a principle that origin-
ates in ancient Greek philosophy: effects resemble their cause.[7] This
means that effects express something of the nature or style of their
cause. The varied compositions and performances of a musician, for
example, express something of her training, skill, and style. Terrestrial
creatures express something of the light and energy of the sun but in a
diverse manner. According to this principle, whilst we maintain the
irreducible difference and asymmetry between creator and creatures,
creation as God's effect expresses something of the eternal nature of
the Godhead. Christian theologians, from Gregory of Nyssa in the
fourth century to the Lutheran theologian Wolfhart Pannenberg in the
twentieth century, have come to the view that the difference between
God and creation is not a capricious and inscrutable act of the divine
will alone; it is an expression of, and participation in, the eternal difference in the Godhead between the persons of the Trinity – Father, Son,
and Holy Spirit. Creation, understood as the gratuitous and loving gift of
being, is not merely an act of the divine will but the expression of the
self-giving love of the eternal Trinity. God is love (1 John 4) and love is a
relation of lover and beloved. As the Father eternally and fully bestows
himself in the begetting of the beloved Son, and the Father and Son
bestow their love in the procession or spiration of the Holy Spirit, so
these eternal emanations, fully constitutive in their perfect unity of the
Godhead's simplicity, are expressed in the gift of creation *ex nihilo*. To
explain this, Aquinas uses the familiar analogy of a craftsman. The
craftsman works through a 'word' or idea in his mind concerning what

---

[7] Aristotle, *Metaphysics* (Books I–IX), trans. Hugh Tredennick (Cambridge, MA:
Harvard University Press, 1996), VII.7, 338–339; *Physics* (Books I–IV), trans. P. H.
Wicksteed and F. M. Cornford (Cambridge, MA: Harvard University Press, 1996),
II.7, 165; Aquinas, *Summa Theologiae*, 1a.45.7.c: 'Every effect in some degree
represents its cause, but diversely.'

is to be made and through his will or loving desire to make the object. 'Word' and 'love' – the knowledge of what is to be made and the will to make it – are integral to our creative acts. This structure is a faint trace and participation in God's creative act: 'Hence also God the Father made the creature through His Word, which is His Son; and through His Love, which is the Holy Ghost. And so the processions of the Persons are the type of the productions of creatures inasmuch as they include the essential attributes, knowledge and will.'[8] The difference between creation and God is not arbitrary; it finds its ground and reason in the eternal processions of the Trinity.

According to the Christian tradition, creation is not the particular act of the Father, Son, or Holy Spirit; it is the singular act of the Trinity. As Gregory of Nyssa puts it, 'every operation which extends from God to the Creation, and is named according to our variable conceptions of it, has its origin from the Father, and proceeds through the Son, and is perfected in the Holy Spirit'.[9] At the same time, the New Testament pays particular attention to the place of the second person of the Trinity – the Son or Word (*Logos*) – in God's act of creation. The Gospel of John, Paul in his letter to the Colossians, and the writer of the letter to the Hebrews state that all things are created in him, through him, and for him; in him all things hold together (Jn. 1:1–4; Col. 1:15–17; Heb. 1:1–3a). These prepositions suggest that creation is an intimate expression of the eternal *Logos*: creation is 'in', 'through', and 'for' the Word or Son of God. Both Augustine of Hippo and Maximus the Confessor write of the *Logos* being present throughout creation in the *rationes seminales* (seeds of reason) or *logoi* (the rational principles) in such a way that every creature bears within itself a seed of the divine Word or Reason.

There is another profound connection between the doctrine of creation and Christology. In Christ the incarnate Word, who is fully divine and fully human in one person, we find a relation of a created

---

[8] Aquinas, *Summa Theologiae*, 1a.45.6.c. A similar idea appears in the thought of the twentieth century Lutheran theologian Wolfhart Pannenberg: 'In the free self-distinction of the Son from the Father the independent existence of a creation distinct from God has its basis, and in this sense we may view creation as a free act not only of the Father but of the trinitarian God.' Wolfhart Pannenberg, *Systematic Theology*, Volume 2, trans. Geoffrey Bromiley (London: T&T Clark, 2004), ch.7, I.§3, 30.

[9] Gregory of Nyssa, 'On Not Three Gods: To Ablabius', in *Nicene and Post-Nicene Fathers of the Christian Church, Second Series*, Volume 5, ed. Philip Schaff and Henry Wace, trans. William Moore and Henry Austin Wilson (Grand Rapids: Eerdmans, 1994), 334.

nature – humanity – to an uncreated nature – divinity – which reveals a
proper understanding of the intimate relation of creation to God. This is
particularly important for our understanding of the theology of providence, namely, how God sustains, orders, governs, and provides for
creatures, guiding them to their proper ends. As we will see in the next
section, the key insight from Christology and the relation of divine and
human natures in Christ is that the relation of creatures to God is non-
competitive. Just as the divine nature of Christ does not displace or
compete with Christ's human nature – Christ is fully human and fully
divine – so divine providential action does not displace or compete with
creaturely action; it is the very ground of creaturely self-fulfilment.

PROVIDENCE

In scripture, we read abundantly about God's provision for creation. The
psalmist writes: 'The eyes of all look to you, and you give them their
food in due season. You open your hand, satisfying the desire of every
living thing' (Ps. 145:15–16). How are we to understand God's providential action in creation, particularly in relation to creaturely action? We
can express the problem with a straightforward example: when I move
my mug across the desk, is it me who moves the mug or God? It is
tempting to suggest that, because God is omnipotent and the creator of
all things, it is really God who moves the mug. After all, God sustains
me and the mug in existence. If we trace all causes back to the beginning of creation, we reach God as the first cause of all things. The view
that only God has genuine causal power is known as 'occasionalism'
because created causes are only the occasion for true divine causation.
For example, it is not really the fire that heats the pan of water but God
in the fire. On this view, created causes, in being merely instrumental,
lack any significance. Occasionalism also absolves human beings of
ultimate responsibility because their actions are really God's actions.
The alternative to occasionalism is deism in which God stands back
from creation and allows it to subsist. On this view, it is only me who
moves the mug. This renders God obsolete within creation. The problem with occasionalism and deism is that they see divine and creaturely
causation as competing for causal space. They are regarded as mutually
exclusive; it has to be me or God moving the mug across the desk, but it
cannot be both.

The classical answer to the problem of divine causation in the
doctrine of providence is to understand that God and creatures have
causal power but in radically different senses. This is because creation is

understood as a hierarchy of causes with God as the primary cause in which all secondary created causes participate. Consider the following simile of the sun that finds its origins in Plato and influences later Neoplatonic and Christian thought. The sun diffuses its energy, causing motion and life on earth. Its causal power extends to everything in the terrestrial domain. But the sun is not the only cause of motion and life on earth. There are other kinds of cause – water, the chemical nutrients of the earth, the climate, human agents, and so on. The sun is, however, the universal primary cause without which there would be no life and motion on earth. All terrestrial creatures receive the causal power of the sun but not in the way that power subsists in the sun – terrestrial creatures are not hot, light-emitting, gaseous bodies. They receive the sun's causal power in a constricted fashion after the manner of their own nature – for example, light for photosynthesis in plants or for sight in animals. In receiving the sun's power, creatures are enabled to be real causes in their own right. Celestial and terrestrial causes do not compete; the latter participate in, and are enabled by, the former.

This simple example helps us to understand that several causes acting differently can bring about a certain effect. Using this as a simile for God's providential causation, we can say that God is the highest or primary cause in creation because God is creator. God diffuses his power to create and sustain causal agents in creation. A long tradition of theological and philosophical reflection claims that God, in being the universal primary cause, infuses himself most deeply into creatures because God is the cause of their being. As Aquinas puts it, God is innermost in each thing according its mode of being, sustaining its existence.[10] At the same time, it is God who causes creation to be other than Godself and so constitutes the independence of creatures and their real causal power.

Crucially, in being the primary cause, God is not just one more very powerful cause amongst all the secondary causal agents in creation. Divine agency and created agency are not univocal, and they do not act on different but comparable planes. Rather, God is the creator whose power to bring about the being of creatures is at every moment the absolute condition of there being any causation within creation. The divine primary cause and created secondary causes do not compete in a zero-sum game; the former wholly constitutes the latter. In the same way, the divine and human natures of Christ do not compete but fully

[10] Aquinas, *Summa Theologiae*, 1a.8.

subsist in Christ. They are not the same kind of thing, so they do not displace each other. The divine nature is the source of the human nature in Christ, just as God is the source of creatures and their causal efficacy in creation.

The distinction between the divine primary cause and created secondary causes allows Christian theology to give an account of how God brings about his loving purposes for creation through created causes. Creatures participate in their own perfecting through a power that is derived from God at every moment but is genuinely their own. They seek their own ends or goals. In this sense, creation is understood to be teleological – ordered to certain purposes and goals that cause the movement and striving of creatures towards those ends. Without such ends or 'final causes' there would be no intelligible agency because, according to a line of thought traceable to Aristotle, all agents act for the sake of some end. The term 'teleological' – referring to the study of final causes or purpose – points us to the apparent design of the universe and the so-called teleological argument for God's existence. Does God design creation as an architect might design a house or a mechanic a car? There is one crucial respect in which God does not design creation in the same way that we design artifacts. The ends or goals of artifacts such as cars and chairs lie outside those artifacts in the mind of the craftsman or designer. The materials of metal and wood do not make themselves into cars and chairs; they are a work of artifice. Metal and wood need to be compelled to take the form of a car or chair. For creatures, on the other hand, their goals or ends are intrinsic to their natures. God forms creatures with their powers and ends already inscribed into their being such that they can pursue those ends for themselves, sustained and guided by God's primary causal power. Whilst God is most intimately infused into the being of every creature as its primary cause, God nevertheless enables creation to seek its own ends and thereby participate in its own fulfilment. The ends of creatures are given by God, but they are intrinsic to the natures of creatures.

As we saw in the book of Genesis, creation is finished in the sense that it is whole and complete, but it is not yet perfected – it has not yet reached its final end, which is God. Whilst creation is an expression of divine love and gratuity, it features sin and evil; it is not yet all that it could be. The work of providence – God's action in creation's ongoing drama and the history of Israel and the Church – brings about the redemption and perfection of all things at the end times. This is why the doctrines of creation and providence are intimately linked to eschatology: at the eschaton, creation will be redeemed such that its full meaning, nature, and perfection will finally be revealed. Only then will creation be all that God intends it to be.

CREATION, SCIENCE, AND THE ENVIRONMENT

Because the doctrine of creation is concerned with the origins, meaning, and purposes of nature, it is often thought to share common territory with the natural sciences. When the modern experimental and mathematical sciences emerged in the seventeenth century, their practices and findings were thought to support belief in God the creator, hence they were known as 'physico-theology'. In the 1660s, the founders of the Royal Society, now the world's most prestigious scientific learned society, believed they could show creation to be an intricate mechanism governed by laws decreed by God. Those laws could be described mathematically; they showed the universe to be an orderly and rational expression of the divine will. Over time, God became increasingly incidental to scientific explanations of the workings of nature. Science and theology parted company, but their relationship would later become antagonistic. In the mid-nineteenth century, the Christian account of creation in Genesis was apparently challenged by Darwin's *On the Origin of Species* and the crystallisation of the idea that species are the result of millions of years of blind evolution rather than a six-day creation. The significance of this challenge is much contested, not least because centuries earlier Jewish and Christian theologians already interpreted Genesis allegorically, not as a piece of natural history akin to Darwin's works. Despite the prevalence of the so-called 'conflict thesis' that regards theology and science as mutually exclusive accounts of the world; in the twentieth century, the rise of Big Bang cosmology supposedly brought modern science into alignment with creation *ex nihilo*.

The relationship between the doctrine of creation and the natural sciences is complex, both historically and conceptually. Apparent conflict or congruence are often the result of a misunderstanding of the nature of the claims made by theology and the natural sciences. A good example concerns creation *ex nihilo* and modern cosmological accounts of the origins of the universe. As we saw, creation *ex nihilo* is not simply about the origins of creation; it describes creation's dependence on God at every moment. Unlike some aspects of the natural sciences, the doctrine of creation does not give explanatory prominence to the temporal origins of the cosmos – to how it all began – but rather looks forward to the final revealing of creation's beauty and meaning in the end times. Meanwhile, the natural sciences are concerned with describing change within nature: the universe expands from a singularity, life develops on earth, and species evolve over millions of years. The natural sciences are necessarily concerned with processes in nature and one thing becoming another. Yet this is precisely what creation *ex nihilo* denies about God's act of creation – it is not one thing becoming another because creation is 'from nothing'. As Aquinas puts it, creation is not a change. In the end, all scientific attempts to describe the Big Bang coming from nothing describe one thing coming from another – the Big Bang coming from a fluctuation in a quantum vacuum, for example. If cosmology were able to give an account of the Big Bang coming from nothing, it would cease to be physics and become metaphysics. So, the doctrine of creation *ex nihilo* is not a rival or complimentary scientific account of cosmic origins. It is what the theologian Janet Soskice calls 'a *biblically compelled* piece of metaphysical theology'.[11] To claim any straightforward congruence or conflict between creation *ex nihilo* and Big Bang cosmology is to confuse the domains and procedures of theology and the natural sciences. This is not to claim that theology and the natural sciences are unrelated. Some claim that the doctrine of creation, in giving an account of the goodness, meaning, and purpose of creation, provides the metaphysical basis for the methods and procedures of truthful science that is adequate to the deep mystery of nature.

The doctrine of creation and providence has also been challenged by the ecological crisis that emerged in the late twentieth century. In the 1960s, a number of historians blamed the crisis on the anthropocentric character of Christianity, particularly the idea that humanity is created in the image and likeness of God and therefore godlike in its power, that nature is for humanity's use, and the teaching in Genesis that humanity is to fill the earth and subdue it, having dominion over other creatures (Gen. 1:27–28).[12] The origins of the crisis are much more complex, of course, not least in the rise of industrial capitalism and the modern conviction that non-human nature is devoid of intrinsic meaning and purpose. Whilst the natural sciences diagnose the ecological crisis, many look to religious traditions, including the Christian doctrine of creation, for resources to address the crisis. One such resource can be creation *ex nihilo*.

[11] Janet M. Soskice, '*Creatio ex nihilo*: Its Jewish and Christian Foundations', in *Creation and the God of Abraham*, ed. David B. Burrell, Carlo Cogliati, Janet M. Soskice and William R. Stoeger (Cambridge: Cambridge University Press, 2010), 25 (emphasis original).
[12] Lynn White Jr., 'The Historical Roots of Our Ecologic Crisis', *Science* 155 (March 1967), 1203–1207.

As we saw above, a core claim of creation *ex nihilo* is that creation is fundamentally a gift (Jas. 1:17–18). This provides a particularly important context for understanding humanity's relation to wider nature. Gifts bear meaning and intrinsic value. According to the twentieth century French anthropologist Marcel Mauss, they bear something of the giver to the recipient and therefore mediate a relationship.[13] As a gift, creation bears something of God to creatures. Moreover, gifts make a moral claim on us: how will we properly receive the gift, enjoy the gift, and share the gift, so as to honour the giver? Gifts must be acknowledged with thanksgiving lest they become mere possessions. All our modes of production are parasitic on what has already been given and received in creation. To recognise this central aspect of the doctrine of creation – that creation is a supremely free and utterly gratuitous gift of divine love – establishes a very different metaphysical and moral framework for the interpretation of Genesis and our understanding the human vocation in the natural world. It suggests that meaning, purpose, and value belong to the whole creation and not just the human domain. Creation is sacred because, as a gift of God, its wholeness, truth, beauty, and goodness covey something of God to creatures. It is not to be the arena of casual exploitation but the cause of delight and thanksgiving.

Further Reading

Anderson, Gary, and Markus Bockmuehl, eds. (2018), *Creation Ex Nihilo: Origins, Development, Contemporary Challenges* (Notre Dame, IN: University of Notre Dame Press).
Aquinas, Thomas (2012), *Summa Theologiae* (Volume 13 Latin/English Edition of the Works of St. Thomas Aquinas; trans. Laurence Shapcote; Lander, WY: The Aquinas Institute for the Study of Sacred Doctrine), 1a.44–46.
Barth, Karl (2004), *Church Dogmatics*, III.1. (ed. G. W. Bromiley and T. F. Torrance; Edinburgh: T&T Clark), §§ 40–42.
Fergusson, David (2018), *The Providence of God: A Polyphonic Approach* (Cambridge: Cambridge University Press).
Harrison, Peter (2015), *The Territories of Science and Religion* (Oxford: Oxford University Press).
Hart, David Bentley (2017), 'God, Creation, and Evil: The Moral Meaning of *Creatio ex Nihilo*'. In *The Hidden and the Manifest: Essays in Theology and Metaphysics* (Grand Rapids: Eerdmans), 338–350.
Jenkins, Willis (2008), *Ecologies of Grace: Environmental Ethics and Christian Theology* (Oxford: Oxford University Press).

[13] Marcel Mauss, *The Gift: The Form and Reason for Exchange in Archaic Societies*, trans. W. D. Halls (London: Routledge, 2002).

Levering, Matthew (2017), *Engaging the Doctrine of Creation: Cosmos, Creatures, and the Wise and Good Creator* (Grand Rapids: Baker Academic).

McFarland, Ian (2014), *From Nothing: A Theology of Creation* (Louisville: Westminster John Knox).

Murphy, Francesca Aran, and Philip Ziegler, eds. (2009), *The Providence of God* (London: T&T Clark).

Oliver, Simon (2017), *Creation: A Guide for the Perplexed* (London: Bloomsbury).

Oord, Thomas J., ed. (2015), *Theologies of Creation: Creatio Ex Nihilo and Its New Rivals* (New York: Routledge).

Tanner, Kathryn (2005), *God and Creation in Christian Theology: Tyranny or Empowerment?* (Minneapolis: Fortress).

Webster, John (2013), '"Love Is Also a Lover of Life": Creation *Ex Nihilo* and Creaturely Goodness', *Modern Theology* 29, no. 2, 156–171.

Williams, Rowan (2018), *Christ the Heart of Creation* (London: Bloomsbury).

3 Humanity

JOHN BEHR

'What is the human being', the Psalmist asks God, 'that you are mindful of him, or the son of man that you attend to him'? (Ps. 8:5, LXX) How, indeed, can we define what it is to be human? Reviewing the diverse ways in which human beings have thought of themselves across the centuries, Charles Taylor concludes: 'I suspect that no satisfactory general formula can be found to characterize the ubiquitous underlying nature of a self-interpreting animal.'[1] Given that we exist in time and, individually and collectively, grow in time, to find a universal definition would perhaps be as impossible as trying to step twice into Heraclitus's river. And yet, that the human being is indeed something particular, worthy of God's mindfulness and attention is presupposed by the Psalmist.

For Christian theology, anthropology is not merely an ancillary topic alongside others in a system of distinct or discrete doctrines. Indeed, if Christian theology proclaims that God has revealed himself uniquely in Jesus Christ, as proclaimed by the apostles in accordance with the Scriptures, then this also speaks to what it is to be human. The Chalcedonian affirmation that Christ is fully divine and fully human does not begin by defining these terms separately, in other ways, to then bring them together; rather, if the one Jesus Christ is 'perfect' or 'complete' (teleios) in his divinity and humanity, then he also defines both, and does so, moreover, in one hypostasis, one concrete being, and one prosōpon, one 'face', such that he is indeed 'the image of the invisible God' (Col. 1:15). To do otherwise, as Barth forcefully pointed out, would be to start with 'God in the abstract ... distant and strange, and thus a non-human if not indeed an inhuman God', and with the human being 'in the abstract', 'sufficient unto himself without God and thus himself to be God'. One must, Barth insists, begin with the point that in Christ

---

[1] Charles Taylor, *The Sources of the Self: The Making of Modern Identity* (Cambridge, MA: Harvard University Press, 1989), 112.

'the fact is once for all established that God does not exist without the human …. In the mirror of this humanity of Jesus Christ the humanity of God enclosed in his divinity reveals itself'.[2] Theology and anthropology thus belong together, and both are grounded in Christology. In the words of Rahner: 'Christology is the end and beginning of anthropology. And this anthropology, when most thoroughly realized in Christology, is eternally theology … unless we think that we could find God without the human Christ, and so without the human being at all.'[3]

JOHN AND IGNATIUS

Given the inseparability of these doctrines, the best place to see a full exposition of what it is to be human is in the earliest unfolding of Christian theology, before these doctrines become thought of as being discrete elements, defined separately, of a larger system. Indeed, what we find there is a rather dramatic understanding of the revelation of God in Christ and of ourselves as being, or rather, called to become human. One of the most striking testimonies to this is the letter of Ignatius of Antioch to the Christians in Rome early in the second century. Journeying under guard to the capital, Ignatius urged the Roman Christians not to interfere with his coming martyrdom:

> Birth-pangs are upon me. Suffer me, my brethren; hinder me not from living, do not wish me to die …. Suffer me to receive the pure light; when I shall have arrived there, I shall be a human being. Suffer me to follow the example of the passion of my God.[4]

Not yet born, not yet living, and, moreover, not yet human, Ignatius sees his impending martyrdom as an opportunity to be confirmed to Christ and his passion, so being born into life as a human being. This birth, moreover, is intrinsically the birth of the body of Christ and so of Christ himself; as Ignatius notes, 'the head cannot be born without the parts' of the body.[5]

The background for this is the final word of Christ from the cross in the Gospel of John: *tetelestai* – 'it is finished, completed, perfected'

---

[2]   Karl Barth, *The Humanity of God*, (London: Collins, 1967), 43, 47, 49.
[3]   Karl Rahner, 'Theology of Incarnation', in Rahner, *Theological Investigations,* Volume 4, *More Recent Writings* (London: DLT, 1966), 105–120, at 117.
[4]   Ignatius of Antioch, *Letter to the Romans*, 6 (ed. and trans. A. Stewart, *Ignatius of Antioch: The Letters*; Yonkers, NY: St. Vladimir's Seminary Press, 2013 modified).
[5]   Ignatius of Antioch, *Letter to the Trallians* in *Ignatius of Antioch, 11.2: The Letters.*

(Jn. 19:30).[6] As has been recognized from the earliest times, John opens his Gospel with the same words as Genesis, 'in the beginning', and then plots the narrative so that it culminates in Christ's exaltation upon the cross. In Genesis, after making heaven and earth, God speaks everything into existence – 'Let there be' – until he comes to the human being, for which the voice switches from an imperative to a subjunctive: 'Let us make the human being according to our image and according to our likeness' (Gen. 1:26). Having set the stage, as it were, God deliberates and announces his own particular project, the particular work of God. That Christ's word from the cross, 'it is finished, completed, perfect', refers back to this is indicated unwittingly by Pilate when, in the final moments before the crucifixion, he presents Christ to the crowd with the words: 'Behold the human being' (19:5). The sabbath during which Christ is in the tomb is the 'great sabbath' (cf. 19:31), when God finally rests, his work being complete.

There are other dimensions to the way in which John presents Christ and his passion that draw further upon the opening chapters of Genesis. Unlike the Synoptics, in the Gospel of John, Christ is always in control; his 'time' is in his hands. When he first addresses 'the woman' in John 2, he tells her 'my hour is not yet'. When he next mentions 'the woman', it is in the words of comfort he gives his disciples as he prepares them for his departure: 'When a woman is in travail she has sorrow, because her hour has come, but when she is delivered of the child she no longer remembers the anguish, for joy that a human being is born into the world' (16:21). And then finally, at the crucifixion, when John narrates the scene, he speaks of 'his [Christ's] mother' being at the foot of the cross, but when he adopts Jesus' perspective, he describes her as 'the mother', and finally, when addressed by Christ it is as 'woman', specifically, 'woman, behold your son'. Already Tertullian pointed out that the way John describes the crucifixion parallels Genesis 2:

> As Adam was a figure of Christ, Adam's sleep sketched out the death of Christ, who was to sleep a mortal slumber, so that from the wound inflicted on his side might be figured the true Mother of the living, the Church. (*De Anima* 43.10)

While the woman in Genesis was called 'Eve' (in Greek *zoē*; 'life'), 'for she was the mother of the living', in fact all her children die; whereas

---

[6] For full exposition, see John Behr, *John the Theologian and His Paschal Gospel: A Prologue to Theology* (Oxford: Oxford University Press, 2019), 194–244.

the woman from the side of Christ is the true mother of the living but requires a birth through death to become a living human being, as understood by Ignatius.

One further intertextual play between Genesis and John is the way in which the figure of 'the woman', Mary, changes after the cross to being a spouse: when Mary first encounters the risen Christ, she supposes him to be the gardener, which is the way in which Adam had been identified in Genesis. As Peter Leithart has forcefully argued, in the two-part royal romance presented across John's Gospel and Revelation, the book of Revelation continues the narrative begun in the Gospel, so that, while the Gospel has presented the Bridegroom, unveiled on the cross, Revelation describes the preparation of the bride, specifically the formation of a human church: 'The incarnation produces the first fully human being – Jesus. Revelation unveils the formation of a fully human church as it describes the cruciformation of witnesses: To be a witness is to be a witness to death, a witness in death.'[7] In this way, Gospel and Revelation are a two-part royal romance, with the wedding intimated at the beginning of the Gospel being consummated at the end.[8]

Importantly, in the Gospel of John, the movement of Christ to the Cross is a movement of love, a love 'to the end' (13:1). This love of Christ in inscribed to the very relationship between Christ and his Father: 'for this reason the Father loves me, because I lay down my life, that I may take it up again' (Jn. 10:17). And it is, moreover, a love that originates from God himself: 'This is the way God loved the world, that he gave his only Son', sending him into the world not for its condemnation, 'but that the world might be saved through him' (Jn. 3.16–17) and a love that is indeed God (1 Jn. 4:8). It is, moreover, a love expected of each: 'Great love has no one than this, that one lay down one's life for one's friend' (Jn. 15:13). If Christ shows us what it is to be God in the way in which he dies as a human being, by laying down his life in love for others, and so showing the whole of his life of ministry and service in the self-offering love, this is also what it is to be human. 'I say you are gods', says the Psalmist in the words quoted by Christ (Ps. 81:7–8 LXX; Jn. 10:34), leaving the following clause unspoken but implicit: 'but you will die like human beings'.

A further reason for the subjunctive in Gen. 1:26 thus emerges: if to be human is to live by taking up the cross in a life of voluntary and

---

[7] Peter J. Leithart, *Revelation 1–11* (T & T Clark International Theological Commentary; London: Bloomsbury, 2018), 224.

[8] Ibid., 22–23.

loving self-offering, this is, to put it bluntly, something that God cannot bring about by an imperative, for the simple reason that it would not thus be an act of voluntary love. God can, however, and does create those – males and females (Gen. 1:27c) – who can learn and grow into such virtue, into 'a perfect man, the measure of the stature of the fulness of Christ' (Eph. 4:13). Having come into existence with no choice of our own ('no one asked me if I want to exist', as Kirillov protests in Dostoyevsky's *The Demons*), an existence in which, moreover, death is inevitably our end, we are, from the beginning of our existence passive victims of mortality; however, the life-giving death of Christ opens up a path for men and women to voluntarily take up the cross in loving self-offering for others, to thereby change the ground of their existence from necessity and mortality, through death, to freedom and love, to become human as Christ has shown this to be, and, indeed, to be gods: 'I say you are gods, sons of the Most-High, but you will die as human beings' (Ps. 82:6–7). The only work of creation described in Genesis as being God's own project but stated with the subjunctive rather than the imperative 'Let there be' requires our own 'Let it be' to be realized. Later theology would speak about this as 'deification' or might even differentiate between 'image' and 'likeness' (the former being given at creation, with a debate about whether it was lost in the 'Fall'; the latter needing to be attained). These early writers see the mystery in becoming human.

IRENAEUS OF LYONS

For Irenaeus of Lyons, a generation later, the whole of the economy from Adam to Christ is a movement, as it was for Paul, from type to reality (cf. Rom. 5:14) and from animation by a breath of life to vivification by the life-giving Spirit (cf. 1 Cor. 15:35–48). The project of God, to make the human being in his image and likeness, is thus a process in which Adam is continuously in the Hands of God, being moulded, to that 'at the end, "not by the will of the flesh, nor by the will of man" [Jn. 1:13], his Hands perfected a living human being [*vivum perfecerunt hominem*], in order that Adam might become in the image and likeness of God'.[9]

The growth from Adam to Christ requires time. As Irenaeus notes, God 'formed the human being for growth and increase, as the Scripture

---

[9] Irenaeus, *Against the Heresies* (=*Haer*) 5.1.3. (ed. and French trans. A. Rousseau et al.; Sources Chrétiennes; Paris: Cerf, 1965–1982), 100, 152–153, 210–211, 263–264, 293–294; English translation (modified here) in *Ante Nicene Fathers, Volume 1* (Edinburgh, 1887; repr. Grand Rapids: Eerdmans, 1987).

says, "increase and grow"' (*Haer*. 4.11.1; Gen. 1:28); and for Irenaeus this is the very difference between God and his handiwork: 'in this respect God differs from the human, in that God indeed makes but the human is made', and while the one who makes remains the same, 'while he who is made must receive a beginning, a middle, addition, and increase. And God indeed makes well, while the human is well made' (*Haer*. 4.11.2). Irenaeus describes the arc of the economy in various ways: as the human being becoming 'harmonized to the symphony of salvation' (*Haer*. 4.14.2) and as God and the human becoming 'accustomed' to each other, with the Spirit becoming accustomed to dwell in human beings, culminating in Christ and then, through Christ, those who are baptized, thereby receiving a 'pledge' of the Spirit preparing them to receive the fulness of the Spirit in the resurrection.[10] The culminating point of this growth is again, for Irenaeus, martyrdom: the martyrs bear their witness not by the weakness of the flesh but by the strength of the Spirit, so that 'when the weakness of the flesh is absorbed, it manifests the Spirit as powerful; and again, when the Spirit absorbs the weakness, it inherits the flesh for itself, and from both of these is made a living human being: living, indeed, because of the participation of the Spirit; and human, because of the substance of the flesh' (*Haer*. 5.9.2; cf. Matt. 26:41).

Irenaeus provides further insight into the dynamics of this growth in *Haer*. 4.37–39, when dealing with the question from his opponents of why it was that God didn't make the human being 'perfect' from the beginning, unable to deviate, without free will and discernment, and 'so unable to be anything other than what they were created' (*Haer*. 4.37.6). Irenaeus begins by pointing out that such a scenario would have benefitted neither God nor human beings: communion with God would have been neither precious, desired, or sought after; being by nature, no pleasure would have been found in it. Moreover, both Christ and Paul have emphasized the need for struggle (citing Matt. 11:12 and 1 Cor. 9:24 27), so that the good found in loving God becomes known (*Haer*. 4.37.7). By way of explanation, Irenaeus points out how sight is more valued by those who know what it is like to be without sight, so also is health prized more by those who know disease, light by contrast with darkness, and life by death (*Haer*. 4.37.7). Elsewhere, Irenaeus uses the example of Jonah to describe how the whole economy, from beginning to end, has been arranged in such a manner that human beings come to

---

[10] Cf. *Haer*. 3.17.1; 3.20.2; 4.5.4; 4.14.2; 4.21.3; 5.5.1; 5.8.1; 5.35.1; and P. Évieux, 'La Théologie de l'accoutumance chez saint Irénée', *RSR* 55 (1967), 5–54.

know their own weakness, for it is here that they simultaneously know the strength of God (cf. 2 Cor. 12:9); and having known the experience of death, they might thereafter hold ever more firmly to the source of life (*Haer.* 3.20).

Irenaeus develops his analysis by contrasting two different types of knowledge: that gained, on the one hand, through experience, and that, on the other hand, learned through hearsay (*Haer.* 4.39.1). It is, he points out, only through experience that the tongue comes to learn of both bitterness and sweetness, and likewise, it is only through experience of both good and evil, the latter being disobedience and death, that the mind receives the knowledge of the good, that is, obedience to God, which is life for human beings. By experiencing both, and casting off disobedience through repentance, the human being (as in the case of Jonah) becomes ever more tenacious in obedience to God, growing into the fullness of life. The alternative, Irenaeus says dramatically, is that 'if anyone shuns the knowledge of both of these, and the twofold perception of knowledge, forgetting himself he destroys the human being' (*Haer.* 4.39.1). Throughout this whole process, Irenaeus asserts, God has shown 'magnanimity' with the human, knowing, as the prophet said, that 'your own apostasy shall heal you' (*Haer.* 4.37.7; Jer. 2:19).

Irenaeus immediately continues by placing this particular action of God within the economy as a whole:

> God, thus, determining all things beforehand for the perfection of the human being, and towards the realization and manifestation of his economies, that goodness may be displayed and righteousness accomplished, and that the Church may be 'conformed to the image of his Son' [Rom. 8:29], and that, finally, the human being may be brought to such maturity as to see and comprehend God. (*Haer.* 4.37.7)

Human disobedience, apostasy, and death is, for Irenaeus, inscribed into the very unfolding of the economy; death results from human action, but it is nevertheless a result that is subsumed and transformed within the larger arc of the economy, as it brings the creature made from mud to share in the very life, glory, and power of the Uncreated, so demonstrating the goodness and righteousness of God. Worked out in and through the life of each individual human being, if they should respond with faith and thankfulness, the conclusion is also corporate. In this way, it is the Church that is conformed to Christ as each human being is brought to see God.

In the middle of this section, Irenaeus analyses the same question from a slightly different angle, suggesting that God could indeed have created the human being perfect or as a 'god' from the beginning, for all things are possible to him. Yet, as created, human beings are initially 'infantile', and so 'unaccustomed to and unexercised in perfect conduct' (*Haer.* 4.38.1). Just as a mother could give solid food to a new-born infant, although it would not do the infant any good, 'so also', Irenaeus continues, 'it was possible for God himself to have made the human being perfect from the first, but the human being could not receive this, being as yet an infant' (*Haer.* 4.38.1). What is needed is, again, growth, a process of accustoming the human being to bear the life and glory of God. And here we return to the issue he identified in his opponents' position: that without freedom and the possibility for growth, the creature would never be able to become something more than they were at first. By definition, of course, the created cannot be uncreated, but this is not a restriction upon the omnipotence of God, for this omnipotence is demonstrated, for Irenaeus, in the way that the created is in fact brought in time to share in the uncreated life of God, a change in the 'fashion' of its existence or the mode of its life, which requires preparation and training, and it is to this that the whole economy has aimed and been tending. God, Irenaeus says, has demonstrated his power, wisdom, and goodness simultaneously: power and goodness in bringing into existence that which was not and wisdom in that he made those things 'rhythmical and harmonious and elaborate', so that they, 'through the superabundance of his goodness, receiving growth and continuance for a long period of time, might obtain the glory of the Uncreated, of the God who ungrudgingly bestows good. By virtue of being created, they are not uncreated; but by virtue of continuing in being throughout a long course of ages, they shall receive the power of the Uncreated, of the God who freely bestows upon them eternal existence' (*Haer.* 4.38.3). With the Father planning and commanding, the Son executing and performing, and the Spirit giving nourishment and growth, the human being 'makes progress day by day, ascending to perfection, that is, approaching the Uncreated One' (*Haer.* 4.38.3). Specifically:

> It was first necessary for the human being to be created;
> and having been created, to increase;
> and having increased, to become an adult;
> and having become an adult, to multiply;
> and having multiplied, to become strong;
> and having been strengthened, to be glorified;
> and being glorified, to see his Master.
>
> (*Haer.* 4.38.3)

What is most striking about this passage, describing the arc of the economy – the growth from Adam to Christ – is that it is patterned upon the life of each human being, the 'seven stages' of life, a pattern of reflection going back to Hippocrates. And, in turn, this means that one can see the lifespan of each human being as recapitulating the whole arc of the economy from the infant Adam to the mature, perfect Christ. It is possible that this pattern of thought goes back to the evangelist John, for Irenaeus records that the elders (Papias is certainly the source) who conversed with John in Asia related that Christ recapitulated all the stages of human life in himself becoming an infant, a child, boy, youth, and, indeed, an old man.[11] That this pattern of thinking does go back to that early period is confirmed by the way Victorinus of Pettau, independently of Irenaeus, affirms that Christ 'consummates his humanity [humanitatem ... consummat] in the number seven: birth, infancy, boyhood, youth, young-manhood, maturity, death'.[12]

GREGORY OF NYSSA

The pattern of thought that we have seen in John, Ignatius, and Irenaeus, continues and is developed most fully by Gregory of Nyssa in his work *On the Human Image of God* (otherwise known as *On the Making of Man*).[13] Here Gregory draws not only upon the prior theological tradition but also the philosophical and medical tradition going back to Anaxagoras and Hippocrates, and especially Plato's *Timaeus*. His work is in fact modelled on the *Timaeus*. Like Timaeus's speech, Gregory divides his treatise into three parts.[14] In the first part (chaps. 1–15), Gregory gives a beautiful picture of the human being as the apex of creation and, more than that, the very image of God. Gregory reads Genesis 1 as Moses providing an 'anthropogony', describing the

---

[11] *Haer.* 2.22.4; the five ages here would increase to seven when one includes birth and death. Cf. John Chapman, 'Papias on the Age of Our Lord', *JTS* 9 (1907), 42–61, which remains the best treatment of these passages.

[12] Victorinus of Pettau, *De Fabrica mundi* (ed. and French trans. M. Dulaey; Sources Chrétiennes 423; Paris: Cerf, 1997), 9.

[13] The text is found in PG 44.125–256, and a translation in *Nicene and Post-Nicene Fathers*, Second Series, Volume 5 (1893; repr. Grand Rapids: Eerdmans, 1994). I have used my own translation, from a forthcoming edition.

[14] Timaeus first presents the 'things crafted by Intellect' (cf. 47e4) but then points out that the world is in fact of mixed birth and so he must also 'give an account of necessity' or 'the straying cause' (48a2–3); and then he brings these two accounts together under 'a final head' (69a7–b12), describing in medical or anatomical terms the constitution of the human being.

evolution of the soul from its initial power of growth and nutrition in plants, then acquiring the power of sense-perception in the irrational animals, and culminating in the human being, whose soul possesses (or rather shares in) the power of the intellect, 'nature making an ascent, as it were by steps, I mean the properties of life, from the lower to the perfect' (*De hom.* 8.4–7). The human body is, in turn, perfectly adapted for the intellect, upright, rather than bent downwards, and with hands, leaving the mouth to articulate speech and so communicate with others (*De hom.* 8.8–93). It is, moreover, in the virtues that it freely exercises that the human being is the living image of the King (*De hom.* 4–5), exercising its sovereignty, as the physically weakest of all the animals, through the cooperation of its subjects (*De hom.* 7). But who this human being is, Gregory does not say.

Gregory opens the second part of his treatise (chaps. 16–29) by taking up again the text of Gen. 1:27 but now asks the question: where do we in fact see the human being in the image of God? For when we look around, what we in fact see is the pitiable wretchedness of human beings, subject to passion and corruption. This leads him into a long discussion, full of digressions and changes of voice, reflecting on who the human being, spoken of in Genesis 1, in fact is, God's prevision of the waywardness of the human will and movement and God's anticipatory provision for this waywardness. There are a number of important points that Gregory makes in this part of his treatise. First, he finds the source of the mismatch between what Scripture claims and the empirical reality we see, in the shift between the two clauses of Gen. 1:27:

'God made', it says, 'the human being, in accordance with the image of God he made it'. The creation of that which came to be 'in accordance with the image' has an end; then it makes a repetition of the account of the formation, and says, 'male and female he made them'. I think it is known to everyone that this is understood to be outside the Prototype, 'for in Christ Jesus', as the apostle says, 'there is neither male nor female' [Gal. 3:28], but the account says that the human being is indeed divided into these. Therefore the formation of our nature is in a sense twofold, that being likened to the divine, [and] that being divided according to this difference; for something like this the account hints at by the arrangement of what is written, first saying, 'God made the human being, in accordance with the image of God he made it', and then, adding to what has been said, 'male and female made he them', something that is foreign to our conceptions of God. (*De hom.* 16.7–8)

In each clause of Gen. 1:27, the word used for God's action is the same: 'made' (*epoiēsen*). For Gregory, as he makes clear in his *Hexameron*, a companion piece to this work, God's act of making is instantaneous, encompassing all that is to be, while what comes into being is 'manifested' in proper order and sequence.[15] Thus, Gregory in the above passage expounds what is 'made' with different words. 'The creation [*ktisis*] of that which has come to be in accordance with the image', Gregory says, 'has an end [*telos*]', that is, a goal or final clause, which is, as he puts it in the next sentence, its Prototype, that is, Christ Jesus. This means, importantly, that it is Christ who is the Prototype, not Adam, who in fact has not yet been mentioned, either by Scripture or Gregory (until *De hom.* 16.16 and 22.3, in both cases specifying that he is not talking about Adam!). Gregory then takes v. 27c as being an 'repetition of the account of the formation [*kataskeuē*]': it is not God's act of making the human being that is in two stages but, rather, the formation of the human being is 'two-fold'.

The two-foldedness of our formation is explicitly spelled out in the following section, where Gregory presents 'the great and lofty teaching of Scripture', that the human being is the 'span' between the divine, incorporeal, and intelligent, on the one hand, and, on the other, the irrational and animal form of life, that is, the in-between embracing both extremes, and, moreover, that each of these aspects 'is certainly in all that partakes of human life'; and, further, that in his anthropogony Moses describes how in the human, the intellectual takes precedence, for the image is mentioned first, so that our participation and kinship with the irrational is 'a concomitant to being human'. All this shows that with regard to the image there is neither male nor female, as there is not in the prototype, Jesus Christ, but that 'the particularities of human nature' are to be male and female (*De hom.* 16.9).

The second point is that having come into existence from non-being, created beings are inherently mutable (*De hom.* 16.12); and on this basis, Gregory responds to the predicament posed at the beginning of the chapter: the lack of 'fit' between the Scriptural assertion and what we in fact see is due to the wavering, mutable will of human beings (the equivalent of Timaeus's 'straying cause'), foreseen by God in his prevision of and provision for the waywardness of the human will. It is this that leads God to 'devise for the image the difference of male and female, which no longer looks to the divine archetype but, as was said,

[15] Gregory of Nyssa, *Hexameron* (trans. Robin Orton; Fathers of the Church, Shorter Works 1; Washington DC: Catholic University of America Press, 2021), 64.

assimilates to the less rational nature' (*De hom.* 16.14). This explanation, it must be noted, is phrased as an aetiological account for what he
has just established as the scriptural teaching regarding the human as a
two-fold being; that is, if the purpose of God is to make a human being
according to his image (Gen. 1:26), and in the Prototype there 'is not
male and female' (Gal. 3:28), why and for what purpose did God also
make the human being 'male and female'? That God has done so, and
that the human being is such, is not in question: the issue is why? And
his answer here is that this assimilation to the less rational is a provision made in anticipation of the divinely foreseen waywardness of the
human will (though, of course, this is ultimately circular: it is because
we are already both that we can tend towards the irrational and
be assimilated to it), though Gregory immediately goes on to say that
he is not stating what comes to his mind but rather writing in the form
of an exercise for his readers (*De hom.* 16.5). That movement and
mutability lie at the basis of human existence, moreover, ensures that
the waywardness of their movements will inevitably come to an end:
evil being inherently finite, compared to the infinity of God, when the
human has run through to the end, their ever-moving nature compels
them to reverse course and return to the good (*De hom.* 21.1–2) but now
with discernment, differentiating between good and evil, a state higher
than mere knowledge (*De hom.* 20.1). The extension of time required for
this is provided by God for the growth of the human being.

But the third and most striking point is that the human being 'made'
in the image of God in Gen. 1:27a includes all humanity (*De hom.*
16.16–19), not simply as a genus but as 'the entire plenitude of humanity'; and this plenitude was, moreover, seen in the prevision of God as a
single human being:

> The human being manifested together with the first formation of
> the world, and he who shall come to be after consummation of all,
> both likewise have this: they equally bear in themselves the divine
> image. For this reason the whole was called one human being,
> because to the power of God nothing has either passed or is to
> come, but even that which is looked for is held fast equally with
> the present by his all-embracing activity. (*De hom.* 16.17–18)

This very strong understanding of the unity of all human beings – past,
present, and future – as one human being is, again, an expression of God's
instantaneous and comprehensive act of making that unfolds through
its own sequence and order. Embracing all that would come to be, the
human being 'manifested' at the beginning and the one who 'comes to

be after the consummation of all' bear the divine image. Here we see the significance of the fact that to this point Gregory has not been speaking of Adam, the first particular human being in the Genesis narrative but only appearing in its second chapter: Adam might well be the first, but he is not the *archē*. The image of God in accordance with whom God makes the human being in Gen. 1.27 is, as we saw in *De hom.* 16.7, Christ Jesus, the 'Prototype'. Yet so too is the one who 'comes to be' at the end, but then, 'after the consummation of all', in 'the entire fullness of humanity' foreseen by God from or in the beginning, the *archē*. Or, as Balthasar more elegantly put it: 'The total Christ is none other than the total humanity.'[16]

In the third and final part of the work (chap. 30), paralleling the third part of Timaeus's speech, in which he brings the two former accounts together and 'puts a final head on his story', Gregory brings his two analyses together in terms of the formation of an actual human being, described in medical and anatomical terms, in terms of the seed deposited and growing in the womb, emerging into the world of sense-perception, where it now grows in its reasoning faculty, recapitulating the stages in the evolution of the soul described by Moses in the opening chapter of Genesis. After providing extensive descriptions of human anatomy, and noting that he has wandered deep into the mysteries of nature, Gregory reflects that his goal was to show that 'from animated and living bodies a being, living and animated from the first, is generated, and that human nature takes it and cherishes it, like a nursling, with her own powers' so that it grows appropriately in each part, 'for it immediately displays, by this artistic and scientific process of formation, the power of the soul interwoven with it, appearing at first somewhat obscurely, but afterwards increasing in radiance concurrently with the perfecting of the organism' (*De hom.* 30.29).

Gregory then goes on to compare this process to the way that a sculptor works on stone, patiently working the figure in mind upon the stone, so that it gradually becomes recognizable to an observer (*De hom.* 30.30). In the same way, Gregory proposes,

we say that nature, the all-contriving, taking from the kindred matter within herself the part that comes from the human being crafts the statue. And just as the form follows upon the gradual

[16] Hans Urs von Balthasar, *Presence and Thought: An Essay on the Religious Philosophy of Gregory of Nyssa* (trans. Mark Sebanc; San Francisco: Ignatius Press, 1995 [1944]), 87.

working of the stone, at first somewhat indistinct, but more perfect after the completion of the work, so also in the carving of the organism the form of the soul, by the analogy, is displayed in the substratum, incompletely in that which is incomplete, and perfectly in that which is perfect; but it would have been perfect from the beginning had nature not been maimed by evil. For this reason our sharing in that impassioned and animal-like coming-into-being brings it about that the divine image does not shine forth immediately in the moulded figure, but, by a certain method and sequence, through those material and more animal-like attributes of the soul, brings to perfection the human being. (*De hom.* 30.30)

It is striking that the 'maiming by evil', which prevented the end result from being perfect from the beginning, refers not to 'our nature' (through a fall, however conceived), but rather to 'nature' as the 'all-contriving', the active agent of the process of that which comes into being (cf. *De hom.* 8.4–7). The 'genesis of evil' is not some primordial event but rather occurs, Gregory pointed out, whenever the intellect turns downwards towards matter and so receives its shapelessness into itself (*De hom.* 12.9–13), and it is this that was played out across the second part of the treatise in terms of the waywardness of the inclination of the human will, learning discernment through experience so that it returns, in the end, to what it was made in the beginning, the *archē*. As such, if the analogy with sculpting is to be followed, then the 'evil' that 'maims' nature, such that the human being is not brought to perfection at the beginning but at the end, is more like the recalcitrance of that upon which nature is working, which in this case is the waywardness of the human will. Like Timaeus's 'straying cause', it needs to be 'persuaded by intellect'.

It is equally striking that Gregory here says that it is not simply by 'sharing in the impassioned and animal-like coming-into-being' that the human race reaches the plenitude foreseen by God (cf. *De hom.* 22.4) but that perfection is attained in a proper order and sequence, and, moreover, this happens '*through* those more material and animal-like attributes of the soul'. If it is 'the evil husbandry of the intellect' that has perverted all their motions and impulses shared with the animals into forms of passion not known amongst the animals, it is the intellect that needs training, to raise all these motions so that they too are 'conformed to the beauty of the divine image' (*De hom.* 18. 4–5), so that the beauty of the divine image in the moulded figure can truly shine forth.

Gregory thus provides us with three coordinated analyses of the human being as the image of God. In the first part of the work (chaps. 1–15), Gregory presents the ideal vision of the ideal human being. In the second part of the work (chaps. 16–29), he offers an analysis of the prevision and provision of God with respect to the wavering inclination of the human will and the evil husbandry of the human intellect, sketching out the economy, or the 'anthropogony', traced in the ascent of nature to the more perfect form of life, on the one hand, and, on the other hand, leading to the completion of the plenitude of the human race as the image of God, the total Christ, a process that requires, and is co-extensive with, time itself, resulting in the final transformation proclaimed by Paul. And in the third part of the work, Gregory describes how this economy is recapitulated in the life of each human being, from the seed being implanted in the womb and growing there through the power of nutrition, then coming into the world of sense-perception, where it continues to grow in both body and soul, learning discernment by experience and growing in virtue. And so he concludes his treatise with the exhortation, using Paul's words, that it is now time to put away childish things, the old human being, and put on instead the one being renewed in accordance with the image of God (*De hom.* 30.33; Col. 3:9–10).

CONCLUSION

The anthropology explored here offers a thoroughly Christological and eschatological understanding of the human being, seeing the whole of the economy as a single coordinated pedagogy bringing God's project, announced at the beginning, to realization at the end. In each case, it is elaborated on the premise of the crucified and risen Jesus Christ as proclaimed by the apostles in accordance with the Scriptures: Ignatius will become human by following Christ in his Passion. For Irenaeus, it is because the Savior exists that creation is brought into being, in a pedagogy that leads from the infancy of Adam to the humanity of Christ. For Gregory, this is played out in grand cosmological terms as the evolution of nature, culminating in the fulness of the body of Christ. In each case, Genesis is read in the light of the end, unveiled in the light of Christ's crucifixion and resurrection. It is the revelation of one who is perfect in divinity and humanity, in one, that not only enables the understanding of how far the human race has fallen short of this from the beginning but also enables seeing our current situation as part of a pedagogy or the 'birth-pangs' of the children of God (Romans 8). It does not imply the lack of an initial perfection, though that 'perfection', as with a new-born infant, is but an initial state, requiring growth into that which they are called to be; in this case, learning to give our own 'let it be' to God's own work and so arrive, individually, at the fulness of the stature of Christ and collectively as his body. The span of growth is both that of the movement from Adam to Christ, the movement of each individual, and the movement of the human race as a whole.[17] It is a growth, moreover, that culminates in the transformation proclaimed by Paul (1 Cor. 15:51–54), the starting point for which, and indeed the first fruits of which, is Christ himself. Theology and anthropology are indeed bound intrinsically together as Christology.

Further Reading

Anderson, Gary A. (2001), *The Genesis of Perfection: Adam and Eve in Jewish and Christian Imagination* (Louisville: Westminster John Knox).
Behr, John (2013), *Irenaeus of Lyons: Identifying Christianity* (CTC; Oxford: Oxford University Press).
Kelsey, David H. (2009), *Eccentric Existence: A Theological Anthropology* (Louisville: Westminster John Knox).
Pannenberg, Wolfhart (1985), *Anthropology in Theological Context* (London: T&T Clark).
Schwarz, Hans (2013), *The Human Being: A Theological Anthropology* (Grand Rapids: Eerdmans).
Spaemann, Robert (2006), *Persons: The Difference between 'Someone' and 'Something'* (Oxford: Oxford University Press).
Zimmermann, Jens (2012), *Humanism and Religion: A Call for the Renewal of Western Culture* (Oxford: Oxford University Press).

[17] Mary LeCron Foster, 'Symbolism: the Foundation of Culture', in *Companion Encyclopedia of Anthropology: Humanity, Culture, Social Life* (ed. Tim Ingold; London: Routledge, 1993), 366–395, at 386: 'both biological evolution and the stages in the child's cognitive development follow much the same progression of evolutionary stages as that suggested in the archaeological record'.

4 Israel

MATTHEW LEVERING

Today, a Christian doctrine of Israel will be worked out under the shadow of Christian persecution of Jews – which prepared the way for the Holocaust – and also in the context of the passages in the New Testament that exhibit harsh polemic against Jews who did not accept Jesus as the Messiah.[1] Traditionally, Christians supposed that the Jewish people who do not accept Jesus as the Messiah are in a condition of covenantal infidelity and covenantal curse. Christians assumed that the Jews' covenants had been revoked so that they no longer are God's people. Christian sermons and writings about the Jewish people, whether in the dreadful stereotypes and violent language employed by Martin Luther, or in Blessed John Duns Scotus's approval of the forced baptism of Jews, or in St. John Chrysostom's poisonous rhetorical invective against the Jewish people of his day, had an impact over the centuries in pogroms, expulsions, and abuse of all kinds.

In contemporary Christian theologies of the Jewish people, fortunately, the guiding assumptions are quite different. A number of new pressing questions have emerged. For example, must Jewish converts to Christianity observe Torah as part of salvific covenantal fidelity?[2] Can Jews be saved without explicitly affirming Jesus as the Messiah? What is

---

[1] See, for example, Robert Michael, *A History of Catholic Antisemitism: The Dark Side of the Church* (New York: Palgrave Macmillan, 2008); Amy-Jill Levine, "Anti-Judaism and the Gospel of Matthew," in *Anti-Judaism and the Gospels* (ed. William R. Farmer; Harrisburg, PA: Trinity International, 1999), 9–36. See also Jonathan Elukin, *Living Together, Living Apart: Rethinking Jewish-Christian Relations in the Middle Ages* (Princeton, NJ: Princeton University Press, 2007).

[2] See, for example, Mark S. Kinzer, *Postmissionary Messianic Judaism: Redefining Christian Engagement with the Jewish People* (Grand Rapids, MI: Brazos, 2005); R. Kendall Soulen, *The God of Israel and Christian Theology* (Minneapolis, MN: Fortress, 1996); Matthew Thiessen, *Paul and the Gentile Problem* (Oxford: Oxford University Press, 2016); Mark D. Nanos, *Collected Essays of Mark D. Nanos*, 4 vols. (Eugene, OR: Cascade, 2017–2018); N. T. Wright, *Paul and the Faithfulness of God* (Minneapolis: Fortress, 2013), chaps. 10–11.

the relationship of specifically Christian names of God (e.g., Father, Son, and Holy Spirit) to the name YHWH?[3] Should Christians support Jewish Zionism and, if so, how would this relate to Christ's fulfillment of the covenants and to Palestinian Muslims and Christians who lay claim to the land and who lack equal status in the State of Israel?[4]

Every Christian theology must have a significant place for such realities as the God of Israel, the exodus, the Torah, the Temple, the Davidic kingship, and the promised land. A covenant-based Christian theology will track God's covenants with Noah, Abraham, Moses, and David, as fulfilled by Christ and the Church.[5] A typological theology will present Christ as the new Adam, the new Isaac, the new David, and so on.[6] Christ is the Torah incarnate; Christ is the Temple embodied and perfected. Christ is the fulfillment of the Akedah (Genesis 22).[7] Incorporated into Christ and filled with his Spirit, Christ's members are a living Temple who share in his perfect fulfillment of Torah through obeying his commandment to love, as spelled out in John 13, Matthew 5, and Matthew 25:31–46, among other places. United to Christ the new Passover Lamb, Christians journey on the new exodus to the true promised land, nourished by the new manna (the Eucharist) and guided by the Spirit.[8]

Additionally, Christian doctrine benefits today through sustained engagement with great Jewish thinkers, including Franz Rosenzweig, Martin Buber, Abraham Joshua Heschel, Joseph B. Soloveitchik, David Novak, Jon D. Levenson, Michael Wyschogrod, Peter Ochs, Jonathan Sacks, and others. Indeed, the Church Fathers themselves benefited – albeit

---

[3] See R. Kendall Soulen, *The Divine Name(s) and the Holy Trinity*, Volume 1: *Distinguishing the Voices* (Louisville: Westminster John Knox, 2011).

[4] See David Novak, *Zionism and Judaism: A New Theory* (Cambridge: Cambridge University Press, 2015); Gavin D'Costa, "Catholic Zionism," *First Things* no. 229 (January 2020), 18–24.

[5] See Joseph Ratzinger, *Many Religions – One Covenant: Israel, the Church, and the World* (trans. Graham Harrison; San Francisco: Ignatius Press, 1999).

[6] For the centrality of typology in the New Testament, see Richard B. Hays, *Echoes of Scripture in the Gospels* (Waco, TX: Baylor University Press, 2016).

[7] See, for example, Edward Kessler, *Bound by the Bible: Jews, Christians and the Sacrifice of Isaac* (Cambridge: Cambridge University Press, 2005); Jon D. Levenson, *The Death and Resurrection of the Beloved Son: The Transformation of Child Sacrifice in Judaism and Christianity* (New Haven, CT: Yale University Press, 1993); R. W. L. Moberly, *The Bible, Theology, and Faith* (Cambridge: Cambridge University Press, 2000).

[8] See Brant Pitre, *Jesus and the Last Supper* (Grand Rapids: Eerdmans, 2015); L. Michael Morales, *Exodus Old and New: A Biblical Theology of Redemption* (Downers Grove, IL: InterVarsity, 2020).

in a competitive fashion – from engagement with Rabbinic viewpoints.[9] Medieval Christian theologians learned from Jewish scholars such as Moses Maimonides even while considering him, along with all other Jews, to be in a spiritual condition of culpable unbelief.[10]

I have tried in many of my earlier writings to practice all of the above aspects of the Christian doctrine of Israel. But for the purposes of the present short essay, I will focus on defending what I consider to be the six necessary foundations of any Christian doctrine of Israel:

(1) Jesus is the divine Messiah of Israel. He is the one sent to inaugurate the promised restoration of Israel and to be the eschatological king of his people. He is the universal Savior, calling Jews and Gentiles into his kingdom.

(2) Jesus came to inaugurate the Messianic Israel, reconfigured around himself. By his Cross, Resurrection, and Ascension to the right hand of the Father, all God's covenantal promises are fulfilled and reconfigured with Christ at the center.

(3) Jesus has poured out his Spirit and established the Church as the eschatological Temple. By his Spirit, believers participate in his sacrificial death in supreme love. United to Christ, believers obey the Messianically reconfigured Torah and participate in the cultic acts of the Messianically reconfigured Temple.

(4) The coming of the Messiah does not revoke or negate God's covenants with the people of Israel, his chosen people. The ongoing Jewish people remain God's beloved, elect, covenantal people.

(5) God has permitted his beloved ongoing Jewish people, as a whole, not to accept Jesus as the Messiah. The Jewish people continue to have a positive place in the economy of salvation. God continues to relate positively to his beloved ongoing Jewish people.

(6) Christians from the outset caused scandal by their polemics against Jews who did not accept Jesus, and the result is that the Jewish people, as a whole, are in a condition of non-culpable invincible ignorance about Jesus's Messianic status. Over the centuries, Jews

---

[9] See, for example, Gary A. Anderson, *The Genesis of Perfection: Adam and Eve in Jewish and Christian Imagination* (Louisville: Westminster John Knox, 2001); Marc Hirshman, *A Rivalry of Genius: Jewish and Christian Biblical Interpretation in Late Antiquity*, trans. Batya Stein (New York: State University of New York Press, 1996); Michal Bar-Asher Siegal, *Early Christian Monastic Literature and the Babylonian Talmud* (Cambridge: Cambridge University Press, 2013).

[10] See, for example, David B. Burrell, C.S.C., *Freedom and Creation in Three Traditions* (Notre Dame: University of Notre Dame Press, 1993).

have generally experienced not charity but the severe counter-witness of hatred and persecution from Jesus's followers. God has permitted his beloved Christian people to cause this scandal. Christians must hope that the Christians who caused this scandal were acting in invincible ignorance against a people whom they did not know.

The remainder of this essay will explicate these six points a bit further. I hope to show why any Christian doctrine of Israel should hold tightly to each of them.[11]

Jesus Is the Divine Messiah of Israel and the Universal Savior

In *The Messianic Theology of the New Testament*, Joshua Jipp demonstrates that the first Christians believed Jesus to be "the Davidic shepherd-king anticipated by Israel's prophets who establishes his just and compassionate reign over Israel."[12] Jesus is the one who inaugurates the Messianic kingdom. This Messianic kingdom is more than the simple extension of Israel's prior way of life. Rather, Jesus as the Messianic king reigns over the whole earth at the right hand of the Father. He fulfills Zech. 9:10's promise that the triumphant Davidic king's "dominion shall be from sea to sea and from the River to the ends of the earth." No one stands outside Jesus's Messianic reign.

Thus, when in Acts 4:12 Peter proclaims to the rulers and elders and scribes in Jerusalem that "there is salvation in no one else [other than Jesus]," Peter is proclaiming the viewpoint of the early Christians. For Paul, too, Jesus is the sole Savior of the world. Paul argues that the salvation brought by Jesus Christ is the necessary path for the forgiveness of our sins. It is the Cross of the Messiah that saves both Jews and Gentiles "from the wrath of God" (Rom 5:9) – not that God was our enemy, but we were God's "enemies" (Rom. 5:10) because we had given ourselves to the bondage of the powers of wickedness. Paul sums up: "The end of those things is death. But now that you have been set free

---

[11] For a much fuller account, see my *Engaging the Doctrine of Israel: A Christian Israelology in Dialogue with Ongoing Judaism* (Eugene, OR: Cascade, 2021). For further clarification, see my "Aquinas and Supersessionism One More Time: A Response to Matthew A. Tapie's *Aquinas on Israel and the Church*," *Pro Ecclesia* 25 (2016), 395–412. Matthew Tapie's criticisms brought me back to these issues and have resulted in a friendship in which he has taught me much.

[12] Joshua W. Jipp, *The Messianic Theology of the New Testament* (Grand Rapids: Eerdmans, 2020), 318–319.

from sin and have become slaves of God, the return you get is sanctification and its end, eternal life" (Rom. 6:21–22).

Jesus's Cross is a supreme kingly act of establishing his people in justice – and thus it constitutes the eschatological inauguration of his holy kingdom. The risen Jesus comes to his disciples as their king, forgiving them and sending them on a mission to the whole world. Christians have the opportunity to share in and to spread Jesus's conquest by communicating to the world the Gospel's message of mercy and triumph over sin and death, not by power but by self-sacrificial love.

If there ever was a New Testament truth, it is that Jesus Christ is now the eschatological king of all nations, Jewish and Gentile. It is not possible, from a Christian perspective, to claim that there is any path of salvation other than union with the Messiah, Jesus. Certainly, Jesus is the Lord and King of God's people Israel, both in the first century and in all centuries since.

Jesus Came to Inaugurate the Messianic Israel, Reconfigured around Himself

Reflecting upon Jesus's choosing of twelve disciples and his promise that they would sit on twelve thrones judging the tribes of Israel (see Lk. 6:13; 22:30), N. T. Wright has commented: "The very existence of the twelve speaks, of course, of the reconstitution of Israel ... for Jesus to give twelve followers a place of prominence, let alone to make comments about them sitting on thrones judging the twelve tribes, indicates pretty clearly that he was thinking in terms of the eschatological restoration of Israel."[13] Yet, this eschatological restoration does not mean that Christ merely adds the Gentiles to the existing Torah, polity, and cult of the people of Israel. Rather, Christ recenters all of these elements around himself.

In the Gospels, Jesus is more than once acclaimed as the one who is to reign in Jerusalem in an earthly manner, taking the place of the Roman interlopers. But Jesus consistently repudiates such a role. He establishes his Church upon the "rock" of Peter, rather than making plans for building a palace or refurbishing the Temple in Jerusalem. His cross bears the inscription "the King of the Jews," but he is no earthly king. Besides, the Davidic kings had ruled the land of Canaan at most, and generally much less territory. In the Torah, specific laws had been

---

[13] N. T. Wright, *Jesus and the Victory of God* (Minneapolis: Fortress, 1996), 300.

given regarding the king and the governance of the land, including the tasks of judging and so on. But Jesus's worldwide kingdom is not organized by these laws. Membership in Jesus's kingdom comes by faith in Jesus and by baptism, not circumcision. The risen Jesus tells his followers to proclaim his worldwide authority and to baptize new believers "in the name of the Father and of the Son and of the Holy Spirit" (Mt. 28:19).

In his public ministry, too, Jesus forgives sins by his own authority rather than by means of the Levitical system for atonement. Jesus heals on the Sabbath and allows his disciples to pick grain on the Sabbath. Even if this may be within the bounds of the Torah, he goes further by adding that "the Son of man [Jesus] is lord even of the sabbath" (Mk 2:28). His followers worship not on the Sabbath but on Sunday, the day of his Resurrection. In the Gospel of Mark, he overturns the Torah's teaching about divorce, replacing it with a much stricter stance. He is regularly accused of blasphemy, of putting himself in the place of God. Indeed, he insists that salvation will entail acknowledging him: "every one who acknowledges me before men, I also will acknowledge before my Father who is in heaven" (Mt. 10:32). He foretells a reconfiguration of the kingdom of God, in which some Gentiles (such as a faith-filled Roman centurion) will stand where some of the "sons of the kingdom" (Mt. 8:11–12) should have stood.

In the parable of the wicked tenants, Jesus depicts a landowner who sends various emissaries to his tenants. The tenants kill the emissaries, finally including the landowner's own son. Jesus draws the moral: "What will the owner of the vineyard do? He will come and destroy the tenants, and give the vineyard to others" (Mk. 12:9). He adds that, in accord with Ps. 118:22, it will be said that the stone rejected by the builders has become the cornerstone. He thus presents himself as the cornerstone of the kingdom of God and also as radically changing the composition of his people. The basic idea is that Gentiles are going to be included in his eschatological kingdom, which is now at hand. His kingdom will be organized no longer around the Torah's sacrificial remembrance of the Passover but around his own Paschal mystery. He gives his followers the Eucharist at his Last Supper and commands that they do this in liturgical remembrance of him.

As a result, the Church that Paul describes as "the Israel of God" (Gal. 6:16) is quite different from the Jewish communities in which Paul grew up and which he knew well. The differences should not of course be exaggerated. Yet, Christ is at the center in a radical way. Paul states, "for just as the body is one and has many members, and all the members of the body, though many, are one body, so it is with Christ. For by one

Spirit we were all baptized into one body – Jews or Greeks, slaves or free – and all were made to drink of one Spirit" (1 Cor. 12:12–13). The assembly gathers not simply around the Torah scroll (though the Scriptures are certainly present) or around the Jewish rites but around the testimonies to Jesus and around the Eucharist, so as to eat "the Lord's supper" (1 Cor. 11:20). There is one "foundation" in these communities: Jesus Christ (1 Cor. 3:11). The point is that the inaugurated kingdom is not a mere extension of the Jewish covenants and community; it is the Messianic fulfillment and reconfiguration of them.

Jesus Has Poured Out His Spirit and Established the Church as the Eschatological Temple

Biblical scholars debate what the intentions of the "historical Jesus" were: Did he think of himself, as Scot McKnight proposes, as "the Passover victim whose blood would protect his followers from the imminent judgment of God against Jerusalem and its corrupt leadership"?[14] Brant Pitre argues that "it is the banquet of the kingdom, and not the earthly Jerusalem or the land, that stands at the center of the centripetal movement being described in Jesus's vision of salvation."[15] I agree with McKnight and Pitre that Jesus offered himself in a sacrificial death for the salvation of his people and that he intended for his self-offering to be shared in by his people: "For the Son of man also came not to be served but to serve, and to give his life as a ransom for many" (Mk 10:44–45).

This is certainly how Paul understood Jesus's actions. Paul thinks that Jesus, in offering "expiation by his blood," perfectly manifested "God's righteousness" (Rom. 3:25). Paul maintains that Christ's supreme act of love perfectly fulfills Torah and thereby removes the covenantal curse (for disobedience to God's Torah) for those who cleave to Christ in faith and love. Paul teaches about Jesus's (and our) fulfillment of the Torah's precepts: "The commandments, 'You shall not commit adultery, You shall not kill, You shall not steal, You shall not covet,' and any other commandment, are summed up in this sentence, 'You shall love your neighbor as yourself.' Love does no wrong to the neighbor; therefore love is the fulfilling of the law" (Rom 13:9–10). For Paul, therefore, Christ on the Cross perfectly fulfills Torah by his supreme love for us. Indeed, nothing other than our own free will can

[14] Scot McKnight, *Jesus and His Death: Historiography, the Historical Jesus, and Atonement Theory* (Waco, TX: Baylor University Press, 2005), 339.
[15] Pitre, *Jesus and the Last Supper*, 471.

"separate us from the love of God in Christ Jesus our Lord" (Rom. 8:39).
Christian life is about being configured to the Messiah's work of love,
through which the Torah's specific commandments are supremely fulfilled. In a real sense, therefore, Paul is able to affirm: "the life I now live
in the flesh I live by faith in the Son of God, who loved me and gave
himself for me" (Gal. 2:20). Paul depicts Christ as a sinless cultic sin
offering. Metaphorically – yet more than metaphorically – Paul states:
"Christ, our Paschal Lamb, has been sacrificed" (1 Cor. 5:7).

Of course, Paul is not alone among the early Christians in holding
this perspective about Christ's cross. The Letter to the Hebrews presents Jesus as a high priest whose cultic offering is himself, in his
sacrificial death. The risen Jesus, having fulfilled by his self-sacrifice
the purposes of the earthly Temple, is able to present his saving sacrifice
to God the Father in the heavenly Temple, of which the earthly
Temple is merely a "copy" (Heb 9:24). With the suffering servant of
Isaiah 52–53 in view, the First Letter of Peter proclaims that Christ
"bore our sins in his body on the tree" and that "by his wounds you
have been healed" (1 Pet. 2:24). The Book of Revelation offers the image
of Jesus as the omnipotent, divine Lamb who has been slain and who
alone gives human history its true meaning by conquering sin and
death. The First Letter of John describes Jesus as the one who came to
"take away sins" (1 Jn. 3:5).

Furthermore, in the Johannine vision, Jesus is the new Temple. The
Gospel of John describes Jesus as not merely predicting the destruction
of the earthly Temple but as predicting his own death and resurrection
by describing his body as a temple that will be destroyed and rebuilt
in three days. For John, as Paul Hoskins has shown, Jesus "abundantly
fulfills the patterns and prophecies connected with the Passover lamb,
the Tabernacle, and the Temple."[16] The Book of Revelation holds that
there is no need for a rebuilt earthly Temple because God and the Lamb
will be the Temple. All the blessed will be sharers in Christ's self-
offering and will thereby share in the divine life of love.

The Pauline vision of Christ's body the Church runs along the same
lines as John's view of the Temple. Indwelt by the Holy Spirit, united to
the Messiah, believers are not only members of Christ's body but also
temples of the Holy Spirit. Together, the whole community of believers
in Christ constitutes the true Temple. Quoting various prophecies
that Christ has fulfilled, Paul states of the members of the Church that

---

[16] Hoskins, *Jesus as the Fulfillment of the Temple in the Gospel of John*, 189.

"we are the temple of the living God" (2 Cor. 6:16). Paul continues to go to the Jerusalem temple, but he does not see it as the center of Christian life, let alone as needed for cultic atonement. Christ has reconciled all things by his perfect self-offering in love, and his body is henceforth the true Temple. For "in Christ God was reconciling the world to himself" (2 Cor. 5:19).

Through the Eucharist, believers participate in Christ's saving sacrifice. Thus, Paul calls the bread and cup a "participation" or "communion" in the body and blood of Christ. Paul compares our communion in the Eucharist to the people of Israel's partaking in the sacrifices of the altar. Just as the Israelites are bound together by this tabernacle-Temple action – sharing in the animal sacrifices whose main purposes were thanksgiving and atonement – so are Christians bound together by our Temple action, communing in Christ's sacrificial self-offering under the cultic forms of bread and wine. In our earthly lives, we are united with Christ our head as his body, constituting the eschatological Temple, so long as we have faith, hope, and love.

All this depends upon Christ's pouring out his Spirit. It is by the grace of the Holy Spirit that we are transformed and united to Christ interiorly. The prophets foretold the outpouring of the eschatological Spirit that would restore Israel and the whole creation. In the Gospel of John, Jesus foretells that the Spirit will come forth from him, and at the end of this Gospel the risen Jesus bestows the Spirit upon his apostles. In the Book of Acts, the ascended Jesus sends the Spirit upon the apostles at Pentecost. Along these lines, Paul rejoices that "God's love has been poured into our hearts through the Holy Spirit who has been given to us" (Rom. 5:5).

The above three points – Jesus is the Messiah of Israel and the universal Savior, Jesus has inaugurated the Messianic Israel which is reconfigured around himself, and Jesus has established the eschatological Temple by reconciling all things and pouring out his Spirit – are utterly necessary parts of the Christian Gospel. They play a role in the Christian doctrine of Israel, insofar as all these elements are, in the Christian view, prepared for and prophesied in the Scriptures of Israel. The very notions of Messiah, Savior, the reconfigured Messianic Israel, the eschatological Temple, reconciliation, and the Spirit all derive from the Scriptures of Israel and are unintelligible without them. Viewed alone, cut off from the people to which he belonged and through which God prepared for his coming, Jesus makes little more sense than a random meteor. In his relationship with his biblical people Israel, expressed in the Torah and in the testimony of the prophets and the

wisdom literature, God conveys the urgency of our need for salvation
from sin and death. Death is most horrible when viewed from the
perspective of one who has felt God's loving presence; this is why Job
recoils so much from his mortal suffering, since he has experienced
God's love and now it seems as though God is coldly preparing Job's
utter destruction.[17] The Christian doctrine of Israel testifies that God,
in the Messiah Jesus, has established an everlasting, glorious communion with his people.

The Coming of the Messiah Does Not Revoke or Negate God's Covenants with the People of Israel

Christian insistence upon the truth and power of the Gospel, upon the
radical and salvific reconfiguration and fulfillment brought by the
Messiah of Israel in inaugurating his kingdom, must not be allowed to
turn into the bad news of persecution. As already noted, for centuries
Christians employed the Gospel as an excuse for persecution of the
ongoing Jewish people. Part of this was due to Jesus's chastisement of
the Jewish leaders of his day; another part was due to the polemics and
violence in the decades after Easter between Jews who accepted Jesus
and Jews who did not, which produced the highly charged rhetoric found
throughout the New Testament.[18] This internal Jewish debate first led
to the persecution of Christians, as, for instance, Stephen's death by
stoning and Paul's endurance of threats and attacks from his fellow
Jews. But soon enough, it flowered into a one-sided and ever sharper
persecution of the Jewish people. Augustine speaks of "the subjection
that the Jews merited when they killed the Lord for their proud kingdom"; and, indeed, the Christian Roman Empire in Augustine's day
increasingly subjected and persecuted its Jewish populace.[19] Things
got even worse in the medieval period.

---

[17] See Jon D. Levenson, *Resurrection and the Restoration of Israel: The Ultimate Victory of the God of Life* (New Haven, CT: Yale University Press, 2006).

[18] See my *Engaging the Doctrine of Israel*, chap. 1. For a broader perspective on polemical rhetoric in Scripture, see Luke Timothy Johnson, *Among the Gentiles: Greco-Roman Religion and Christianity* (New Haven, CT: Yale University Press, 2011).

[19] Augustine, *Answer to Faustus, a Manichean* (trans. Ronald Teske; Hyde Park, NY: New City, 2007), XII.12, 133. For discussion, see Paula Fredriksen, *Augustine and the Jews: A Christian Defense of Jews and Judaism*, 2nd ed. (New Haven, CT: Yale University Press, 2010). For critical responses to Fredriksen's argument, see Jeremy Cohen, "Revisiting Augustine's Doctrine of Jewish Witness," *Journal of Religion* 89, no. 4 (2009): 564–578; Ra'anan S. Boustan, "Augustine as Revolutionary? Reflections

In the light of the history of Christian denigration and persecution of the Jewish people, contemporary Christian doctrine of Israel attends with particular care to Romans 9–11, even if the meaning of this dense passage is still contested among biblical scholars.[20] Paul speaks longingly of his "brethren," his "kinsmen according to the flesh" who "are Israelites," to whom "belong the sonship, the glory, the covenants, the giving of the law, the worship, and the promises," and of whose race are the patriarchs and Christ himself (Rom. 9:3–4). It is precisely this people who, as Paul observes with deep sorrow, have by and large rejected the Messiah. Paul credits them with a "zeal for God" though not an "enlightened" one (Rom. 10:2).

He goes on to insist, however, that God has not "rejected his people" (Rom. 11:1). On the one hand, this is because a graced "remnant" (Rom. 11:5) of the Jewish people has accepted Jesus as the Christ. But, on the other hand – and this is most important for my purposes – even the Jewish people who have rejected Jesus, says Paul, have not "stumbled so as to fall" (Rom. 11:11). Paul observes that they may be opponents of the Gospel, but they remain in God's eyes his elect people, "beloved for the sake of their forefathers" (Rom. 11:28). Their election as God's beloved people has not been canceled or revoked by their rejection of Jesus as the Messiah. Paul hammers home the point to his largely Gentile audience: "For the gifts and the call of God are irrevocable" (Rom. 11:29).

The fact that the ongoing Jewish people, having rejected Jesus's Messianic status, still retain the status of being God's chosen and covenantal people is of the utmost importance for the Christian doctrine of Israel. The ongoing Jewish people have not, in this sense, been replaced or superseded by Christians. Just as much as ever, the ongoing Jewish people are God's chosen people. They still bear their special covenants regarding their people, land, and Torah; they still today await the Messianic Davidic king, since they know that God will be faithful to his covenants.

on Continuity and Rupture in Jewish-Christian Relations in Paula Fredriksen's *Augustine and the Jews*," *Jewish Quarterly Review* 99, no. 1 (2009): 74–87.

[20] For recent contributions to the debate, see, for example, Jason A. Staples, *The Idea of Israel in Second Temple Judaism: A New Theory of People, Exile, and Israelite Identity* (Cambridge: Cambridge University Press, 2021); Florian Wilk and J. Ross Wagner, eds., *In Between Gospel and Election: Explorations in the Interpretation of Romans 9–11* (Tübingen: Mohr Siebeck, 2010); Pablo T. Gadenz, *Called from the Jews and from the Gentiles: Pauline Ecclesiology in Romans 9–11* (Tübingen: Mohr Siebeck, 2009).

64 MATTHEW LEVERING

Paul is painfully aware that his largely Gentile audience is failing to recognize God's powerful love for the ongoing Jewish people. Paul describes the Jewish people who have rejected Jesus as being like branches broken off temporarily from an olive tree. Employing this image, he says that Gentile Christians must not "boast over the branches" (Rom. 11:18). Their boasting would show that they have failed to treat the Jewish people as God's "beloved" and that they have become arrogant and proud, blinded by their own election. Paul urgently warns against such a disaster. He does so not least by changing the metaphor from an olive tree's broken-off branches to that of an olive tree's "root" (Rom. 11:18). The Jewish people, even after having rejected Jesus, are still the root of the Church; they have not been replaced or displaced but remain at the foundation of God's plan of salvation.

God Has Permitted His Beloved Ongoing Jewish People, as a Whole, Not to Accept Jesus as the Messiah, but the Jewish People Continue to Have a Positive Place in the Economy of Salvation

The fact that the covenants have not been revoked leads to a second point regarding the ongoing Jewish people, as part of formulating a Christian doctrine of Israel that does not turn the good news into an excuse for hatred and persecution of God's beloved people. Namely, the rejection of Jesus by most of his fellow Jews is not some sort of colossal failure in God's providential plan for his chosen people. It is not as though God, having prepared the Jewish people in every way and having sent his Son, was then simply thwarted by his chosen people. Rather, the Jewish rejection of Jesus belongs mysteriously to the economy of salvation that God planned from the outset. Christians can find some intimations of this in the prophets – as, for example, Isa. 53:3, "he was despised, and we esteemed him not," or Zech.12:10, "and I [God] will pour out on the house of David and the inhabitants of Jerusalem a spirit of compassion and supplication, so that, when they look on him whom they have pierced, they shall mourn for him." But for my purposes here, it is not central to identify specific prophetic texts. Rather, the central elements come from the words of Paul in Romans 11.

These words are difficult to interpret since they may seem to implicate God in doing evil. Paul argues that the Jewish rejection of Jesus belongs to God's plan for the salvation of Gentiles and involves a divine "hardening" of his beloved people (Rom. 11:25). For centuries, it was the Jews who received all the privileges (as God's chosen people), while the Gentiles were in darkness about God's identity. Now, says Paul, it is the Jews who experience darkness about God's identity (in Christ). Paul concludes that God wishes Jews and Gentiles each to owe something to each other, so that each contributes something to the other's salvation – and also so that each experiences serious disobedience and is compelled to rely solely upon God's mercy for salvation.

Let me explore these claims further. Paul knows that the Gentile Christians are boasting over the Jews who have not accepted Jesus. Such boasting reveals a terrible blindness on the part of the Gentile Christians to the reality of God's unbreakable love for the ongoing Jewish people. Paul therefore says to his Gentile audience: "Lest you be wise in your own conceits, I want you to understand this mystery, brethren: a hardening has come upon part of Israel, until the full number of the Gentiles has come in, and so all Israel will be saved" (Rom 11:25–26). Two things follow: God's salvific purposes for his beloved Jewish people are still ongoing; and their rejection of Jesus flows from a divine "hardening," whose purpose is ultimately in favor of salvation.

Paul underlines the mutuality of the relationship of Jews and Gentiles. He does this with his characteristic emphasis that no human being has any right to boast. Indeed, spiritual boasting, which is what the Gentile Christians are doing against the Jews, is consistently the sin that Paul most abhors. He tells the Gentile Christians in Rome, "just as you were once disobedient to God but now have received mercy because of their disobedience" – because the Gospel is now being preached primarily to the Gentiles rather than to the Jews – "so they have now been disobedient in order that by the mercy shown to you they also may receive mercy" (Rom. 11:30–31). In God's plan, there is an ongoing mutuality of Jew and Gentile, each offering gifts to the other. It is precisely the fact that both groups have been disobedient that is an opening for real salvation, which depends upon the refusal to boast spiritually and upon the recognition that all depends upon the divine mercy. Despite what is on the surface a dismaying situation, Paul concludes joyfully: "For God has consigned all men to disobedience, that he may have mercy upon all" (Rom. 11:32).

This is an extraordinary statement. God has "consigned" both Jews and Gentiles to "disobedience"; a divine "hardening" has come upon both at different times; and the reason for the whole plan is not divine condemnation of either Jews or Gentiles but rather divine mercy and the recognition that each has been a gift to the other.

How grieved would Paul have been to know of the future centuries of Christian (mainly Gentile Christian) hatred and persecution of God's beloved Jewish people! Yet, Paul observed its seeds and warned forcefully against it in Romans 11. Clearly, Christians over the centuries have in a real sense been spiritually blinded vis-à-vis the ongoing Jewish people. What then of the centuries of Rabbinic Judaism? Is it the mere unfolding of the "trespass" (Rom. 11:11)? For Paul, the Jewish people continue to have a positive role in the history of salvation, which will become clear at the eschaton. As Paul puts it, "now if their trespass means riches for the world, and if their failure means riches for the Gentiles, how much more will their full inclusion mean!" (Rom 11:12). But what should Christians say about Rabbinic Judaism, about the development of Judaism during the twenty centuries since Paul wrote his letter?

On the one hand, this history of God with his ongoing Jewish people (Rabbinic Judaism) is not part of Christian doctrine. It is not the task of Christianity to make determinations about the presence and power of God to his beloved Jewish people over the past two millennia. But, on the other hand, Paul suggests that this history cannot, from a Christian perspective, be one of mere judgment and condemnation. The ongoing Jewish people remain the "root" (Rom. 11:18); and if the root were (spiritually) dead, the "olive tree" could hardly be alive. The ongoing Jewish people continue to receive "the gifts and call of God" (Rom. 11:29). Surely, these must bestow spiritual benefits, even if, as in the centuries prior to Christ, they are mingled with human disobedience (as is everything human, including the Church). Besides, we Christians can see with our own eyes the spiritual fruit borne within the Jewish people. In the twentieth century, the amazing spiritual endurance and vibrancy of the Jewish people after the horror of the Holocaust shows that the "root" is powerfully and graciously alive, as do the writings of the many great Jewish scholars drawing upon the Written and Oral Torah, even if Christians do not affirm the latter as divinely inspired in the way that Jews do.

Christians from the Outset Caused Scandal by Their Polemics against Jews Who Did Not Accept Jesus, and the Result Is That the Jewish People, as a Whole, Are in a Condition of Non-culpable Invincible Ignorance about Jesus's Messianic Status
I have now arrived at my final point for the Christian doctrine of the Jewish people. Thomas Aquinas and other Christian theologians developed the concept of non-culpable "invincible ignorance," grounded in such biblical texts as Lk. 12:47–48; Jas. 4:17; 1 Tim. 1:13; Acts 3:17; 17:30; and Rom. 10:14. For example, Lk. 12:47–48 compares two servants, one who knows "his master's will" and the other who

does not know; it is only the former who is gravely culpable, despite both servants doing what was wrong. In the *Summa theologiae*, Aquinas states that "it is not imputed as a sin to man, if he fails to know what he is unable to know. Consequently ignorance of such like things is called *invincible*, because it cannot be overcome by study."[21] There are various situations that can cause someone to be unable to know something. For example, when Christians proclaim that the Messiah has come in Jesus of Nazareth and has poured out the eschatological Spirit of self-sacrificial love and mercy – and when these same people vilify, persecute, and kill Jews as scapegoats in a display of hatred and overweening power – then it becomes impossible for Jewish persons, in general, to recognize Jesus as the true Messiah.

If so, then notable implications follow. Most importantly, the Jewish people as a whole are warranted in continuing to observe their covenantal obligations as though the covenants had not been fulfilled and reconfigured by the Messiah. Non-culpably unaware that the Messiah has in fact come, the ongoing Jewish people bear spiritual fruit today by seeking to obey Torah and to obey the covenantal commandment to dwell in and govern the promised land. They practice circumcision and the kosher laws, ask God for the grace to obey the Decalogue, observe the Sabbath and the festivals, engage in regular repentance and worship, follow the procedures laid down by the Rabbis in Oral Torah for observing the Temple sacrifices, and pray for the coming of the Messiah and the restoration of the Temple. As the Catholic theologian Gavin D'Costa comments, for Christians "Rabbinic Judaism's practices can be understood as God given, efficacious, with their covenant intact, God's fidelity to it 'objectively' operating to those who are subjectively living in period one of the *tria tempora* – epistemologically, before the coming of Jesus Christ."[22] From a Christian perspective, insofar as the Jewish people continue to yearn for the coming of the Messiah, they may be united to Jesus Christ by what Aquinas describes as "implicit" faith, through which people who for whatever good reason have not been able to hear the gospel are joined to the Savior.[23]

---

[21] Thomas Aquinas, *Summa theologiae* I-II, q. 76, a. 2 (trans. Fathers of the English Dominican Province; Westminster, MD: Christian Classics, 1981).
[22] Gavin D'Costa, *Catholic Doctrines on the Jewish People after Vatican II* (Oxford: Oxford University Press, 2019), 44. See also Emmanuel Perrier, O.P., "The Election of Israel Today: Supersessionism, Post-Supersessionism, and Fulfilment," *Nova et Vetera* 7, no. 2 (2009): 485–504, at 493.
[23] On implicit faith, see Aquinas, *Summa theologiae* I-II, q. 103, a. 2; I-II, q. 106, a. 1, ad 3; II-II, q. 2, aa. 7–8.

To a non-Christian, the above account may seem patronizing or supersessionist. But for Christians, who in faith believe that the Messiah has come, the doctrine of invincible ignorance and implicit faith ensures that the Jewish rejection of Jesus need not be taken to be culpable unbelief. Awareness of God's overlapping dispensations militates against offensive supersessionism. The Jewish rejection of Jesus is (not least) a product of the Christian boasting that Paul already observed, generated in part by the earliest intra-Jewish polemics that were an unavoidable element of the proclamation of the crucified and risen Messiah. Christians are thus deprived of any excuse for boasting over the Jewish people but rather must approach the Jewish people with repentance and – as should always have been the case – with a profoundly humble gratitude.

CONCLUSION

Christians continue to disagree with Judaism about the identity of the Messiah, as well as about all that follows from this central point. The Christian doctrine of Israel must confess Jesus Christ as incarnate Torah and his body as the eschatological Temple. The Messiah's coming has effected a radical reconfiguration of the central elements of Israel's life, not merely an extension of Israel's life to the Gentiles (pace some Messianic Jewish theologians). Likewise, the Christian doctrine of Israel should affirm that the Christological fulfillment of the covenantal land promise means that the whole world – indeed the whole cosmos – is now under the reign of the Messiah. According to the Christian doctrine of Israel, too, Christ is the new Passover Lamb and the new manna by which believers are nourished on the journey of the new exodus to the true promised land, the new creation. The Christian doctrine of Israel's God includes Christ and the Spirit as Creator, without, however, compromising the divine unity or the distinction between God and creatures.

Today, however, Christians have the opportunity to reflect upon the doctrine of Israel in a real conversation with Rabbinic Judaism.[24] Whereas Christians in the past supposed that the ongoing Jewish people are no longer God's covenantal people or are under a curse that will continue until they confess Jesus as the Messiah, Christians now recognize that it is not a choice between explicit faith and culpable unbelief.

[24] See my *Engaging the Doctrine of Israel*.

Contemporary Christians are much more aware of the positive notes in Romans 9–11 about God's irrevocable relationship with his beloved Jewish people. Instructed by great Jewish thinkers,[25] Christians must continue to strive to overcome the horrors caused over the centuries by shameful Christian boasting against the Jewish people.[26] On this basis, Christians may return to Paul's conclusion in hope: "For God has consigned all men to disobedience, that he may have mercy upon all" (Rom 11:32).

Further Reading

D'Costa, Gavin (2019), *Catholic Doctrines on the Jewish People after Vatican II* (Oxford: Oxford University Press).

Fredriksen, Paula (2010), *Augustine and the Jews: A Christian Defense of Jews and Judaism*, 2nd ed. (New Haven, CT: Yale University Press).

Jipp, Joshua W. (2020), *The Messianic Theology of the New Testament* (Grand Rapids: Eerdmans).

Kinzer, Mark (2005), *Postmissionary Messianic Judaism: Redefining Christian Engagement with the Jewish People* (Grand Rapids, MI: Brazos).

Levering, Matthew (2021), *Engaging the Doctrine of Israel: A Christian Israelology in Dialogue with Ongoing Judaism* (Eugene, OR: Cascade).

Levering, Matthew, and Tom Angier, eds. (2021), *The Achievement of David Novak: A Catholic-Jewish Dialogue* (Eugene, OR: Pickwick).

Marshall, Bruce (1997), "Christ and the Cultures: The Jewish People in Christian Theology," in *The Cambridge Companion of Christian Doctrine* (ed. Colin E. Gunton; Cambridge: Cambridge University Press), 81–100.

Pitre, Brant (2015), *Jesus and the Last Supper* (Grand Rapids: Eerdmans).

Ratzinger, Joseph (1999), *Many Religions, One Covenant: Israel, the Church, and the World* (San Francisco: Ignatius).

Soulen, R. Kendall (1996), *The God of Israel and Christian Theology* (Minneapolis, MN: Fortress).

Wilk, Florian, and J. Ross Wagner, eds. (2010), *In between Gospel and Election: Explorations in the Interpretation of Romans 9–11* (Tübingen: Mohr Siebeck).

[25] See, for example, *The Achievement of David Novak: A Catholic-Jewish Dialogue*, ed. Matthew Levering and Tom Angier (Eugene, OR: Pickwick, 2021), which includes extensive responses by David Novak to each of the essays.

[26] For further examples, see Cyril Hovorun, *Political Orthodoxies: The Unorthodoxies of the Church Coerced* (Minneapolis, MN: Fortress, 2018).

5 Christ

KATHERINE SONDEREGGER

"In the fullness of time, God sent His Son, born of a woman, born under the Law, to redeem those under the Law, that we might receive adoption as children." So the Apostle Paul teaches his community in Galatia (Gal 4.4–5). Christology, in all its height and breadth, is caught up in these few brief rounded phrases. The Apostle joins together a particular notion of time – that is, gathers to a fullness, pleroma – with a Divine action, to send or send out. This sending comprises elements of the life of Jesus Christ, His existence as a mortal, a child of Eve, and as a Jew, one born under the Law. The Apostle gathers this whole complex into a single purpose: to redeem creatures from the structure of the cosmos, the *stoicheai*, and to adopt us as children, both Jew and gentile, as Divine heirs. Other crystalline verses from Holy Scripture – the Prologue to the Gospel of John; the *Carmen Christi* or Christ hymn, as it is often styled, in Philippians 2; or the Annunciation by the Archangel Gabriel to Mary or from angelic hosts to shepherds, keeping night watch – have been taken by theologians, early and modern, as touchstones for Christology. These must find their way into any full examination of the structure and *telos* of this doctrine. But Galatians 4 remains the keystone.

Chief among the reasons for this architectonic role is the prominence given to the central verb: to send. Paul places God as the Subject of this verb, and it is here that Christology properly begins. To affirm this starting point is to take the entire articulated whole of Christology into the Doctrine of God – more properly, into the Doctrine of the Holy Trinity. Primordially, the early Church ventured to exegete the very idea of "Son" as an element, a motion or "procession," within the Godhead. To read the treatises of the Fathers is to enter into a thought-world in which the biblical notions – titles, in a later age – of the Son of God or Son of David or Son of Man – were understood to apply ultimately and principally to God, the Inner Life of Procession and Begetting. One way to interpret, in the words of the Patristic historian R. P. C. Hanson, the "search for the Christian Doctrine of God" is to see it as an extended debate over the proper exegesis of the term, "Son", and its relation to the keystone, "sending." All the positions later determined to be dogmatic, or creedal, and those that were heterodox or unschooled, can be viewed as differing and conflicting interpretations of the words, "God sent His Son." In this larger sense, the doctrinal area we speak of as Christology is in its structure, history, and purpose, an element within the Doctrine of Trinity and is most properly understood within its contours.

The conflict we know as Arianism, after an Egyptian cleric, Arius, emerged from the undifferentiated joining of "Son" to "being sent." The Arian party understood the Godhead to encompass a mediating figure, a Son, whose constitution spanned the Eternal One and the temporal realm of generation and sending forth. That this seemed a congenial way to understand Deity can be attributed, of course, to contemporary forms of Platonism, particularly influential in Alexandrian circles and visible in the greatest exegete and intellectual of the third century, Origen. Indeed, the very notion of "Neo Platonism," some historians argue, can be attributed in good measure to the exuberant work of Origen. But this picture can be overdrawn. In Arianism or in Origenism (and we should not conflate the two), we do not encounter a Hellenism that has overswept the biblical record. Rather, we see contemporary thought-forms being harnessed to explicate the central mystery of Christology: How can a Divine Son be sent? Is there a property or nature ingredient in the Son that makes possible His presence among us, His descent into the world of unlikeness? These early Christian exegetes knew that Christ was styled the Mediator in 1 Timothy, and they took with full seriousness the Wisdom literature and its praise of the One "created by the Lord as the beginning of all His ways." The Son is the "First-born of all creation," Colossians teaches, and it seemed persuasive to argue that such a One stood between Heaven and earth as a Divine-creature, or an Image that possessed the disposition for being sent, being temporal and of the earth. These early schools are often styled "Subordinationists," and it is certainly true that the Son who is sent is subordinate to the Sender, the Transcendent and Invisible One. But I think we might be closer to the mark to describe them as Commissionists, if we can bear the term, for the fundamental impulse is to take with full seriousness the steady insistence of Scripture that the Son is the One sent into this world. And their questions and proposals are by no means antiquarian or foolish.

To imagine that sending belongs to the essence of the Son is to conceive of the Only-Begotten as the Divine Person whose very nature is to be given, donated to the world. It is to think that Deity can have an aptitude for the creaturely, what the twentieth-century dogmatician Karl Barth called a "positive relation" with creation. Might this be the very nature, the structure, so to say, of the Divine Son? Could He be the God for whom time is compatible, a moving image of His own Eternity? Is this, in truth, what the "fullness of time" means? Could He have a capacity for enfleshment, a nature that does not compel but could incorporate a humanization in the likeness of sinful flesh? Could the events we see in the Gospels, and in promise, in Covenant Israel, find their possibility in the very constitution of the Son who is sent? If not, how can we even sketch out conceptually the Divine turn toward Incarnation? What could be the possible ground for such an act?

We can see some of the force of these questions in the remarkable Christology of Karl Rahner, a twentieth-century Jesuit and systematician. Rahner held that in the Incarnation we see something distinct, something proper, to the Son Himself. Not simply "God incarnate" but rather the "Son incarnate": the Incarnation teaches us something unsurpassed and particular to the Second Person of the Triunity. Not every Person is Incarnate, Rahner reminds us, and more daringly, he asserts that not every Person can be incarnate. It is the *proprium* of the Son to take flesh of Mary, His mother. On this score – though not on every score – Rahner departs from scholastic teaching. But this is not to say that either Rahner or Barth were Arians or Subordinationists! Certainly, both Barth and Rahner were fully Nicene Christians, and they would reject Subordinationism (though, for Barth, not Subordination) directly. But their profound wrestling with the singular nature of the Son demonstrates to us that the questions posed by the third-century Alexandrians are not otiose. They remain central conceptual challenges to Christology, taken as an element within Trinitarian dogma and tied to the sending of such a Son.

The fourth-century debate over the nature of the Son – His full equality with the Father – that begins among Alexandrians such as Athanasius and extends to North Africans such as Augustine turned on the proper reading of the cardinal texts from Scripture, in the Gospels, in the letters of Paul, and in the Books of Isaiah and Proverbs. Just how should these references to creation be exegeted? How should the sending be understood? It fell to these theologians, the "Nicene party," to develop concepts and vocabulary to affirm both the full equality of the Divine Son, and His work of grace among us, as the One sent from God. What this required over many decades of bitter polemic was the re-conceptualization of the term "nature" and a re-direction of the Scriptural theme "sending." The golden text for this work was the *Carmen Christi*, the eloquent reflection upon the "mind of Christ" Paul lays out in Philippians 2. In this section of the letter, considered by many modern exegetes to be an ancient hymn – it is set forth in strophes in the NRSV – Paul speaks of a particular kind of *emptying*, a movement from a realm of glory to one of lowliness, a form of God that was exchanged for a form of human likeness, an enslavement that brought in its train a profound humiliation, bearing down on obedience and to cruciform death. This wedding of emptying with humiliation turns over into exaltation, where Christ's resurrection is understood in the language of the Psalmist, as a "going up with a shout," a raising into dominion that is captured in the Name given Him, the Lord.

For some modern exegetes such as Richard Bauckham, it is this passage above all that proves a "high Christology" in the earliest sediments of the New Testament, associating Jesus with the Lord God, or, in Kendall Soulen's innovative reading, bestowing upon Him the Tetragrammaton, the Ineffable Name of the Holy One of Israel. (Not all exegetes read this passage in such direct, metaphysical fashion. It might refer to Paul's favored Adam-Christ typology, some argue, with "form" serving as synonym for "image and likeness." Or it might, as Luther thought, refer to the proper shape of the Christian life, one of humility and self-giving to the neighbor.) This passage, for the metaphysically inclined, joins ancient and modern exegesis, signaling a central Christological dynamic within Scripture itself.

For the Nicene party, and for Augustine in particular, the critical term in this Pauline passage is *morphe, forma*, shape, character, or form. What the Nicenes spied there was a contrast that consisted in an emptying, a height followed by a depth, a glory followed by an enslavement to the elements of the cosmos, to human frailty, mortality, and failing, and to a death that tasted the deepest humiliation and shame. Doctrinally, we begin to see the rudiments of later Christological debate: a fresh concept of nature, when used of Christ, and a fresh reconsideration of the relation of Christ's sojourn among us to His life in glory. The Son who is sent, that is, is now seen to undergo two stages – what later Reformed theologians would call, "statuses" – one heavenly and one earthly, or in the Alexandrian and Origenistic idiom, the Inner, Immanent, "Theological" life of the Son as opposed to His external or "Economic" life in the wilderness of this world. What is coming into sharp focus in the fourth century, then, is the conviction that the Incarnate Son must be of two "forms" or "natures." He must have a

Deity, they argued, that is fully and simply God, *Deitas*, without diminution or reserve; and He must have a humanity that is ours and like ours, including a temporality and most importantly, a mortality. But these two forms are not unrelated or simply sequential. Rather, the *forma Dei* stands to the *forma servatus* in a relation of emptying: the "mind of Christ" is realized fully when one sees that the Son who possesses Divine Glory can shed Himself of it, and on His gracious Self-donation, take on what He did not first possess, the likeness of humankind.

God is the Agent here, and the Son, though sent, must be seen not as a passive secondary being, but rather as the Initiator, the Glory of the Father who strips Himself of what is truly His in order to carry out the Economic work of redemption. This is the heart of Cyril of Alexandria's Christology: God the Word must be the sole Acting Subject of the life of Christ. He saw in the Antiochene exegesis, typified in the Metropolitan of Constantinople, Nestorius, a threat to this sole agency and thus, Cyril said, to the unity of Christ. Cyril's Christology was firmly crowned victor in later Ecumenical Councils in Constantinople and thus entered the Latin Church through John of Damascus and Thomas Aquinas, who studied these later Councils intensively. Thomas translated the Cyrillian emphasis upon the Word as Agent into the scholastic metaphysics of the 'suppositum'. There is one only in Christ, Thomas argued, and that suppositum, or *esse* (act of being) is the Divine Son. All that Christ does is the work and purpose of the Divine Son; his humanity accompanies and executes instrumentally the will of the Deity.

These later Patristic and Scholastic developments can be found in germ in the Augustinian notion of form. These forms or natures, in the One Son, are twinned with the states of lowliness and exaltation. The Son begins in exalted glory; He lowers Himself into human flesh; He is exalted once again to His heavenly realm. This interlocking pattern of nature and status gives to early Christology the language of descent. In the words of the Nicene Symbol: He comes down from heaven and is incarnated of the Holy Spirit and the Virgin Mary. This, in the idiom of later theologians, is a "Christology from above," and it is one of the lasting elements of the debate over the Divine sending that the Doctrine of the Person of Christ can be seen as a movement, a lowering from Above to below, to carry out the work of redemption. For the Father "to send," for these theologians, comes to mean for the Son "to assume": to take on human flesh. It means to become "visible," as Irenaeus styles it. Augustine insists in *De Trinitate* that the Son does not "go anywhere" when He descends to the earth; rather He manifests Himself in His

Person, taking flesh as the medicine that alone can cure the fever in our blood. God manifested or visible as enfleshed Son, Savior: this is the descent and emptying that just is the Economy of God, God with us.

Only in the modern era is this distinct motion, from Above to below, upset and overturned. We may take the great German academic Pietist, Friedrich Schleiermacher, and the post-war systematican, Wolfhart Pannenberg, as two prominent advocates of a "Christology from below." (Not surprisingly, these phrases themselves are of modern origin.) The aim of such Christologies is to uncover a point of departure in the earthly life of Jesus, His teaching, example, His testimony in trial and in conflict, His luminous presence in the confused night of sin and need. Not simply His Passion, but rather His entire Self-witness, the whole run of His life, should serve as proper anchor for Christology. Here we see the marked influence of the higher criticism of the Bible, the so-called *LebenJesuForschung*, the "quest for the historical Jesus," as Albert Schweitzer's memorable history of these labors is titled. The controlling thought-form here is not the Economy, as the Fathers would have it, but rather the plausible, compelling testimony of a historical life, One that heralds and manifests the nearness of the Kingdom of God. Some trait within this historical existence would warrant the early confession that God was in Him, reconciling the world to Himself, or the later confession that this Man was God. As might be imagined, this required some heavy lifting. But the instinct that underlay the whole was the suspicion that a Christology from Above never actually touched earth: the figure of Jesus in the classical tradition was simply "docetic," a Divine Being who appeared to be human.

Theologians who worked from below pointed to Patristic and Scholastic Christologies that taught Christ's perfect knowledge, a kind of human omniscience, or to His Divine Agency, which made of his human suffering and sorrow a mere example or teaching for the crowds; these were fundamentally docetic, they said. The Jesus of the Gospels, in contrast to all that, they held, possessed a limited historical perspective: He was a Jew of the first century who saw the world through the eyes of One born under the Law. He palpably learned from his surroundings, underwent terror and torment He could not foresee, died a death reserved for rebels and slaves, a cruelty of Imperial pacification. Such Christologies open a wide door to critical findings of historical research: there is much in the Gospel record that historians cannot verify or countenance, and these constrain the judgments made on behalf of this singular Jew. The nineteenth-century's agonized struggle to determine whether Jesus had a "messianic consciousness" lives on in the quest for a Christology from below, for this is a Son who knows Himself simply to be an observant Jew and a prophet of the Immanent Reign of God. For Pannenberg, or for Paul Tillich, it is this very austerity, Christ's refusal to call Himself God, that makes Him the true Son, the living Symbol of the Transcendent, Eschatological God. Perhaps the most radical and enduring legacy of this path to Christology is the profound encounter with Jesus's Jewishness, His identity within and not against or above, this Covenant People, and His teaching that belonged to and not over against the Scriptures of Israel. The scourge of anti-Judaism and later, racialized anti-semitism that marred Christian witness to this One Jew, both early and late, can be healed only by a clear-eyed and happy confession of this Son of God as Son of David, a member of the Eternal People.

We must say, however, that the relation of this movement to the Patristic and Medieval and Reformation Christologies is strained; perhaps we spy the rupture of the modern here in a stark dogmatic form. The pronounced predilection of modern theologies to treat Christology as an autonomous topic, freed from its Trinitarian home, and preoccupied with matters of faith and history, can be traced to this devotion to a Christology from below. Such Christologies can sit lightly on the dogmatic tradition: Christ's perfect sinlessness, considered an axiom of His birth of the Holy Spirit, could in these modern accounts be treated as "contingen" – a happy but not necessary fact – or even set aside altogether as a sign of Christ's thoroughgoing and unimpeded solidarity with a sin-laden humanity. Of course, a Christology from below need not depart from tradition in such stark ways, and in its greatest practitioners, does not. It remains a school that has weighed its doctrine against the "tribunal of conscience and truth," in Karl Rahner's incisive phrase, and has opened a path to full, unanxious acknowledgment of a developed world, shaped by history and by science. But a full examination of Christology can only complete its round by taking up the Scriptural and Patristic theme of "descen'" in which the vast majority of Christologies have taken their compass.

These pre-modern theologians would pursue at some length the Pauline word, central to the Philippian's hymn, of "emptying." What would it mean for the Divine Son to empty Himself? Because God is the Agent here, the question drives right to the heart of the metaphysics of Incarnation. Might the human nature of the Incarnate Son possess traits or powers that could be hidden and displayed only in brief epiphanies? One thinks here of the "nature miracles," as these manifestations of dominion over wind and seas are sometimes styled in the Gospel accounts, or supremely of the Transfiguration where, perhaps, the hidden glory of the Lord was revealed to amazed disciples. Or might it be that the human nature of the Son could renounce such gifts and properties? Does "emptying" mean that though a Son by nature and right, Christ yielded up these prerogatives and was content to be mortal flesh for the sake of mortal sinners? These were Lutheran speculations, associated with schools in Giessen and Tübingen and theologians such as Johannes Brenz and Martin Chemnitz.

In the nineteenth century, both English and German theologians began a more daring exploration into the very Deity of the Son. Could the Divine Agent empty Himself of His own Attributes, in order to be very flesh of our own kind? What might those Attributes be? Perhaps what Gottfried Thomasius termed the "relative attributes," Omniscience, Omnipotence, Omnipresence. Or perhaps as C. E. Raven and later Sergei Bulgakov proposed, the Glory that was once His, and even, more daringly, His own awareness of His Deity – though the Incarnate Christ remained God throughout. Though the Hegelian I. A. Dorner scornfully referred to such hypotheses as the *"kenosis* of reason,"* we might cast a more friendly eye on the structural dilemmas that led to such proposals. The distinction between the Son and His sending, the emergence of distinct natures or properties, human and Divine, and the whole of it bent toward Golgotha makes of the status of the humble Son of God a profound mystery. In virtue of what properties, in Deity or humanity, can the portrait of Jesus of Nazareth, found in the Gospels, in truth be the life of the Incarnate God? Of course, the problems of historical criticism of the Bible are palpable in these later *kenotic* speculations. But they derive their force from the Nicene insistence upon a descent of a True Son.

Now, such a schema comes at a cost. It appeared that the integration of sending with descent threatened the unity of the Triune Godhead. Could a Divine Person in truth leave the Inner Divine Life and dwell wholly on earth? Could the Uncontainable God be contained in human flesh? Or, on the other hand, could there be a Divine Son *extra carnem*, beyond the flesh? Athanasius felt this problem keenly. In his treatise on the Incarnation, *De Incarnatione* (of uncertain date, perhaps after 325 AD), Athanasius boldly asserts that the Son rules the stars all the while he sojourns on earth. The Son must be understood to "take on a body" as an instrument, a creaturely tool by which a besieged city is freed, taught, renewed, and healed. Later generations of theologians – the sixteenth-century Protestant Reformers – returned to this problematic with real vigor. The "extra" of Athanasius's treatise was now dubbed the "extra Calvinisticum," as the Swiss Reformers followed Calvin in affirming Athanasius's commitment to the Heavenly Son. The Lutheran party considered such a teaching fatal to Christology as a whole. Though this debate is sometimes organized around the logical and metaphysical question of whether "finite substance can encompass the infinite," we might better see this as a struggle to determine just what this manifestation, or descent, demands in Christology. Is it proper, in light of the Divine sending, to conceive of the Son apart from His flesh? Is the Pauline teaching – to know nothing but Christ and Him crucified – to be interpreted as both an epistemic and a metaphysical truth, such that the Son *post natum* is wholly and without reserve the Incarnate One? One can readily see the early Church debates about the constitution and nature of the Son in these Reformation disputes over the Son's existence *extra carnem*. Is the Divine Son always the *Incarnandus*, the One who will, in the fullness of time, be sent in the likeness of human flesh? For the Reformers and their later descendants – often called the "Protestant Scholastics" – these discussions took place within the matrix of the Lord's Supper and Christ's presence within that ordinance. But later Protestant dogmaticians considered the proper locus for this debate to be firmly placed within the Doctrine of God.

Is there in truth such a reality as the *Logos asarkos*, the Word beyond or without the flesh? For Karl Barth, despite his Reformed heritage, the answer was a complex but nevertheless bold, No. In a celebrated section of the *Church Dogmatics*, Barth exegetes the Prologue to John, one of our golden texts, as referring, from beginning to end, to Jesus: He just is the Word. In the hands of some English, North American, and German theologians, this amounted to a denial of the Son's "pre-existence." There is only this earthly Son who, on various accounts, is declared or recognized or identified with God. There is no *Logos asarkos*, no Son *extra carnem*, though there may be a Divine "ground" or "narrative" or "counter-factual" that underlies the Incarnate One. Robert Jenson, an American, and Wolfhart Pannenberg, a German, both Lutherans, develop robust Christologies of the enfleshed Son, the *Logos ensarkos*, with special metaphysical verve.

Under the conditions of high scholasticism, these Nicene debates about Divine nature, agency, and sending were given technical vocabulary. The fundamental structure of Christology in the *Summa Theologica* of St. Thomas Aquinas is built from the distinction between Procession and Mission, the latinate form of "sending." In this classical, Latin form, Christology finds its anchor in what Thomas calls the "temporal goal" of the Eternal Procession of the Son. There is no hesitation in this account of a *Logos asarkos*; indeed, the very notion of the Divine Mission of the Son is predicated upon it. What is debated among the Schoolmen is the relation of this Divine Son to His human nature. Is this *relatio* something like a soul in the human body? Or is it perhaps more akin to an Aristotelian "accident," a non-necessary property of a self-standing "substance"? Though to modern ears these may strike us as odd analogs, they in fact throw in bold relief the complex freedom and necessity of a Divine act. It has struck many philosophers, ancient and modern, as well as theologians from many eras that the Divine Nature, *Deitas*, demanded a necessity to all His Attributes – indeed for Thomists, an identity among them – and an existence that was necessary, *simpliciter*. How is such a Being, the Most Necessary Being, to "become" anything at all? This is the question the twentieth-century historian of dogma Alyois Grillmeier grouped under the heading "making" (*Homo factus est*), which must properly accompany the heading of "assuming."

We might translate this debate about the Son's Mission into temporal terms. The Apostle Paul affirms that God sends His Son in the fullness of time. How can such a Mission be conceived of God understood as Eternal, and how can the relation of the humanity to the Divine Son be anything but necessary? Hard won was the insight that the act of creation could be freed of necessity – or so it was thought – by the introduction of the Divine will. God freely determined to create the cosmos, as His will is moved by nothing other than His own good pleasure. Could this also open the iron cage of necessity in the Incarnation? In a deft move, Thomas Aquinas interwove the two modal properties, declaring that the Father eternally – hence, necessarily – willed the temporal – hence, free or contingent – Mission of the Son. That this solution did not win the day wholly can be seen in Thomas's later contemporary, Duns Scotus, for whom the Incarnation is frankly affirmed as the Eternal purpose of God, bestowing a certain form of necessity – predestination – to the human nature of Christ, but tempered always by the Divine Will, a position that makes the saving work of Christ secondary to the Eternal Election of the Incarnation. In this way, Scotus carries forward a Franciscan tradition, sharpens and extends it, in which Christ is Primary, the Center and Structure and Goal of all creation. We can see the Galatians passage here, with its pronounced emphasis upon the Son's sending as salvific – He is sent in order that we be adopted – interpreted now in light of Colossians and Ephesians where doctrines of Creation and Election predominate. Of course, Scotus does not deny that Christ is Savior! But He is so under the conditions of the Fall; necessarily, the Son is Incarnate, contingently, He is Savior. Though controversial among Barth specialists, this Scotist position appears the natural outcome of Barth's denial of the *Logos asarkos*, twinned with the innovative Doctrine of Election he sets forth in *Church Dogmatics* II.2. Barth however brings Christ's obedience and salvific Self-giving into the determination of God's own life, such that the Son remains necessarily Savior, though resting entirely upon the Good Pleasure, and hence, loving freedom of God.

But, however we settle matters of Divine Self-determination in the Mission of the Son, we may quickly see that such Triune resolutions do not touch the heart of the matter. For it remains unclear how the humanity of the Incarnate could relate to the Deity in such a way that the Deity was not entangled necessarily in the ways of the flesh. Was not "becoming" a fresh attribute now of Deity, and was not the Godhead immersed in the sea of temporal change, the fatal tides of passion, and of decay? To these dangers the Schoolmen proposed the analogs of soul to body, and accident to substance, or even part to whole. There must be something discretionary, they reasoned, about the Incarnation, such that the flesh assumed did not become nor was ever seen to be, necessary to the Divine Son. The instrumental language, first voiced in Athanasius, found its home, too, in Thomas's *Summa*, playing a substantial role in the *Tertia Pars* of the *Summa* in the Treatise on the Incarnation. We may think of another tagline from the Patristic era – One of the Trinity suffered in the flesh – as an earlier expression of this same conceptual puzzle. The early Church Fathers, in the midst of all their profound differences and animosities, recognized the signal fact of Golgotha as the deepest mystery of Divine becoming. In the words of the Nicene Symbol, the Word became flesh, and nothing confirmed that temporal unfolding as did the death on a Roman Cross of the Lord of Glory. Here again, all sides recognized a certain necessity (perhaps hypothetical) to this event: the salvation of the world required this terrible cost. But early Alexandrians proposed language that appeared to mitigate the conceptual contradiction that clung so closely to the Passion. They taught that something God does can take place in something else – in human flesh. God the Son remains Agent here, the Principal of the whole, but He can enact His own will in another nature, another substance, His own body. Later Alexandrians such as Cyril of Alexandria heightened this already vivid language to paradox: The Divine Son, he wrote, suffered impassibly, a suffering without suffering. In the modern era, paradox was a term favored by those influenced by the nineteenth-century Danish theologian, Soren Kierkegaard; Paul Tillich may be taken as chief exemplar.

But it fell to the modern era to question the fundamental structure of Patristic and Medieval Christology. The delicate interplay of "forms" or "natures" and their relation to lowliness and exaltation became conceptually unworkable to many schools of modern Christologists. Robert Jenson spoke for many when he boldly asserted that the entire history of early Christological debates turned on the dilemma posed by Divine Immutability in a suffering Son. To preserve God's Impassibility and Immutability, an entire edifice of distinctions, paradoxes, and notional relations must be erected to shield Deity from the passionate mortality of the Son of Man. But what if, these moderns dared to ask, Deity is not Impassible, not Immutable, at least in the traditional Scholastic sense? What if suffering can be a Divine Attribute? Perhaps, the Supreme Attribute? The most widely read Protestant dogmatician of the postwar era, Jürgen Moltmann, dared to asked these questions directly in the influential work, *The Crucified God*. His motivation, however, was not purely metaphysical; he did not consider such fine-grained speculative questions primary to proper Christian theology. Rather, Moltmann's aim was pastoral and evangelical: to speak to a generation that had witnessed, and done, unspeakable things, creating and undergoing suffering on a scale unimaginable in earlier days. The only God who can save, Moltmann wrote, echoing Dietrich Bonhoeffer's haunting phrase, is the God who suffers. Moltmann emerged from Allied prisoner of war camps as a Christian, and his dogmatic enterprise is defined by a world seared by fire – the Holocaust, the flames of hatred and violence and cruelty, the stubborn light of hope that flickers through it all. Christology must lie at the very heart of that suffering and that hope. God acts in Christ, but it is a God who suffers in the sending of the Son, a God who in death suffers the terrible silence of His Father, a God of hope who raises, vindicates, and restores the suffering Son to the Passionate Love of the Father. In this way, Moltmann brings Christology deep within Trinitarian dogmatics and re-structures the whole of Christian teaching about the descent of the Son.

He is not alone. We might take contemporary Christology to be an expansion and parallel development of these Moltmannian themes. Liberation Theology, as it developed in Latin America after the Second Vatican Council, took the suffering of Christ, His love of enemy, His proclamation of a Divine Realm of justice, to be the governing dynamism of theology. For Gustavo Gutierrez, the principle systematician among the Liberationists, Christ was Savior in this expansive sense: He was Liberator, both internally and externally, a Mission sent within the heart of the oppressed, the burst of hope, and into a world of poverty and despoliation, to free from the sin of oppression and despair, to be the luminous heart of a new humanity, a true humanism at the last. In just this way, Gutierrez deftly re-works a Thomistic theme in which the external Mission of the Son is paired, indeed bested, in the interior Mission of the Son into the believer's heart. We might also consider some North Americans who have worked in the wake of Gutierrez and who take up the theme of a Suffering God into the racialized and gendered world of current society. James Cone understood Christ as the Liberator of the African diaspora, the One who had tasted the depths of degradation and contempt, who preached revolution over every tyranny and empire, and died a convict, lynched by the callous, the smug and cruel who in later days would become White, the White segregationists, bigots, and supremacists.

Feminist and Womanist theologians have turned this motif of suffering in fresh directions, finding in Christ the Liberator, yes, but One who overturns, resists, and re-makes a colonizing, suffocating world of suffering and self-sacrifice. So much of gendered success among Western women has been proclaimed to be the quiet endurance of suffering, ennobled, as was thought, by a readiness to put others before self, to sacrifice, to give and forgive, to simply withstand the diminution and contempt that is women's lot. Such, the first wave of feminist theologians argued – we think of Rosemary Ruether, Elizabeth Schüssler Fiorenza, and Sallie McFague as exemplars – was the toxin at the heart of the sentimental vision of a suffering Christ. Kathryn Tanner, in an influential collection of essays, defends these early feminist claims, finding in Christ One who is not so much sacrifice – or sacrifice as classically understood – as gift, a bestowal upon the needy world of God's own goodness, not as cost but rather as beneficence. More recently, Sarah Coakley has defended a complex in the suffering Son of God, a certain form of sacrifice, one in which a carefully qualified form of dependence, of need, and of passion is not incompatible with agency but indeed represents a deeper, more liberative expression of true creaturely flourishing. We may expect further systematic outworkings of this novel emphasis in Christology to appear in the work of Postcolonial and Queer theologians.

So far, we have undertaken a sounding of the depths of Christology drawing upon Scriptural texts and the Nicene conceptual development of those idioms. Much of the ground of medieval and modern Christology appears to have been traversed in this way. But as any student of the history of theology can tell us, a central gear appears to

have fallen out of the assembly: the Council and Definition of
Chalcedon. Now, this may strike the reader as a special idiosyncrasy
for many, many treatments of Christology as a dogmatic structure take
their leave and their compass from Chalcedon. The terms of art of
Christology – hypostatic union, two natures, their relation, unmixed
and unseparated – and the various impedimenta of the Acta, the anath-
emas, the affirmations, most especially of the technical, Cyrillian term,
Theotokos, the rejection, at least in name, of Nestorius: these have been
treated as the very constituents of Christology and the point of departure for any dogmatic consideration of the locus.

Of course, moderns had objections to Chalcedon! The language of
"nature" and "hypostasis" were unworkable in the modern era, it was
said, and worse still, the condemnation of Nestorius seemed ill-
considered and unworthy of the aims he in fact espoused. More recently,
scholars of the early Church, such as Rowan Williams and Brian Daley,
have wondered out loud whether Chalcedon should be taken as the final
word, the destination, for Christological reflection. Might it not be
better seen as a way station or point of debarkation, a companion rather
than a *vade mecum* to dogma? That this has been a growing instinct
among historians is manifest as early as the English Kenoticists, especially in the collection on Christology, *Lux Mundi*, published toward
the end of the nineteenth century; and traces of this view can be seen in
the magisterial survey, *Christ in Christian Tradition*, by Alyois
Grillmeier, whose influence we have already registered to other ends.

And certainly it cannot be ignored that several branches of the
Christian Church registered dismay at the Council's Definition and
considered it a betrayal of Cyril and the phrase strongly associated with
him, the One nature of the Incarnate Son. These Miaphysites never
denied human characteristics amid the Divine – indeed an early
Alexandrian such as Gregory Nazianzus could speak boldly of a "mixture" of the two – but these were notional in the One Person of Christ,
distinguished as Cyril often said, in "theory" within the vibrant agency
of the One Christ.

Whatever the merits of these historical claims, the theologian who
remains committed to the Ecumenical Councils of the Church and
perhaps also to the traditions emerging from them, scholastic and devotional, the place of Chalcedon cannot be denied or overlooked. What a
theologian anchored by tradition and magisterial teaching might argue,
instead, is that Chalcedon understood itself to be simply an extension
and interpretation of Nicaea: its Definition unfolds the logic of Christ's
Person within the thought-forms and idiom of the Holy Trinity. This

essay has attempted to follow this pattern, treating Christology as a Trinitarian matter and setting forth its central terms and preoccupations from this Conciliar threshold. But it is time, now, to take up directly the idiom and interpretation that Chalcedon bequeaths to dogmatic theology.

In full view now are the rudiments Nicene theologians inaugurated: nature, Person, mission, unity. After some wavering, the Fathers of the Council settled on the language we now see in the Definition: One Person in, and not simply from, two natures. Christ must be understood to possess a full humanity, body and rational soul, that is *homoousios* – the determinative term of Nicaea – that is, of one substance with us. So too He must be in His Deity *homoousios* with the Father, very God of very God. His existence must be governed by a twin birth, an Eternal Generation as Divine Son and an earthly begetting by the Holy Spirit and the Virgin Mary. The fateful term, *Theotokos*, God-bearer, so vital in Cyril's pamphlet war with Nestorius, is now affirmed directly; it sets the high-water mark of Cyrillianism in the Decree.

But there are other elements within the Definition that appear to some ears, at least, to support Nestorius's central conviction, that the Divine and human natures must remain unmixed, distinct, and intact. Though it is a matter of some scholarly debate, the influence wielded by the papal letter sent to the Council, the "Tome of Leo," the Council echoed one of the Tome's most striking phrases: the "natures of Christ doing what is proper to each." We reach the heart of the Definition in its measured and balanced depiction of the natures in their relation, one to the other. They are "unmixed, unconfused; unseparated, undivided." Much to the dismay of its opponents, these phrases appeared to make "nature" the governing category in Christology and not Person. It is not self-evident that two distinct natures, acting out of their own powers and habits, can compose a single Person: much of the Christological debates before and after Chalcedon can be summed up in this worry.

In the Tome, and in Cyril's many letters and treatises, we begin to see a form of unity between these two natures that is governed by a form of exchange, predicates of one nature being assigned to the other. Later given a Latin title by the medieval logicians, the *"communicatio idiomatum,"* this drive toward the unity of distinct natures became, in the sixteenth and seventeenth centuries, a central testing ground for the new Protestant dogmatics. Between the Swiss Reformed and the German Lutherans, a lively, at times bitter, debate turned on the forms of this exchange: its grammatical and metaphysical presuppositions, its appeal to predicates abstract and concrete, and its natural refulgence into Eucharistic theology. To honor the distinctiveness of the natures, to preserve them unconfused, yet to take their properties and apply them to what each is not, is no mean feat. To affirm that "God is dead," or that "Man is God" trains a piercing light on the complex legacy of Chalcedon and the continuing search for the proper Nicene reading of this discourse on nature. All the same, Chalcedon has more to say than to simply list these four adverbs, prominent as they are.

The ostinato of the whole is the ringing phrase, One and the Same – One and the Same Son, Lord, Only Begotten, Jesus Christ. This One Son is the Agent of the earthly life of Christ, and it is He who was sent into the world to suffer and to save. From this stern emphasis upon unity spring the Scholastic debates about the mind, will, and obedience of the earthly Christ. The natures, human and divine, are joined in the Person of the Son – "hypostatically," another Nicene leitmotiv – but the human nature must "follow" or "obey" or be "conformed" to the Divine. The human mind of Christ, affirmed since the condemnation of Apollinarius in the fourth century, now took center stage. Can this rational soul, having no proper independence – it is "impersonal" – be understood to have faith? Can it disobey? Does it enjoy during its earthly life the direct vision of God, the Beatific Vision? Is it a "comprehensor" or a "wayfarer" in its earthly mission to the Cross? Can it direct meritorious deeds for the human life of Jesus before God? To these questions, Thomas roughly answered, no, no, yes, yes to both, and yes; but other of the Schoolmen disagreed.

Such metaphysical and spiritual questions have not fared well in the modern era; indeed, they are often accused of subverting the very Gospel narrative they aim to interpret. But the legacy of Chalcedon, and its Cyrillian interpretation at Constantinople II and III, will not allow these Scholastic questions to die away. They are the perennial questions, in medieval idiom, raised by the combustion of the great themes of the Definition, Person, Nature, and relation as they spark off one another in the life of the One who was sent in the fullness of time by God to a sin-sick world.

We have surveyed Christology from its beachhead in the Apostle Paul, through the outworking of Nicaea in the teaching and constitution of the Son, to His descent and emptying and assumption of human flesh, to His reality and purpose as Savior, born of a woman, born under the Law. To take up the Doctrine of the Person of Christ is to take into one's hands the burning core of Christian confession about God's ways with us, the brilliant Light that has come into the world. It is a demanding, exact science, the task of Christology; but it is also much,

much more. It is the ground of Christian discipleship, a path we may and must follow, to contemplate, confess, and teach, but also, and supremely, to adore.

Further Reading

Aquinas, Thomas (1947–1948), *Summa Theologica*, Third Part (trans. Fathers of the English Dominican Province; New York: Benziger Bros.).

Barth, Karl (1956–1967), *Church Dogmatics*, Volume IV (ed. and trans. G. Bromiley; Edinburgh: T&T Clark).

Bulgakov, Sergius (2008), *The Lamb of God* (trans. B. Jakim; Grand Rapids: Eerdmans).

Cross, Richard (2019), *Communicato Idiomatum: Reformation Christological Debates* (Oxford: Oxford University Press).

Douglas, Kelly Brown (1994), *The Black Christ* (Maryknoll: Orbis).

Daley, Brian (2018), *God Visible: Patristic Theology Reconsidered* (Oxford: Oxford University Press).

Gutierrez, Gustavo (1988), *A Theology of Liberation* (ed. and trans. C. Inda and J. Eagleson; Maryknoll: Orbis).

Rahner, Karl (1978), *Foundations of Christian Faith: An Introduction to the Idea of Christianity* (trans. W. Dych; New York: Seabury Press).

Schleiermacher, Friedrich (2016). *The Christian Faith* (ed. and trans. T. Tice, C. Kelsey, E. Lawler; Louisville: Westminster John Knox).

Tanner, Kathryn (2010), *Christ the Key* (Cambridge: Cambridge University Press).

Welch, Claude (1965), *God and Incarnation in Mid-Nineteenth Century German Thought: G Thomasius, IA Dorner, AE Biedermann* (Oxford: Oxford University Press).

Williams, Rowan (2018), *Christ the Heart of Creation* (London: Bloomsbury).

6 Atonement and Sin

ADAM JOHNSON

The doctrine of the atonement is the church's work of exploring the meaning and significance of the death and resurrection of Jesus Christ as the triune God's chosen way of reconciling all creation to himself. This chapter unearths some of the key doctrinal commitments essential to providing a sufficiently expansive account of Jesus's work – one equipped to do justice to the range of causes leading to, and effects flowing from, the death and resurrection of Jesus as described in Scripture and the history of doctrine. As such, it is a work of faith seeking understanding, in which we use the range of tools available to us (biblical, historical, theological …) to understand a reality greater than but utterly consequential to ourselves.

An alternative approach, birthed in the nineteenth century and culminating in the emphasis upon linguistic plurality and the role of metaphor, is evident in views that describe a range of "theories" or metaphors for the atonement. This family of approaches (1) acknowledges a necessary plurality of metaphors (2) and orders these metaphors in relation to each other or (3) selects one of these to provide the preeminent account of the work of Christ for theological or culturally specific reasons. At their best, such approaches facilitate the appreciation of the breadth of the scriptural and historical thinking about the saving work of Christ and, at their worst, minimize much of this diversity, limiting its significance by polarizing what were meant to be complementary perspectives.[1]

---

[1] For representative texts employing metaphor-based approaches, see Mark D. Baker and Joel B. Green, *Recovering the Scandal of the Cross: Atonement in New Testament and Contemporary Contexts* (Downers Grove, IL: InterVarsity Press, 2003); Colin E. Gunton, *The Actuality of Atonement: A Study of Metaphor, Rationality, and the Christian Tradition* (Grand Rapids: Eerdmans, 1989). My own approach has minimized the role of this perspective in order to ground an explanation of the diversity in the biblical and historical understanding of the atonement in God himself, namely his divine attributes. Adam Johnson, ed., *T&T Clark Companion to*

The present account anchors the range of perspectives on the work of Christ in a properly theological understanding of the diversity proper to the triune life of God, balanced with an appreciation of the creaturely nexus of causes and effects at play in Jesus's death and resurrection. Jesus's death, that is to say, is a uniquely complex event: a range of causes (physical, psychological, social, religious, political, spiritual, and theological) contribute to bringing about his death, and the resurrection results in a correspondingly abundant array of effects (in keeping with Gregory Nazianzus's axiom that "the unassumed is unhealed"). This chapter explores six theological commitments central to the work of Christ which are vital for a full appreciation of this fundamental doctrine of the Christian faith.

Each section concludes with a reflection on the nature of sin: that which is exposed, condemned, and done away with in the work of Jesus – for this is what sin is: any creaturely perversion or distortion of the character and will of God exposed and judged in the saving work of Christ. As such, sin should be treated in a distinctly secondary way, as that which (following Augustine) has meaning only as a privation, only as that which exists by perverting or distorting some good which precedes it.

THE DOCTRINE OF GOD

"It was the will of the Lord to crush him" (Isa. 53:10); and "for God so loved the world" (Jn. 3:16)

The death of Jesus was more than an accident, more than the natural outcome of God-made-man living among sinful human creatures. Though Jesus died as the result of many causes (the machinations of the Pharisees, politics of the Romans, betrayal of Judas, and work of Satan), behind them all stands the will of the Father. God gave his only Son who must be "lifted up" just as "Moses lifted up the serpent in the wilderness" (Jn. 3:13–17). The Father sent Jesus, that we might feed on his flesh and blood (Jn. 6:52–59). Jesus "gave himself for our sins to

---

the Atonement (New York: T&T Clark, 2017); Adam Johnson, Atonement: A Guide for the Perplexed (New York: T&T Clark, 2015).

On the origins of "theories" of the atonement, cf. Adam Johnson, "Theories and Theoria of the Atonement: A Proposal," International Journal of Systematic Theology 23, no. 1 (2021), 92–108; Oliver D. Crisp, "Methodological Issues in Approaching the Atonement," in T&T Clark Companion to the Atonement (ed. Adam Johnson; New York: T&T Clark, 2017), 315–334.

deliver us from the present evil age, according to the will of our God and Father" (Gal. 1:3–4). Behind the wills of the powers and principalities, nations, leaders, and individuals stands the unified will of Jesus and his Father: a united willing to send and be sent. For that is the will of Jesus: to do the will of his Father (Jn. 4:34) – and the cross is what the Father willed, for it was "the will of the Lord to crush him" (Isa. 53:10).

Considerable theological resources stand behind such a claim – for ultimately questions about the atonement are really questions about the doctrine of God – the trinity, divine attributes, and election. First, this is the action of the triune God. This is not the action of three gods, three independent centers of willing and acting, a tri-theism or polytheism in which the superior and more powerful god wills that a lower, lesser god do a lowly and painful work. These are not separate and distinct gods with different and even opposed wills, as we find so commonly asserted in "divine child-abuse" critiques of traditional views of the atonement. Rather, this is the one unified work of the one God: Father, Son and Holy Spirit. To borrow classic and medieval categories, God wills to be the material, efficient, formal, and final cause of our salvation – God uses himself, makes himself the means of our salvation, for the sake of his glorious name. The incarnation, life, death, and resurrection of Jesus is the work of the one God, for us and for our salvation: God wills himself to act, wills to obey himself, and empowers himself to do this work for us, employing the riches and resources of the triune divine life for us and for our salvation, taking up the human dilemma into the relationship of Father, incarnate Son, and Holy Spirit, that we might be saved.[2]

Why, then, the cross? Only a full account of the divine character will suffice for a proper understanding, in response to the problem of human sin. Theologies of the cross derive their power and insight from the divine attribute they emphasize – for the logic of the atonement fundamentally revolves around the character of God, not metaphors. Is

[2] Cf. Fleming Rutledge, *The Crucifixion: Understanding the Death of Jesus Christ* (Grand Rapids: Eerdmans, 2015); Nicholas E. Lombardo, *The Father's Will: Christ's Crucifixion and the Goodness of God* (New York: Oxford University Press, 2013). On the subject of feminist critiques, cf. Marit Trelstad, *Cross Examinations: Readings on the Meaning of the Cross Today* (Minneapolis: Fortress, 2006); Brad Jersak and Michael Hardin, eds., *Stricken by God? Nonviolent Identification and the Victory of Christ* (Grand Rapids: Eerdmans, 2007); Thomas H. McCall, *Forsaken: The Trinity and the Cross, and Why It Matters* (Downers Grove, IL: IVP Academic, 2012). On the unified acts of God, or "inseparable operations," see Adonis Vidu, *The Same God Who Works All Things: Inseparable Operations in Trinitarian Theology* (Grand Rapids: Eerdmans, 2021).

this a work of God's love? Wisdom? Justice? Power? Incorruptibility?
Theologians throughout history have developed each of these (and
others), and each offers a unique and theologically fruitful vantage point
from which to understand Christ's saving work – but only together, in
honor of the unity and simplicity of God, do they truly help us understand Christ's saving work. For in Christ the fullness of God was pleased
to dwell (Col. 1:19), and in him is the whole character of God, the
fullness of the divine attributes enacted for us and for our salvation.
The love, wisdom, patience, holiness, power, constancy, presence of
God ... everything God is, he is in, toward and for Jesus. We are
welcome to meditate on the role of any divine attribute in shaping the
doctrine of the atonement – so long as we do so as part of a larger work,
integrating the fullness of the divine attributes into our understanding.
Much harm comes from imbalanced approaches that emphasize one
divine attribute at the expense of others, whether that be mercy, righteousness, or any other attribute. All fruitful work on the atonement
comes from the tensions created by integration, rather than segregation,
of divine attributes. The tension of justice and mercy is but the beginning of this synthetic project, so fruitful within the doctrine.[3]

But, again, why does God will the cross? If this is a work of, by, and
for the triune God, then why the crushing, why this suffering and death?
The cross is God's response to human sin, God's extension or enactment of the immanent divine life for us and for our salvation, within the
circumstances of fallen creation, in opposition to sin, death, and the
devil. In other words, this is not a glimpse into the immanent life of
God, the love of Father, Son, and Holy Spirit portrayed as such on a
human stage that we might know and be shaped by such a grand vision
of love. Or rather, it is such, for God has nothing greater to give us than
himself; but it is such in a different key, under the circumstances of sin,
corruption, and death. In Christ, we see the response of the triune God
to sin. It is here, therefore, that the whole witness of Scripture to God's
response to sin coalesces. The patience/long-suffering, the unleashing of
anger and wrath, the destruction and annihilation, the promises and

---

[3] On atonement and simplicity, cf. Stephen R. Holmes, "A Simple Salvation?
Soteriology and the Perfections of God," in *God of Salvation* (ed. Ivor J. Davidson
and Murray A. Rae; Burlington, VT: Ashgate, 2011), 35–46; Johnson, Atonement;
Adonis Vidu, *Atonement, Law, and Justice: The Cross in Historical and Cultural
Contexts* (Grand Rapids: Baker Academic, 2014), 255–272; Ken Oakes, "The Divine
Perfections and the Economy: The Atonement," in *Theological Theology: Essays in
Honour of John Webster* (ed. R David Nelson, Darren Sarisky, and Justin Stratis;
London: T&T Clark, 2015), 237–246.

covenants, the forgiveness and mercy .... It is in the death and resurrection that the whole tumultuous picture of God's covenantal relationship with Israel, and through Israel all humankind, coalesces into a unified, self-consistent and saving act. We see here that the Lord our God, the Lord is one (Deut. 6:4–5) – for it is here that the will of the Lord to judge and annihilate sin and sinful creation that opposes him, and the will of the Lord to love and bless his creation, are revealed to be in harmony, a single unified will enacted in Jesus Christ: a will in which the negative response to sin is fully accomplished in the death of Jesus but subsumed within the greater and more comprehensive and eternal will to love and bless, in his resurrection. Why does God will the cross? That in Christ, he might destroy sin and fallen creation, judging and annihilating the evil that opposes him – that he might restore creation through its participation in himself, in the resurrection of Jesus Christ.[4]

What, then, is sin from this perspective of Christ's saving work? It is any power that is antithetical to God's power, or love that is foreign to God's love – realities made abundantly clear, for instance, in the portrayal of power and love in Ovid's *Metamorphoses*, or Twain's depiction of justice in the feud between the Grangefords and Shepherdsons in *Huckleberry Finn*. But more specifically, sin is that which grasps one aspect of God's character, separating it from the united and simple whole that is God. God's righteousness, holiness, patience, mercy, and kindness, when isolated from each other, deprived of the unity within which each is what it is, cease to be the character of God. A "holiness" unqualified by mercy and patience, a "forgiveness" that knows no omniscience or righteousness, a "love" that knows no covenant faithfulness (and vice-versa) – these are the dynamics of sin, which

---

[4] The logic of God's judgment on sin, rooted in the divine attributes of justice, wrath, and righteousness as witnessed throughout the Old and New Testaments, grounds a proper understanding of the negative aspect of Christ's saving work. Cf. Jeremy J. Wynne, *Wrath among the Perfections of God's Life* (New York: T&T Clark, 2010). It also raises the question of Christ's descent and suffering in hell. Cf. Hans Urs von Balthasar, *Mysterium Paschale: The Mystery of Easter* (trans. Aidan Nichols; San Francisco: Ignatius Press, 1990); Edward T. Oakes, "The Internal Logic of Holy Saturday in the Theology of Hans Urs Von Balthasar," *International Journal of Systematic Theology* 9, no. 2 (2007), 184–199; Alyssa Lyra Pitstick, *Light in Darkness: Hans Urs Von Balthasar and the Catholic Doctrine of Christ's Descent into Hell* (Grand Rapids: Eerdmans, 2007); Matthew Y. Emerson, "*He Descended to the Dead*": an Evangelical Theology of Holy Saturday (Downers Grove, IL: IVP Avademic, 2019).

destructively unleash a perverted imitation of the divine life by creating
separations and divisions in that which, properly speaking, is what it is
only by its unity.[5]

REPRESENTATION/SUBSTITUTION

"He is the image of the invisible God . . . . All things were created
through him and for him . . . and in him all things hold together" (Col.
1:15–17); "He made him to be sin who knew no sin, so that in him we
might become the righteousness of God" (2 Cor. 5:21)

Christology is a matter of establishing that Jesus is fully God and fully
man – but just as important is the utterly unique kind of man this happens
to be, a uniqueness due in part to humankind's relation to him: "All things
were created through him and for him . . . and in him all things hold
together' (Col. 1:15–17; cf. Ephesians 1–2). Jesus is not merely one of us,
though he is that – we are who and what we are in him, for we were chosen
in him, created in him, and our purpose lies in him. He is the representative, the archetype, the one in whom creation's fate hangs in the balance.
And Jesus is this as faithful Israel: the one in whom Israel accomplishes
the Exodus from Egypt and crosses the river Jordan; he is the giver and the
fulfiller of the law, the one who spoke by, and fulfills, the words of the
prophets, the true king of Israel, the one who fed and nourished Israel in
the wilderness (1 Cor. 10:4). Yes, Jesus is a man – but he is a Jew, the son of
David, the Covenant God with whom and in whom Israel keeps covenant.
    And the will of the Father is that Jesus, the representative of Israel
(and therefore all humankind), be the substitute. God "made him to be
sin who knew no sin, so that in him we might become the righteousness
of God" (2 Cor. 5:21), "he himself bore our sins in his body on the cross"
(1 Pet. 2:24), he is the "lamb of God who takes away the sin of the
world" (Jn. 1:29), he is identified with the "record of debt" that stood
"against us with its legal demands," which he "nailed to the cross"
(Col. 2:14), he is the one who bore "our griefs and carried our sorrows,"
the one on whom the Lord "laid the iniquity of us all" (Isa. 53:4–6; cf.
Matt. 8:17). These verses do not settle the matter – they are the matter
to be settled. But central to the doctrine of the atonement is the relationship between our sin and Jesus Christ – the relation or connection

---

[5] See Stephen J. Duby, *Divine Simplicity: A Dogmatic Account* (New York: T&T Clark,
2015).

between Christ and our sin should constitute the explanatory core of any theory, model, or account of the atoning death of Christ. Irenaeus and Athanasius established the logic of the great exchange; Augustine spoke of the exchange of debts that occurs within a marriage covenant; Maximus wrote of Jesus bearing the punishment of Adam's nature, thereby converting the use of death; Anselm offered his alternative to sin-bearing in his account of vicarious satisfaction; Calvin adopted at times a more forensic/legal approach of imputation; and Barth and Torrance explored the grounding of humanity in Christ such that Jesus is, in the words of Luther, the "one great sinner." Central to most accounts of the atonement throughout the history of the church (in Orthodox, Catholic, and Protestant teaching) is an understanding that Jesus bears, takes upon himself, or in some sense has a real connection to or identification with the sin and/or punishment of humankind such that Jesus does something for us, sparing us from doing that work ourselves.[6]

Who is Jesus? He is the one who represents us, whose work includes and remakes us. And he is our substitute, the one who does his work for us, instead of us, in our place. Both substitution and representation are biblical, and neither can be excluded from our atonement theology without distortion. And together, Jesus's representative and substitutionary bearing of our sin find their telos in our relation to, or being remade in, the image of Jesus, who is the "image of the invisible God" (Col. 1:15). The doctrine of the atonement deals with God's relation to sin only in reference to its primary business, the goal of re-creation: that we might be "transformed into the [image of God] from one degree of glory to another" (2 Cor. 3:18), that we might be "filled with all the fullness of God" (Eph. 3:19), that God might abide in us and his love be perfected in us through our abiding in God and he in us (1 Jn. 4:9–16). The telos of substitution and representation lies not merely in Jesus's vicarious death but in his resurrection: our ongoing life transformed in him through his life-giving Spirit.

From this standpoint, what emerges of the character of sin? The doctrine of the atonement revolves around a twofold account of participation:

---

[6] For recent creative alternatives to the tradition, see Eleonore Stump, *Atonement* (Oxford: Oxford University Press, 2018); Marilyn McCord Adams, *Christ and Horrors: The Coherence of Christology* (Cambridge: Cambridge University Press, 2006); Darrin W. Snyder Belousek, *Atonement, Justice, and Peace: The Message of the Cross and the Mission of the Church* (Grand Rapids: Eerdmans, 2012). For a recent defense of the traditional view, cf. Rutledge, *The Crucifixion*. On the relationship between substitution and representation, see Jeannine Michele Graham, "Substitution and Representation," in *T&T Clark Companion to Atonement* (ed. Adam J. Johnson; London: Bloomsbury, 2017), 763–768.

Christ in us and our sin; we in Christ and his glory (as a shorthand for the fullness of the character of God) – as Athanasius put it in *On the Incarnation* §54, "he was incarnate that we might be made god." As the logic of Christianity is participation, so that of sin is isolation, independence, of curving in on ourselves, to live by our own power and strength. Sin is the experience not of a triumphant Prometheus or Dr. Frankenstein but of a broken isolation – one in which the participatory logic of the Trinity, extended to the creature in the participatory logic of humanity in Christ, is stretched to the vanishing point of existence: Jesus's cry of forsakenness, the fulfillment of Jonah's descent into the depths for three days, the descent of Israel into Egypt, of Samson into his blind captivity in the prison of the Philistines. And it is worth noting that this independence and curving in on oneself can take a communal form – a demonic Orwellian unity that rejects the difference essential to representation.

RESURRECTION

> "If Christ has not been raised, your faith is futile and you are still in your sins" (1 Cor. 15:17)

God is not the God of the dead, but of the living (Matt. 22:32). The doctrine of the atonement seeks to give an account of the work of this living One, Jesus Christ – the one who was dead, but is now alive, risen and ascended to the right hand of the Father. It seeks to explain the reasons for his incarnation, his becoming man, and give an account of the many reasons for his death; but as the joyful counterbalance to this, and in a recapitulation of the doctrine of creation, it explores the meaning of his resurrection – for it is as the risen One that his incarnation, ministry, and death take on their decisive meaning. As the Apostle tells us, "if Christ has not been raised, your faith is futile and you are still in your sins," and "we are of all people most to be pitied" (1 Cor. 15:17–19). But "he has been raised for our justification" (Rom. 4:25) and is the "first fruits of those who have fallen asleep," the one in whom "shall all be made alive" (1 Cor. 15:20–22), the one who brings glory, power, life in the Spirit, and who remakes us in his image (1 Cor. 15:42–49). The resurrection is a work of power that changes the human predicament, the human condition and fate – death is no longer final.[7]

---

[7] See Ingolf U. Dalferth, *Crucified and Resurrected: Restructuring the Grammar of Christology* (Grand Rapids: Baker Academic, 2015); Thomas F. Torrance, *Space, Time, and Resurrection* (Grand Rapids: Eerdmans, 1976).

Given this understanding, why did the risen one need to die? Why was his incarnation alone insufficient – for isn't the resurrection merely a return to the sinless existence of the God-man (in the sense of no longer being the sin-bearer)? We frame the question this way to expand the conceptual footprint of the doctrine of the atonement. While the doctrine attends to the causes and implications of Jesus's death, at its very core it does far more than this, for the fundamental reason that the atonement is not a negative or destructive but a positive and creative doctrine: an account of the work of the living and creative God, a God who is the faithful covenant keeper, a God who uses this surprising manner of establishing his identity with his creation, of establishing the identity of his creation by its proper relation to him. Atonement, a word unique to the English language, is therefore delightfully appropriate, pulling our attention to the one-ness, the making-at-one of which this doctrine seeks to give account. This is a oneness involving separation, judgment, punishment, and destruction for anything opposed to the character and will of God but whose telos is that we may be one as God is one – that we may be in God, receiving the glory of God, that we may be one even as the Father and Son are one, for Jesus is in us and the Father is in him, that we may be perfectly one (Jn. 17:21–23), abiding as a new creation in him. The goal, the purpose of the doctrine of the atonement is the free gift of that which we sought to take in the garden of Eden: "you will be like God" (Gen. 3:5) – but not merely a likeness: a union, a participation. The goal of Christ's resurrection is our union with him, our participation in God by grace and glory – a doctrine known as divinization or *theosis* – a creaturely participation in which we are not subsumed or simply incorporated into God but in which we, through the gift of the Spirit, become the image of God by creaturely participation in him.[8]

Sin, seen from this vantage point, is the attempt to seize that which God seeks to give us freely. It is the desire to be like God apart from

---

[8] This fundamentally positive vision of the atonement rooted in resurrection stands as the impetus for the idea that God would have become man even apart from sin and the fall. See Edwin Chr. van Driel, *Incarnation Anyway: Arguments for Supralapsarian Christology* (Oxford: Oxford University Press, 2008); Justus H. Hunter, *If Adam Had Not Sinned: The Reason for the Incarnation from Anselm to Scotus* (Washington, DC: Cathlolic University of America Press 2020).

On theosis/divinization, see the numerous edited works on the subject, and Norman Russell, *The Doctrine of Deification in the Greek Patristic Tradition* (Oxford: Oxford University Press, 2004); Khaled Anatolios, *Deification through the Cross: An Eastern Christian Theology of Salvation* (Grand Rapids: Eerdmans, 2020).

God, over and against God, by our own power and understanding. It is the attempt to be wise apart from God's wisdom, to become powerful apart from his might, like Milton's Satan to create law and kingdom alien to his law and kingdom. And this distortion and disorder within God's creature leads it, both by punishment and the natural outcome of the path we choose, to fragmentation and death. For as God is the God of the living, so to separate ourselves from God, to seek to be like him apart from and as rivals to him, is to seek life apart from life, a demonic perversion in which every creaturely portrayal of the attributes of God becomes a parody, a vice-unto-death, no matter how good or pure it may seem. In fact, it is precisely that impossible and unattainable pursuit of the pure, the holy, and the good apart from God and his will, that unleashes the greatest evil in the world around us.

HOLY SPIRIT

> "Being therefore exalted at the right hand of God, and having received from the Father the promise of the Holy Spirit, he has poured out this that you yourselves are seeing and hearing" (Acts 2:32)

The baptism of Jesus was a trinitarian affair: the Spirit descended upon Jesus in the form of a dove, "and a voice came from heaven, 'You are my beloved Son; with you I am well pleased'" (Lk. 3:22). But Jesus was baptized not once but twice: in foretelling his death (Mk. 10:32–45), Jesus asked James and John: "Are you able to . . . be baptized with the baptism with which I am baptized?" – and Paul too thinks of the Passion as Jesus's baptism, into which we are baptized (Rom. 6:3–4). The role of the Holy Spirit is the most neglected aspect of the doctrine of the atonement, a lacuna between the doctrines of the Trinity and atonement. Scripture tells us that Christ offered himself "through the eternal Spirit . . . without blemish to God" (Heb. 9:14) and that upon his ascension and exaltation to the right hand of God, Jesus received and thence poured out "the promise of the Holy Spirit" (Acts 2:33) but says little more, and most works on the atonement have little to say about the Holy Spirit. Christian piety nonetheless demands faithful reflection on the Holy Spirit's work here as elsewhere.

We begin by noting that there is a difference between the two baptisms of Christ, a difference between "this is my Son with whom I am well pleased," and "my God, my God, why have you forsaken me?" – a difference understood partly in terms of the Holy Spirit who descended upon Jesus at the river Jordan but was again given to Jesus upon his resurrection and exaltation (Acts 2:33). My own sense is that

Jesus, the true Israelite, empowered by the Spirit after the pattern of Moses, Samuel, and David, recapitulates his nation's history. He bears in himself the judgment of the Spirit upon Israel and receives the full blessing of the Spirit in his resurrection as the new temple built in three days, sharing with those united to him by faith the promised Spirit. In that sense, Jesus recapitulates the role of the Spirit in the history of Israel, being baptized twice: (1) an inaugural gifting of the Spirit akin to God's gift of the Spirit to Israel as part of its calling and establishment and (2) a full and complete gifting of the Spirit after Christ's ascension, fulfilling the promises saturating the prophets. Between those two baptisms stands the death of Jesus, the fulfillment of the Spirit's cleansing judgment upon the representative of unfaithful Israel.[9]

If the purpose of the atonement is for Christ to become the recipient and sharer of the promised Holy Spirit with those that are baptized in him, what does this reveal about the nature of sin? To sin is to think and act as if our identities, natures, and possibilities are completely our own to know, shape, and control. But the ultimate guide to our self-understandings, possibilities, and purposes is found not merely in ourselves, in personal or social constructs, but in the way our purpose and therefore nature is bound up with the work of the indwelling Holy Spirit made possible by the death and resurrection of Jesus Christ. To sin is to refuse our identity and vocation as given by God, to reject human nature as bound up with the work of God, and to seek its meaning and possibilities in the sphere of human activity and self-definition, apart from the indwelling of the Holy Spirit.

CREATED ORDER

> "In him we have redemption through his blood ... according to the riches of his grace ... which he set forth in Christ as a plan for the fullness of time, to unite all things in him, things in heaven and things on earth" (Eph. 1:7–10); "For the creation was subjected to futility ... because of him who subjected it, in hope that the creation itself will be set free from its bondage to corruption and obtain the freedom of the glory of the children of God" (Rom. 8:20–21)

The complexity proper to the atonement means that one of the grave dangers attending the doctrine is that of reductionism: making the

---

[9] See Frank D. Macchia, *Jesus the Spirit Baptizer: Christology in Light of Pentecost* (Grand Rapids: Eerdmans, 2018); Carolyn E. Tan, *The Spirit at the Cross: Exploring a Cruciform Pneumatology* (Eugene, OR: Wipf & Stock, 2019); Kathryn Tanner, *Christ the Key* (Cambridge: Cambridge University Press, 2010).

doctrine smaller, so to speak, in order to make it more manageable. Limiting one's focus to the Father and (incarnate) Son at the expense of the Holy Spirit, to mercy and justice while ignoring or minimizing the full range of divine attributes at play in Christ's work, limiting an account of sin to just one of its dimensions ... such reductionism abounds in the doctrine of the atonement. One such temptation is to reduce the effect of Christ's atoning work to humankind alone – to make us the exclusive aim of Jesus saving work. But Scripture and the history of its interpretation demand more of us.

The mystery of God's will, Paul tells us, is set forth in Christ: a plan "to unite all things in him, things in heaven and things on earth" (Eph. 1:10), while in Romans he briefly explores the way that creation itself has been bound up with the fate of humankind, and awaits our freedom, our "attaining the freedom of the glory of the children of God" (Rom. 8:21). The doctrine of the atonement, we might say, is the hinge upon which the doctrine of creation swings. Since the fall of Adam and Eve, creation has been compromised, subjected to futility, disorder, and chaos, a futility bound up with those who were meant to be its care-takers (Genesis 3), a futility that ceases only when creation is made whole again through being united to the one by whom all things were made. The atonement, in short, is the at-one-ment of creation, the making whole of creation. But this unifying of creation is ordered, revolving around the work of the Messiah in fulfilling the calling of Israel, that through him (and them) the Gentiles might be saved, and through humankind's reconciliation to its maker, all things in heaven and earth might be re-ordered, recapitulated.

The atonement is not merely about guilt – neither is it merely about systemic patterns of oppression or the need to cultivate civic virtue. It is about all of these – but much more. The doctrine, as envisioned by the Old and New Testaments, is about the uniting of all things in Christ; the fulfillment of a cosmic harmony that entails the overcoming of sin, death, and the devil through Jesus Christ; and the establishment of God's will and ways throughout a graced and Spirit-renewed creation, the kingdom of God. As such it includes environmental and ecological concerns, matters of guilt and shame, individual and systemic/commu-nal dimensions. In short, it is as well-rounded and comprehensive as creation itself – but it is so in an ordered way, recognizing humanity's central place within the drama of creation.[10]

---

[10] See David Clough, *On Animals*, Volume 1: *Systematic Theology* (London: T&T Clark, 2012).

Accordingly, we must understand the incarnation not merely as God becoming man but as God becoming creature. Jesus is a microcosm of creation – in him is the dust and mineral of Israel, and he, standing midway between angel and beast, represents both. Christ's resurrection from the dead, Paul tells us, is the man of dust becoming the man from heaven, the perishable putting on the imperishable – and we and creation in him, such that "when the perishable puts on the imperishable ... then shall come to pass the saying that is written: 'Death is swallowed up in victory'" (1 Cor. 15:54).

From this perspective, the doctrine of sin and its consequences is far from an exclusively human problem, limited to religious and psychological dimensions (vices, addictions, habits ...), with a range of sociological entailments. Scripture connects sin directly to the various forms of disorder plaguing creation. While ecological systems did not sin, for instance, they have been "subjected" as an extension or divine response to the fall of humankind, a visible and tangible manifestation of the chaos introduced into creation by our sin against God. This is not the main problem, as Scripture sees it – but it is a real problem, awaiting the ordered solution provided by its maker: creation will be released from its futility, as we will be freed from the sufferings of our bodies, when we obtain the freedom of the glory of the children of God, when we too (and creation in and with us) participate in the glory of the resurrected Christ (1 Cor. 15).

Sin is a violation of the order of God. It is a violation of the centrality of humankind in God's creative purposes, relegating our status to that of fallen creatures, if not that of a virus or infection in an otherwise good creation, or an equally perverse over-emphasis on humankind as the sole focus for ourselves and for God, as if the rest of creation were of no particular consequence for God's plan and purpose in Christ, the creator of all things. Sin is equally invested in de-centralizing or displacing humankind, on the one hand, and making humankind the sole concern, on the other hand, the sole measure of meaning and action in creation.

SPIRITUAL REALM

"He disarmed the rulers and authorities and put them to open shame, by triumphing over them in him" (Col. 2:15)

Nineteenth-century liberal theology shaped the doctrine of the atonement by positing the existence of competing views or theories of the

work of Christ throughout the history of the church. This, combined
with Enlightenment critiques of Christianity, led to the relegation of
Christ's defeat of Satan to the status of an obscure relic – one that
Gustaf Aulén sought to reestablish to its proper dignity in his famous
book, *Christus Victor*.[11] But, with notable exceptions, the church has
generally held to the existence of spiritual beings, both fallen (demons)
and unfallen (angels), which play a significant role in Scripture – and has
likewise held that Jesus overcame the power of demons through his
death and resurrection (though it did so with a variety of explanations –
a family of theories, one might say). Contra Aulén, one finds such views
throughout the writings of the medievals, including Anselm, Bernard,
Abelard, and Aquinas, as well as modern and contemporary theologians.
In fact, apart from Enlightenment critiques of the spiritual and the
miraculous, such views continue to be present in the teaching of the
church, though not necessarily as the central aspect of its teaching. (No
church father made it the exclusive feature of their account of Christ's
atonement.)

Several points should guide our thinking. First, Scripture clearly
assumes the existence of Satan and demons: real though fallen spiritual
beings, with powers and agency.[12] Second, Satan's relation to fallen
humankind is complex: to some degree we are his slaves or property,
for he is the prince of this world (Jn. 12:31), but he is a usurper who has
been judged and disarmed (Col. 2:15). In other words, as a creature loved
by God, Satan has certain rights before God in relation to us – but only
within God's order and justice, as a part of his love for and rule of his
creatures. Third, spiritual beings have a complex role within God's
purposes for creation. To some degree, they seem more central to
God's creative purposes than humankind (Job is a player on the stage
of God's interaction with Satan; cf. 1 Jn. 3:8). But given the incarnation
and ascension of the Son of God as a man, humankind seems preeminent, and we will judge the angels (1 Cor. 6:3). Finally, Christ's defeat of
Satan should not be understood as a theory of the atonement (a self-
contained and sufficient explanation of his work) but an ingredient vital

---

[11] Gustaf Aulén, *Christus Victor: An Historical Study of the Three Main Types of the
Idea of Atonement* (trans. A. G. Hebert; New York: Macmillan, 1951).

[12] René Girard's influential contribution is best understood not as a demythologized
alternative to traditional accounts, but as an anthropological appreciation of the
particular kind of power Satan often employs. René Girard, *I See Satan Fall Like
Lightning* (Maryknoll: Orbis, 2001). For a more traditional account of the powers
and principalities, see Esther Acolatse, *Powers, Principalities, and the Spirit:
Biblical Realism in Africa and the West* (Grand Rapids: Eerdmans, 2018).

to any proper understanding of Christ's saving work. Whether Christ's victory is explained in terms of justice or honor, individuals or nations, through an emphasis on representation or substitution ... there is more to the atonement and therefore the Christian life than our relationship with God – Scripture and the history of doctrine are clear that God became man to free us from the power of Satan, to restore order and justice not only in humankind but in the spiritual realm – a work not only of power but of love and wisdom meant to both honor and put in its proper place, all levels of power and authority.

Sin is not merely a problem of breaking God's laws or a lack of charity, a problem of the will or the heart. And neither is it merely a social or systemic problem, arising from deeply flawed structures of financial, judicial, and political injustice (though it certainly includes these). Sin, according to Scripture, has to do with powers and principalities, with real though fallen spiritual beings at play within creation that actively seek to undermine and oppose the kingdom of God. A Christian theology that takes the biblical witness seriously will in some way grapple with an account of sin that transcends the psychosomatic boundaries of the individual and the larger community. Sin, as is unmistakably clear from the Gospels, involves Satan and demons; powers and principalities of creation; involves allegiances, authorities, and boundaries; is a matter of kingdoms, laws, and rules that far transcend individual or social human intentions, actions and consequences.

CONCLUSION

The doctrine of the atonement is a synthetic doctrine, a whole formed by a range of interrelated theological commitments. It is by careful attention to this synthesis, the role of the various doctrines within the atonement, that our understanding of Jesus's death and resurrection comes to life in its full complexity and beauty. This is one of the great challenges for the doctrine today: to refuse simplistic or one-dimensional accounts of the work of Christ as we seek to understand the full scope of the doctrine, all the forces at play in bringing about the death of Jesus, and the full range of blessings stemming from the power of his resurrection. To this end, an appreciation of the whole Trinity (and not just the Father and incarnate Son), of the full range of divine attributes (and not simply mercy and justice), of Christ's relation to the sin of humankind – in short, of the full range of factors mentioned in this chapter, will facilitate a fruitful reading of both Scripture and the Christian tradition.

Further Reading

Primary Sources

Anselm (1998), "Why God Became Man." In *The Major Works* (ed. Brian Davies and G. R. Evans; New York: Oxford University Press).

Athanasius (2011), *On the Incarnation* (trans. John Behr; Yonkers, NY: St Vladimir's Seminary Press).

Aquinas, Thomas (1964), *Summa Theologiae: The Passion of Christ (3a. 46–52)* (trans. Dominican Order; Volume 54; New York: Blackfriars).

Barth, Karl (1988), *Church Dogmatics IV/1: The Doctrine of Reconciliation* (Edinburgh: T & T Clark).

Calvin, John (1960), *Institutes of the Christian Religion* (Philadelphia: Westminster Press).

Secondary Sources

Hart, Trevor A. (2019), *In Him Was Life: The Person and Work of Christ* (Waco: Baylor University Press).

Johnson, Adam (2015), *Atonement: A Guide for the Perplexed* (New York: T&T Clark).

ed. (2017), *T&T Clark Companion to the Atonement* (New York: T&T Clark).

Rivière, Jean (1909), *The Doctrine of the Atonement: A Historical Essay* (trans. Luigi Cappadelta; 2 Volumes; London: Kegan Paul, Trench, Trubner & Co.).

Rutledge, Fleming (2015), *The Crucifixion: Understanding the Death of Jesus Christ* (Grand Rapids: Eerdmans).

7 Holy Spirit

DANIEL CASTELO

INTRODUCTION

The person and work of the Holy Spirit are central to visions of the Christian doctrine of God, the Christian gospel, and the Christian life. This judgment is not simply based on a single biblical episode (such as the Pentecost narrative in Acts 2 or the Farewell Discourses of the Gospel of John). Rather, the centrality of the Spirit is grounded in the very logic of how the God of Christian confession, YHWH-Trinity, acts in the world and how this One goes on to be known and worshipped by followers of the Risen One. Christian initiation, the availability of grace, the remembrance of Jesus, the transformation of the heart, the eucharistic life of the church, the reading of Scripture, growth in holiness, the embodied mission of the people of God with "power" and "authority," the sustained hope of living a cruciform existence in the eschatological "last days" – in short, every feature of God's self-manifestation and work in the economy of salvation history is not just pneumatologically related but pneumatologically constituted and driven. Gordon Fee captures this sentiment well when he remarks of Paul's pneumatology: "'salvation in Christ' not only begins by the Spirit, it is the ongoing work of the Spirit in every area and avenue of the Christian life."[1] The disciples of Jesus, then, are those called to be a people of the Spirit, ones who walk according to the Spirit and those who bear the gifts and fruit of the Spirit. As Kallistos Ware has so compellingly suggested, "The whole aim of the Christian life is to be a Spirit-bearer, to live in the Spirit of God, to breathe the Spirit of God."[2]

These claims about the Spirit's centrality stand in tension with the everyday speech-practices and understandings of many Christians, for

---

[1] Gordon D. Fee, *God's Empowering Presence* (Peabody, MA: Hendrickson, 1994), 869.
[2] Kallistos Ware, *The Orthodox Way* (Yonkers, NY: Saint Vladimir's Seminary Press, 2018), 126.

historically and customarily, the Holy Spirit has been neglected in both
academic and lay (or "pew") theology. Occasionally, theologians of
various persuasions have brought attention to this neglect because it
is so blatant, and sometimes they do so via memorable phrases: In 1957,
C. J. Sirks spoke of the doctrine of the Holy Spirit as the "Cinderella of
theology"[3] – often forgotten or left behind in favor of other topics; in
1993, in reference to the sustained (though it is important to note, not
complete) avoidance of the Spirit in the theology of Karl Barth, Robert
W. Jenson mused, "you wonder where the Spirit went"[4]; and in 2005,
Eugene Rogers suggested the following as an upshot of the last two
centuries of trinitarian revival: "Anything the Spirit can do, the Son
can do better."[5] Over the last few decades, some scholars have recognized this neglect, and pneumatological work has been on the rise. On
the whole across the Christian academy and church, however, pneumatological neglect continues to be obstinately perduring. On its face,
neglect of the Holy Spirit is unjustifiable: Trinitarian Christians confess
belief in Father, Son, and Holy Spirit. Why, then, have so many
Christians repeatedly ignored the Holy Spirit?

This state of the matter cannot be attributed simply to theological
ignorance or malfeasance. Those are surface diagnoses that may be
somewhat pertinent on a case-by-case basis, but they would not take
us very far in understanding and addressing the severity of this pneumatological deficit. Rather, it can be argued that this neglect is symptomatic of something deeper and more endemic to the field of Christian
pneumatology. Put pointedly, the topic of the Holy Spirit is beset with
several receptive challenges, especially for Westerners. These challenges are oftentimes not identified or explored even by theologians of
the highest caliber, yet they have a consequential and deleterious
impact upon pneumatology's role in formal and informal theology.

How should one go about assessing the impact of this neglect? Let
us take a sensitive matter for north-transatlantic Christianity: If the
Spirit is the One who renews the face of the earth and the life of the
church, what impact does neglecting the Spirit have on Christian vitality? This question is a very difficult (and uncomfortable) one to consider. Alongside their pneumatological neglect, Western Christians

---

[3] G. J. Sirks, "The Cinderella of Theology: The Doctrine of the Holy Spirit," *Harvard Theological Review* 50 (1957), 77–89.
[4] Robert W. Jenson, "You Wonder Where the Spirit Went," *Pro Ecclesia* 2 (1993), 296–304.
[5] Eugene F. Rogers Jr., *After the Spirit* (Grand Rapids: Eerdmans, 2005), 33.

often find their faith in retrenchment in their environs. This situation is in contrast to other parts of the world – including what is deemed "the Global South" – where Christian revivals are taking place that many consider unprecedented in terms of their scope and momentum. As it so happens, this revival is overtly pneumatological and charismatic, as Philip Jenkins has reminded us.[6] Could it be, then, that the present and future health of the Christian church is tied to its self-consciously pneumatological orientation?

This question will loom over the following chapter. Rather than directly answering it, we will allow the question to stand as a strategy for generating a kind of disquietude – one that hopefully will lead to curiosity and change. As a way forward, we will identify five receptive issues that contribute to the Spirit's neglect (especially in the West) and in turn offer some alternatives – all with the aim of contributing to doctrinal remediation for the sake of Christian vitality.

DOCTRINAL TAXONOMY

A basic receptive challenge to pneumatological vibrancy that may appear on first blush moot or insignificant is the way doctrines are ordered and listed. Let us call this topic "doctrinal taxonomy." In formal theological works, one usually finds that reflection on the Spirit takes place after much doctrinal formulation has already taken shape along the lines of theological authorities, the doctrine of God, creation, and so on. In this arrangement, the Holy Spirit is most often connected to the Christian life – an important theme to be sure, but one that is typically quite removed from more foundational and orientating considerations because of its casting as a culminating theme.

This particular taxonomy is not "wrong," and it has significant precedent as well. As to the first point, doctrinal taxonomies are arrangements and patterns that convey something theological by their very expression. Each represents a certain kind of logic – a kind of "take" on the Christian meta-narrative; therefore, each should be given space to resonate and "make its theological case," so to speak. As to the second point, this taxonomy has significant precedent, especially when we look to creedal expressions within Christianity. In both the Apostles' and Nicene Creeds, the Spirit is mentioned in the third (and final) article. This taxonomy, then, is both viable and prominent.

---

[6] Philip Jenkins, *The Next Christendom* (rev. and expanded ed.; Oxford: Oxford University Press, 2007), 8.

As a kind of interpretation and account, however, a doctrinal taxonomy should be taken as one among other possibilities. In fact, one
could say that alternative taxonomies are required for the cultivation of
a robust doctrinal imagination since one taxonomy can only do so much
to convey the fullness of the Christian gospel. For instance, if the Spirit
is persistently placed after many other doctrines in works of theology,
the ordering can come to convey a theological valuation that can
become problematic over time. The theological assumption can be
made on account of this taxonomy that the Spirit only has to do with
the Christian life and so is less fundamental than other theological
topics that get the theological enterprise off the ground. This assumption, of course, is patently false, but the prevalence of this taxonomy
does not help us see that.

What is a way forward from this pneumatological challenge? Quite
obviously, alternative taxonomies are needed. One possibility that has
relatively recently emerged is called "Third Article Theology" (or TAT).
TAT places the Holy Spirit as first (rather than third) in a different kind
of doctrinal taxonomy, one that is explicitly and fundamentally Spirit-
oriented. A significant prompt for this reorientation has been the work
of Lyle Dabney,[7] and the tendency has been developed further under the
tutelage of Myk Habets.[8] The general achievement of this taxonomical
sensibility is that it focuses on the Spirit both methodologically and
thematically as integral to the dogmatic task; in other words, the centrality of the Spirit mentioned earlier in this essay is now displayed and
at work in how theology is executed and sustained. How one secures
theological knowledge (via an "inspired" text and/or a "Spirit-logic"),
how one thinks of the doctrine of God (God as spirit, the Spirit as triune
person), how one considers the constitution of human persons (that is,
those who are "in-spirited" beings), how one thinks of sin (as grievances
and rejections of the Spirit's moral shaping) – these and other topics are
proposed as thoroughly pneumatological in TAT. From this taxonomical viewpoint, then, all doctrines require a pneumatological orientation
in order to be understood expansively, faithfully, and compellingly.

[7] D. Lyle Dabney, "Otherwise Engaged in the Spirit: A First Theology for a Twenty-first
    Century," in *The Future of Theology: Essays in Honor of Jürgen Moltmann* (ed.
    Miroslav Volf, Carmen Krieg, and Thomas Kucharz; Grand Rapids: Eerdmans, 1996),
    154–163.
[8] Myk Habets, ed., *Third Article Theology: A Pneumatological Dogmatics*
    (Minneapolis: Fortress, 2016).

CLASHING WORLDVIEWS

Another receptive challenge that must be considered straightaway is the role different worldviews have in facilitating or complicating the task of pneumatological consideration. For instance, many of the Christians who live in sub-Saharan Africa are part of an environment in which a "spirit-world" is very much constitutive of their "social imaginary" (to use Charles Taylor's phrasing).[9] For these Christians, speaking of the Holy Spirit on Christian terms does not require a kind of intellectual leap or suspension of the plausibility structures and intellectual frameworks characteristic of their contexts. Quite the contrary, such speech would simply be a starting point for further discussion, including the character of such a spirit and the power it has in relation to other spirit-entities.[10]

Westerners, on the other hand, cannot affirm the existence of the Holy Spirit without brushing up against many features of their own worldview as it has taken shape over the last few centuries. So much of the intellectual momentum of the West since the late medieval period has been to "naturalize" the world – to make it disenchanted, demythologized, and desacralized. A "spirit-world" in this context is largely unintelligible and so implausible and irrational. Deism rose to prominence under these conditions, and of course, deism is non-trinitarian and so non-pneumatological. Deists cannot affirm belief in One who will be with and in the disciples of Jesus (cf. Jn. 14:17). The vision of individuality within modernity has also created a solipsistic mood that has had an impact on pneumatological reflection. Time and again, considerations of *Geist* have been anthropologically orientated; therefore, pneumatic language in modernity typically exudes an anthropological – rather than properly theological – tenor. Those inclined in this direction would find it difficult to affirm belief in One who will clothe believers 'with power from on high' (cf. Lk. 24:49).

This all-too-brief contrast suggests that some worldviews are more accommodating to the language and thought requirements of a "spirit-reality" than others. This varying quality influences directly how reference to and belief in a "Holy Spirit" would "work" in a given context. Westerners in particular do not simply have to explore one topic among

[9] Charles Taylor, *A Secular Age* (Cambridge: Belknap, 2007), 171–176
[10] For more on this topic, see Daniel K. Darko, "Perspectives on the 'Spirit' in Africa," in *T&T Clark Handbook of Pneumatology* (ed. Daniel Castelo and Kenneth M. Loyer; London: Bloomsbury T&T Clark, 2020), 269–279.

others when considering spirit-matters; rather, they have to contend
with pushing up against the pillars and conventions of their thought-
world. This process is exceedingly challenging. At some level, it is also
unappealing if one is wishing to make a case for a topic that will draw
largescale, public support within one's immediate context. In light of
such formidable challenges, Westerners generally and Western theologians particularly may intentionally or unintentionally neglect the Holy
Spirit in favor of another topic that simply "makes more sense" and in
turn is "much more available."

A response to this challenge would be for Western Christians to
reconsider boldly some of the premises surrounding the regnant worldviews that dominate their environs, especially at a popular level.
Assumptions surrounding the natural-supernatural distinction and
what constitutes "naturalism" more specifically, the diminished sense
of what empiricism can mean, the equivocation between "science" and
"truth," the Newtonian straightjacket that dominates public perception
of how the physical world works – these and other topics require
significant theological exploration, and this not simply as a way for
theologians to speak into those conversations, but more pressingly for
our purposes, as a strategy for them to cultivate a more "Spirit-friendly"
worldview for church and society in which miracle, surprise, and
change/transformation (or what one could call "evidences of the
Spirit") are deemed as very much part of our reality.[11]

WIDE-RANGING TERMS

One suspects that those holding Western commitments also have receptive difficulties as they go on to appreciate the shape of biblical pneumatology. Whereas Westerners must contend with a severely diminished
role for spirit-language in their contexts, they find a different sensibility
at work in "the world of the Bible." The terms *ruach* in Hebrew and
pneuma in Greek are exceedingly wide-ranging in the ways they are
deployed in Scripture. No fitting analogates exist in English that
approximate this range of usage – a situation that may make it difficult
to imagine how this language can be understood and used today.

---

[11] This work has begun to emerge, but more must be done. See such volumes as James
K. A. Smith and Amos Yong, eds., *Science and the Spirit* (Bloomington: Indiana
University Press, 2010); Amos Yong, *The Spirit of Creation* (Grand Rapids:
Eerdmans, 2011); and Oliver Davies, *Theology of Transformation* (Oxford: Oxford
University Press, 2013).

Consider the following biblical uses: these terms can refer to sentient entities such as the "spirit" of both individuals[12] and collectives;[13] qualities of character and mood states of individuals (e.g., Ps. 142:3; Isa. 57:15); negative spirits (some of which are even sent by God);[14] visionary creatures (e.g., throughout Ezek. 1); particular theological names and titles through combinations with "Elohim,"[15] "YHWH,"[16] "God,"[17] "the Father" (e.g., Matt. 10:20), "Christ" (e.g., Rom. 8:9; Phil. 1:19; 1 Pet. 1:11), "the Lord" (e.g., Lk. 4:18; Acts 5:9; 2 Cor. 3:17), and so on; and cases where renderings exceedingly vary, such as "wind" (possibly Gen. 1:2 and many instances in Ecclesiastes), "breath" (the parallelism of Job 27:3; 32:8; 34:14), and "life" (Job 33:4; Rom. 8:10). These examples simply represent a sampling of biblical pneumatology – a fact that pushes against the perception that pneumatology is a minor topic in the Bible! With this extensive range of uses for the words *ruach* and *pneuma*, how can Westerners manage these cases fittingly and compellingly?

An obvious first strategy before this challenge would be to acquaint oneself with these many instances of spirit-talk in the Bible. This strategy, however, is complicated by the way English translators have sometimes diminished the prominence of spirit-talk in their renderings. In some cases, one would not even know that *ruach* or *pneuma* was present in the text.[18] For instance, the NRSV (a popular English translation, especially among academics) renders Exod. 28:3 as follows: "And you shall speak to all who have ability, whom I have endowed with skill, that they make Aaron's vestments to consecrate him for my priesthood." The phrase "endowed with skill" can be translated more literally as "filled with the spirit of wisdom" (a translation that is in

---

[12] For example, Gen. 41:8; Exod. 35:21; Num. 14:24; Deut. 2:30; Judg. 15:19; 1 Sam. 1:15; 1 Kgs. 10:5; 2 Kgs. 2:15; 1 Chron. 5:26; 2 Chron. 36:22; Ezra 1:1; Job 7:11; Ps. 31:5; Isa. 26:9; Dan. 2:1; Hag. 1:14; Lk. 1:17; 1 Cor. 2:11.
[13] For example, Exod. 6:9; Josh. 5:1; 2 Chron. 21:16; Ezra 1:5; Isa. 19:3; Jer. 51:11; Matt. 5:3; 1 Thess. 5:23.
[14] For example, Num. 5:14, 30; Judg. 9:23; 1 Sam. 16:14-16; 1 Kgs. 22:21; 2 Chron. 18:20; Hos. 5:4; Zech. 13:2; Matt. 12:43; Mk. 1:23; Lk. 9:42; Acts 19:15; 2 Tim. 1:7; Rev. 18:2.
[15] For example, Gen. 1:2, 41:38; Num. 24:2; 1 Sam. 10:10; 2 Chron. 24:20.
[16] For example, Num. 11:29; Judg. 11:29; 1 Sam. 10:6; 1 Kgs. 18:12; 2 Kgs. 2:16; 2 Chron. 20:14; Isa. 11:2; Ezek. 37:1; Mic. 3:8; Zech. 4:6.
[17] See Matt. 3:16; Rom. 8:9; 1 Cor. 2:11; Eph. 4:30; 1 Jn. 4:2.
[18] Translational variation is a long-standing issue that extends even to the Septuagint: "Of 378 occurrences of *ruach* in the Hebrew OT, 277 appear in the LXX as *pneuma*" (Marie E. Isaacs, *The Concept of Spirit* [London: Heythrop Monographs, 1976], 10). By implication, then, 101 instances of *ruach* were not translated as *pneuma* by the Septuagint translators.

effect in the Authorized or King James Version). At some level, there is
value in the way the NRSV has rendered the phrase since it connects
pneumatology with the cultivation of skill.[19] The difficulty with
this connection, obviously, is that it is unknown to the English reader
of this one translation. Other relevant instances in which spirit-
language is present but not evident in the NRSV include examples
related to affective and internal language, such as depression
(1 Kgs. 21:5), anger (2 Chron. 21:16), thoughts (Prov. 1:23), temper
(Prov. 14:29, 16:32), self-control (Prov. 25:28), breath (Isa. 40:7;
Rev. 11:11), and mind (2 Cor. 2:13). And of course, we have the case of
Gen. 1:2, which the NRSV translators rendered "while a wind from God
(ruach Elohim) swept over the face of the waters," whereas the
Authorized Version preferred a more literal (and capitalized) option:
"the Spirit of God moved upon the face of the waters." In this specific
case, the AV/KJV allows for specific theological readings that the NRSV
does not.[20] In short, simply the work of translation may be an impedi-
ment to familiarizing oneself with the range of spirit-talk in Scripture.

Why would certain translators downplay spirit-talk in Scripture? As
the maxim goes, "every translation is an interpretation," and once
again, we see plausibility structures and worldview concerns having a
role in pneumatological prominence – in this case within the pneumatological imaginations of translators. The commitments and decisions
of translators in turn have an impact upon the pneumatological imaginations of readers. As a result, specific terms, renderings, cases of non/
capitalization, references, and so on are all affected, leaving readers in
many instances with a pneumatological deficit in relation to what they
literally see in the biblical text itself.

Once readers of Scripture are able to familiarize themselves with
the range and many instances of spirit-talk in the text, a subsequent act
of remediation would be to use spirit-talk more openly in their speech-
practices, using Scripture as a template and guide. Admittedly, some
cases are difficult to implement, given Western sensibilities. Other
cases, however, are less so. In the latter camp could be examples of
character formation and spiritual endowments (the various gifts/fruit
lists one finds in the Bible, including Isaiah 11, Romans 12,

---

[19] John R. Levison wishes to make this connection in this passage and in others so as to
resist the interpretive predominance of thinking of *ruach/pneuma* cases as strictly
instances of charismatic endowment. See *Filled with the Spirit* (Grand Rapids:
Eerdmans, 2009), 36–41.

[20] One possibility could be an Irenaean proposal per the "two hands" imagery; see
Against Heresies, passim, including IV.20.1–4 (*ANF* 1:487–488).

1 Corinthians 12, and Galatians 5), the endowment and development of skill sets (as we noted in Exodus 28), the sharing of leadership and spiritual authority (per Numbers 11 as well as other texts that highlight prophecy and generational transition), and many more. The biblical patterns are available to make this remediation both viable and significant. Such a change has the potential to impact not only the reading of Scripture but also the engagement of certain pneumatological strands of church tradition. Relatively recently, more works in church history and historical theology are assessing the ascetic, pastoral, spiritual, and mystical dimensions of Christian expressions from the past (in contradistinction to the privileged place polemical theology has received within the theological academy). As a result, pneumatology has played a prominent role in this renewed interest.[21]

THE FEARS OF DECEPTION AND LOSING CONTROL

On some level, pneumatology can serve as the linchpin to denote the dynamic relationality between God and humans. This prospect is both promising and risky. Plenty of biblical passages would allow for a kind of constructive exploration of this topic. In fact, one could say that the language that typically does this work – namely, the terms "image" and to a lesser extent "likeness," both from Genesis 1 – is not as well-suited to fulfill this role as is a pneumatological option. This suitability is not simply registered in terms of the imagery of Gen. 2:7, where God dispensed the "breath" (different Hebrew term here: *nishmat*) of life upon the first humans but also the many instances in which God's Spirit and human spirit are intricately connected. Part of the risk is that a categorical divide must always be preserved: humans are not God. When the divide is not vigilantly preserved, humans tend to want to divinize themselves.

And yet, within Christian theological proposals, the God-human divide is bridged repeatedly in a certain way from God's side in terms of creation, sustainment, providence, Christology, and yes, pneumatology. In the case of pneumatology in particular, that connection is relational[22] and can be penetratingly intimate – that is, within the registers

---

[21] Plenty of works could be cited in this vein, but an important one would be Thomas L. Humphries Jr., *Ascetic Pneumatology from John Cassian to Gregory the Great* (Oxford: Oxford University Press, 2013).

[22] For a helpful survey of this point, see John McIntyre, *The Shape of Pneumatology* (Edinburgh: T&T Clark, 1997), ch. 7 ("Relational Pneumatology," 172–210).

of the deepest aspects of individual selves, including hearts, minds, sub/consciousness, wills, motives, feelings, intuitions, character, desires, and so on. Accompanying that kind of intimacy are the sundry challenges we associate with subjectivity. As a result of this connection, the challenges of subjectivity become the challenges of pneumatology, thereby presenting us with a fourth constellation of matters that make pneumatology difficult to receive on the contemporary scene.

One challenge of subjectivity as it relates to pneumatological neg-lect is deception. This topic comes to the fore in one of the most scathing warnings Jesus offers us: "Not everyone who says to me, 'Lord, Lord,' will enter the kingdom of heaven, but only the one who does the will of my Father in heaven. On that day many will say to me, 'Lord, Lord, did we not prophesy in your name, and cast out demons in your name, and do many deeds of power in your name?' Then I will declare to them, 'I never knew you; go away from me, you evildoers'" (Matt. 7:21–23, NRSV). Jesus's warning has to do with a kind of spiritual deception. The remedy offered by Jesus for spiritual deception is to do the will of Jesus's Father, which is properly an appeal to objectivity (that is, not our will but the Father's will). What is interesting about this passage for our present purposes is that those works cast by Jesus as unreliable are ones deemed to be charismatic, Spirit-phenomena: proph-esying, casting out demons, and performing deeds of power.

How is it that people can call upon Jesus as "Lord" and apparently perform these Spirit-phenomena and still (1) not enter the kingdom, (2) not be known by Jesus, (3) and be labeled by Jesus as "evildoers"? Ultimately, Jesus is pointing to a gap: on the one side, a nominal devotion to Jesus and an apparently charismatic form of ministry and, on the other, a lack of wholistic conformity to the will of the Father. Therefore, to cast this matter pneumatologically, the harrowing pro-spect of Jesus's remarks is that a person may claim to be acting according to the Spirit and look to be so – and yet not be. Spiritual appearances can be deceiving – to ourselves and to others. In light of this danger, some may opt to "play it safe" and resist all charismatic works and appearances of Spirit-phenomena so as to attempt to avoid this kind of deception; however, this move would be fallacious, given the charis-matic shape of Jesus and his disciples' ministry. The more general point to be taken here is that deception is a challenge as it relates to Spirit-matters.

Another challenge of subjectivity as it relates to pneumatological neglect is the overall theme of losing control. This issue has been highlighted by Sarah Coakley, who stresses it as central for how models of trinitarian theological reflection that highlight experience, affectivity, and desire – in short, those models that emphasize the Spirit as having a leading role – were often put to the side historically in favor of others that were more ecclesiastically and hierarchically "stable."[23] In Coakley's rendering, the temptation to "subordinate the Spirit" was at work in these instances because a pneumatologically incorporative approach to prayer and the divine life could lead to two deemed dangerous matters: sectarian or purist tendencies (as often represented by the Montanists) and the messy, "problematic entanglement" of spiritual and sexual desires.[24] Both represent a kind of loss of control, one ecclesiastical and the other sexual. In the midst of an emerging consensus and ecclesiastical hierarchy – one dominated by males – these kinds of threats were deemed as excessively dangerous. Their resistance led to a species of pneumatological neglect that pivoted on the rationale that losing control was simply too risky of a prospect.

Plenty of fear surrounds pneumatological topics in particular, and the above examples perhaps only exacerbate it: deception and losing control sound like awful prospects, ones that suggest an overwhelming and inescapable abyss. Rather than resist the contributions of pneumatology in the midst of these possible predicaments, we are best served here in reassessing the source of our "theological security," so to speak. Deception and losing control are to be avoided, yes, but avoiding them well (that is, in a way that is not prohibitive of future growth and challenge) requires divine assistance. In other words, theologians – as all Christians – are a needy people, ones who depend upon a Paraclete/ Advocate/Comforter (cf. Jn. 14:16, 26) who is both with us and in us so as to "de-subjectify" and "re-subjectify" our very selves at different constitutive registers, including the affective.[25] We have been promised by Christ that his departure will not leave us orphaned (cf. Jn. 14:18). Matters as these are the tension points where we come to see the value of that promise. We must give space and be receptive to the Spirit's help (Rom. 8:26) in order to carry on faithfully and courageously before our fears.

---

[23] Sarah Coakley, *God, Sexuality, and the Self* (Cambridge: Cambridge University Press, 2013).
[24] Ibid., 102.
[25] Affectivity has gradually been emphasized more in theological work, especially as it relates to the intersection of spirituality and theology. For a suggestive recent effort on the topic, see Simeon Zahl, *The Holy Spirit and Christian Experience* (Oxford: Oxford University Press, 2020).

CHRISTOLOGY OVERSHADOWING PNEUMATOLOGY

We will conclude with a fifth receptive challenge to pneumatology. This example is perhaps the most difficult one of those surveyed because on the surface it appears to be not so much a challenge as a salutary doctrinal strategy. In short, Christology has often been put to service as a way of concretizing and keeping "in line" what are deemed to be the more difficult aspects of pneumatology. If pneumatology is generally understood to be dangerous, risky, ambiguous, and unreliable, then the doctrinal recourse of choice for this predicament has been Christology. After all, Christ said that the Spirit would bring to the disciples' remembrance the things that he said (Jn. 14:26), and whereas it may not seem clear to many if and how the Spirit speaks, it is more than clear what Jesus teaches, commands, and exhorts in passages of Scripture. Furthermore, the Johannine community makes it exceedingly clear that the way of discerning the Spirit from other spirits is through a christological criterion: "By this you know the Spirit of God: every spirit that confesses that Jesus Christ has come in the flesh is from God, and every spirit that does not confess Jesus is not from God" (1 Jn. 4:2). Christology, then, has been put to use to bolster pneumatology in light of the latter's deemed weaknesses.

What this strategy tends to promote over time, however, is a pneumatological dependence upon Christology that typically is not seen as mutual – in this arrangement, pneumatology needs Christology, but Christology does not need pneumatology. As a result, this approach – true to form with the other complicating receptive challenges surveyed – tends to subordinate the Spirit, and this subordination leads to avoidance and neglect. Rogers's claim quoted above ("Anything the Spirit can do, the Son can do better") puts the matter in a certain, christologically capacious way; another characterization of the situation is simply to admit rhetorically the functional dispensability of the Spirit by asking, "Who needs the Spirit when one has the Son?"

The roots of this particular issue stem from the very origins of trinitarian pneumatology, which are often highlighted as emerging during the fourth century via the work of such figures as Athanasius and the Cappadocians. One should mention, however, that Christian pneumatology did exist before the trinitarian debates took on full form. In its most nascent stages, it drew from Jewish-Hellenistic tendencies stemming from the intertestamental period. These tendencies were wide-ranging from case to case.[26] Major figures in the second and third centuries, such as Irenaeus and Tertullian, also had important things to say about the Spirit. But as more formal pressures emerged to distinguish Father, Son, and Spirit amidst monarchical tendencies, a taxis or order emerged that began placing the Spirit "at the end" of a more dyadic preoccupation, one that had to do with the Father and the Son.

Of course, that preoccupation took concrete and pressing form with responses to the Arian controversy and the work both culminating and beginning at the Council of Nicaea in 325 CE. Infamously, the Creed emerging from Nicaea simply affirmed belief in the Holy Spirit – it took until Constantinople in 381 CE for a more expansive statement on the Spirit to be included, one that referred to the Spirit as "the Lord and Giver of life, who proceeds from the Father, who with the Father and the Son together is worshiped and glorified, who spoke by the prophets." This addendum is clarifying on many levels in that it establishes the divinity of the Holy Spirit and suggests roles for the Spirit within the economy and salvation history. Of course, this amplification is not without its own controversy, in that a further addendum (per the East)/clarification (per the West) was made by the West years after Constantinople, one that involved inserting the Latin term *filioque* ("and the Son") to the procession clause, a move the East took as out of ecclesiastical-political order and as theologically disrupting the taxis of the triune life, but one the West thought logically befitting the consubstantiality of the divine persons.[27] One of the ironies of this significant controversy is that it has to do with changes in the oft-neglected "third article," yet one could make the claim that in this case the question was more properly trinitarian than pneumatological.

The point to press for our purposes here is that the trinitarian debates tended to focus mostly on the relationship between the Father and the Son because of the threat of Arianism, yes, but the "personhood" of the Spirit was a matter of considerable difficulty from the very start of the Christian tradition.[28] The challenges relate to a host of

---

[26] For a brief history and secondary literature reference guide, see the "General Introduction" of Athanasius the Great and Didymus the Blind, *Works of the Spirit* (trans. Mark DelCogliano, Andrew Radde-Gallwitz, and Lewis Ayres; Yonkers, NY: St. Vladimir's Seminary Press, 2011).

[27] For a definitive history of this controversy, see A. Edward Siecienski, *The Filioque* (Oxford: Oxford University Press, 2010).

[28] A helpful chapter along these lines is Jörg Frey, "How Did the Spirit Become a Person?," in *The Holy Spirit, Inspiration, and the Cultures of Antiquity* (ed. Jörg Frey and John R. Levison; Berlin: Walter de Gruyter, 2014), 343–371.

matters, including interrelating the spirit-talk of both testaments and distinguishing the Spirit's individuation, agency, and speech. Even today, English speakers especially feel this pressure as they are burdened (without the necessity of grammatical consequence) to decide which pronouns they are to use in reference to the Spirit. Furthermore, a kind of non-self-referential modesty surrounds the Spirit in both Scripture and church tradition, as the Spirit works to make available the effects of Jesus's life and ministry and in turn works in and through the church. All of this means that the Spirit is never "center-stage" in the way Christ is (via such things as the four canonical gospels and the explicit liturgical life of the church broadly). On these grounds, it is easy to see why Christology has overshadowed pneumatology.

One possible remediation before this receptive challenge is quite subtle, in that it requires us to rethink the basis and shape of Christology. If the central question of the New Testament is, Who is Jesus?, then the opening chapters of all four canonical gospels make the answer quite plain: He is the Spirit-baptizer (Matt. 3:11; Mk. 1:8; Lk. 3:16; Jn. 1:33). Admittedly, it is strange that this identifier was not more manifest in the outworking of the gospels, but the unified focus of the Baptist's proclamation about the "One who is to come" at the beginning of the four gospels eventually finds its apogee in the opening chapters of Acts (see the explicit reference to the Baptist's message in Acts 1:5). We can also make a different pneumatological move here in answer to this central question. If Jesus is the "Messiah" (Hebrew) or the "Christ" (Greek) – both titles suggesting "the anointed One" – then a further question can be pressed: And this One is anointed with what/whom? Again, it is fascinating that in the opening chapters of the gospels, the Spirit plays a prominent role in Jesus's own baptism (Matt. 3:16; Mk. 1:10; Lk. 3:22; Jn. 1:32), which is a public display of this anointing. Furthermore, this particular theme of anointing does receive development in the NT witness (for instance, Jesus's recitation of Isaiah 61 in Lk. 4:17–21). In short, one can answer this second question with the reply: Jesus is anointed with the Spirit of God.[29]

These gestures indicate something basic to Christology: One cannot understand who Jesus is apart from the presence and work of the Spirit – both at the historical point of the intelligibility of Jesus's own life and at the contemporary point of reception (that is, people knowing and accepting who Jesus is today). This first point is especially pressed by

[29] See Myk Habets, *The Anointed Son: A Trinitarian Spirit Christology* (Eugene, OR: Pickwick, 2010).

Luke in his gospel, for in this account, Jesus is depicted as the quintessential charismatic figure who operates in accordance to the promptings and in the power of the Spirit (cf. Lk. 4:1, 14, 18–19); the second point is prominent in Paul (cf. Rom. 8:9–17).

This pneumatological sensibility in Christology often goes by the name of "Spirit Christology," and a number of wide-ranging (and sometimes disparate) proposals have been offered recently under this heading. They can vary in theme and emphasis – some may raise the contrast between this model and a "Word" or "Logos Christology," whereas others may create schematics that highlight various themes of soteriological significance. They often call into question conventional christological thinking, which may lead to some of the incongruity along doctrinal lines.[30] For instance, some may build on Chalcedon, while others may resist it. In light of this variability, each proposal should be evaluated on its own terms. Such work, however, should inspire both a skill set of theological criticism and a constructive and creative tendency that is much needed. In the latter camp, for instance, is Clark Pinnock's "experimental" suggestion in his work *Flame of Love*, one that continues to be relevant today: "Let us see what results from viewing Christ as an aspect of the Spirit's mission, instead of (as is more usual) viewing Spirit as a function of Christ's."[31] Pinnock's invitation need not be taken as a christological subordination so as to counter or "even the score" of a pneumatological subordination; rather, Pinnock's suggestion can be cast as an exercise of taking seriously the organic intertwining of Christology and pneumatology, a point that tends to bind many proposals in Spirit Christology together in common cause. An analogous kind of intertwining is on display in the work of Thomas Weinandy, who has made a number of suggestive trinitarian proposals that have considerable generative possibilities, including overcoming some of the more entrenched aspects of the *filioque* controversy.[32]

Simply put, rather than pitting one doctrine (or, for that matter, one triune Person) as the sole criterion of another (which runs the risk of setting up a hierarchy), what is needed moving forward is a sense of how doctrines constitute and amplify one another – a "doctrinal

---

[30] See various essays in Habets, *Third Article Theology* as entry points for the discussion; also note the many works by Leopoldo A. Sánchez M. on the theme, including *Sculptor Spirit* (Downers Grove, IL: IVP Academic, 2019).

[31] Clark H. Pinnock, *Flame of Love*, 2nd ed. (Downers Grove, IL: IVP Academic, 2022), 88.

[32] Thomas Weinandy, OFM Cap., *The Father's Spirit of Sonship* (Edinburgh: T&T Clark, 1995).

trinitarianism," if you will. Pneumatology requires Christology, yes, and Christology requires pneumatology.

CONCLUSION

A rising interest in pneumatology has marked the last few decades of theological scholarship. Additionally, as noted, the church on a global scale has been experiencing a kind of unprecedented charismatic revival during that span. And yet, significant segments of the theological academy and the church continue to be untouched by these developments. The running argument of this chapter is that this neglect has an underlying logic, one that presses deeply into the receptive viability of pneumatology as a field, especially for Western audiences. This chapter has exposed key aspects of this underlying logic and in turn offered remediating steps – all with the aim of aiding its readers in the academy and the pew to be more attuned to the One who is the source of our life, peace, and joy.

Further Reading

Athanasius the Great and Didymus the Blind (2011), *Works of the Spirit* (trans. Mark DelCogliano, Andrew Radde-Gallwitz, and Lewis Ayres; Yonkers, NY: St. Vladimir's Seminary Press).

Briggman, Anthony (2012), *Irenaeus of Lyons and the Theology of the Holy Spirit* (Oxford: Oxford University Press).

Coakley, Sarah (2013), *God, Sexuality, and the Self* (Cambridge: Cambridge University Press).

Habets, Myk, ed. (2016), *Third Article Theology* (Minneapolis, MN: Fortress Press).

Humphries, Thomas L. Jr. (2013), *Ascetic Pneumatology from John Cassian to Gregory the Great* (Oxford: Oxford University Press).

Pinnock, Clark (2022), *Flame of Love*, 2nd ed. (Downers Grove, IL: IVP Academic).

Rogers, Eugene F. Jr. (2005), *After the Spirit* (Grand Rapids: Eerdmans).

Sicienski, A. Edward (2010), *The Filioque* (Oxford: Oxford University Press).

Weinandy, Thomas (1995), *The Father's Spirit of Sonship* (Edinburgh: T&T Clark).

Zahl, Simeon (2020), *The Holy Spirit and Christian Experience* (Oxford: Oxford University Press).

8 Holy Scripture

KEVIN J. VANHOOZER

INTRODUCTION

To describe the Bible as "Holy Scripture" is to identify it as set apart by a holy God for the purpose of generating and governing a "holy nation," a description applied first to Israel (Exod. 19:6) and later to the church (1 Pet. 2:9). The word of God and the people of God exist in a symbiotic relationship, though there is some dispute over which has priority: Does the word of God proceed from the people of God or vice versa? Either way, a doctrine of Scripture must have recourse to more than history or sociology, for its main task is to say how both the word of God (the Bible) and the people of God (the Church) are of God. The present essay reflects theologically on the nature, attributes, purpose, and interpretation of the Christian Bible, examining each of these aspects in relation to God and God's acts. Viewed theologically, Scripture is a human constituent in the communicative activity of the triune God: the voice, word, and breath that speaks forth the light, life, and love of God himself.

Scripture holds a distinctive place in Christian doctrine, as it is both one doctrine among others and the principal source and norm for all other doctrines: "the Christian tradition [is] what the church of Jesus Christ believes, teaches, and confesses on the basis of the Word of God."[1] Scripture's double-edged sword presents a challenge of where to locate it in the system of theology and in confessions of faith. Some Christians locate Scripture in the doctrine of the church inasmuch as it is the product of the apostles and prophets. Others locate it under the doctrine of revelation, as an element in the way God makes himself known. The approach taken here is to consider God, the word of God, and the people of God as together constituting "first theology" and to locate Scripture in this organic pattern.

---

[1] J. Pelikan, *The Christian Tradition: A History of the Development of Doctrine*, Volume 1 (Chicago: University of Chicago Press, 1975), 1.

With these big picture concerns in mind, we begin by examining the difference between the concepts of "Bible" and "Holy Scripture." We then explore the nature of Holy Scripture: what it is. The third section examines further three qualities that make Scripture "holy." Having said what Scripture is and is like, the fourth section explores the purpose or teleology of Holy Scripture: what it is for. The final section turns to the vexed question of biblical interpretation (how to read it) and the conflict of interpretations (whose reading is right and why).

"BIBLE" VS. "HOLY SCRIPTURE"

Human Words

It is of course possible to approach a community's sacred writings non-theologically, in a way that brackets out questions concerning the presence, activity, or even reality of God. This is, in fact, the tendency of modern academic approaches that treat the Bible not as the authoritative Scripture of a believing community but as a document of the university: "Textual naturalism is not simply a literary strategy but a metaphysic, one that suggests that the explanatory setting for the biblical writings is not divine revelation and its creaturely instruments but a set of principles about cultural production, including the production of religious texts."[2]

There are many ways to describe the Bible as a document of the university. Perhaps the most common is to regard it as a historical source from which to reconstruct "what actually happened." History is not the only academic interest, however; courses in the "Bible as literature," where students learn to read the Bible like any other book, as "a document that can speak volumes to humans about their own humanity,"[3] have also become popular.

Scripture lost its "holy" status in early modernity when scholars began to view it as a merely human artifact, shaped decisively by its varied historical contexts. The discipline of modern biblical studies employs its vaunted "historical-critical" method to describe the historically and culturally conditioned nature of the texts. To read the Bible in its ancient Near Eastern and Greco-Roman contexts – to explain it in terms of this-worldly, "secular" factors only – is effectively to drain it of its

---

[2] J. Webster, "On the Inspiration of Scripture," in *Conception, Reception, and the Spirit: Essays in Honour of Andrew T. Lincoln* (ed. J. G. McConville and L. K. Pietersen; Eugene, OR: Wipf & Stock, 2015), 247.

[3] J. Gavel and C. Wheeler, eds., *The Bible as Literature* (Oxford: Oxford University Press, 1986), xii.

divine authority: "Scripture died a quiet death in Western Christendom sometime in the sixteenth century."[4] The growing awareness that the biblical authors were time-bound – "weak like any other man" as was Samson shorn of his locks (Judg. 16:13) – has led biblical critics, and others, to question the accuracy of the Bible's historical accounts, the reliability of its knowledge claims, and the relevance of its moral tenets.

We also discover the Bible as a document of the university in the context of religious studies, including the anthropology, psychology, and sociology of religion. Even here, however, the accent is on the words of men, for modern students of religion view the Bible as an expression of human religious experience. Here too, the focus is on humanity inasmuch as "religion" is something people do to orient themselves to or commune with some higher power. Moreover, the various Marxist, Freudian, and postmodern critiques of religion pertain equally to the Bible. These forms of sociopolitical criticism routinely accuse the Bible of fostering unhealthy and oppressive ideologies like patriarchy and ultimately of using religion to sanction various kinds of violence.

The Voice of God

Upon hearing Scripture read in the context of worship, the traditional Christian response is, "Thanks be to God." Christian theologians approach the Bible with a different set of assumptions that proceed from a hermeneutic of trust rather than academic suspicion. It is appropriate that both doxology and dogmatics, in describing Scripture, should give special attention to Scripture's own self-presentation as a human means of divine address. From the perspective of Christian faith, the Bible is Holy Scripture not because religious people venerate it but because it has been appointed by God for divine use.

In his *Commentary on Romans* (1922), Karl Barth criticized biblical critics for not being critical enough. They fail to discern the true subject matter of the Bible, which is not religion but revelation: the self-presentation of God or, as Barth liked to describe it, the Word of God in the words of men. Barth acknowledges the human character of the biblical texts – they are fully human witnesses – but insists that God co-opts these words such that they "become" revelation, an event in which God addresses readers. For example, Barth can say about the book of Romans not that *Paulus dixit* ("Paul has spoken") but *Deus dixit* ("God has spoken").

---

[4] M. Legaspi, *The Death of Scripture and the Rise of Biblical Studies* (Oxford: Oxford University Press, 2010), 3.

Barth retrieved in his own way a deep theological conviction that has persisted since the early church, namely, that the Bible is itself an instance of a phenomenon it repeatedly describes, the "word of the Lord" coming to particular persons like Abraham (Gen. 15:1) and the prophets (see, for example, 1 Sam. 15:10; 1 Kgs. 18:1; Isa. 38:4; Jer. 1:2). While some prophets predict the future in the name of the Lord, the bulk of what the prophets actually say pertains to the covenant promise that God would make of Abraham's seed a great nation through which all families of the earth would be blessed (Gen. 12:3). The "word of the Lord" comes to Israel in the form of law and gospel but always for the sake of advancing this covenant promise.

The Word of God

Barth insisted that the one word of God has three forms: the definitive revelation of God in the person and history of Jesus Christ (the living Word), the commissioned witness to Christ in the prophets and apostles (the written word), the preaching of the Scriptural witness (the proclaimed word). Each form can become a means of experiencing "God with us" (Matt.1:23).

Like other doctrines, the doctrine of Scripture must be biblical. It is therefore important to see that a claim like Barth's has biblical precedent. In addition to the frequent mentions of the "word of the Lord" in the OT, the Gospel of John presents Jesus Christ as the Word of God made flesh (Jn. 1:14). The Letter to the Hebrews begins by reminding its Christian readers, "God spoke to our fathers by the prophets, but in these last days he has spoken to us by his Son" (Heb. 1:1). The whole letter is a kind of sermon, based on various passages from the Old Testament, that argues for the superiority of Jesus Christ over all other prophets, priests, and kings. The *Catechism of the Catholic Church* alludes to Heb. 1:3 in Article 3 (on "Sacred Scripture"): "Through all the words of Sacred Scripture, God speaks only one single Word, his one Utterance in whom he expresses himself completely": Jesus Christ.

The author of Hebrews is conscious that the church community, like Israel before it, is on a journey toward its own Promised Land, the kingdom of God. The church is a covenant community, like Israel, charged with faithfully trusting and obeying God's word, a word that the author describes as "living and active" (Heb. 4:12). The general idea is that God uses the biblical text to communicate what humans need to know in order to fulfill their vocation as persons made in God's image, the template for which is Jesus's own humanity. What unifies the Bible's overall message is the Creator God's desire to have fellowship with his human creatures and, more specifically, to create a people to be "a kingdom of priests and a holy nation" (Exod. 19:6; cf. 1 Pet. 2:9), an embassy to the world as it were of the kingdom of God.

NATURE: WHAT SCRIPTURE IS

Christian theologians throughout church history have tended to regard the Bible as a linguistic, literary, and canonical medium of divine self-communication, God's loving address to intelligent creatures.

Language: Written Discourse

At its most basic level, Scripture is made up of human language – words written primarily in Hebrew and Greek, with a smattering of Aramaic. These languages root the biblical documents in particular places and times, and translators have found it helpful to know as much as possible about both the original historical contexts and various cognate languages. From the start, Christianity has expanded largely through an impulse to translate the gospel, a message at whose heart is the news of a "translation" of God's Word into human flesh: "Incarnation is translation. When God in Christ became man, Divinity was translated into humanity, as though humanity were a receptor language."[5] Christianity is distinct among the world religions for having its Scriptures written in a language other than that of its founder (Jesus spoke Aramaic) and for encouraging its translation and proclamation "to the ends of the earth" (Acts 13:47).

Scripture (Lat. *scriptura*) means writing, and the Greek translation *graphe* is used some fifty times in the New Testament to refer to some or all of the Old Testament, as in Jesus's oft-cited formula, "It is written" (e.g., Mk. 14:27; Lk. 4:4). The early church theologian Augustine held that written words are signs that can both transmit thoughts (inner words) to others and refer to things, some of which may signify higher things (e.g., eternal truths): "words were instituted among men ... so that anyone might bring his thoughts to another's notice by means of them."[6] In his *On Christian Doctrine*, Augustine argues that God brings his thoughts to the attention of humanity via the Scriptures, earthly signs of heavenly realities. Language is an interpersonal medium for

---

[5] A. F. Walls, *The Missionary Movement in Christian History: Studies in the Transmission of the Faith* (Edinburgh: T&T Clark, 1996), 27.

[6] Augustine, *Enchiridion* 22.7.

sharing love and knowledge, an intelligible communication oriented to social communion.[7]

The emphasis on language communicating thoughts led some theologians to view Scripture as "propositional" revelation. On this view, language makes known or reveals cognitive content, making Scripture a divine deposit of truth – what sinners need to know about salvation. Barth countered this view by insisting that biblical language is less information about God than a means by which the triune God brings about a personal encounter with God's Word, which is to say God himself.

Language is a complex phenomenon that may be studied on different levels, from individual words and the way they are combined in sentences (morphology and syntax) to the function of words in the context of whole texts (text linguistics). Descriptions of what Scripture is fall short unless and until they do justice to these higher levels. One all-encompassing category that has proven useful is "discourse": what someone says about something in some way to someone for some purpose. Discourse analysis studies the sign/thing relationship but does so in the context of inquiring what writers are doing using just these words in just this way.[8] Discourse accounts for both the propositional and the personal aspect of language use.

Literature: Written Works

Scripture is made up of language, yes, but it is not a theological textbook, with propositions logically set out in a system of axioms, theorems, and proofs. Nor will one find technical jargon, as is common in the writings of some professional theologians. On the contrary, what theology there is – talk about God – often comes in the ordinary forms of speaking and writing of the day: wisdom sayings (Proverbs), poetry (Psalms), love songs (Song of Solomon), stories (Esther), and so forth.

The Bible is literature, then, just not the modern kind. Scripture's versification – the conventional dividing up into chapters and verses – sometimes obscures its literary nature. A preoccupation with isolated verses is liable to miss the forest for the trees, where the forest is the form – the particular genre or literary kind to which a verse belongs. Do

---

[7] See further R. A. Markus, "Signs, Communication, and Communities in Augustine's *On Christian Doctrine*," in *De doctrina Christiana: A Classic of Western Culture* (ed. Duane Arnold and Pamela Bright; Notre Dame, IN: Notre Dame University Press, 1995), 97–108.

[8] See J. L. Austin, *How to Do Things with Words*, 2nd ed. (Cambridge, MA: Harvard University Press, 1975).

we understand what we are reading? In order to avoid misunderstanding, one has to do more than identify words; one has to say what an author is doing in this kind of literary work. To imagine one can ignore form and read only for content is to fall prey to a flat-footed literalism. That Scripture employs certain literary forms that are no longer in use complicates the process of interpretation. Yet even here there are analogies: biblical apocalyptic, like the book of Revelation, is not entirely unlike dystopian fiction like *The Hunger Games*. To read with understanding, one has to become familiar with their respective literary conventions, the rules of the game that govern a particular type of discourse.

The most prevalent form of biblical discourse, narrative, is arguably also the most important, for several reasons. First, the narrative form figures prominently in literature and history alike. Second, the narrative form is well-suited to the Christian faith inasmuch as Christianity is less a system of ideas or morality than it is an account of what God has done in the history of Israel and, climactically, in the history of Jesus Christ. Scriptures from other religions (with the exception of Judaism) are nowhere near as reliant on narrative as is Christianity. That is because Holy Scripture is most fundamentally the story of what the Creator God has done in the history of salvation, and particularly the history of Jesus Christ, to put a fallen creation right. Third, narrative is an especially suitable form for coming to know a person. To know someone, we need to know more than vital statistics – place of birth, height, weight, eye colors, etc. – we need to know his or her story. If theology is the teaching of God by God (so says Thomas Aquinas), then Scripture is God's autobiography. Jesus himself taught in narratives (the Bible calls them "parables"), ordinary stories that help listeners appreciate the way God works with ordinary people in ordinary situations to do extraordinary things – things that put the world upside-down and testify to the coming kingdom of God. Still, while not every religion privileges narrative the way the Bible does, not everything in Scripture can be reduced to narrative. The foundation of Christianity is not a mere story but story made flesh – a drama that centers on Christ and that unfolds through many kinds of discourse, including direct speech from God, particularly in the form of promise and command.

Library: Canonical Collection

The Bible (from Greek *biblia*, "books") is an anthology or collection not of propositions, or verses but literary works of assorted kinds and sizes, some sixty-six, according to the typical reckoning of English Bibles.

This is the "common core" on which most Christians agree. Canonical Holy Scripture is the result of a remarkable consensus, namely, that Old and New Testaments, though written centuries apart in different languages, belong together, and together constitute a unified whole: "Concerning Scripture, little controversy emerges in the church's orthodox tradition: The Biblical texts together comprise one unified (form of the) Word of God."[9] The early church, following the example of the apostles and Jesus himself, read Israel's Scriptures as veiled testimony to a messianic figure and new covenant embodied and fulfilled in the person and work of Jesus Christ. Augustine puts it well: "The New Testament is in the Old concealed; the Old Testament in the New revealed."

The term "canon" originally denoted a measuring rod, something like our modern ruler. Christians speak of Holy Scripture as canon in two senses. It refers, first, to the library of writings acknowledged by the people of God as the written products of prophets and apostles, appointed by God, who together testify to a single subject matter: God's gracious promise to bless all the families of the earth through the seed of Abraham, eventually fulfilled centuries later in Jesus Christ (Gal. 3:16, 29). Canon means, secondly, that just these texts serve as the "rule" (kanon) of Christian faith and life. This is the godly purpose for which they have been set aside and deemed "holy."

Critics of canon, both the concept and the resultant list, point to the messy history of its formation. Agreement about precisely which books should be included in the canon was a long time coming. Indeed, there is still no consensus, with Roman Catholics accepting "deuterocanonical" (i.e., "second canon") books like 1 and 2 Maccabees that Protestants refuse to recognize as having canonical status. Modern skeptics describe the process of canon formation in naturalistic, political terms. On this view, the walls that separate Holy Scripture from other texts of the time are arbitrary social constructions, erected by those who had the power to do so: to the victor go the spoils (i.e., canonical Scripture). It is nevertheless important to remember that all Christians acknowledge a common core, including all the books of the New Testament.

From a Christian theological perspective, however, the canon is ultimately an article of faith, confessed partly on the basis of its own

[9] D. J. Treier, "The Freedom of God's Word: Toward an 'Evangelical' Dogmatics of Scripture," in The Voice of God in the Text of Scripture: Explorations in Constructive Dogmatics (ed. O. Crisp and F. Sanders; Grand Rapids: Zondervan Academic, 2016), 22.

self-attestation. The Bible gives intrinsic reasons to think that its texts should indeed be set apart. Many of the biblical books display a canon-consciousness, an awareness of their set-apart status. For example, a written version of the Ten Commandments was kept in the holiest place: the Ark of the Covenant. Moreover, toward the end of the declaration of God's law, Moses tells Israel: "Everything that I command you, you shall be careful to do. You shall not add to it or take from it" (Deut. 12:32; cf. Rev. 22:18–19). The prophets claimed to be speaking a word that had come to them, not of their own devising. In the New Testament, Jesus repeatedly cites Israel's Scriptures with the formula, "It is written," connoting their intrinsic authority. Similarly, the apostle Paul insists that there is no other gospel than the one he delivered to the church (Gal. 1:6–9). Peter refers to Paul's letters in conjunction with "the other Scriptures" (2 Pet. 3:16), implying that his writings are on a par with the authoritative writings of Israel.

To call a set of writings "Holy Scripture" is to imply their canonical status. It was actually Marcion, a second-century bishop, who inadvertently served as a catalyst for canonization by judging the wrathful God of the Old Testament inferior to the loving Father of Jesus in the New Testament. The early church quickly realized that the Old Testament is essential to identifying Jesus as the Christ. No less than 10 percent of the New Testament consists of quotations, paraphrases, and allusions to the Old Testament. The church has recognized just these texts as the ones the Spirit has impressed upon their consciousness and corporate worship: "one Lord, one faith, one baptism" (Eph. 4:5), yes – and one canon, with two testaments, four Gospels, and many distinct books. The doctrine of Holy Scripture deploys the category of canon to describe the "collected works" of their divine author – and the christological center of the collection.[10]

HALLMARKS: WHAT QUALIFIES SCRIPTURE AS "HOLY"

Scripture is prophetic and apostolic discourse fixed by writing of different genres and collected in a two-testament canon, a library of manuscripts all having to do with God's plan for the whole world, worked out in the history of Israel and culminating in Jesus Christ and the history of his effects. The present section examines further three aspects of that discourse that lead Christians to confess it as "holy."

---

[10] See further J. C. Peckham, *Canonical Theology: The Biblical Canon, Sola Scriptura, and Theological Method* (Grand Rapids: Eerdmans, 2016).

Inspired Authorship

Discourse involves someone saying something to someone about some-thing. Scripture is discourse, yes, but *whose?* The prophets' and apostles', to be sure, but according to them they speak and write on behalf of God, not themselves. For example, Paul refers to the Old Testament as "the oracles of God" (Rom. 3:2). He thanks God because the church at Thessalonica received the gospel he delivered "not as the word of men, but as what it really is, the word of God" (1 Thess. 2:13), and he tells the church at Corinth that he writes "in words not taught by human wisdom but taught by the Spirit" (1 Cor. 2:13). The technical term for God authoring by means of human authors is "inspiration," and it is associated with the work of the Holy Spirit: "but men spoke from God as they were carried along by the Holy Spirit" (2 Pet. 1:21).

Before discussing inspiration proper, it is worth noting the emphasis in Scripture on God's speaking. Unless God actually speaks, it is impos-sible to say what God is up to in the world, which is why when Scripture records divine deeds it also records the divine words that accompany and explain them. Only speech disambiguates behavior: either God has spoken or his presence and activity are, at best, matters of speculation or ignorance. Moreover, unless God speaks, he cannot make promises, issue commands, teach wisdom, or forgive sinners. The entire story line of the Bible depends on God saying things and then proving himself true and faithful by keeping his word. It is therefore not surprising that a God so intent on communicating would make provisions for preserving his most important pronouncements.

Scripture is divinely inspired not because it is inspiring but because it is *expired*, mysteriously breathed out (not into) by God: "All Scripture is inspired by God [Gk. *theopneustos* = "God-breathed"]" (2 Tim. 3:16). Thomas Aquinas's view is representative of the Christian tradition: "The author of Holy Writ is God."[11] Later Protestant confessions concur, typically emphasizing that Scripture is inspired rather than saying how, though the fourth-century Nicene Creed ascribes the authorship to the Spirit in particular, "who spake by the prophets." Various models have been proposed to account for the dual authorship of Scripture. The notion of "mechanical" inspiration, which depicts God using the human authors as ventriloquist's dummies to give word-for-word dictation, is but a caricature. The traditional view focuses on the product, not the process, and acknowledges the genuine

---

[11] Thomas Aquinas, *Summa Theologiae* I, Q. 1, art. 10.

contribution of the human authors: "It is God who speaks through them; at the same time, it is they themselves who speak and write."[12] God providentially superintends and perfects the creaturely process of writing via the Holy Spirit, a means of cognitive grace that ensures a correspondence of human and divine communicative action: "for it is God who is at work in you, enabling you both to will and to work for his good pleasure" (Phil. 2:13).

In brief, to say that Scripture is inspired is to affirm the real yet secondary human authorship of Scripture in its service to God, its principal author. What is holy and inspired is not the individual authors but their discourse or speech act (what someone does in speaking). Verbal inspiration means that the "one" doing things with biblical words is ultimately the triune God, via the words or discourse of his human aides-de-camp (Ward).[13]

Infallible Authority

The authority of Scripture is distinct from that of other books. Biblical authority is shorthand for "the authority of God speaking in Scripture," for the divine authority of Scripture is a consequence of divine authorship. Holy Scripture is set-apart, authoritative divine discourse. God speaks with authority – rightful say-so – because he is Author of all things. It is therefore important not to confuse the authority of Scripture with an oppressive authoritarianism. God's discourse, like everything God does, is qualified by everything God is – the sum total of the divine perfections, including wisdom, goodness, and love.

What, then, is God saying/doing in Scripture? Most basically, he is relating to his people as their Creator and covenant Lord. He is using language to identify himself and make known his plan of salvation: to sum up all things in Christ (Eph. 1:10) – to establish his reign and place his enemies under his feet (Eph. 1:22; 1 Cor. 15:25). God in Scripture is pledging his troth, staking his truth on the certainty of his promises.

Biblical infallibility is the traditional idea that God's word cannot fail, "but it shall accomplish that which I purpose, and shall succeed in the thing for which I sent it" (Isa. 55:11). Scripture's infallibility implies its truth: Scripture is authoritative because readers can rely upon its teachings. Augustine's view of Scripture's truth set the tone for historic Roman

[12] H. Bavinck, *Reformed Dogmatics*, Volume 1: *Prolegomena* (Grand Rapids: Baker Academic, 2003), 432.
[13] T. Ward (2009), *Words of Life: Scripture as the Living and Active Word of God* (Downers Grove, IL: InterVarsity Press).

Catholic and Protestant orthodoxy alike: "of these alone [the canonical books of Scripture] do I most firmly believe that the authors were completely free from error."[14] Martin Luther says something similar: "I and my neighbor and, in short, all people may err and deceive. But God's Word cannot err."[15] The *Catechism of the Catholic Church* acknowledges that the biblical books "without error teach that truth which God, for the sake of our salvation, wished to see confided to the Sacred Scriptures."

In recent Protestant Evangelical discussions, "infallibility" has come to mean the trustworthiness of Scripture as concerns faith and salvation only – the message about God's love poured out for the world on the cross of Christ – whereas "inerrancy" is the term preferred by those who believe that Scripture speaks truly in all things it affirms, regardless of the subject matter, a bridge too far for those who see potential conflicts with modern science or historiography. The way forward in these important discussions is to distinguish textual meaning (what Scripture says) from readers' interpretations (what we think or would like Scripture to say), a point to which we will return below.

Illuminating Efficacy

To this point we have examined the divine authorship and trustworthy content of Scripture, which we can relate to God the Father and God the Son respectively. The final moment in written communication (and divine revelation) is reception, the moment when readers receive the message sent. Usually, this part of the process is beyond an author's control. Not so with Holy Scripture, where the Spirit who speaks is also the power enabling right reception, "'the Lord of the hearing,'" to use Barth's fine phrase.

The Bible is holy but not magical. Unlike witches' spells, its words have no mysterious power of their own. Rather, the human discourse of the Bible is the creaturely means for the triune God – Father, Son, and Spirit – to do things with words, and the emphasis here is on the Spirit's ability to minister understanding by providing cognitive lumens: illuminating power. It is not that the Spirit adds new content to the Scriptures; rather, the Spirit enables readers to understand that content and feel its full force, especially the summons to surrender false understandings of God and self. The biblical texts are "fields of the Spirit's activity in the publication of the knowledge of God."[16]

---

[14]   Augustine, *Letter 82* (to Jerome).
[15]   *Large Catechism* IV, 57.
[16]   J. Webster, *Holy Scripture: A Dogmatic Sketch* (Cambridge: Cambridge University Press), 27.

The Reformed tradition in particular, following John Calvin, is known for its insistence on the inseparability of word and Spirit. The Spirit is the "internal witness" to the biblical text. The word without the Spirit is inert; the Spirit without the word is unintelligible. Scripture and Spirit together, however, make for an internally persuasive witness to the living Word, Jesus Christ. The apostle Paul speaks of "the sword of the Spirit, which is the word of God" (Eph. 6:17). The Westminster Shorter Catechism well captures Calvin's basic insight: "The Spirit of God maketh the reading, but especially the preaching, of the Word an effectual means of convincing and converting sinners."[17]

PURPOSE: WHAT SCRIPTURE IS FOR

Discourse is something someone says for some purpose. The present section examines the end for which God sent his word. To anticipate: the word of God generates and governs the people of God.[18] God communicates his light, life, and love in Christ in order to form a people – citizens of the gospel – who can respond in faith, hope, and love. God gives Holy Scripture to a holy nation to serve as its covenantal constitution.

Orientation: Love's Knowledge

The earliest Christians were called the Way (Acts 9:2), disciples who followed Jesus, who described himself as "the way, the truth, and the life" (Jn. 14:6). Jesus also identified himself as the "light of the world" and promised those who follow him that they would not walk in darkness but would have "the light of life" (Jn. 8:12). The light in question concerns knowledge of God. The Psalmist describes God's word as "a lamp to my feet and a light to my path" (Ps. 119:105) because it provides orientation, showing us the way to walk.

Think of the canon as an atlas, a collection of different maps – maps of meaning. These maps provide a precious orientation for the people of God. Thanks to these maps, they know where they have come from (Genesis; creation), where they are going (Revelation; consummation), and how to get there. Thanks to Holy Scripture, disciples are no longer

---

[17] *Westminster Shorter Catechism* (1648), Question 89.
[18] D. Kelsey argues that theologians appeal to Scripture to shape Christian identity (*Proving Doctrine: The Uses of Scripture in Recent Theology* [Harrisburg, PA: Trinity Press International, 1999]).

in the dark about the meaning of life and can therefore walk as "children of light" (Eph. 5:8).

What do Christians need to know in order to follow the way of Jesus Christ? The principal thing that disciples need to know, and that Scripture gives, is the big story of which Israel, Jesus, and the church are all a part. Christianity is not a system of ideas but a testimony to what God did in the history of Jesus Christ (the climax of the story of Israel) to make good his promise to Abraham to bless all the nations of the world through his seed. The Bible provides a wide-angle lens on human history, from creation and fall to salvation and reconciliation in Christ, ending with the Last Judgment and the kingdom of God established in a new earth. Throughout this story, Scripture identifies God by what he does and God's people by what they should do in response. God is the gracious one who loves in freedom: "In this is love, not that we have loved God, but that he loved us and sent his Son to be the atoning sacrifice for our sins" (1 Jn. 4:10). The people of God respond in gratitude and free obedience. The story depicts humans as created for fellowship with God, alienated from God by their senseless rebellion, then reconciled to God by God, the one whose love stands fast.

In many and various ways, the diverse texts of the Bible all contribute either to telling this story, a grand narrative, or to contemplating its implications. The Bible does not necessarily contradict the story modern science tells but puts it in a larger, supernatural framework informed by a scriptural imaginary and symbolic universe: a "worldview." A worldview "functions like a compass or road map. It orients us to the world at large, gives us a sense of what is up and what is down, what is right and what is wrong."[19] The diverse books of the Bible together comprise a multi-lensed worldview, a storied way of approaching the core questions of human history and existence in relation to God. The grand story at the heart of Scripture orients the people of God to their new reality in Christ, providing citizens of the gospel everything they need to know to work out their salvation "with fear and trembling" (Phil. 2:12), which is to say, with all seriousness.

Adjudication: Light's Wisdom

The second purpose of Scripture, related to the first, is to serve as a means of adjudicating between true and false religion, which is to say, true and false doctrine (teaching). Recall that Christian Scripture is both

---

[19] A. Wolters, *Creation Regained: Biblical Basics for a Reformational Worldview*, 2nd ed. (Grand Rapids: Eerdmans, 2005), 5.

a discrete doctrinal locus and the source and norm of Christian doctrine in general. The canonical story of what God is doing in Christ serves as stimulus and standard of faith's search for understanding (i.e., theology).

Theology is the attempt to distinguish the way of wisdom, the way of Jesus Christ. It is the attempt to speak of God and what God has done on the basis of the prophets and apostles. Christian doctrine is largely the result of biblical reasoning, the attempt to follow the way the biblical words go. In particular, it is the attempt to understand the grand story of Scripture: its characters, themes, and plot developments. Doctrines tell us who God is, what's wrong with humanity, and what God has done in Christ to set things right.

That the people of God have to make judgments about what to believe and how to behave is a constant theme in Scripture. The Lord God prohibits idolatry (Exod. 20:3–5) because idols are worthless, unable to speak or do anything for the people who worship them. Moreover, the worship of anything other than the one true God is foolish; and whereas wisdom leads to life and flourishing, foolishness leads to death and destruction (Prov. 10:14). Consequently, the appeal to Scripture to distinguish true from false doctrine is ultimately a matter of life and death.

The key question for Christian theology is the one Jesus posed to his disciples: "Who do you say that I am?" (Matt. 16:15). Christology is the pursuit of an answer to this question, and here too Scripture is the authoritative guide. It is clear that the authors of the New Testament were concerned to get this right, as evidenced by their polemic against wrong answers, particularly the quasi-Gnostic teaching that Jesus only appeared to be human: "For many deceivers have gone out into the world, those who do not confess the coming of Christ in the flesh" (2 John 7). The identity of Jesus Christ is also the main issue at stake in the doctrine of the Trinity, another doctrine that matters because it affects how one reads the story of the gospel. True doctrine is needed for Christians to walk as children of light, that is, in accordance with the story of Jesus Christ, which is to say "in accordance with the Scriptures" (1 Cor. 15:3–4; cf. Exod. 34:27). A "heresy" is a falsehood so egregious that one who holds to its teaching is no longer reading the same story the prophets and apostles are telling.

Edification: Life's Hope

In addition to orienting the people of God to the world and indicating ways in which they should (and should not) speak, think, and act, the word of God written is a means of grace that encourages believing individuals and communities to persevere in the way of faith.

The church looks to Scripture not simply for information but for trans-formation, specifically, to cultivate the mind of Christ in the body of Christ (the church). The purpose of Scripture is to inform faith, direct love, and sustain hope.

Holy Scripture is the God-breathed constitution of the new coven-ant community, given to make God's people wise unto salvation. The apostle Paul says that Scripture "is useful for teaching, rebuking, cor-recting and training in righteousness, so that everyone who belongs to God may be proficient, equipped for every good work" (2 Tim. 3:16–17). Put differently: Holy Scripture is useful for forming citizens of a holy nation.

The Bible is realistic enough to know that walking the way of Jesus Christ is often difficult. The kingdom of God may be the destination, but the people of God are not there yet. Israel wandered in the wilder-ness for forty years in search of their Promised Land; no time frame is given the church as to when Jesus will return. Christians therefore look to God's promises and his faithfulness through the centuries for support. What the apostle Paul wrote to the Romans continues to be the watch-word for Christians in our time: "For everything that was written in the past was written to teach us, so that through endurance and the encour-agement of the Scriptures we might have hope" (Rom. 15:4).

INTERPRETATION: READING THE BIBLE AS HOLY SCRIPTURE IN THE CHURCH

To interpret the Bible correctly one has to know what it is. Christians read the Bible as Holy Scripture, a means of coming to know God and being formed in Christian faith, hope, and love. The church is the social domain of the word, the assembly that gathers to celebrate, understand, and communicate the fundamental truths of Scripture, in particular the good news that the promised Messiah has fulfilled God's purpose to bring about reconciliation and renew creation.

At the same time, Scripture has given rise to diverse and sometimes divergent interpretive traditions and reading communities. The 1963 Faith and Order report on "Scripture, Tradition, and Traditions" distinguishes between "Tradition" (the gospel passed on from gener-ation to generation), "tradition" (the process of passing on), and "trad-itions" (the particular doctrinal interpretations that distinguish, say, the Lutheran from the Reformed). The differences pertain not only to what Scripture means but also to how various church traditions understand its light in relation to other sources of divine light, with some seeing the church as "creature of the Word" while others insist the church precedes Scripture. Everything depends on how one sees each leg of this three-legged stool – Scripture, tradition, church –functioning in relation to the other two.

Orthodox Tradition: Light Reflected

The emphasis in Eastern Orthodoxy (a communion of churches that recognize the patriarch of Constantinople as "first among equals") is on Scripture's use and interpretation in liturgy, for Christian life and theology are fundamentally expressions of personal and corporate prayer. John Chrysostom compares reading Scripture to opening the gates of heaven. Moreover, Scripture is itself a by-product of the liturgical life of the church. Tradition on the Orthodox view is a matter of being caught up in the living Spirit's ministry of the living Christ, a matter of getting life from the giver of life. Tradition is not a dead deposit of doctrinal truths but the living into the mystery of divine grace.

The use of Scripture in Orthodoxy is strongly mystical: truth and beauty, right doctrine and right worship, come together in icons (for the invisible God became visible in the incarnate Christ) compared to which doctrinal propositions appear rather colorless. Orthodoxy trusts Jesus's promise that the Spirit would guide the church into all the truth (Jn. 16:13). In Orthodox reckoning, the Spirit traditions both tradition and Scripture by abiding in the church. This is why the Orthodox view themselves as the true heirs of the church's seven ecumenical councils. For it is in these councils that "the faith that was once for all delivered to the saints" (Jude 3) was correctly understood. Jesus's promise that the gates of hell will not prevail against the church (Matt. 16:18) provides additional assurance that the Orthodox tradition is trustworthy and true.

According to the Orthodox, then, Scripture is rightly read in the context of a worshiping community in communion with the (Greek) Fathers and ancient ecumenical councils. Tradition provides the rule or "canon" that forms the "mind of the church" to read the canonical Scriptures rightly, namely, in ways that usher the community deeper into the mystery of life in Christ.[20] Tradition is Scripture rightly understood, an accurate reflection of Scripture's light.

---

[20] See further G. Florovsky, *Bible, Church, Tradition: An Eastern Orthodox View* (Belmont, MA: Nordland, 1972).

Roman Magisterium: Light Filtered

The Roman Catholic church parses Scripture and tradition differently, viewing both as forms of the one apostolic ministry. The original apostles left behind not only their writings but also bishops as their successors, whom they invested with their own teaching authority.[21] Tradition stands alongside Scripture, the written transmission of God's word, as a living transmission of this same word. Sacred Scripture and Sacred Tradition proceed from one common source, the word of God, in two distinct modes of transmission.[22]

Though the word of God has been entrusted to the whole Church, the task of providing an authoritative interpretation of the word of God, either in its written or living form, falls to the teaching office of the Church alone: the Magisterium, which is to say, the bishops in communion with the Pope at Rome. Unlike the Orthodox, who look back to the ecumenical councils for such teaching authority, the Roman Magisterium continues to provide readings with binding authority. It is not that God gives new revelation, only that the Church may come to a fuller understanding of its truth.

According to Joseph Ratzinger (later Pope Benedict XVI), Scripture is born "from the womb of the Church by the power of the Spirit."[23] Ratzinger contrasts this with the Protestant understanding (see below), for which Scripture is an independent reality that stands over against the Church. Roman Catholics are unwilling to separate Scripture from the Church that is its living Tradition and whose teaching office guarantees its right reading. The light of God's word shines on a holy nation but only when filtered through a Roman prism, the Magisterium.

Protestant Priesthood of All Believers: Light Enough

In the Protestant pattern of authority, Scripture outranks tradition and the church as does a text its interpretation. The Reformation emphasis on *sola scriptura* ("Scripture alone") means that the Bible is the supreme but not the only authority for Christian faith and life. Scripture is the sole magisterial authority, for it alone enjoys the status of set-apart divine discourse. Creedal formulas and confessional statements have ministerial authority, however, insofar as they correspond to biblical teaching. There is room in the Protestant pattern of authority for the church's tradition and teaching ministry. Protestants see

---

[21] "Dogmatic Constitution on Divine Revelation: *Dei Verbum*," 7.
[22] See *Catechism of the Catholic Church*, Article 2.
[23] Benedict XVI, *Verbum Domini*, 32.

Scripture as the "norming norm" (*norma normans*) and tradition as a "normed norm" (*norma normata*).

Protestants deny the need for an official teaching authority (e.g., the Roman Magisterium) to tell them what Scripture means. Instead, they affirm "Scripture interprets Scripture": "the infallible rule for interpretation of Scripture is Scripture itself."[24] This principle assumes the essential clarity of Scripture, meaning not that every passage is as easy to understand as another, but that what is obscure in one place is explained in another, and the parts in light of the whole. Scripture alone explains clearly enough what every Christian needs to know to find salvation and follow Christ.

Martin Luther affirmed the priesthood of believers, citing Peter's description of the church as "a royal priesthood" (1 Pet. 2:9). This is not a charter for individual interpreters to do with Scripture what is right in their own eyes only (cf. Judg. 17:6) but rather Luther's alternative to the Roman Catholic magisterium. The priesthood charged with reading and interpreting Scripture is the whole congregation, incorporated as the body of Christ by the Holy Spirit and guided by the Spirit into the truth of the written word: "The unfolding of your words gives light; it imparts understanding to the simple" (Ps. 119:130).

CONCLUSION: A LAMP UNTO OUR PATH

Holy Scripture is the word "of God" in three ways: it has the Father for its author, the Son for its content, and the Spirit for its interpreter. The one who dwells in unapproachable light and is the "Father of lights" (Jas. 1:17) has sent his light into the world in the person of his Son (Jn. 8:12) and, thanks to the illumination of the Spirit, "has shone in our hearts to give the light of the knowledge of the glory of God in the face of Jesus Christ" (2 Cor. 4:6). Holy Scripture is that creaturely servant by which the word of the triune God gathers, governs, and galvanizes the believing community, "children of light" who walk in the light (Eph. 5:8) in order to extend the light of Christ to all nations. In this way, the word of God and the people of God indwell one another: "In your light we see light" (Ps. 36:9).

---

[24] *Westminster Confession of Faith*, I, 9.

Further Reading

Benedict XVI (2010), *Verbum Domini: The Word of the Lord* (Boston: Pauline Books & Media).

Berkouwer, G. C. (1975), *Holy Scripture* (Grand Rapids: Eerdmans).

Carson, D. A., ed. (2016), *The Enduring Authority of the Christian Scriptures* (Grand Rapids: Eerdmans).

Crisp, O., and Sanders, F., eds. (2016), *The Voice of God in the Text of Scripture: Explorations in Constructive Dogmatics* (Grand Rapids: Zondervan Academic).

Gordon, J. K. (2019), *Divine Scripture in Human Understanding: A Systematic Theology of the Christian Bible* (Notre Dame, IN: University of Notre Dame Press).

Holcomb, J. S., ed. (2006), *Christian Theologies of Scripture: A Comparative Introduction* (New York; London: New York University Press).

Loughlin, G. (1996), *Telling God's Story: Bible, Church and Narrative Theology* (Cambridge: Cambridge University Press).

Stylianopoulos, T. (1997), *The New Testament: An Orthodox Perspective*, Volume 1: *Scripture, Tradition, Hermeneutics* (Brookline, MA: Holy Cross Orthodox Press).

Swain, S. (2011), *Trinity, Revelation, and Reading: A Theological Introduction to the Bible and Its Interpretation* (London: T&T Clark).

Ward, T. (2009), *Words of Life: Scripture as the Living and Active Word of God* (Downers Grove, IL: InterVarsity Press).

Webster, J. (2003), *Holy Scripture: A Dogmatic Sketch* (Cambridge: Cambridge University Press).

9 Church and Sacraments

TOM GREGGS

The church is in one sense unique among the loci of Christian doctrine: the church is not only the subject of believing but also an object of belief; the church formulates and articulates doctrine while at the same time itself being an object of doctrinal reflection. It is the church universal that formulates the creeds ('We believe'); yet part of what is believed involves certain dogmas about the church (that it is 'one, holy, catholic, and apostolic' and that it acknowledges 'one baptism for the forgiveness of sins'). We call the discipline of reflecting on what we believe about the church 'ecclesiology'. That we have beliefs about the church indicates, moreover, that while in certain ways the church shares the same forms and conditions of its empirical existence as other societies and organisations in the world (for example, it is observable and spatio-temporal), the church is also unique as an organisation by virtue of its oneness, holiness, catholicity, and apostolicity. Indeed, the church is (with Israel) a community that is different from all others in that it is a community directly created by God: the church (as with Israel) is that body of people about whom we believe God speaks the words, 'I shall be your God and you shall be My people' (Jer. 30:22). We have faith that the church is God's people – faith in the invisible activity of God within the visible, empirical society of people called 'church'.

BIBLICAL

The biblical origins of the church are found in the recurrent narrative that God reveals Godself to a particular people. The manner in which God is the God of the whole of creation is as the God of a particular people – a holy people who are to be a light to the world (cf. Isa. 49:6). This concept is picked up in the New Testament not in relation to the political and ethnic people of Israel but in relation to those who are now incorporated into God's people in Christ and through the Spirit. When we look to Christ, we are confronted with crowds and assemblies that gather round him.

These groups around Jesus formed the earliest recorded communities. But the earliest discussion of the church can be found in Pauline literature. In his writings, Paul refers to what we come to think of as the 'church' as the *ekklēsia*. The term denotes the popular assembly of citizens entitled to vote in the ancient world and is commonly used to denote crowds, groups, and gatherings; but it is best to imagine that Paul's usage relates to the Septuagint's use of *ekklēsia* over one hundred times for the underlying Hebrew word, *qahal* (assembly). There is a likelihood, therefore, of Paul seeking both to express the gatherings that arise from faith by the Holy Spirit in Christ and to draw directly from Israel's self-identification as God's people. There is no hint in Paul that the term *ekklēsia* had some sort of polemical antithesis over against *synagōgē* (synagogue). It may well be that both served distinct and different purposes and that there was a contrastive but not necessarily antithetical relationship. George Lindbeck makes this point well: 'Christ is depicted as the embodiment of Israel .... Thus, in being shaped by the story of Christ, the Church shares (rather than fulfils) the story of Israel.'[1] Furthermore, these two communities (in different ways) still understand themselves as unfulfilled as even the Christian community anticipates the future and final coming of God in God's Kingdom, in that time when there will be no temple since God Himself will be the temple (Rev. 21:22).

Therefore, as much as there is a continuity in the New Testament from the Old Testament idea of God having a specific people, there is no sense of a complete fulfilment: the church, after all, is not the Kingdom of God. Ephesians 1 makes plain that those in Christ are by the Spirit 'God's own people' but also that this is a 'promise', 'seal', and 'pledge' of an inheritance that awaits since in the fulness of time all things in heaven and on earth will be gathered up in Christ (Eph. 1:8–14). The church as a people awaits its own fulfilment in God's own future for creation: the church is not yet the complete realisation of this but only a provisional anticipation and representation of this future that it awaits.

The idea of the church as a new 'people' has its *locus classicus* in 1 Pet. 2:9–10: God creates a people for God's purposes here – 'God's own people' – to be a priesthood and a nation with the purpose of

---

[1] G. Lindbeck, 'The Story-Shaped Church: Critical Exegesis and Theological Interpretation', in *The Theological Interpretation of Scripture: Classic and Contemporary Readings* (ed. Stephen E. Fowl; Oxford: Blackwell, 1997), 43.

proclamation of God's economy. This people is comprised not of national or ethnic origins: after all, this people was previously not a people before receiving God's mercy. This people is the people of God who are created such through God's salvific purposes. While the trinitarian principle that every economic activity of the trinity involves all members of the trinity, it is most fitting to appropriate the cause of the creation of the church to the person of the Holy Spirit. In Acts 1, we have something that has the 'semblance' of a church: there is worship, some kind of sermon, an election of officers, and so forth. But it is only in Acts 2 that the church actually comes into existence. The cause of the creation of the church is the coming of the promised Holy Spirit; and the effect of this coming is that the people discover their purpose – to proclaim the Gospel beyond the confines of the upper room. The Spirit forms God's people for God's purposes. The form that this people takes is the form of Jesus. The Spirit who rested fully on Christ now rests on Christ's people, forming them into the likeness of Christ in the world in the time between Christ's ascension and His return. It is in this analogical or metonymous sense that Scripture speaks of the church as 'the body of Christ'.

There is a particular relation in the New Testament between the idea of the body of Christ and, what we come to understand to be at later points in the church, the sacraments. Ephesians 4:5 speaks of 'one Lord, one faith, one baptism' while 1 Cor. 12:13 speaks of baptism into one body. Similarly, there is identification between the bread and wine of the Last Supper with the body and blood of Jesus Christ. In terms of the New Testament, it is easiest to understand sacraments as dominical ordinances accompanied by signs or actions and associated words; the idea of these actions stems from the Latin word *sacramentum* meaning 'sign'. Some churches also seek ordinances (around such matters as ordination and marriage as sacraments) in the Old Testament as well. Within the New Testament, baptism by water (commanded by Christ as He ascended) is one such sacrament (or 'sign'), as is the command by Christ to repeat in remembrance of him the actions of the Lord's Supper. These actions continue throughout the Acts and are referenced clearly in Paul's writing. Confession is also debated as a sacrament: 'If you forgive the sins of any, they are forgiven them; if you retain the sins of any, they are retained' (Jn. 20:23); the question relates to the 'action' or 'sign' in this case. And others have pointed to foot washing as fulfilling the conditions set for sacraments as well.

Alongside the imagery of the church as a new people created by the Spirit and as the body of Christ, and not unconnected to the administration of these ordinances, the New Testament also points towards the manner in which the body orders itself and in which particular parts of the body have particular roles. The New Testament, in fact, contains multiple structural forms that the earliest churches had: one based on elders or what are later called 'priests' (*presbuteroi*) who occasionally gather as a council (Acts 15); one in which elders and what we later call 'bishops' or overseers (*episkopoi*) are interchangeable (Acts 20:17–18; Tit. 1:5–7; 1 Pet. 2:25; cf. 5:1); one based on what we later call 'deacons' (*diakonoi*) and bishops (1 Timothy 3; Philippians 1); and one based on the apostles and functions members of the body fulfil – prophets, teachers, miracle workers, evangelists, pastors, administrators (Eph. 4:11; 1 Cor. 12:28). It is worth noting, in relation to these matters, that at no point are officers of the church called by the title *hiereus* (priest, the term used for priests of the temple in Greek); and it is also worth noting that the terms *diakonos, presbuteros, episkopos* do not carry the sacerdotal connotations they later receive and could be variously translated. Furthermore, certain terms are quite rare within the New Testament: *episkopos*, for example, is only used five times, and it is not clear that it is demarcated from *presbuteros* in the text.

THE DEVELOPMENT OF 'ECCLESIOLOGY' TO THE REFORMATION

Development of Clergy

In tracing what the church believes about itself as a locus of theological reflection, there is inevitably a requirement to reflect on the history of the church itself. Indeed, very often we are required to reflect on the operant theology (with all its inevitable apologetic tones from the 'given' church's form and practice) about the church at work within the history of the church's own life. This is not least the case in relation to the development of the threefold office of deacon, priest, and bishop. The origins of this can be traced to Ignatius, and particularly his letter to the Smyrneans. There is, however, an apologetic tone even to Ignatius (himself a 'bishop') in his writing, and – as one who is potentially contemporary to later New Testament writings – it is worth, again, noting that the terms here did not necessarily have sacerdotal tones and were not reflected in the practice of the church, which was much more varied. Nor, indeed, does the work of Ignatius mark a final arrival at the idea of a set aside 'clergy' with ontological understandings of ordination akin to the priesthood in the Old Testament or the pagan world.

The shift in focus from Christ and the whole church as a united body to the clergy begins to take place with Tertullian in the third century.[2] In a Greek-speaking world, Hippolytus begins to use language of priesthood in relation to the apostles. By the time that Origen is writing, it appears normal to refer to bishops and presbyters as priests and high priests.[3] It is, however, Cyprian who most develops these themes, linking unity and the efficacy of the sacrifice (eucharist) to a set aside clergy who are now considered the priesthood: for him, a single group exclusively within the church grounds its unity, and this group alone is related only to the Aaronic priesthood that has passed from Moses to Christ to Peter to the pope. This is clearly a development from the NT's and the very early church's understanding of priesthood, and some theologians (especially Protestants) have noted this.

Alongside this focus on clergy comes a focus on the relationship of the clergy to the primacy of one diocese within the Christian church – that of Rome. Associated as a city with the martyrdom of the primus inter pares of the disciples (St Peter to whom the keys of the kingdom were given by Christ) and of the leader of the gentile churches, St Paul, the primacy of Rome as a civic centre quickly also saw the primacy of the Roman see as an ecclesial centre. Not only were the legates of the see of Rome the first on the list of signatories at the Council of Nicaea (indicating pre-eminence); but in 378, the Emperor Gratian granted a decree granting the bishop of Rome (the pope) authority over bishops of every province and made the church subject to the discipline of Rome. The popes who followed this decree began to take a greater and greater sense of the authority they had with a dignity distinct from even the greatest metropolitans and patriarchs of the church. This approach of papal primacy remains the polity of the Roman Catholic Church.

Although there was a primacy afforded the successor of Peter, there were nevertheless in the Roman Empire five patriarchs who governed over their synods: the Patriarchs of Rome (the pope), Constantinople, Alexandria, Antioch, and Jerusalem. Throughout the history of the church from the origins of Roman primacy, there had been struggles between this more 'synodical' approach of territorial patriarchy and Roman primacy. The schism in 1054 between Western and Eastern churches over the *filioque* clause augmented these tensions, which themselves were contributory to the division. As Christianity spread, areas that followed the rites of the Constantinopolitan Church (such as

---

[2] *De baptismo*, 17.1.
[3] E.g., *Homiliae in Leviticum*, 2.3.

Bulgaria and later Russia) followed the pattern of patriarchy and synod, with a structure of king/emperor-patriarch-church-nation. This polity is called *autocephaly* and the churches *autocephalous*. In practice, the Patriarch of Constantinople is often considered primus inter pares, though this is a matter of contention particularly for the Russian church.

Constantinople and the Marks of the Church

The primary dogmatic reflection on the church came in the Council of Constantinople (381), which adopted what we now tend to call the Nicene creed, adding to it articles particularly following from the 325 Council of Nicaea's statement of the church's belief in the Holy Spirit:

> I believe in the Holy Spirit, the Lord, the giver of life,
> who proceeds from the Father and the Son,
> who with the Father and the Son is adored and glorified,
> who has spoken through the prophets.
> I believe in one, holy, catholic and apostolic Church.
> I confess one Baptism for the forgiveness of sins;
> and I look forward to the resurrection of the dead
> and the life of the world to come.

Four things are of particular interest in this statement. The first issue is the location of the discussion of the church. Crucially, the church is not an independent article, as is the case for the articles relating to the three persons of the trinity. As Congar puts it:

> In the West ... the preposition *eis* or *in* has usually been omitted before *ecclesiam* and this fact has often been accorded a religious or theological significance .... When the great Scholastic theologians, then, came to consider the formula 'Credo in Spiritum Sanctum ... et in unam ... Ecclesiam' in the Niceno-Constantinopolitan Creed, they provided the following commentary: I believe in the Holy Spirit, not only in himself, but as the one who makes the Church one, holy, catholic and apostolic.[4]

Discussion of the church follows the third article of the creed (on the person of the Holy Spirit) in the same way the event of creation follows from the Father's acts and the event of salvation or reconciliation from

---

4 Y. Congar, *I Believe in the Holy Spirit*, Volume 2 (New York: Crossroad, 2013), 5.

the Son's act. This is reflected in Irenaeus's words: 'Where the Spirit of Christ is, there the Spirit of God is, and where the Spirit of God is, there is the church and the fullness of grace.'[5]

The second revolves around the fourfold description (or four marks) of the church – that it is one, holy, catholic, and apostolic. The unity of the church ('one') indexes that there is only one true church since there is only one body, one Spirit, one Lord. This has either been understood in terms of visible unity around the eucharist (and thereby dependent on relation to a bishop standing in historic succession) or else in terms of the invisibility or hiddenness of the whole church as a community to believers since the church is to be believed in and whose members and extent are known only to God. The holiness of the church is an indication that it is a creation of God who alone is holy and that – as the church shares in the body of Christ by the power of the Spirit – it is sanctified. For Roman Catholics and the Orthodox, this holiness is related to the institution itself that is granted authority and made holy in its own creation as an institution to be used by God; for most Protestants, the holiness of the church rests alongside a knowledge of its creaturely form as an institution before the return of Christ that is both holy and (in not being fully realised and complete) fallen in parallel to the sense in which the believer is *simul iustus et peccator*.

The catholicity of the church indexes the church's universality. This is related to the church's oneness, global reach, and the idea of the whole company of all Christians across local differences of practice. For some churches, such as the Roman Catholic Church, this idea revolves around being in full communion with the bishop of Rome or might involve commitment to a particular polity. For other churches, such as Magisterial Protestant churches, catholicity speaks of the shared faith and practices that mark those who hold to apostolic faith and doctrine expressed in continuity with the ecumenical creeds and councils, particularly the first seven of these. Catholicity relates, therefore, to the apostolicity of the church. Apostolicity describes the church's continuity with the teachings of Christ known and passed on by the disciples and earliest believers. For churches that are episcopally structured and claim a historic succession for their bishops from the earliest disciples, apostolicity is expressed principally through personal means related to the office of the bishop, which stands in apostolic succession and guards the apostolic deposit of faith. Non-episcopal

---

[5] Irenaeus, *Adversus haereses*, 3.24.1 (PG 7:966).

churches tend to focus more on the deposit of faith itself: the church is founded upon the apostles (Eph. 2:20), but there are no personal successors of them; and, instead, apostolicity is orientated towards the teaching of the apostles contained in Scripture (though this may well be guarded and upheld through the teaching office of the church however these are ordered).

The third matter of note from the creed is that the visible bounds of church are expressed in relation to the action (sacrament) of baptism. While other sacraments (such as holy communion) are not listed in the credal statements about the church, it is very clear that the creed affirms one baptism as that which defines concretely the life of the church. Although certain denominations (such as the Salvation Army or the Quakers) do not practice the sacrament and although some (such as Baptists) practice 'believers' baptism, correctly performed with the correct trinitarian formula, all baptisms are true. Over the years, some denominations have practised provisional baptism for those who moved from one denomination to another (usually with the baptism preceded by the words, 'If this person not already be baptised'); this diminishing practice was usually related to episcopal understandings of the marks of the church.

The fourth issue to note is that the creed emphasises that the church is not the realisation of God's eschatological purpose or, in other words, that the church is not the same as the Kingdom of God. The church is 'on the way' to redemption and not synonymous with the redeemed community. Immediately following the discussion of the church and baptism is the anticipation of the fulfilment of the redemption. Crucially, this is not in the present with the church but in the future: 'I look forward to the resurrection of the dead and the life of the world to come.' This is a reminder of the provisionality of the church in time and space even as the church as the community of the redeemed is related to the eschatological completion of God's salvific purposes.

The Reformation

While there were disputes about the meaning of the marks of the church, and the extent to which they were synonymous with the empirical, institutional church (especially from the perspective of monastic movements), the mainline position until the Reformation in the sixteenth century was that the visible, institutional church was the locus within which the church's unity, holiness, catholicity, and apostolicity was located. What was believed about the church (invisibly) was visibly present in direct correspondence to the church's institutions and polity. Citing the Bible as the absolute authority that ruled sovereignly over the church, the Reformers challenged the idea that the church (particularly through the authority of the pope, bishops, and clergy) knew and determined the extent of God's people – that the church could decide on who those are who are outside the people of God and, thereby, salvation since *extra ecclesiam nulla salus est* ('outside the church there is no salvation'). Luther and the other Reformers challenged the identification of the hidden (or invisible) church with the visible church from two angles. First, they claimed that the visible church might well simply have the 'semblance' of a church and not be a true church at all; and, second, they claimed that the church itself (and its officers) could not determine those who were within the bounds of God's elect and who would receive God's salvation. Ultimately Protestants, therefore, came to understand the visible church(es) as subsisting within the ultimately hidden unity, holiness, catholicity, and apostolicity of the church; in comparison, Roman Catholics have seen the invisible church (with its marks) as subsisting within the visible institutions of the church, albeit with elements of truth and sanctification elsewhere. This has determined that Protestant churches have tended to be wedded less to ideas of episcopacy (or a given polity) as an essential aspect of the church; albeit certain Reformation Episcopal churches (such as the Anglican Church or the Church of Sweden) have continued to claim apostolic succession and episcopacy as beneficial (*bene essentia*) for the church's life.

The focus for Protestant churches has often been on the existence of the church as *creatura Verbi* (a creature of the Word). The church is brought into being by the living Word of God and as a locus of the Word. In the church, the Word is heard and preached in both the preaching of the Word and in the visible enactments of the Word in the sacraments. It is the preaching of the true word of God (in sermon and sacrament) that is the condition of the church's existence and that makes the church visible. Indeed, Calvin wrote: 'Wherever we see the Word of God purely preached and heard, and the sacraments administered according to Christ's institution, there, it is not to be doubted, a church of God exists [cf. Eph. 2.20].'[6] The Augsburg Confession (the primary confession of the Lutheran Church) states: 'The Church is the congregation of saints, in which the Gospel is rightly taught and the Sacraments are rightly administered.'[7] Baptism and holy communion are considered the *verba visibila* (visible words) and together with the

---

[6] Calvin, *The Institutes of the Christian Religion* (1536), 4.1.9 (trans. McNeill; Philadelphia: Westminster, 1960), 1023.

[7] *Augsburg Confession* (1530), 7.

proclamation of the pure Word of God (*verba invisibila* or invisible word) are the basis of the church's existence and the means by which a true church can be identified. Added to these identifiers of the church is also church order. The reason for this is not a claimed historic succession of episcopacy or a view of a particular form of polity as necessary for the church's veracity. Instead, the reason for this is that the Gospel (the Word) orders itself. As a result, while there might be variance in forms of polity or in issues of discipline, Magisterial Protestants see church order and discipline as a key factors in the church's existence and in identifying the church. However, these matters of polity and discipline were for the sake of order and did not imply necessarily a 'set aside' clergy: emphasis was on the shared priesthood of the baptised body of believers from within which certain officers were appointed for the public teaching of the Gospel and to aid the self-ordering of the Word.

Alongside the Magisterial Reformation, there was a more funda-mental rejection of the traditional structures of the church and of the church's historical ecumenical and synodical confessions. These move-ments were grouped together under the title 'Radical Reform'. These churches considered the traditional organised and institutional forms of the church as unbiblical. Rejecting infant baptism and at times trad-itional forms of institution of the Lord's supper, these communities of believers or brethren saw themselves as opposed to the world and the other ecclesial institutions in the world. They saw the adoption of Christianity by the Roman Empire as a great apostasy. They considered themselves alone to be the true church, a tiny remnant; and they identified themselves through believers' baptism and as congregations of believers that often did not appoint public ministers of the Gospel because of a strong commitment to the shared priesthood of believers. Ironically, in seeing themselves as the only true, separated remnant of the Christian church, these churches rejected the Magisterial Reformation's key separation of the visible and invisible (hidden) church and the inability humans have to see perfectly the continuity between these.

SACRAMENTS

Key to many of the distinctions that exist in the church's ecclesiological self-understanding is the church's understanding of sacraments. The word 'sacraments' comes from the Latin word *sacramenta* – a secular word that means either 'sacred thing' (according to Cicero) or a 'sacred oath' (according to Dionysius of Halicarnassus). In Greek, the word is rendered *mysterion* or mystery. In the early Christian church, this term came to be associated with several practices and rites of the church. Building on Augustine, *The Book of Common Prayer* refers to these as 'outward and visible sign[s] of an inward and spiritual grace'. However, there is hardly an area of theology that has been surrounded by so much controversy and division. While these signs of grace should be rites that unify the church, they have continued to be those that divide the church.

The first area of division is related to the number of sacraments. Following Peter Lombard and systematised by Thomas Aquinas, Roman Catholics identify seven of these: baptism, confirmation, communion, matrimony, penance, extreme unction, and ordination. These are considered sacraments, according to Lombard, on the basis of being both the visible sign of invisible grace (following Augustine) and also the cause of grace it signifies. Aquinas required each institution of a sacrament to be by Christ but understood this institution in the promises and death of Christ rather than necessarily the initiation of the sacrament by Christ.[8] The Orthodox Church also identifies seven sacraments, though identifies these slightly differently: baptism, chrismation, communion, ordination, penance, anointing of the sick, and marriage. In these rites, according to the Orthodox Church, the whole church participates in God through cooperation or 'synergy'; the basis for this participation is an extension of the work of God's incarnation in Jesus Christ. For the Magisterial Reformers, the primary condition for something possessing the status of a sacrament was that it was associated with dominical ordinance (an instruction from Jesus) – a sign and the associated words with that sign. Generally speaking, most Protestant churches have considered there to be two sacraments – baptism and holy communion, as commanded by Jesus. Luther, however, postulated that penance might also be a sacrament, seeing it as dominically commanded on the basis of Matt. 18:15–20, albeit it lacked the associated sign required.[9] Calvin offered a twofold account of sacraments: both a broad understanding of sacraments as signs of God's covenants and a narrower one in relation to the church and the 'ordinary' sacraments of the church's ceremonies, ceremonies that again stem from dominical ordinance (and he identifies these as baptism and the Lord's supper).[10]

---

[8] *Summa Theologica*, 3.62.5; 3.64.2.

[9] *D. Martin Luthers Werke* (WA), 120 volumes (Weimar, 1883–2009), 546, 572.

[10] See Calvin, *Institutes*, 4.14.

There is general ecumenical agreement amongst those churches that engage in sacramental worship around the two principal sacraments (what Augustine considered *sacramenta maiora* or *principalia*)[11] of the eucharist (or holy communion or Lord's supper) and baptism.

As already noted, there has in recent years been a growing unity around baptism within the ecumenical movement. Baptism is the Christian act of sprinkling, dipping, or immersing someone in water, accompanied by the words 'in the name of the Father, Son and Holy Spirit' (though some churches use 'in the name of Jesus Christ'). The World Council of Churches Faith and Order Commission paper, *One Baptism: Towards Mutual Recognition* concludes with the following observation:

> The member churches of the World Council of Churches ... affirmed together that baptism is the basis of their commitment to one another within the ecumenical movement. And more than that, they committed themselves to draw the full consequences from the existing mutual recognition of baptism.[12]

While there are differences of meaning and of practice for this act, the symbolism associated with it involves entry into the church through dying to self (in the water) and being raised again to life in Christ. This might be an enactment that emphasises the objectivity of what Christ has done for us, carried out in promise in infancy; or else, it might be a subjective expression of the decision of faith through believers' (or adult) baptism. With a background in the Old Testament and the use of water for purification, and set against the actions of John the Baptist in the New Testament, for Christians baptism is not simply for the remission of sin but also for the receipt of the Holy Spirit: John the Baptist demarcates his baptism with water from that of Jesus's with the Spirit. St Paul speaks of baptism with a number of overlapping images: we are baptised into Jesus's death (Rom. 6:3); baptised into one body and given the same Spirit to drink (1 Cor. 12:13); baptised into Christ (Gal. 3:27); and, buried with Christ in baptism, raised with Him through faith (Col. 2:11–12). Luke connects baptism with repentance and the gifts of the Spirit (Acts 2:38). One of the most controversial texts in the Bible about baptism is Jn. 3:5 in which it is argued no one can enter the Kingdom unless being born of the Water and of the Spirit. For some, this verse has been used to

[11] Augustine, '*In Johannis Evangelium Tractatus CXXIV*', in *Patrologia Latina*, 35.1375–1970 (ed. J.-P. Migne; Paris, 1861), 80.3.
[12] Faith and Order Paper, No. 210 World Council of Churches (Geneva, 2011), 20.

point towards the need for baptism to purge humans from original sin. St Augustine is the most famous exponent of this position. In his *Treatise on the Merits and Forgiveness of Sins*, he argues that original sin is universal and arises through birth (I.20) and that only God's grace can save from sin. For him, this grace is conferred through baptism (I.10). To protect unbaptised infants from the stain of original sin (and condemnation should they die in infancy), it is necessary to baptise infants (I.22). For others, such as those who profess believer's baptism, the need to be baptised by water and Spirit is expressed in the public declaration of faith enacted in the choice of adult baptism.

While there are certainly contentious aspects to baptism, the theological understanding, practice, and even name of holy communion is even more divisive: it remains the hope of the ecumenical movement, indeed, that all Christians can share full eucharistic communion and share the Lord's Supper together.

Roman Catholic understandings of the eucharist revolve around two principal themes. The first is the issue of *ex opere operato*. This Latin term means 'out of the work performed' and indicates that sacraments (particularly the eucharist) find their efficacy, not from the merits of the priest or recipient, but from the sacrament itself, independent of any faith or merit. To ensure that the sacrament is valid, it must be performed by an ordained minister in full communion with Rome: 'The ordained priesthood guarantees that it really is Christ who acts in the sacraments through the Holy Spirit for the Church.'[13] Thus, while at least minimal openness to grace is required of the recipient, the cause of the sacrament's efficacy is not that openness or faith but Christ Himself as the author of the sacrament with the priest acting in Christ's place (*in persona Christi*). The second key theme for Roman Catholic understandings of the eucharist is that of transubstantiation. This is the belief that the bread and wine actually become in the sacrament the body and blood of Christ, by transubstantiation as ecclesially defined in the First Canon of the Fourth Lateran Council (1215).[14] The key point to understand about transubstantiation is that the elements' substances are changed, miraculously, from being bread and wine to being the body and blood of Jesus; but the accidents (such as the taste and appearance of the bread) are not changed. The bread and wine (the accidents) are now in substance the body and blood of Christ, but if one were to

---

[13] *Catechism of the Catholic Church*, 2.1.1.2.2 (1120).
[14] This theme is unpacked by Aquinas, *Summa Theologica*, III.75.5–8.

perform scientific experiments on the elements, since the accidents are unchanged, the material make-up of the bread and wine would remain as bread and wine.

Orthodox theologians have also come in recent centuries to describe their eucharistic doctrines in terms of transubstantiation. For them, there is the real presence of Christ in the eucharist and, through the calling down of the Holy Spirit (*epiclesis*) onto the elements, the bread and wine become the body and blood of Jesus. One distinctive issue to note for Orthodox approaches is that the Orthodox believe that in the celebration of the Divine Liturgy they are united to the church in eternity and thereby to all churches throughout time – past, present, and future. There is an eschatological component to their eucharistic theology that emphasises that the many celebrations of communion and the many loaves and cups are actually one – joined to the eternal eucharistic fellowship in which the individual celebrations participate.

Within Protestant Churches, there are a variety of theological perspectives concerning the Lord's supper. While certain denominations, such as Quakers and The Salvation Army, do not celebrate communion in the traditionally understood, institutional sense, the majority of churches subscribe to one of the three possible theological positions, associated with three major sixteenth-century reformers. All of these reject the doctrine of transubstantiation as unbiblical and dependent on Aristotelian thought rather than scriptural exegesis. Lutherans affirm the real presence of Jesus in the sacrament but not in a manner that involves a transformation of the elements. For them, Christ is 'truly and substantially present in, with and under' the forms of the consecrated bread and wine. This idea trades on the Christological belief in the *genus majestaticum* whereby the humanity of Christ is enhanced after the ascension and through the communication of idioms becomes ubiquitous and particularly present in the church (in the Word preached and on the table). There is a sacramental union but it is beyond that which is visible in the forms of bread and wine.

At the opposite end of the Protestant spectrum is the position of Zwingli, who could not agree with Luther. For Zwingli, there is no other avenue to salvation than through faith, and there is thereby a relativisation of the importance of sacramental practices. However, Zwingli emphasised the command of Christ to engage in the celebration of the Lord's supper 'in remembrance' of what Christ had done uniquely, once-and-for-all in Christ's life, death, and resurrection. Holy communion is the most precious symbol of this act of Christ and the most powerful means of its remembrance. Zwingli uses the image of the wedding ring given by a king to his wife, the queen. Of all the queen's jewels, it may be the least valuable in its material form (a simple band of gold), but in its meaning and symbolism, it is of the greatest worth since it is a sign of what makes the queen a queen – that she is married to the king. Its power is symbolic and is based in who it is who gives the ring and the change of status the ring signifies.

John Calvin's position is often considered to mediate between the Lutheran and the Zwinglian. Calvin fundamentally disagrees with the Lutheran commitment to the ubiquity of Christ through the communication of idioms. However, he also disagrees with the idea that holy communion is only a memorial. For Calvin, there is a real, spiritual presence of Christ in the church's sharing in communion. The crucial bond between Word and Spirit determines that not only is the eucharist a sign of the believer's spiritual union in Christ, but it is also, through the Spirit, the means of grace by which the believer participates in the 'spiritual banquet' and is nourished in faith in their soul. In holy communion, through the Spirit, 'the body of Christ is really (as is commonly said), that is, truly given to us in the Supper'.[15] Crucially, this is by the actualisation of the Spirit in the believer and the community through the means of grace of the supper, rather than by the physical presence of Christ in the elements.

CONCLUSION: RECENT AND CONTEMPORARY DEVELOPMENTS

The fields of ecclesiology and sacramentology have particularly flourished in light of the rise of the ecumenical movement that has led churches and theologians once again to reflect on their self-understanding, polity, and sacramental practices as they seek for full visible, eucharistic unity. Vatican II's reflections on the church have also offered fresh impetus to a generation of theologians seeking to understand the nature of the church, particularly in the context of globalisation and the realities of an ecumenical and pluralistic context. In service of understanding the differences between underlying ecclesiologies in an ecumenical context, outwith the divisions of denominations and the historical-political contexts in which they arose, Cardinal Avery Dulles famously offered a typology of ecclesiologies beyond the confessional contexts of individual denominations. He sought in his *Models of the Church* to trace the distinct emphases

---

[15] Calvin, *Institutes*, IV.17.32.

different ecclesiological traditions have in relation to particular aspects of
Scripture and the great tradition of the church. Using distinct denominational statements, but seeking to go deeper into the underlying theological schematics, Dulles identified five potential conceptualisations of
the church, each with a particular emphasis for particular churches and
families of churches: mystical communion, sacrament, servant, herald,
and institution. More recently, the approach of receptive ecumenism has
pioneered the practice of seeking to recover from other traditions recep-
tively what emphases might have been lost or forgotten in particular
denominations and ecclesiological self-understandings.

   Recent ecclesiologies have also sought to integrate other theological
commitments or academic disciplines into discussions of the church.
Karl Barth's Christocentric theology provided impetus for theological
redescription of the life of the church apart from issues of institutional
polity. John Zizioulas has used his account of the doctrine of the trinity
to develop a highly influential social trinitarianism through which to
describe the life of the church. Others have sought to offer a strongly
pneumatological account of the church as flowing from the life and
activity of the Spirit,[16] while others have drawn on the theodrama of
God's salvific work.[17] Recent engagements with the church in relation
to the realities of 'lived' ecclesial faith and practice have also sought to
draw on social scientific methodologies, including particularly ethnography to attend to the actual social dynamics and practices of the
church alongside (and sometimes in contradiction of) formal and doctrinal theological reflection.[18]

   Perhaps the greatest developments in ecclesiology in recent years
have arisen in light of the contemporary contexts within which the
church exists: the church does not exist *in abstracto* but *in concreto*
in a given place and a given time. In this way, the church will always in
its self-description have to give account for itself in relation to the
contexts in which it exists. Over the last century, there has been particular attention in ecclesiology given to the role of women in the life of
the church in light of critiques of patriarchy. A greater awareness of the
global context of Christianity has given rise to distinct and contextual
expressions of the life of the church while criticism of the church's

[16] T. Greggs, *Dogmatic Ecclesiology*, Volume 1: *The Priestly Catholicity of the Church*
     (Grand Rapids: Baker Academic, 2019).
[17] N. Healy, *Church, World and the Christian Life: Practical-Prophetic Ecclesiology*
     (Cambridge: Cambridge University Press, 2000).
[18] See, for example, Pete Ward, ed., *Perspectives on Ecclesiology and Ethnography*
     (Grand Rapids: Eerdmans, 2012).

complicity in issues relating to racial oppression has heightened the need for the church to reflect on its own life in relation to matters of racial power dynamics. The growth of global Pentecostalism has seen new expressions of ecclesiology that speak to this ever-expanding global phenomenon, and the navigation between fresh expressions of church communities and traditional institutional understandings of the church has demanded serious ecclesiological reflection. It is certainly the case that alongside wonderful opportunities, the fast-changing contexts in which the church exists bring challenges. But it has been the role of the church in every generation to be faithful to the inheritance of the one, holy, catholic, and apostolic church within the givenness of the world for which the church exists and to discover what the continued purpose of the church's existence is in every given age. To end where this chapter began, the church will inevitably share some of the same forms and conditions of its empirical existence as other societies and organisations (and to that extent reflect the paradigms in which they exist), but in so doing the church will also continue to understand in faith itself as unique, as a community that ever becomes the body of Christ by the Spirit's grace.

Further Reading

Congar, Y. (2013), *I Believe in the Holy Spirit*, Volume 2 (New York: Crossroad).
Dulles, A. (1976), *Models of the Church: A Critical Assessment of the Church in All Its Aspects* (Dublin: Gill & Macmillan).
Greggs, T. (2019), *Dogmatic Ecclesiology*, Volume 1: *The Priestly Catholicity of the Church* (Grand Rapids: Baker Academic).
Hardy, D. W. (2000), *Finding the Church* (London: SCM).
Healy, N. (2000), *Church, World and the Christian Life: Practical-Prophetic Ecclesiology* (Cambridge: Cambridge University Press).
Küng, H. (1968), *The Church* (London: Burns & Oates).
Moltmann, J. (1977), *The Church in the Power of the Spirit: A Contribution to Messianic Ecclesiology* (London: SCM).
Murray, P., ed. (2008), *Receptive Ecumenism and the Call to Catholic Learning: Exploring a Way for Contemporary Ecumenism* (Oxford: Oxford University Press).
Ramsey, M. (1990), *The Gospel and the Catholic Church* (London: SPCK).
Torrance, J. B. (1996), *Worship, Community and the Triune God of Grace* (Downers Grove, IL: InterVarsity Press).
Torrance, T. F. (1993), *Royal Priesthood* (Edinburgh: T&T Clark).
Ward, Pete, ed. (2012), *Perspectives on Ecclesiology and Ethnography* (Grand Rapids: Eerdmans).

10 Eschatology

IAN A. MCFARLAND

In line with the meaning of the Greek word from which it is derived, eschatology deals with *eschata*: the last things. Yet because this way of speaking can easily suggest a future that is indefinitely distant (and thus less than pressing), the import of the doctrine is arguably better conveyed by the traditional Latin phrase *de novissimis*: literally, the newest things – the definitive revelation of God's lordship as already breaking in upon the world. Such language appropriately echoes Jesus Christ's own proclamation that God's kingdom is "at hand" (Matt. 4:17 and pars.). For although the kingdom is not included among the four "last things" – death, judgment, heaven, and hell – that are the traditional topics of eschatological treatises, the hope of the kingdom does summarize their collective content: the end of the present order of creation and the inauguration of a new order of redemption, in which God's will is done "on earth as it is in heaven" (Matt. 6:10 and par.). Moreover, because for Christians the realization of this promise is defined by Jesus's return in glory, the Christian hope for the kingdom is identical with hope for Jesus, who for this reason is rightly called (in the words of Origen of Alexandria) the *autobasileia* – God's kingdom in person. The life of the kingdom is just the communion of creation with the Creator that has been made possible by God's assuming a creature's life in Jesus of Nazareth. It follows, as Karl Barth famously declared, that, "if Christianity be not altogether thoroughgoing eschatology, there remains in it no relation whatever with Christ."[1]

A key implication of eschatology's christological focus is that there is no difference for Christians between hope's present form and its

[1] Karl Barth, *The Epistle to the Romans*, 6th ed. (trans. Edwyn C. Hoskyns; Oxford: Oxford University Press, 1968 [1932]), 314.

future content: both are defined by Jesus of Nazareth.[2] It is precisely for this reason – because the one whose coming we "wait for" is none other than he who long ago "gave himself for us that he might redeem us from all iniquity" (Tit. 2:13–14) – that Scripture calls Jesus "our hope" (1 Tim. 1:1). To hope in Jesus is thus to live in confidence that the commitment to our lives that he showed forth in giving his life "as a ransom for many" (Matt. 20:28 and par.) will be vindicated when (in the words of the Nicene Creed) "he will come again in glory to judge the living and the dead."[3] For this reason, the hope for Jesus that is the essential content of Christian eschatology is also "the hope of glory" (Col. 1:27; cf. Tit. 2:13).

THE HOPE OF GLORY

But what is glory? In English translations of the Bible, the word is used to translate two distinct terms: the Hebrew *kabod* and the Greek *doxa*, which connote "weight" and "splendor," respectively, and which are used by the biblical writers to refer to the visible manifestation of God's divinity. Although God's glory is eternally displayed in heaven (Pss. 113:4; 148:13; Acts 7:55), within the realm of time and space, its revelation is episodic, as in the theophany to Moses on Mount Sinai (Exod. 24:15–18), Solomon's dedication of the temple (2 Chron. 7:1) or Jesus's transfiguration on Mount Tabor (Matt. 17:1–13 and pars.). By contrast, the promise of the eschaton is that the experience of God's glory will extend permanently throughout the whole of creation, such that "the earth will be filled with the knowledge of the glory of the LORD, as the waters cover the sea" (Hab. 2:14; cf. Rev. 21:23) and creatures will share by grace in the glory God possesses by nature (Rom. 8:21; 2 Cor. 3:18; 1 Pet. 5:4). In his resurrection, Jesus became the first to enter this life of glory (1 Tim. 3:16), in which he has left death definitively behind him and now lives on new and different terms: no

---

[2] In this context, it is worth noting that the ancient Christian acclamation, "Maranatha" (1 Cor. 16:22) can be understood as having either a past or a future reference, depending upon whether the Aramaic is read as *maran'athā* ("Our Lord has come"), or *maranā thā* ("Our Lord, come!").

[3] Based on its use in biblical passages like Matt. 24:3, 27, 37, 39; 1 Cor. 15:23; 1 Thess. 2:19; 3:13; 4:15; 5:23; 2 Thess. 1:8; Jas. 5:7–8; 2 Pet. 3:4; and 1 Jn. 2:28, the Greek word *parousia* has been appropriated in English to refer to Jesus's return, although the word literally refers not to motion but rather to presence or "at-handedness," thereby stressing the sudden and unexpected character of his appearing (see 1 Thess. 5:2; 2 Pet. 3:10; Rev. 3:3; 16:15; cf. Matt 24:36–44 and pars.).

longer "according to the flesh" (2 Cor. 5:16 alt.), but "to God" (Rom. 6:10; cf. 2 Cor. 13:4), beyond time and its vicissitudes. When he comes again, this glory will be universally disclosed (1 Cor. 1:7), with the result that all who belong to him will share in it, also living to God as those who have been made alive in Christ (Col. 3:4; cf. 1 Cor. 15:22; Heb. 2:10–11) in what the Western churches describe as the "beatific vision" and the Orthodox tradition as "deification" (or *theosis* in Greek). Indeed, Paul contends that because believers are already in receipt of the Spirit of the risen Jesus as a "pledge of our inheritance" (Eph. 1:14; cf. 2 Cor. 1:22; 5:5), they are even now "being transformed into the same image from one degree of glory to another" (2 Cor. 3:18).

In order to make sense of this final claim, it is necessary to reflect a bit more on the difference Christian eschatology posits between human life now and in the age to come, or as created and redeemed, respectively. Because human beings are created from nothing, their existence is already sustained fully and exclusively by God's grace. But this grace of creation is indirect, mediated through a network of created causes that include the physical laws that give our bodies their structure and keep them anchored to earth, as well as the ecological and social relationships whereby we concretely live, move, and have our being in time and space.[4] This dependence of human life as created on myriad physical interactions with other creatures renders it subject to disruption (for example, by the absence of food or the onset of disease) and thereby vulnerable to suffering and death. By contrast, to be "alive to God" as Jesus is, is to live by the grace of redemption: then we shall no longer be subject to death, because we shall no longer derive our life from God indirectly, through the mediation of relationships with other creatures, but directly – "face to face" (1 Cor. 13:12; cf. 1 Jn. 3:2), as those who do not "live by bread alone, but by every word that comes from the mouth of God" (Matt. 4:4 and par.; cf. Deut. 8:3). We anticipate this state in the present in that while we continue to depend on other creatures ("bread") for our quotidian existence, the gospel declares that even now our lives are not defined by the legacy of our (invariably sinful) relationships with other creatures but solely by God's word of promise (cf. Phil. 2:16).

[4] It is important to note that, at least according to the Thomist theological tradition, the lives of angels are not characterized by relationships with other creatures but are from the outset sustained directly by God. This may be taken as another dimension of the contrast in the Lord's Prayer between the realization of God's will already in heaven but not yet on earth.

And yet if in this way we have already a foretaste of the kingdom (Eph. 1:14), the fact that life in glory remains a matter of hope, glimpsed only "in a mirror, dimly" (1 Cor. 13:12) and obscured by the ambiguity of our relationships with other creatures (where experiences of love, beauty, and joy are all too often overwhelmed by cruelty, stupidity, and pain) means that the fulness of the kingdom has not yet arrived. This tension points to eschatology's limits. For although the kingdom Jesus will consummate in glory is the same as the one he proclaimed in Palestine, the shape of the former cannot simply be read off of the latter, because Jesus's life was lived in history, where the place of evil – and thus its final significance before God and for us – remains opaque. To be sure, in light of Jesus's resurrection from the dead, evil's ultimate defeat is not in doubt; the question is how its destruction affects the destiny of human beings, whose actions give rise to so much of the confusion, sorrow, and suffering that constitute evil's legacy. Does Jesus's promise of abundant life (Jn. 10:10) apply to all? Or are there some for whom Jesus's final word will be, "I never knew you?" (Matt. 7:21–23)? In short, as much as the confession that Jesus will come again defines the Christian hope, exactly what that coming will portend for the world remains beyond present sight (1 Pet. 4:17). At the same time, if Christians are to speak of hope at all, they must be prepared to venture at least some claims about what will transpire upon Jesus's return. To ask what Christian hope is, is to ask what it means to see the Lord's glory; and in this context the "four last things" of classical eschatology – death, judgment, heaven, and hell – continue to provide a serviceable framework for eschatological reflection.

DEATH

Strictly speaking, death is not one of the "last things," if that designation is meant to refer to things that all human beings will confront as the result of Jesus's return. On the contrary, Paul is very explicit that Jesus's return preempts any claim that death has any universal claim on humanity: "We will *not* all die, though we will all be changed" (1 Cor. 15:51). Death may be the lot of the majority of humankind, but the eschaton is defined not by death but by advent: Christians do not look forward to cosmic extinction but to the return of Jesus – who is alive (cf. Lk. 24:5). This distinction is important, because it highlights the fact that Jesus's second coming is not (any more than was his first) the culmination of any inner-worldly process of physical, cultural, or spiritual evolution but rather the gracious irruption of God's presence into the midst of worldly processes. To understand eschatological hope in this way decouples it both from (more optimistic) postmillennial theories of Christ's advent being prompted by the success of human missionary activity and from (more pessimistic) extrapolations of contemporary scientific cosmology, according to which the cosmic evolution terminates in universal extinction, whether via a gradual "heat death" or a more sudden "Big Rip."

With this correction in mind, "death" can nevertheless serve as an appropriate starting point for eschatological reflection insofar as it is understood as a synecdoche for the individual's coming into the presence of the living Lord, whether at the end of her earthly life or at the end of the age. Understood in this sense, "death" signifies the essential finitude of human life, which is bounded by a temporal beginning and end. To be human is not to live forever (see Gen. 6:1–3) but to be granted a definite life-span, which concludes, whether by way of death or the parousia, with every person's coming into God's presence in Jesus.[5] It is that encounter, that seeing face to face (1 Cor. 13:12; cf. 1 Jn. 3:2), which is the most appropriate designation for the first of the "last things" that form the substance of Christian hope – first, because it is the presupposition and ground of the other three.

To see why this is the case, it is necessary to return to the idea that human life has an end and is therefore bounded. Again, Paul's insistence that not all will die serves as a reminder that this characteristic of human life is not simply a by-product of sin, as though human beings would have had endless life apart from their violation of God's primordial commandment in Eden (see Gen. 2:16–17; 3:22). Death is the particular form taken by human finitude in the wake of the fall, and insofar as it signifies nonexistence, and thus absence from God's presence (see Ps. 6:5; Isa. 38:18), it is indeed "the last enemy" (1 Cor. 15:26); but to have a life with temporal boundaries is not in itself a result of sin but inherent to humans' (and all worldly beings') condition as creatures. And to meet Jesus, the world's Lord and Savior, when life's further temporal boundary has been reached is simply to be confronted with the fact of one's status as a creature: a being whose existence is from

---

[5] Importantly, if death has come to be the context in which most Christians imagine their encounter with Christ, this was not always the case. In his first letter to the Thessalonians (the earliest Christian document we possess), Paul clearly views the Christian experience of death as anomalous. His claim that "we who are alive, who are left until the coming of the Lord, will by no means precede those who have died" (1 Thess. 4:15) indicates that (at least at this point in his ministry) Paul does not envision either himself or most of his fellow believers as dying before Jesus returns.

start to finish and in every respect both founded and upheld exclusively by God and whose ultimate destiny is therefore in God's hands alone. To identify death as the first of the "last things" is thus to confess that the ultimate fate of human beings, whether good or ill, depends entirely on the One in whom "we live and move and have our being" (Acts 17:28).

JUDGMENT

It makes good logical sense for judgment to be listed as the second of the last things, since it is only once a life that has run its full course that it may be judged. The only appropriate judge is God, since only the Creator is in a position to provide a truly comprehensive assessment of a creature's life. And that the task of judgment should be given to the Second Person of the Trinity in particular follows from the fact that it is just this person who has assumed flesh and is therefore able to have the kind of personal encounter with the creature that judgment (as opposed to the operation of impersonal forces like fate or karma) entails.[6] Taken together, these principles provide the conceptual framework within which to interpret the biblical teaching that "all of us must appear before the judgement seat of Christ, so that each may receive recompense for what has been done in the body, whether good or evil" (2 Cor. 5:10; cf. Acts 10:42; 17:31; Rom. 14:10).

It has become a matter of broad agreement among Christians that this "appearance" happens for most people at the time of their death, but the point has been a matter of dispute. After all, when Paul speaks of Christians who have died in 1 Thess. 4:13–15, it is not clear that he thinks that they have already encountered Jesus; indeed, the fact that he uses here the euphemism "to fall asleep" (*koimasthai*; cf. Jn. 11:11–14) rather than the normal Greek word for dying (*apothanein*) might be taken to suggest that he understands death as a state of unconsciousness rather than encounter. Although Paul elsewhere does explicitly state that to die is to "be with Christ" (Phil. 1:23), the presence of biblical language that describes death and resurrection in terms of sleep and waking (e.g., Dan. 12:2; Matt. 27:52) raises questions over the status of the dead prior to Jesus's return. In the Western church, the notion of "soul sleep" (i.e., that the dead subsist in an unconscious state prior to the parousia) was definitively rejected only in 1336 in the papal decree

---

[6] Cf. the witness of Jn. 5:27 that the Father "has given [the Son] authority to execute judgement, *because* he is the Son of Man" (cf. 5:22).

Benedictus Deus, which declared that the souls of the blessed "immediately after death … have been, are and will be with Christ in heaven."[7] At the same time, the belief that judgment comes for the majority of individual human beings when they encounter Jesus at death does not negate the Christian belief in the promise of a universal judgment that will follow upon Jesus's return: the biblical "day of the Lord," when "the Son of Man … will sit on the throne of his glory," and "all the nations will be gathered before him, and he will separate people one from another as a shepherd separates the sheep from the goats" (Matt. 25:31–32; cf. Rev. 20:11–12). Belief in a "Last Judgment" therefore remains a cornerstone of Christian confession.

There are, however, two theological problems raised by the idea of a Last Judgment. The first is that the biblical witness often makes it difficult to view the prospect of a final divine judgment of the world as a matter of hope. Isaiah is typical:

> Wail, for the day of the LORD is near;
>   it will come like destruction from the Almighty!
> Therefore all hands will be feeble,
>   and every human heart will fail,
>   and they will be dismayed.
> Pangs and agony will seize them;
>   they will be in anguish like a woman in labour.
> They will look aghast at one another;
>   their faces will be aflame.
> See, the day of the LORD comes,
>   cruel, with wrath and fierce anger,
> to make the earth a desolation,
>   and to destroy its sinners from it.
>   (Isa. 13:6–9; cf. Jer. 46:10)

If that prospect were not dismal enough, Amos specifically rebukes those who would make the day of the Lord an object of hope:

> Alas for you who desire the day of the LORD!
>   Why do you want the day of the LORD?

---

[7] *Benedictus Deus*, in *Compendium of Creeds, Definitions, and Declarations on Matters of Faith and Morals* (ed. Heinrich Denzinger, Peter Hünermann, et al.; 43rd edn.; San Francisco: Ignatius Press, 2012), §1000; a similar position was defended by John Calvin in his first theological treatise, *Vivere apud Christum non dormire animis sanctos, qui in fide Christi decedunt* (1542; later translated into French with the title *Psychopannychie*).

It is darkness, not light;
   as if someone fled from a lion,
   and was met by a bear;
or went into the house and rested a hand against the wall,
   and was bitten by a snake.
Is not the day of the LORD darkness, not light,
   and gloom with no brightness in it?

(Amos 5:18–20)

To be sure, not all will succumb to the terror of the day. The "separation" of people described in Matthew 25 includes the assurance that Jesus will declare to some, "Come, you that are blessed by my Father, inherit the kingdom prepared for you from the foundation of the world" (v. 34; cf. Jn. 5:29), but even here, the fact that the saved no less than the damned are seemingly surprised by the results of this final assize (see Matt. 25:37–38, 44) seems to cast a pall of uncertainty and dread over the whole process (cf. 1 Pet. 4:17).

The second problem is the inverse of the first, for if the vast majority of human beings encounter Jesus – and thus have their eternal destiny decided – at the moment of death, then it would seem that the Last Judgment, far from being marked by uncertainty, will be supremely anticlimactic. While the few "who are left until the coming of the Lord" (1 Thess. 4:15) might be surprised by the consequences of Jesus's return, for the rest it would appear to be superfluous. A little further reflection, however, suggests that there is no reason to suppose that the expectation of an immediate post mortem encounter with Jesus renders the promise of the Last Judgment redundant. Indeed, if the Last Judgment comes later in time, it is prior in significance, because the countless lines of relationship that connect every human life with myriad others across space as well as time means that a definitive reckoning of any individual cannot be made apart from the context of the whole, which will only be known when history comes to an end. Yet the claim that the full and final significance of any one life can only be known at the end of time does not undermine the significance of the individual's encounter with Jesus upon death. The difference between the two may be stated as follows: if one's encounter with Jesus at death reveals that one is saved, only the Last Judgment reveals what it means to have been saved. In light of the incalculable effects of even the most seemingly trivial of sins, only when the full accounting of each person's errors is manifest will the magnitude of God's grace likewise be disclosed – and with it the meaning of the biblical principle that it is only by God's word that we live. As Joseph Ratzinger says: "Even though the definitive truth of an individual is fixed in the moment of death, something new is contributed when the world's guilt has been suffered through to the bitter end. It is at this point that one's final place in the whole is exhaustively determined: after what one might call the solidification in their finished state of all the effects to which one has given rise."[8]

This essential continuity between post mortem and final judgment is suggested by the writer of Hebrews: "just as it is appointed for mortals to die once, and after that the judgement, so Christ, having been offered once to bear the sins of many, will appear a second time, not to deal with sin, but to save those who are eagerly waiting for him" (9:27–28). From this perspective, the Last Judgment is an occasion for hope, not because we deserve the salvation that will there be revealed – for, "If you, O LORD, should mark iniquities, Lord, who could stand?" (Ps. 130:3) – but because God justifies the ungodly (Rom. 4:5). Nevertheless, the warnings of Amos and Isaiah are perfectly justified, for the burden of our sinfulness is such that if we are saved, it can and will be "only as through fire" (1 Cor. 3:15).

HEAVEN

The result of this work of salvation is nothing less than life with God, which is the focus of the third of the traditional "last things": heaven. To be sure, like death, "heaven," too, is synecdoche, for the Christian hope is not for heaven alone but rather for a "new heavens and a new earth, where righteousness is at home" (2 Pet. 3:13; cf. Isa. 65:17; 66:22; Rev. 21:1). Far from envisioning an eschatological future in which life with God means that we "fly away" from earth up to some distant plane, the Bible's climactic eschatological vision is that of "the holy city, the new Jerusalem, coming down" from heaven to earth, accompanied by the divine declaration that "the home of God is among mortals" (Rev. 21:2–3). That this renewal of the whole creation should be abbreviated as "heaven" reflects again the principle implicit in the third petition of the Lord's Prayer: that heaven refers to that realm where God's will is done immediately and transparently – which will extend with Christ's coming to the whole created order, including earth

[8] Joseph Ratzinger, *Eschatology: Death and Eternal Life*, 2nd ed. (Washington, DC: Catholic University of America Press, 1988), 207.

as well as heaven.[9] In this sense, the millenarian insistence that the Christian hope not be consigned to an otherworldly sphere is fully justified, even if the idea of Christ returning to reign within history (following a literal reading of Rev. 20:4–6) has been rejected by most Eastern and Western church traditions.

The comprehensive character of God's redemptive activity at the eschaton is reflected in the Christian confession that life in glory entails the resurrection of the body, for the body is that by which each human being is inseparably linked (albeit with varying levels of immediacy) to all the rest of material creation. Through our bodies we are constantly interacting with the external environment, drawing matter and energy from it and releasing both back into it. Our dependence on the rest of creation includes the cosmological processes long antedating our emergence that gave rise to second-generation planetary systems like our own, as well as the physical, chemical, and biological systems that provide the earth with an oxygenated atmosphere sustaining (and sustained by) unfathomably diverse ecologies of mutually interdependent organisms. Nor are our somatic connections with other creatures merely external: within our own bodies there are as many bacterial as human cells, and their presence is integral to our well-being.[10] To confess that the eschaton is marked by the resurrection (i.e., that life in glory is inherently embodied) is thus to affirm that the vindication of human life (individual eschatology) is inseparable from the vindication of the whole of the material universe (cosmic eschatology), in line with Paul's insistence that "the creation itself will be set free from its bondage to decay and will obtain the freedom of the glory of the children of God" (Rom. 8:21). In this context, Ernst Käsemann rightly notes that for Paul "life always has a cosmic dimension, since it is always integrated

---

[9]   In this context, it is important to note that the promise of a "new heaven" does not refer to the place where God dwells in glory (see Matt. 5:34), since that heaven, as the place where God's will is already done, does not need to be created anew. It refers rather to the physical heavens, which form part of the earthly (i.e., visible) realm that does require renewal (see, e.g., 2 Pet. 3:12–13, where the claim that "the heavens will be set ablaze and dissolve" immediately precedes the promise of "a new heavens and a new earth").

[10] While some earlier studies had suggested ratios of bacterial to human cells in the human body as high as 3:1, the best current estimates suggest a ratio of 1:1, with the bacterial component accounting for around 0.3 percent of total body weight. See Ron Sender, Shai Fuchs, and Ron Milo, "Revised Estimates for the Number of Human and Bacteria Cells in the Body," *PLoS Biology* 14, no. 8 (August 2016): e1002533.

in creation," even if it is also true that "nature plays a very small role" in the apostle's thought.[11]

And yet to affirm that the resurrection of the body is bound up with the hope for a new heaven and a new earth does not mean that the life of glory is simply a continuation of the present form of human existence under new and improved circumstances. As already noted, death (or, for those alive at the time, Jesus's second advent) marks the definitive end of a human life. Resurrection does not change this fact. As opposed to resuscitation – the kind of temporary restoration to earthly life experienced by Jairus's daughter (Mk. 5:22–24, 35–43 and pars.) or Lazarus (John 11) – resurrection does not mean an indefinite extension of life but rather the definitive vindication of a human life precisely as bounded by the limits of birth and death.[12]

But if risen life is no longer sustained by those relationships with other beings that are both the condition of earthly existence and the source of its pain and vulnerability, that does not mean that such relationships are absent, and this for two reasons. First, the risen life is above all a life in relationship with God, whose own triune life, though not a temporally extended series of events, is nevertheless one of mutual relationship in the eternal perichoresis of the divine persons. If in glory we, too, participate in this life, which according to Scripture is love (1 Jn. 4:8), then it follows that glorified existence will include a more profound experience of relationship than we do or can experience now.[13] Second, although in glory we, along with the whole of the new creation, will live by virtue of this primary, divine relationship (that is, "by every word that comes from the mouth of God"), the fact that we will no longer depend on other creatures to live does not mean that we will live without them. For since no creaturely life can be known and celebrated apart from the network of relationships that define it as the life it was, to live in glory is to live in and with the whole of the renewed creation. Once again, individual eschatology is inseparable from cosmic eschatology.

---

[11] Ernst Käsemann, *Commentary on Romans* (trans. and ed. Geoffrey W. Bromiley; Grand Rapids: Eerdmans, 1980), 233.

[12] See Karl Barth, *Dogmatics in Outline* (trans. G. T. Thompson; New York: Harper & Row, 1959), 154.

[13] Maximus the Confessor used the deliberately paradoxical language of *aeikinētos stasis* – "ever-moving rest" – to characterize the life of glory. See his *Quaestiones ad Thalassium* 59 (CCSG 22:53) and 65 (CCSG 22:285); *Opuscula Theologica et Polemica* 16 (PG 91:185A); and *Ambigua ad Iohannem* 67, PG 91:1401A).

HELL

But does this inseparability of one from all mean that all are raised to life with God? The witness of Scripture would seem to suggest not, since it teaches that of those who have died, "some" will be raised "to everlasting life, and some to shame and everlasting contempt" (Dan. 12:2). The churches have traditionally followed this teaching by acknowledging as a possible destiny for human beings the fourth and final of the traditional "last things": hell, defined as "a place of torment, in which [the damned] suffer, according to the degree of their ungodliness, in bodily and spiritual pains, for their sins, eternally."[14] That the Bible (and, more specifically, Jesus) speaks of a place of post mortem torment for the wicked is undeniable (e.g., Matt. 13:49–50; 25:41–46; Mk. 9:47–48; cf. Rev. 20:10, 14; 21:8). Paul, on the other hand, nowhere speaks of eternal torment but rather seems to envision the resurrection as limited to believers (1 Cor. 15:42–44; Phil. 3:11; 1 Thess. 4:13–17) and to view the punishment of the wicked as consisting in their destruction (see Phil. 3:19; 2 Thess. 1:9; 1 Cor. 15:24; but cf. Rom. 2:8–9) – a position that has come to be known in the modern period as "annihilationism." And the situation is further complicated by the fact that still other biblical passages appear to support the idea that all people are indeed saved (Rom. 11:32; 1 Tim. 4:10; Tit. 2:11; cf. 1 Cor. 4:5): the doctrine of universalism or *apokatastasis* (the Greek word for "restoration").[15]

The exegetical debates over the interpretation of these and similar passages remain unresolved and are probably unresolvable. Something of their futility is evident in the often tortured character of arguments on both sides. Among universalists, for example, much energy is spent trying to show that the post mortem torment described by Jesus is not eternal. The effort turns on the force of the Greek word *aiōnios*, which, though rendered "eternal" in most English translations, literally means "of an age," and so might be taken to suggest a long but nevertheless limited period; but such arguments face the difficulty that in

---

[14] Heinrich Schmid, *Doctrinal Theology of the Evangelical Lutheran Church*, §67, 3rd ed. (trans. Charles A. Hay and Henry E. Jacobs; Minneapolis: Augsburg, 1899), 656. While this definition is taken from a Lutheran text, there would be no appreciable difference in one drawn from Reformed or Catholic sources.

[15] The word *apokatastasis* occurs once in the Greek New Testament, when Luke records Peter teaching that Jesus "must remain in heaven until the time of universal restoration [*apokatastaseōs pantōn*] that God announced long ago through his holy prophets" (Acts 3:21). While the sentence is certainly patient of interpretation in a universalist sense, it is less explicit in support of universal salvation than passages that speak directly of salvation being extended to all.

passages like Matt. 25:46 the threat of *aiōnios* punishment occurs in parallel with the promise of *aiōnios* life – and no one suggests that the latter is anything other than everlasting. Contrariwise, those who insist that not all are saved must resort to considerable ingenuity to explain how in the various passages that speak of all people being saved, "all" does not really mean all but only some human beings.

Equally unsatisfactory are efforts to frame the debate in terms of the demands of God's mercy, on the one hand, and God's justice, on the other, as such approaches invariably trade on general sensibilities regarding kindness and cruelty unmoored from specifically Christian theological considerations. When the latter are kept in the foreground, there are good reasons to think that with the topic of hell theology confronts its limits, since fundamental Christian commitments give rise to two opposing theological perspectives on hell that are at once thoroughly compelling on their own terms and completely irreconcilable.

The first of these takes its cue from the doctrine of creation, with its insistence on the unstinting generosity and love by which God both brought the world into being and continues to sustain it in being. Because the utterly gracious character of creation means that no creature could exist for an instant if God's love for it were interrupted (since the creature is sustained by nothing except that love), and because divine wrath would entail such an interruption, evil cannot be regarded as a factor capable of separating any creature from God, whether now or in eternity.[16] Instead, before God evil must finally be regarded as an absolute nullity and hell, correspondingly, as an impossibility; for although sin is real, whatever alienation from God to which it gives rise can be understood as existing only on the creature's side. Consequently, the incarnation neither can nor does change anything in God's relation to the world; it simply reveals in a definitive way God's unbreakable love for it (see Jn. 3:16), which has never been severed and never can be.

And yet as compelling as this perspective may be, its insistence on the absolutely unbroken character of God's love makes it impossible to give forgiveness the place in the divine economy that the gospel message seems to require. The gospel is, after all, the proclamation of the forgiveness of sins: release from the condemnation to which human beings would be justly consigned apart from God's gracious determination to meet the sinner's refusal of life under God with mercy in the saving mission of Jesus. And such forgiveness is genuinely good news

---

[16] See Julian of Norwich, *The Showings of Julian of Norwich* (ed. Denise N. Baker; New York: W.W. Norton, 2005), 67 (ch. 49).

only if the threat of damnation to which the sinner would otherwise be consigned is real.[17] In other words, to insist on the transformation of the sinner's situation before God carries with it, as its presupposition and shadow, the conviction that the alienation from God produced by sin is not restricted to the human side but is a rupture for God as well, such that the same God who promises life to those who receive his grace also intends the destruction of those who refuse it.

The problem here is that however much one may insist that human beings should focus their theological attention exclusively on the will of God as revealed in Christ, the "hidden God" of wrath and condemnation remains the background, and thus – as with any background – invariably comes to appear as the more fundamental reality, from the specter of which the believer cannot turn away in spite (and indeed precisely because) of its inseparability from the confession of Christ as the one who saves from wrath and judgment. The logic of this perspective, too, is unimpeachable on its own terms, since speaking a word of forgiveness presupposes the presence of a genuine fault that requires forgiveness; and yet this emphasis on the reality of God's wrath seems invariably to rob the gospel of its essential content: that God is in no respect other than who God shows God's self to be in Jesus. This tension is visible in the work of Martin Luther, who writes that "we have to argue in one way about God ... as preached, revealed, offered, and worshiped [in Christ], and in another way about God as he is not preached, not revealed, not offered, not worshiped," because to "the extent that God hides himself and wills to be unknown to us, it is no business of ours." And yet as much as Luther insists that this hidden God must "be left to himself in his own majesty, for in this regard we have nothing to do with him, nor has he willed that we should have anything to do with him," Luther's own example shows how difficult in practice it is to keep this advice.[18]

To the extent that each of these two positions pursues to its logical end a central insight into what God has revealed, both accounts are at

---

[17] Julian of Norwich recognizes the problem here: "I toke [based on church teaching] that the forgevenesse of his wrath shulde be one of the pryncypall poyntes of [God's] mercy. But for oughte that I might beholde and desyer, I culde nott see this point in all the shewyng." Julian, *Showings*, 65 (ch. 47); cf. 67 (ch. 49): "oure Lorde God as a neynst [with respect to] himself may not forgeve, for he may not be wroth."

[18] Martin Luther, "On the Bondage of the Will," in *Luther and Erasmus: Free Will and Salvation* (ed. E. Gordon Rupp and Philip S. Watson; Philadelphia: Westminster, 1969), 200–201.

once profoundly compelling and burdened with implications that are theologically troubling. The theological vision of the invariant and unbroken character of God's love for all humankind cuts against the gospel message that Jesus came to secure the forgiveness of sins (Matt. 26:28; cf. Lk. 24:27; Acts 5:31; Col. 1:14) and thereby to deliver human beings from God's wrath (1 Thess. 1:10; cf. Col. 3:6; Rev. 14:9–11). By contrast, the contrasting focus on Christ as the agent of forgiveness who saves us from divine wrath ends up driving a wedge between God and God's word that contradicts the biblical claim that God's word is God (Jn. 1:1; cf. Col. 2:9) and thereby undermines the conviction that what God reveals in Jesus Christ is precisely the divine intention that all people be saved (1 Tim. 2:4; cf. Rom. 11:32; Tit. 2:11).

And yet the ability to identify the shortcomings in each position provides no clue as to how to arrive at a more satisfactory solution to the challenge of reconciling God's revelation in Christ with the power of evil and sin. If neither position is finally satisfactory, the power of the theological insights that fund them both suggest that their respective shortcomings reflect the inherent limits of eschatology rather than any failure in theological imagination. Both presuppose that Jesus is the revelation of the one, true God; however, both also find themselves compelled to acknowledge that there remain things hidden in God that are not revealed in Jesus, so that although in Jesus we see only divine forgiveness and mercy, we have to allow that in Jesus we do not see everything about God. And yet this does not mean that there exists any source of knowledge of God other than Jesus, since it is just the revelation of God's love for us in Christ that defines the content of what remains hidden: namely, the mystery of evil, death, and damnation.

This brings us back to the promise of the inbreaking of the kingdom that was the focus of Jesus's earthly ministry and, correspondingly, the essential content of Christian eschatological hope. The tension in Jesus's own proclamation between the kingdom as at once already "among you" (Lk. 17:21) and as something not yet for which we must pray (Matt. 6:10 and par.) may be taken as an index of the fact that in the present age definitive knowledge of how the kingdom will look eludes us. For although the picture of God we see in Jesus is full – to the extent that to look for God elsewhere than in Jesus is inevitably not to see God at all – it is not final, such that the light of glory in which all will be made plain at the end of the age is not reducible without remainder to the light of grace that has already been revealed. Martin Luther put the problem in the following terms:

Let us take it that there are three lights – the light of nature, the light of grace, and the light of glory . . . . By the light of nature it is an insoluble problem how it can be just that the good man should suffer and a bad man prosper [the "problem of evil" in its typical sense]; but this problem is solved by the light of grace [viz., with its revelation of post mortem punishment and reward]. By the light of grace it is an insoluble problem how God can damn one who is unable by any power of his own to do anything but sin and be guilty. Here both the light of nature and the light of grace tell us that it is not the fault of the unhappy man, but of an unjust God . . . . But the light of glory . . . will show us hereafter that the God whose judgment here is one of incomprehensible righteousness is a God of most perfect and manifest righteousness.[19]

The reason that the light of glory is not reducible to the light of grace is not because the Lord who will come will be anyone other than the Jesus who has already come, but because the final disclosure of what it means for just this one to be Lord remains outstanding. Yet although we do not yet see this Lord "face to face" (1 Cor. 13:12), nevertheless, we do know this: "when he is revealed, we will be like him, for we will see him as he is" (1 Jn. 3:2).

Further Reading

Hart, David Bentley (2019), *That All Shall Be Saved: Heaven, Hell and Universal Salvation* (New Haven, CT: Yale University Press).
Moltmann, Jürgen (1996), *The Coming of God: Christian Eschatology* (Minneapolis: Fortress).
Ratzinger, Joseph [Pope Benedict XVI] (1988), *Eschatology: Death and Eternal Life*. 2nd ed. (Washington, DC: Catholic University of America Press).
Sauter, Gerhard (1999), *What Dare We Hope? Reconsidering Eschatology* (Valley Forge, PA: Trinity Press International).
Schwarz, Hans (2000), *Eschatology* (Grand Rapids: Eerdmans).

---

[19] Luther, *Bondage of the Will*, 331–332.

Part II

Movements

11 Feminist Theology

SHELLI M. POE

In her landmark book, *Beyond God the Father* (1973), feminist theologian Mary Daly wrote that "as the women's movement begins to have its effect upon the fabric of society, transforming it from patriarchy into something that never existed before . . . it can become the greatest single challenge to the major religions of the world, Western and Eastern."[1] Some fifty years later, it remains to be seen whether "the women's movement" might reach this potential. Christian feminist theology has at least begun, however, to challenge lines of thought and practice that have been dominant throughout Christian history and to construct new ways of thinking and living by attending to the experiences of women, along with scripture and tradition.

In this chapter, my aim is to show the impact of feminist theology on Christian doctrine and to suggest areas of thought that would benefit from further feminist treatment. In the first section, I survey the history of feminism, giving particular attention to its religious and theological history. I highlight the diversity of the movement and leading feminist theologians' attempts to grapple with that diversity. In the second section, I offer a summary of some important themes within feminist theology, which have changed the landscape of Christian doctrine. In the third section, I identify a few areas of thought that are ripe for further feminist development.

A BRIEF HISTORY OF FEMINISM

A persistent misunderstanding about feminism writ large is that its adherents wish only to garner equal rights for women: equal pay for equal work, equal job opportunities, equal access to education, and so on. While this focus on equality is certainly true for certain historical

[1] Mary Daly, *Beyond God the Father: Toward a Philosophy of Women's Liberation* (Boston: Beacon, 1973), 13–14.

and political manifestations of feminism, a broader view reveals that many feminists wish to do much more than "add women and stir." To understand the diverse aims and adherents of feminism and to see feminist theology as one manifestation of the feminist movement, we turn to the three "waves" in which feminism has appeared in the ocean of history.[2]

First Wave: Which Women?

The first wave of the feminist movement is generally dated from the late 1700s to the 1920s in England and the United States, where women sought rights to education, to hold property, to employment, and to vote.[3] Their arguments included both an appeal to women's equal humanity and to the need of mothers to educate their children. Mary Wollstonecraft's *A Vindication of the Rights of Woman* (1792), for instance, argues for the education of women in England on the basis of women's shared humanity with men and points out the many ways that women's education would benefit society as whole. Through education, women could become more virtuous citizens, wives, and mothers. As she writes in the dedication of the work:

> The more understanding women acquire, the more they will be attached to their duty, comprehending it, for unless they comprehend it, unless their morals be fixed on the same immutable principles as those of man, no authority can make them discharge it in a virtuous manner. They may be convenient slaves, but slavery will have its constant effect, degrading the master and the abject dependent.[4]

In this way, Wollstonecraft argues that because of the interdependence of each member of society, women's education would be like a rising tide that lifts all boats. The last sentence of this passage may lead the reader to believe that Wollstonecraft would have been focused just as

---

[2] See Margaret Walters, *Feminism: A Very Short Introduction* (Oxford; New York: Oxford University Press, 2005), 6–16.

[3] As Rosemary Radford Ruether notes, however, feminist theology "was not born ex nihilo." For a brief account of proto-feminist writers of the Medieval, Renaissance, and Reformation periods, see "The Emergence of Christian Feminist Theology," in *Cambridge Companion to Feminist Theology* (ed. Susan Frank Parsons; New York: Cambridge University Press, 2002), 4–5.

[4] Mary Wollstonecraft, *A Vindication of the Rights of Woman: With Strictures on Political and Moral Subjects* (London: Printed for J. Johnson, No. 72, St. Paul's Church Yard, 1792), x–xi.

much on equality for women of color as for white women. However, her argument primarily takes its perspective and evidence from a society in which elite white women were physically weak, concerned with beauty and fashion, and had "susceptibility of heart, delicacy of sentiment, and refinement of taste."[5] That is to say, her argument did not adequately take into account the concerns or perspectives of women of color and lower-class white women. Wollstonecraft's focus on upper- and middle-class white women was extended by another early activist, Elizabeth Cady Stanton, who with Lucretia Mott organized the Seneca Falls Convention of 1848. That convention is typically recorded as marking the beginning of the women's rights movement in the United States.

However, Black women had been working for voting rights in the United States since the 1830s in various cities' interracial female anti-slavery societies. In fact, the early women's movement and the abolitionist movement were heavily intertwined. Formerly enslaved activist and itinerant preacher Sojourner Truth (1797–1883), for example, argued that Black men and Black and white women should receive the right to vote simultaneously. While feminist Christian theology as a distinct discipline had not yet emerged during the first wave of feminism, many key figures in first wave feminism drew on biblical themes and made theological claims in the course of making their arguments for women's rights, and Sojourner Truth stands out among them. She includes theological reflection in her famous "Ain't I a Woman?" speech in 1851:

> I have heard the bible and have learned that Eve caused man to sin. Well if woman upset the world, do give her a chance to set it right side up again. The Lady has spoken about Jesus, how he never spurned woman from him, and she was right …. And how came Jesus into the world? Through God who created him and woman who bore him. Man, where is your part?[6]

In this and other speeches, Truth simultaneously points to her own experience as a Black woman and to biblical texts to subvert common Christian narratives about both women's inferiority and Black women's marginalization. Sarah Grimké (1792–1873) and Angelina Grimké Weld (1805–1879) also joined the abolitionist movement to the cause for women's rights and often used biblical and theological reflection in so

---

[5] Ibid., 6.
[6] "Women's Rights Convention. Sojourner Truth," *Anti-Slavery Bugle* (Salem, Ohio: June 21, 1851). Available through the Library of Congress: https://chroniclingamerica .loc.gov/lccn/sn83035487/1851-06-21/ed-1/seq-4/.

doing. Sarah Grimké offered a series of lectures in 1837 on the abolition of slavery and was condemned by the Congregationalist clergy of Massachusetts. She responded, in part, by writing,

> Woman I am aware stands charged to the present day with having brought sin into the world. I shall not repel the charge by any counter assertions, although, as was before hinted, Adam's ready acquiescence with his wife's proposal, does not savor much of that superiority in strength of mind, which is arrogated by man. Even admitting that Eve was the greater sinner, it seems to me man might be satisfied with the dominion he has claimed and exercised for nearly six thousand years, and that more true nobility would be manifested by endeavoring to raise the fallen and invigorate the weak, than by keeping woman in subjection. But I ask no favors for my sex. I surrender not our claim to equality. All I ask of our brethren is that they will take the feet from off our necks and permit us to stand upright on that ground which God designed us to occupy.[7]

Inspiring though such words might be, when Black men were granted the right to vote in 1870 with the passage of the fifteenth amendment, many white women's commitment to justice for Black women was tested and found wanting. In part as a result of white women's resentment that Black men were given the right to vote before them, white women began to more fervently seek women's right to vote while at the same time marginalizing and excluding Black women, often requiring Black women to march behind them in demonstrations, barring Black women from leadership, and in some cases excluding Black women altogether. Black women therefore founded their own organizations. Journalist and activist Ida B. Wells-Barnett (1862–1931), for instance, founded the National Association of Colored Women's Club, which sought both civil rights for people of color and women's right to vote. When the nineteenth amendment was passed into law in 1920, granting all women the right to vote, it remained the case that Black women were effectively barred from voting in the US South. Black women continued to work to secure the voting rights that had been established in the fifteenth amendment, and their work culminated in the Voting Rights Act of 1965.

---

[7] Sarah Grimké, *Letters on the Equality of the Sexes and the Condition of Women* (Boston: Isaac Knapp, No. 25, Cornhill, 1838), 9–10.

Native women in North America and women of color around the world were also active in the struggle against gender-based oppression. For these women in particular, that struggle was heavily intertwined with the oppression they endured because of European colonial expansion across the globe. Gender oppression and colonialism were explicitly intertwined because colonialists used the differences they noticed about how women were treated in other countries in order to evaluate various peoples and motivate their further domination. Estelle Freedman notes that "native practices such as foot binding in China, polygyny in Africa, and the veil in the Middle East provided evidence that so-called primitive peoples needed guidance to elevate women's status."[8] In response, women across the globe have been politically active in opposing colonial rule. Friedman illustrates how independence movements and movements for women's rights often accompanied one another:

> Sarojini Naidu, who worked with Gandhi and in 1925 served as the first woman president of the Indian National Congress, campaigned for the right of widows to remarry and for woman suffrage. During the 1920s Indian women achieved local suffrage and created the All India Women's Conference, which joined Muslim and Hindu women. The members took the lead in arguing for legislation to abolish child marriage by raising the age of consent.[9]

This example illustrates how women of color across the globe have been active in resisting oppression of a variety of sorts, and it is important to remember that such oppression includes that wrought by white feminists. Asian feminist and postcolonial theologian Kwok Pui-Lan notes that "women's contexts, though diverse, are closely connected with one another because of the legacy of slavery, colonialism, and genocide."[10] Kwok is pointing here to the interlocking systems of oppression that characterize women's lives, where gender oppression is joined by racial discrimination, colonial expansion and violence, unjust economic structures, and so on. As such, women of color in the United States and around the world have signaled the need to ask not only about the condition of women in a society but also to ask about which particular women are in view.

---

[8] Estelle B. Freedman, *No Turning Back: The History of Feminism and the Future of Women* (New York: Ballantine, 2002), 97.

[9] Ibid., 100.

[10] Kwok Pui-Lan, "Feminist Theology as Intercultural Discourse," in *Cambridge Companion to Feminist Theology* (ed. Susan Frank Parsons; New York: Cambridge University Press, 2002), 28.

SECOND WAVE: WHICH FEMINISTS?

Feminism became a widely recognized global movement during the second wave of feminism, typically dated from the 1960s to the 1980s. While New Zealand granted women the right to vote in 1893 and Finland in 1906, most women have had to wait until well into the twentieth century to enjoy that right. The United Nations "Decade for Women" propelled women's cause forward from 1975 to 1985, followed by The Beijing Conference on Women in 1995. International forms of feminism are as varied as the people who comprise them and are held together by the concern for women's full human rights. However, many politically active women outside of Europe and the United States during the second wave did not call themselves feminists. Freedman explains that for them, "the term feminism could still evoke a narrow focus on [women's] equal rights," in contrast to "broader human rights and social justice campaigns that address the needs of both men and women in developing countries."[11]

Beginning in the 1970s, Latin American, African, and Asian theologians organized the Ecumenical Association of Third-World Theologians (EATWOT), and in 1983 women theologians founded the Women's Commission of EATWOT, which "supported a process by which Third World women could contextualise their own theological reflections in their national and regional situations."[12] Other organizations for women theologians also emerged during this time. For instance, the Korean Association of Women Theologians was founded in 1980, and African women theologians organized the Circle of Concerned African Women Theologians in 1989. In the United States, the second wave of the feminist movement coincided with the Civil Rights movement, the enforcement of the Voting Rights Act of 1965, and protests against the Vietnam War. In 1971, feminist theologians and biblical scholars gathered at the American Academy of Religion and the Society of Biblical Literature to form a Woman's Caucus.

During this period, feminism became more theoretical and a number of distinct feminist camps emerged, including liberal feminism, radical feminism, socialist feminism, and difference (or cultural) feminism. Liberal feminists worked toward women's equal inclusion and leadership in society. Radical feminists argued for a revolutionary remaking of societal structures. Socialist feminism drew on radical

[11] Freedman, *No Turning Back*, 5.
[12] Ruether, "The Emergence of Christian Feminist Theology," 14.

feminism and added a particular focus on women's oppression within capitalist economic systems. Difference feminists embraced what they identified as the differences between men and women and celebrated women's qualities. Feminist theologian Serene Jones demonstrates that the variety between these four feminist camps illustrates two primary points of contention among feminists.[13] First, feminists are divided on the topic of what makes someone a woman. The conversation has been framed in terms of the nature/nurture debate. Are there character traits that are natural and essential to being a woman, which all authentic women embody? Or is the idea of womanhood socially constructed and therefore changeable? Those who hold the former view are called "essentialists" and those who maintain the latter are called "constructivists." A second difference that emerged among feminists during the second wave concerns the way community is envisioned. The conversation that coalesces around these questions is called the liberal/communitarian debate. On the one hand, liberal feminists claim that the ideal community begins with the individual engaged in a social contract, which has public (i.e., political, legal, economic, etc.) and private (i.e., familial, religious, cultural, etc.) spheres that are kept separate for the good of each. Communitarian feminists, on the other hand, maintain that individuals are always already part of and heavily influenced by specific, existing communities in particular social locations. They usually begin their reflections by providing a "thick description" of a local community, including their diverse and sometimes conflicting values, and advocate interpersonal conversation as a means to establish life together.

Early works in feminist theology reflected the diversity of feminist theory. Valerie Saiving Goldstein wrote a landmark article in 1960, called "The Human Situation: A Feminine View." Therein, she argues that "there are significant differences between masculine and feminine experience and that feminine experience reveals in a more emphatic fashion certain aspects of the human situation which are present but less obvious in the experience of men."[14] Relating this form of difference feminism to Christian theology, Saiving writes that contemporary doctrines of love have "been constructed primarily upon the basis of masculine experience and thus view the human condition from the

---

[13] Serene Jones, *Feminist Theory and Christian Theology: Cartographies of Grace* (Minneapolis: Augsburg Fortress, 2000), 22–48.

[14] Valerie Saiving Goldstein, "The Human Situation: A Feminine View," *The Journal of Religion* 40, no. 2 (April 1960), 101.

male standpoint."¹⁵ She goes on to demonstrate her claim by using the anthropological work of Margaret Mead to analyze the views of Anders Nygren and Reinhold Niebuhr. Radical feminist theology, for its part, found an early leader in Mary Daly (1928–2010). In her early work, she drew on her own Roman Catholic training and Paul Tillich's work (among others) to argue that God should be reconceived as a Verb (Being) who calls forth human liberation. She writes that "the entire conceptual systems of theology and ethics, developed under the conditions of patriarchy, have been the products of males and tend to serve the interests of sexist society."¹⁶ As such, she works on the boundary of both philosophy and theology to "study the potential of the women's revolution to transform human consciousness and its externalizations, that is, to generate human becoming."¹⁷ As these examples show, while second wave feminists were varied in their theories and methods, they nonetheless rallied around gender oppression.

   Further, it continued to be the case that white, educated, middle- or upper-class feminists generally ignored the concerns of women of color and their own white privilege, assuming that one's identity as a woman would be more basic than one's racial identity. As Daly writes in reference to Black theology, "the Black God and Black Messiah apparently are merely the same patriarchs after a pigmentation operation – their behavior unchanged."¹⁸ She maintains that "a transsexual operation upon 'God,' changing 'him' to 'her,' would be a far more profound alteration than a mere pigmentation change."¹⁹ In this way, Daly thinks of gender as more basic to human experience than race. As such, she and other second wave feminists overlooked white women's perpetration of oppression against people of color and their complicity in and privilege gained from systems of white supremacy. Black women who were active in working for women's interests therefore struggled not only for their perspectives to be recognized by men but also by white women. Audré Lorde wrote an open letter to Mary Daly in 1979 that illustrates this struggle. After reading Daly's *Beyond God the Father* (1973) and *Gyn/Ecology* (1978), Lorde writes:

   The history of white women who are unable to hear Black women's words, or to maintain dialogue with us, is long and discouraging.

¹⁵ Ibid.
¹⁶ Daly, *Beyond God the Father*, 4.
¹⁷ Ibid., 6.
¹⁸ Ibid., 25.
¹⁹ Ibid., 19.

But for me to assume that you will not hear me represents not only history, perhaps, but an old pattern of relating, sometimes protective and sometimes dysfunctional, which we, as women shaping our future, are in the process of shattering and passing beyond, I hope . . . . In this spirit I invite you to a joint clarification of some of the differences which lie between us as a Black and a white woman.[20]

Lorde goes on to point out the various ways that Daly's work needs correction. For example, she writes that to imply "that all women suffer the same oppression simply because we are women is to lose sight of the many varied tools of patriarchy. It is also to ignore how those tools are used by women without awareness against each other."[21] What Lorde and other Black women found was that although their concerns over-lapped with white feminists in their efforts, for instance, to establish childcare and address violence against women, Black women's experi-ences and perspectives nonetheless continued to be ignored and/or distorted by a number of white feminists during the second wave. In this way, the concerns of first wave feminism continued alongside the further theoretical diversification of second wave feminism.

Third Wave: Which Identities?

By the 1990s, when the third wave of the feminist movement began, women of color had already begun naming themselves using other labels that are now in use. Feminist theologians are now joined by womanist (Black women) theologians; *mujerista*, Latina, and *mestiza* (Hispanic women) theologians; and women who describe their work in relation to their ethnicities (e.g., Asian women, Asian-American women, African women, Middle-Eastern women). In addition, theolo-gians concerned with gender identity and expression, sexuality, and sexual orientation have initiated lesbian and gay theologies and developed queer theology. While lesbians, in particular, were part of the feminist movement from its early days and have been leading voices in the movement (e.g., Mary Daly, Carter Heyward, Sallie McFague), the particular perspectives and experiences of lesbian women as lesbians had not been put front and center in feminist theology. Carter Heyward and Mary Hunt, for example, argued in 1980 that "the significance of

---

[20] Audré Lorde, "An Open Letter to Mary Daly," found at: www.historyisaweapon.com/defcon1/lordeopenlettertomarydaly.html.
[21] Ibid.

lesbianism warrants critical attention by all feminist theologians. Pushing against the structure of heterosexism, lesbian love represents the antithesis of men's control over women's bodies and, as such, signals a challenge to fundamental tenets of patriarchal religion."[22] Without occluding the importance of lesbian experiences, queer theory subsequently challenged the binary of "heterosexual" and "homosexual," arguing that these categories themselves ought to be recognized as socially constructed.[23] Only in the twenty-first century have the insights and experiences of trans women made significant strides in affecting the field of feminist theology.[24] While women engaged in these diverse forms of theology may be informed by, engaged in, and have a stake in feminist theology, they also claim distinct identities apart from the label "feminist" by self-naming in other ways and sometimes by challenging feminist notions of "womanhood."

Third wave feminist theologians embrace the proliferation of such self-naming and are distinctive for their increased and sustained attention to the intersecting concerns of gender, sex, race, class, colonialism, ethnicity, and sexual orientation. Whereas white, Western feminists in the previous waves of the movement may have dismissed or neglected the experiences and views of women of color, third wave white feminists have characteristically attempted to become educated about and to integrate into their own work the concerns of women of color across the globe as well as lesbian, bisexual, and trans women. For example, in the new introduction to Rosemary Radford Ruether's book, *Sexism and God-Talk*, which was originally published in 1983 and republished in 1993, Ruether writes that "this cross-cultural, multivocal dialogue has enriched my own thinking and exposed its limitations. Such diverse perspectives put my own thought in its appropriate cultural context, as the work of one feminist theologian among others, functioning in an Anglo-American context."[25] Likewise, in 1992, we see Elizabeth Johnson reflecting in her book, *She Who Is*, on her own social position

[22] Carter Heyward, Mary E. Hunt, Burnadette J. Brooten, Clare B. Fischer, Delores S. Williams, and Evelyn Torton Beck, "Roundtable Discussion: Lesbianism and Feminist Theology," *Journal of Feminist Studies in Religion* 2, no. 2 (Fall 1986), 95.

[23] See Kathy Rudy, *Sex and the Church: Gender, Homosexuality, and the Transformation of Christian Ethics* (Boston: Beacon, 1997).

[24] See Siobhan M. Kelly, "Multiplicity and Contradiction: A Literature Review of Trans* Studies in Religion," *Journal of Feminist Studies in Religion* 34, no. 1, Transing and Queering Feminist Studies and Practices of Religion (Spring 2018), 7–23.

[25] Rosemary Radford Ruether, *Sexism and God-Talk: Toward a Feminist Theology* (Boston: Beacon, 1993), xvi.

and her desire to write in a way that embraces the experiences of more women than those in her own location. She writes, "the ecumenical, interracial, and international spectrum of women's theological voices ensures that the ways of speaking about God are many. Within this symphony of voices, sharply discordant at times, my own stance is inevitably shaped by my social location as a white, middle-class, educated and hence privileged citizen of a wealthy North American country."[26] Moreover, she states that for her, "the goal of feminist religious discourse pivots in its fullness around the flourishing of poor women of color in violent situations."[27]

Contemporary feminist theologians are also now recognizing the field as a global phenomenon that goes beyond Christianity. Feminist theologians are to be found in a number of religious traditions, including Judaism (e.g., Judith Plaskow), Islam (e.g., Riffat Hassan), Buddhism (e.g., Rita Gross), and neo-paganism (e.g., Carol Christ). Moreover, Sheila Briggs and Mary McClintock Fulkerson argue that globalization is "the foremost characteristic of the context in which we do feminist theology today."[28] They highlight three features of globalization that have serious implications for women's lives: global capitalism, transnational power dynamics, and condensed cultural flows allowed by rapid communication. Because of these globalizing trends, women's lives are now connected across the globe in unprecedented ways.

Some historians see a fourth wave of feminism taking shape, which began as a response to the gang-rape of an Indian woman in 2012, the 2014 Gamergate harassment campaign, and Donald Trump's 2016 derogatory comments about women during and after his presidential campaign. The 2017 March on Washington and the #MeToo Movement are cited as significant moments in the fourth wave. It remains to be seen how feminist theology will develop in concert with such recent events.

FEMINIST THEOLOGY AND CHRISTIAN DOCTRINE

Like the broader feminist movement, Christian feminist theology is a diverse and varied field about which generalizations cannot easily be

---

[26] Elizabeth A. Johnson, *She Who Is: The Mystery of God in Feminist Theological Discourse* (New York: Herder & Herder, [1992] 2002), 11.

[27] Ibid.

[28] Sheila Briggs and Mary McClintock Fulkerson, "Introduction," in *Oxford Handbook of Feminist Theology* (ed. Sheila Briggs and Mary McClintock Fulkerson; New York: Oxford, 2011), 2.

made. However, there are a number of Christian doctrines that feminist theologians have challenged and about which they have offered constructive proposals. Both the challenges and constructive proposals offered are various in their details, but some shared concerns can be discerned, which have changed the terrain of contemporary Christian doctrine.

First, many feminist theologians are concerned about the way the divine is portrayed in Christian doctrine as masculine, patriarchal (or kyriarchal),[29] and otherworldly. Early on, Daly argued for a reconsideration of the doctrine of God that would avoid divinizing masculinity, since she maintains that "if God in 'his' heaven is a father ruling 'his' people, then it is in the 'nature' of things and according to the divine plan and the order of the universe that society be male-dominated."[30] In short, "if God is male, then the male is god."[31] Instead, Daly offers an understanding of God as a Verb, which points to divine dynamism and activity along with the ability for humanity to participate (i.e., to "live, move, and have our being") in the divine.[32] In 1992, Elizabeth Johnson also challenged commonplace depictions of God in contemporary Christian doctrine by arguing that the exclusive, literal, and patriarchal use of masculine language for the divine is not only oppressive but idolatrous: "It functions to justify social structures of dominance/subordination and an androcentric world view inimical to the genuine and equal human dignity of women, while it simultaneously restricts the mystery of God"[33] Drawing on the work of Thomas Aquinas and the Jewish and Christian Wisdom (in Greek: *Sophia*) traditions, Johnson makes the case for speaking of God as "She Who Is," who can be named Spirit-Sophia, Jesus-Sophia, and Mother-Sophia. Other feminist theologians turn to the work of Julian of Norwich or the Cappadocians, for

[29] In 1994, Elisabeth Schüssler Fiorenza argued that feminists should replace their focus on "patriarchy" with "kyriarchy," which is "the rule of the emperor/master/lord/father/husband over his subordinates." She introduced this term in response to the inadequacy of "patriarchy" to describe the exploitation of women along with those who are not "elite Western educated propertied Euro-American men" and to focus on those who live "at the bottom of the kyriarchal pyramid and who struggle against multiplicative forms of oppression." Elisabeth Schüssler Fiorenza, *Jesus: Miriam's Child, Sophia's Prophet: Critical Issues in Feminist Christology* (New York: Continuum, 2004; originally published in 1994), 14.

[30] Daly, *Beyond God the Father*, 13.

[31] Ibid., 19.

[32] Ibid., 34. Other feminists have also taken up process theology as a way to emphasize this point using a different metaphysic. For example, see Donna Bowman, *The Divine Decision: A Process Doctrine of Election* (Louisville: Westminster John Knox, 2002).

[33] Johnson, *She Who Is*, 40.

example, to envision the divine through a "baffling of gender literalism," that sees God as Mother as well as Father, Christ as Mother as well as Lover, Spirit as Love as well as Lord.[34] By speaking of the this-worldly presence of God the Verb, foregrounding the Spirit, and lifting up Sophia as a suitable name for the divine essence, feminists have helped to raise Christian theologians' awareness of the social and political implications of the doctrine of God and trinitarian thought, and they have contributed to remedying a doctrinal neglect of the Holy Spirit and the Wisdom tradition.

A second doctrinal locus around which feminist theology has coalesced is the person and work of Jesus Christ. Particularly at issue has been the significance of Jesus's maleness for redemption and ordination and substitutionary interpretations of his death. With regard to the first theme, Rosemary Radford Ruether poignantly asks in her 1983 *Sexism and God-Talk*, "Can a Male Savior Save Women?" She famously writes:

> The maleness of Jesus has no ultimate significance. It has social symbolic significance in the framework of societies of patriarchal privilege. In this sense Jesus as the Christ, the representative of liberated humanity and the liberating Word of God, manifests the kenosis of patriarchy, the announcement of the new humanity through a lifestyle that discards hierarchical caste privilege and speaks on behalf of the lowly.[35]

In a different vein but to the same effect, Mercy Amba Oduyoye reflects on African women's Christologies, saying that in Jesus, "they find an affirmation of their personhood and worth in the person of Jesus, born of a woman without the participation of a man. The significance for them is that 'womanness' contains the fullness of 'humanness.' By this they counter earlier assertions that a woman by herself is not fully human."[36] Oduyoye summarizes the view of Rosemary Edet, a founding member of the Circle of Concerned African Women Theologians: "What Edet says about the humanity of Jesus was that it is the humanity of woman, and African women should and do claim Jesus as their

---

[34] Janet Martin Soskice, "Trinity and Feminism," in *Cambridge Companion to Feminist Theology* (ed. Susan Frank Parsons; New York: Cambridge University Press, 2002), 146.

[35] Ruether, *Sexism and God-Talk*, 137.

[36] Mercy Amba Oduyoye, "Jesus Christ," *Cambridge Companion to Feminist Theology* (ed. Susan Frank Parsons (New York: Cambridge University Press, 2002), 164.

liberator."[37] On the whole, feminist theologians have affirmed that Jesus's maleness is not of ultimate significance for his redemptive work. People of any sex and gender may adequately represent Christ in Christian congregations insofar as they continue his ministry. In concert with that view, many Protestant denominations now recognize the call of women to ordained ministry. Although Roman Catholic, Eastern Orthodox, and most evangelical Protestant denominations currently do not ordain women and these groups comprise well over half of the global Christian population, the work of feminist theologians has nonetheless resulted in a large-scale reconsideration of the significance of Jesus's maleness for both redemption and ordination.

As for interpretations of Jesus's death, Black feminist and womanist theologians have been at the forefront of questioning the common interpretation of Jesus's cross as a vicarious atonement for sin. In *Sisters in the Wilderness* (1993), Delores S. Williams reflects on the forced and voluntary surrogacy roles that Black women have played throughout history, in which they have acted as substitutes for others (e.g., as "mammies," field laborers, or sexual objects). Interpreting the cross of Jesus as a substitute for others, Williams argues, serves only to reinforce and valorize Black women's suffering in surrogacy roles. She maintains that "the spirit of God in Jesus came to show humans life – to show redemption through a perfect ministerial vision of righting relations between body (individual and community), mind (of humans and of tradition) and spirit."[38] Williams interprets Jesus's cross as "the response to this invitation by human principalities and power."[39] In 2006, Traci C. West extended Williams's argument in order to show that to some degree,

> atonement theology expressed in church rituals like communion could merge with and inform white people's sense of entitlement. It could teach them that reaping the benefits of forgiveness and absolution ... is due them because of God's intentional sacrifice of a person for their sake. Communion could function as a kind of

---

[37] Ibid., 165. Feminist theologians also highlight women liberators within their own cultures as a way of demonstrating that "women can be fully human and can represent the sort of liberative human we all want to be" (Rosemary Radford Ruether, *Women and Redemption: A Theological History* [Minneapolis: Fortress, 1998], 278).

[38] Delores S. Williams, *Sisters in the Wilderness: The Challenge of Womanist God-Talk* (Maryknoll: Orbis, 1993), 165.

[39] Ibid., 165.

liturgical reinscribing of the privileges of whiteness, possibly fostering a lack of concern for the systemic ways they may benefit from the sacrifice of the health, safety, and well-being of "alien others."[40]

Arguments like these challenge theologians reflecting on atonement theories to take into consideration their effects on the lives of women, and especially women of color. While Jesus's suffering on the cross is recognized by feminist and womanist theologians, its significance lies in the fact that Jesus was willing to risk his life because of his commitment to the coming reign of God. Radford Ruether points to the role that suffering has in feminist theologies: "Suffering is a factor in the liberation process, not as a means of redemption, but as the risk that one takes when one struggles to overcome unjust systems whose beneficiaries resist change."[41] By highlighting the negative effects of substitutionary atonement theory, feminist and womanist theologians have begun to change the landscape of Christian doctrinal reflection on redemption.

Third, feminist theologians have made significant contributions to Christian doctrine by attending to embodiment and creation. Sallie McFague, for example, offered an "ecological theology of liberation" for twenty-first century North American Christians that she argued could "free us from insatiable consumerism and, as a result, liberate others, including the natural world, for a better, healthier life."[42] As this passage suggests, McFague draws economics into her ecotheology, arguing that neo-classical economics and its consumer society disregard two key values: "distributive justice to the world's inhabitants and the optimal scale of the human economy within the planet's economy."[43] To remedy this situation, McFague offers an ecological economic model, which begins with distributive and planetary justice, rather than with competition among individuals.[44] In 2003, Catherine Keller published *Face of the Deep*, wherein she offers an extended reflection on the chaotic waters (*tehom*) of Genesis 1:2, its history in Christian thought, and the "lasting correlation between tehomophobia [i.e., fear of the chaotic waters] and gynophobia [i.e., fear of women]."[45] She presents a

[40] Traci C. West, *Disruptive Christian Ethics: When Racism and Women's Lives Matter* (Louisville: Westminster John Knox, 2006), 124.
[41] Ruether, *Women and Redemption*, 279.
[42] Sallie McFague, *Life Abundant* (Minneapolis: Fortress, 2001), 33.
[43] Ibid., 77.
[44] Ibid., 100.
[45] Catherine Keller, *Face of the Deep: A Theology of Becoming* (New York: Routledge, 2003), xix.

form of panentheism that "retains what all theism desires: a 'Thou' different enough and intimate enough to love and to be loved," and it also affirms "creation as incarnation," where "divinity unfolds 'in' the all .... The all in the divine, the divine in the all."[46] In these ways, feminist theologians are offering new doctrinal insights into the relation between God and the world. Further, ecowomanist theologians have drawn out the correlation between planetary injustice and racism. In 2017, Melanie Harris argued that "earth justice is and has always been a justice priority for black women" because of "the deep value of the earth as sacred, and the interconnection of black women's bodies to the body of the earth."[47] Ecowomanists, she explains, "engage, ecology, religion, and gender and how these interconnections raise important questions regarding the impact of globalization in the lives of women, the impact of climate change on indigenous communities and other communities of color around the planet, in a way that is prophetic and committed to peacemaking in an era of violence."[48] The upshot of ecofeminist and ecowomanist theologies like these is to re-envision the relationships between humanity (and especially its most vulnerable members), the planet, and the divine.

These are just three areas of Christian theology to which feminist theologians have made significant doctrinal contributions. Yet these three areas show the pervasive reach of feminist theologies on central doctrines within the Christian tradition: the doctrine of God, trinitarian thought, Christology, atonement theory, pneumatology (i.e., doctrine of the Holy Spirit), and the doctrine of creation.

AREAS FOR FURTHER DEVELOPMENT

There are at least three areas of doctrine that would benefit from further feminist treatment. The first regards the doctrine of God, and specifically the question of how God ought to be described in relation to "personhood." To my knowledge, no feminist theologians are suggesting that God is "a person" in a literal sense, that is, an embodied being that exists somewhere outside of the universe (seated on a throne, for example). On the other side of the spectrum, neither are most feminist theologians suggesting that God is a purely mechanistic force within

---

[46] Ibid., 219.
[47] Melanie Harris, "Ecowomanism: An Introduction," in *Ecowomanism, Religion and Ecology* (ed. Melanie Harris; Boston: Brill, 2017), 4.
[48] Ibid., 9.

the universe. Between these two extremes, many feminist theologians have offered the idea that the divine is enacted through right relation or that God is the power of right relation.[49] What, exactly, this might mean could be explored in any number of ways. What would it mean for God to be neither an individual person nor an impersonal force, but "personal"?[50] How is the divine "matrix" to be understood in feminist Christian thought? What does it mean to affirm a panentheistic view of the relation between God and the world? While these questions would undoubtedly require feminist theologians to treat ontological matters that many have sworn off, the opportunity is open for a new generation to wade into classically forbidden waters to critically address the question, "What is God?"[51]

Feminist theologians could also beneficially expand their work in the field of ecclesiology (i.e., theory of the church), which has begun in the scholarship of Elisabeth Schüssler Fiorenza, Rosemary Radford Ruether, and Letty Russell, among others. Since the 1980s, feminist Christians, especially from the Roman Catholic tradition, have been part of the Women-Church movement. The movement has been active in the United States and across the globe as small groups of women meet together to worship and converse about their own experiences of being church. In concert with these communities that are focused on ritual and justice, feminist theologians could now ask with Natalie Watson, "whether the theological language and ideas traditionally used by male theologians speak about the church in a way which is meaningful for women and describes the church as a liberating and life-giving reality for women and enhances the celebration of women's being church."[52] Similarly, feminists could explore with Susan A. Ross, "what kinds of organizational structures most enhance love and justice."[53]

---

[49] See Richard Grigg, "Enacting the Divine: Feminist Theology and the Being of God," *The Journal of Religion* 74, no. 4 (October 1994), 506–523.

[50] See Shelli M. Poe, *Essential Trinitarianism: Schleiermacher as Trinitarian Theologian* (New York: T&T Clark, 2017), 95–114.

[51] For an entrance into that discussion, see Lyn Miller, "What Has Divinity to Do with Democracy? Metaphysics, Transcendence, and Critical Theology of Liberation," *Journal of Feminist Studies in Religion* 25, no. 1, Special Issue: In Honor of Elisabeth Schüssler Fiorenza (Spring 2009), 65–83.

[52] Natalie K. Watson, "Feminist Ecclesiology," *The Routledge Companion to the Christian Church* (ed. Gerard Mannion and Lewis S. Mudge; New York: Routledge, 2008), 465.

[53] Susan A. Ross, "Church and Sacrament – Community and Worship," in *Cambridge Companion to Feminist Theology* (ed. Susan Frank Parsons; New York: Cambridge University Press, 2002), 237.

Especially because feminists have been at the forefront of efforts to join ethnography with theology, the field is ripe for further theoretical development in this area. Such theoretical projects are an important bulwark for the practical work already taking place in and among Christian communities that are attentive to women's experiences.

Finally, there is room in the current doctrinal landscape for further feminist work on eschatology (i.e., the doctrine of last things). Most feminist theologies do not offer much by way of reflection on the eschaton, primarily because for feminists it is important to foreground this life rather than focus on another world. Many therefore offer what has been called "realized eschatology," which works to establish the kin-dom of God here and now. A key scriptural passage is Jn. 17:3: "And this is eternal life, that they may know you, the only true God, and Jesus Christ whom you have sent." As important as this insight remains, feminist theological discussion could also benefit from a square acknowledgment of the significance of the notion of an afterlife for many Christians and its force within their lives.[54] Feminist theologians could expand their doctrinal impact by fully explicating their eschatologies in order to show how their work is compatible and/or incompatible with the maintenance of an afterlife, to draw out more fully the implications of feminist theology's focus on the here and now, and to constructively address Christian hope for full redemption and community.

In this chapter, we have seen that feminist theology is a diverse field, corresponding to the diversity and development of the feminist movement as a whole. While women have been reflecting on their Christian faith since the beginning of Christian history, the academic field of feminist theology did not emerge until the second wave of feminism in the 1960s to 1980s, when it became a significant site for doctrinal criticism and construction across the globe. Feminist theologians of all manner of races, ethnicities, classes, societies, and cultures have contributed to the changing terrain of Christian doctrine primarily through their insights related to the doctrine of God (along with trinitarian thought and pneumatology); Christology and theories of redemption (including implications for ordination); and to the relation between

---

[54] For an instructive effort in this direction, see Deanna A. Thompson, "Hoping for More: How Eschatology Matters for Lutheran Feminist Theologies," *Transformative Lutheran Theologies: Feminist, Womanist, and Mujerista Perspectives* (ed. Mary J. Streufert (Minneapolis: Fortress, 2010), 225–236. See also Kathryn Tanner's detemporalized eschatology in, for example, "Eschatology and Ethics," in *The Oxford Handbook of Theological Ethics* (ed. Gilbert Meilaender and William Werpehowski; Oxford: Oxford University Press, 2007), 41–56.

God, humanity, and creation. While feminist theologians have not wholly transformed Christian communities around the world, they have certainly challenged and reconstructed Christian doctrine in significant ways that are sure to have concrete effects into the future.

Further Reading

Coleman, Monica A. (2008), *Making a Way Out of No Way: A Womanist Theology* (Minneapolis: Fortress Press).

Copeland, M. Shawn (2009), *Enfleshing Freedom: Body, Race, and Being* (Minneapolis: Fortress).

Fulkerson, Mary McClintock (1994), *Changing the Subject: Women's Discourses and Feminist Theology.* (Minneapolis: Fortress).

Hampson, Daphne (1990), *Theology and Feminism* (Oxford: Blackwell).

Isasi-Diaz, Ada Maria (1996), *Mujerista Theology: A Theology for the Twenty-First Century* (Alexandria: Alexander Street Press).

Pui-Lan, Kwok, ed. (2010), *Hope Abundant: Third World and Indigenous Women's Theology* (ed. Kwok Pui-Lan; Maryknoll: Orbis).

Schüssler Fiorenza, Elisabeth (1994), *In Memory of Her: A Feminist Theological Reconstruction of Christian Origins* (New York: Crossroad).

12 Theological Interpretation of Scripture

ANDREA D. SANER

Through Scripture, readers encounter the Word of God: this is the central principle of theological interpretation. Such interpretation is teleologically ordered toward knowledge and love of God – however partial that knowledge and love might be on this side of the veil – and reaching out toward knowledge and love of neighbor. Thus understood, theological interpretation is a task not restricted historically or geographically; it is as old as the church and as global as Christians' reading of the Bible, when their reading is oriented toward participation in the divine life.

In addition to being a perennial task of the church, "theological interpretation of scripture" denotes a contemporary movement. In the judgment of one prominent theologian, "the return of biblical scholars to the theological reading of Scriptures, and the return of systematic theologians to sustained engagement with the scriptural texts – in a phrase, the return of both to theological readings of the Bible – is *the most significant theological development in the last two decades.*"[1] To speak of theological interpretation in this way is to identify a contemporary phenomenon: a movement within English-language mainline Protestant, evangelical, and Catholic[2] biblical and theological scholarship. Though there is debate about whether this contemporary phenomenon is a movement, hermeneutic,[3] method, or something else,[4]

[1] M. Volf, *Captive to the Word of God: Engaging the Scriptures for Contemporary Theological Reflection* (Grand Rapids: Eerdmans, 2010), 14.

[2] I use "Catholic" to refer to the communion (i.e., "Roman Catholic") and "catholic" to refer to a wider, unifying impulse among Christians toward other Christians throughout time and place.

[3] S. Porter, "What Exactly Is Theological Interpretation of Scripture and Is It Hermeneutically Robust Enough for the Task to Which It Has Been Appointed?," in *Horizons in Hermeneutics: A Festschrift in Honor of Anthony C. Thiselton* (Grand Rapids: Eerdmans, 2013), 234–267.

[4] Fowl likens theological interpretation to "a large and somewhat chaotic party." See S. E. Fowl, *Theological Interpretation of Scripture* (Eugene, OR: Cascade Books, 2009), x.

I suggest that the range of family resemblances among those who identify themselves as doing theological interpretation, by that wording or
the closely related "theological exegesis," "theological hermeneutics,"
and "theological reading," legitimate its recognition as a loose movement. Not all theological interpreters have all of the traits evident
throughout the family, but they each have some. Further, some of those
who do not identify their work with the movement nevertheless
share some of the family resemblances. This is the case in part because
the trends and predecessors that brought about theological interpretation as a movement have had influence beyond the movement and, in
part, because theological interpretation as task reflects the reading
practices of Christians. Thus, fuzzy boundaries around what constitutes
theological interpretation are to some extent appropriate to the nature,
goals, and historical development of the movement.

   After a brief account of the origins of theological interpretation,
I will describe some of the distinctive features of it – namely, what is
theological about theological interpretation – before attending to theological interpretation's relationship(s) to historical criticism.

ORIGIN OF THE MOVEMENT

Theological interpretation of scripture emerged in the 1990s, as shifts in
the theological disciplines fostered renewal of biblical interpretation,
manifested in collaborative projects including the anthology
Theological Interpretation: Classic and Contemporary Readings (ed.
Fowl) in 1997; "The Scripture Project" of the Center of Theological
Inquiry (Princeton) from 1998–2002, which led to the publication of
The Art of Reading Scripture;[5] and the Scripture and Hermeneutics
Seminar, based in Gloucestershire from 1998–2007 and published as
the Scripture and Hermeneutics series (Zondervan). First, as narrative
criticism of the Bible gained prominence in the 1970s and 1980s, it
brought with it echoes of the kinds of protests against historicism that
were common among new critics decades prior; texts were meant to be
read, not dissected.[6] Second, the growing independence and prominence
of hermeneutics as a discipline in its own right provided professional

---

[5] E. F. Davis and R. B. Hays, eds., *The Art of Reading Scripture* (Grand Rapids:
     Eerdmans, 2003), 1.
[6] S. D. Moore, "Biblical Narrative Analysis from New Criticism to the New
     Narratology," *The Oxford Handbook of Biblical Narrative* (ed. D. N. Fewell;
     Oxford: Oxford University Press, 2016), 27–50.

legitimacy and institutional support for philosophical and theological inquiry into the task of interpretation. Third, the explosion of newer biblical criticisms in the 1970s and 1980s, especially those that forefront the identity, social location, and/or particular concerns of the reader, opened space for theological interpretation; if there can be feminist hermeneutics and post-colonial hermeneutics, there can be ecclesial hermeneutics. Fourth, biblical theology, which Childs declared to be "in crisis" in 1970,[7] continued to be practiced but was much contested; some theological interpreters drew on critiques of biblical theology in order to forge a new path, while some biblical theologians saw the two as naming the same project.[8]

Treier traces the movement's theological patrimony from Karl Barth. Barth's Romans commentary engaged with historical criticism but only as subservient to the subject matter of the text. This focus on the subject matter "resulted in unique attention to the particularity of [biblical texts'] language and theological possibilities, using the mode of conceptual paraphrase that in his own way he found modeled in John Calvin."[9] Barthian influence is evident, variously, in the works of B. Childs, D. Kelsey, H. Frei, G. Lindbeck, S. Hauerwas, R. Jenson and others who in turn fueled the development of theological interpretation, particularly in mainline Protestantism, which has felt the challenges of modern biblical criticisms acutely while retaining stake in academic theology and historical theological traditions.

This genealogy, Treier argues, is complicated by Catholics and evangelicals who have been involved in theological interpretation. While historical criticism came in the twentieth century to be embraced fully by Catholic scholars, giving rise to the need to articulate again the necessity of theological reading, some communities of evangelicals in the United States have been less involved in academic biblical criticism and so have not felt to the same degree the disillusionment that has given rise to the movement. In the United Kingdom, evangelicals have remained more closely connected to universities; Treier observes a fuller embrace of theological interpretation among British evangelicals. Catholic interest in theological interpretation stems not only from a critique of exclusively historical criticism but

---

[7] B. S. Childs, *Biblical Theology in Crisis* (Louisville: Westminster Press, 1970).

[8] See D. J. Treier, "Biblical Theology and/or Theological Interpretation of Scripture? Defining the Relationship," *SJT* 61, no. 1 (2008), 16–31.

[9] D. J. Treier, "What Is Theological Interpretation? An Ecclesiological Reduction," *IJST* 12 (2010), 149.

by Scriptural and ecumenical trends in the spirit of Vatican II and by *ressourcement* theologians including especially Henri de Lubac. Treier connects the retrieval of premodern biblical interpretation to the widespread recovery of ancient Christian practices in American religion in the 1990s, felt within evangelicalism.[10] Catholic biblical interpretation has also retained an important place for spiritual reading throughout its history.

WHAT IS THEOLOGICAL ABOUT THEOLOGICAL INTERPRETATION?

I have suggested that the task of theological interpretation of scripture is teleologically ordered toward knowledge and love of God and that one can identify the movement given the family resemblances among various accounts and acts of theological interpretation. Four of these family resemblances are (1) a theological understanding of the Bible as scripture; (2) prioritization of the church as the location most appropriate to scripture reading; (3) attention to premodern biblical interpretation as resource for modern theological readings; and (4) critical reception of modern historical criticism. The first three of these will be discussed in this section of the essay, and the fourth, in the next.

The Bible as Scripture

As indicated in the name of the movement, theological reading requires the reader to approach scripture as locus of divine revelation and continual source of nourishment for those who attend faithfully to it. We read the Bible theologically because God reveals himself through it, drawing those who attend to the Word by the Spirit into communion with the Father. Thus, scripture is rightly understood within the Triune God's work in the world; the designation "scripture" is not code for a certain kind of human attention (though it does demand a certain kind of human attention). In the words of the English Anglican theologian John Webster, who has been perhaps the single most influential voice on the subject for theological interpretation: "What Scripture is as sanctified and revelatory activity is God's triune being in its external orientation, its gracious and self-bestowing turn to the creation."[11] This is not to say that one ignores human processes of authorship, transmission,

---

[10] D. J. Treier, *Introducing Theological Interpretation of Scripture* (Grand Rapids: Baker, 2008), 39.
[11] J. Webster, *Holy Scripture: A Dogmatic Sketch* (Cambridge University Press, 2003), 9.

and reception of biblical texts in theological interpretation but that one must acknowledge God's providential use of the same in God's reconciling, saving, and sanctifying acts.[12]

Ecclesial Location

If God's use of it in giving himself to be known and loved constitutes scripture as such, then in Christ's body, in union with which we are sanctified by the Holy Spirit, one understands scripture rightly. In the mode of "faith seeking understanding," the reader journeys further into the mysteries of faith through scripture. This is to say neither that only Christians can read the Christian Bible nor that the Bible cannot be read as a wide range of ancient religious texts but that reading Christian scripture as such is an ecclesial act (in addition to whatever else it may also be).

The ecclesial location of the theological interpreter may be sketched in a variety of ways. Sociologically, the church is the location that cultivates the faith and virtues necessary for theological reading. Participation in the church develops in the reader understanding of the text's subject matter through catechesis, worship, prayer, service, truth seeking/telling, repentance, forgiveness, reconciliation, patience, advocacy, and so on.[13] Such pre-understanding of the text does not foreclose the interpretive process but rather renders theological understanding recognizable and intelligible.

Moreover, in the church, readers recognize and participate in the text's effects. The language of "effective history" or *Wirkungsgeschichte* calls to mind the twentieth-century German philosopher Hans-Georg Gadamer's discussion of classic texts as those that shape the pre-understandings of readers across generations, informing the ways that they think about the text's subject matter even if they have not read the classic work firsthand. This way of speaking acknowledges that the significance of past events develops or unfolds over time; the reader grasps the events to which the text gives witness by participating in the stream of its effects.[14] Such participation in the subject matter of the text can also be brought out with striking immediacy. Reminiscent of the way in which Barth argued that the Apostle Paul's concerns should be the contemporary reader's concerns, Joel Green suggests that, for example, "theological interpretation inquires whether we are ready to be the 'you' in whom

---

[12] See M. Levering's essay in this volume (Chapter 4).
[13] See Fowl, *Theological Interpretation*, 64–70.
[14] M. A. Rae, *History and Hermeneutics* (London: T&T Clark, 2005), 135.

James addresses his letter and to be sculpted in terms of this theological vision."[15] Green's "you *are* the addressee of James" is bracing in its directness, drawing attention to the immediacy of the speaking of the Word through the text in the ever-present today of faith. In so hearing and responding by the Holy Spirit, readers are joined to all those who have likewise been so moved by the Spirit across time and place.

Therefore, attention to the ecclesial location of biblical interpretation opens into wider reflection on the nature of the reader in relation to the revealing and saving work of God the Father, Son, and Holy Spirit. This is not simply a question about faith and presuppositions, nor about the reader's social relationships, but about theological anthropology: What is the human reader of scripture? How does the reading of scripture relate to the identity, mission, and end of the human person as *imago Dei*? A fuller account of the reader in the interpretive act requires not only attention to the role of faith and presuppositions and the social realities of ecclesial location but attention to the intellect and will of the embodied soul who reads and the ways reading forms her imagination and desire.[16]

Interlude: Is "Theological" Too Vague?

At this point one may argue that the discussion of the doctrinal and ecclesial locations of scripture and its reading run roughshod over significant questions historically debated in and between Christian traditions. Surely a Baptist will understand the doctrinal location of scripture differently than an Anglican, and a Catholic, the ecclesial location of scripture differently from a Methodist. "Whether in postliberal or evangelical guise, fashionably mellifluous talk of 'ecclesial communities' may conveniently cloak tough questions both of history and of tradition," writes Markus Bockmuehl.[17] Further to, "what is "theological" about "theological interpretation"? one might ask, "what *kind of theology* is entailed in theological interpretation?" To some degree, I sought to answer this question in the origin story: it emerges from a neo-Barthian, mainline Protestant, Anglophone theology, influenced by

---

[15] J. B. Green, *Practicing Theological Interpretation: Engaging Biblical Texts for Faith and Formation* (Grand Rapids: Baker, 2011), 42.

[16] See L. Ayres, "The Soul and the Reading of Scripture: A Note on Henri de Lubac," *SJT* 61, no. 2 (2008), 189.

[17] M. Bockmuehl, *Seeing the Word: Refocusing New Testament Study* (Studies in Theological Interpretation; Grand Rapids: Baker Academic, 2006), 58; quoted in W. Hill, "In Defense of 'Doctrinal Exegesis': A Proposal, with Reference to Trinitarian Theology," *JTI* 14, no. 1 (2020), 21.

the "Yale School" (if ever there was such a thing).[18] But this central current in the movement does not account for the whole of the stream and its tributaries, because theological interpreters converse with the inflections of their particular communities and traditions, even if these distinct inflections are unacknowledged. Fowl reflects, "after participating for fifteen or more years in debates and arguments over theological interpretation, I am beginning to wonder if some of the current arguments over methods and theories arise more from confessional differences than methodological differences."[19] At this point, I simply mark ambiguity regarding the "theological" nature of "theological interpretation." By the conclusion of the essay, I will offer some suggestions for ways forward.

Retrieval of Premodern Biblical Interpretation
At the broadest level, ancient and medieval readings of scripture offer an antidote to modern naturalistic historical approaches and connect to modern theological interpretation with regard to the ends of interpretation. While significant questions remain regarding how to integrate premodern with modern reading strategies, three central commitments or practices of premodern (especially ancient) Christian interpretation nourish modern theological interpretation: reading scripture as a unity, in light of the rule of faith, and according to its literal and spiritual senses.

Unity of Scripture
Whereas much modern historical investigation seeks differentiation between texts (e.g., between the christological portrait of Mark versus Matthew or the theology of P versus JE), theological reading requires attending to scripture as a coherent whole, in the light of faith. That which initially seems to be contradictory may not be so on final analysis. This is not special pleading but appropriate to the unity and the mystery of faith. The mystery cuts both ways, though: if faith is genuinely a mystery into which we are invited to enter and think, then any quick or reductive harmony would be insufficient to reflect it.

It may be said that scripture is a unity because of the coherent story that it tells; scripture's unity may be found within this story.[20] Though

---

[18] M. Root, "What Is Postliberal Theology? Was There a Yale School? Why Care?," *Pro Ecclesia* 27 (2018), 399–411.

[19] Fowl, *Theological Interpretation*, 73–74; quoted in Hill, "In Defense," 22 n. 5.

[20] R. Bauckham, "Reading Scripture as a Coherent Story," in *The Art of Reading Scripture* (ed. E. F. Davis and R. B. Hays; Grand Rapids: Eerdmans, 2003), 27–53.

much of the Bible is narrative, obviously large portions of it are not. The psalms find their coherence in the history of Israel, the letters of Paul, and in the life of Christ. These two stories of the Old and New Testaments in turn converge, as Jesus takes up the history of Israel into himself, fulfilling it. This complex story is also the story of the world, from creation to eschaton, for it is the story of God's loving creation, judgment, redemption, and sanctification of the world, and it is the story in which the reader finds herself. "Nothing falls outside of its scope."[21] So the unity of scripture is also in the unity of its divine author, who providentially orders the many human words of scripture to God's own Word.

The Rule of Faith

The rule of faith, *regula fidei*, is what grounds the unity of scripture. Discussions of the rule often begin with Irenaeus, while the term predates him and the concept further developed in Tertullian, Clement of Alexandria, and Augustine. Fowl concisely introduces the rule:

> Irenaeus develops an account of God's economy of salvation, which has its definitive and climactic moment in the incarnation, death, and resurrection of the Word. By clarifying the economy of salvation in the light of a crucified and risen Lord, Irenaeus can give a coherent account of the various movements of God's economy. This summary account of the whole of God's economy is what he calls the apostolic faith, a faith that is formally represented in the creed. This then provides the framework within which the diversity of Scripture can be rightly ordered so that it can be directed toward advancing the apostolic faith in the life, teaching, and worship of the church – a life, teaching and worship that is acknowledged throughout the world (1.10.1–13).[22]

Irenaeus refers to both the rule of faith and the rule of truth, and in either case, the point is that the rule is the truth (or faith).[23] Whether in scripture or the proclamation of the church (e.g., the creeds), the rule is

---

[21] R. L. Wilken, *The Spirit of Early Christian Thought: Seeking the Face of God* (New Haven: Yale University Press, 2003), 63.

[22] Fowl, *Theological Interpretation*, 29–30.

[23] This point dates at least to D. Van den Eynde, *Les Normes d'Enseignment Chrétien dans la Littérature patristique des trois premiers siècles* (Paris: J. Ducolot, 1933), 283; quoted in L. Ayres, "Irenaeus and the 'Rule of Ruth': A Reconsideration," in *The Rise of the Early Christian Intellectual* (ed. L. Ayres and H. C. Ward; Boston: De Gruyter, 2020), 145–164.

that truth or faith that these expressions provide, and this rule in turn allows the reader to order the reading of scripture toward the apostolic faith. Thus, there is a complex relationship that obtains between the rule, scripture, and the church's proclamation of her faith.

Many theological interpreters have looked to the rule of faith to guide interpretation or at least to delimit its boundaries. This seems appropriate, but attention to the rule as boundary marker, and especially to the creeds as articulating the rule, can unduly narrow the range of interpretive issues one might wish to address theologically. Attention to the rule of faith could serve in two additional ways: first, to garner confidence regarding the central unity of the Christian faith in all its aspects, such that one can think theologically from the particularity of a range of biblical texts into the central mystery of faith – the life of the Triune God – and second, to engage Christian faith in such a way that the reader's attention is turned back toward scripture in its entirety. The logic here is circular, but it need not viciously be so, because it is appropriate that the faith of the church both follows from scripture and leads back to it as an ever-new fount of refreshment for the church's life.

Spiritual Reading, Typology, and Figuration

The convergence of the stories of the Old and New Testaments in Christ suggests a simultaneity of time. Old and New Testament events are joined in the divine economy. In this way, attention to the unity of Scripture leads to reading it spiritually. Within the two-testament canon and the economy of salvation, the Passover lamb, for example, is a type of which Christ, in his salvific offering of himself, is the antitype. In faith, the reader can think the type and antitype together. Such types or figures can be traced throughout the canon: to the slaughtered but victorious lamb in Revelation, extending perhaps back to the ram offering in place of Isaac in Genesis 22, to the good shepherd who lays down his life for his sheep, and so on. Such paths of figures through scripture rely on God's ordering of the sacred text and the Holy Spirit's leading the reader into contemplation of the mysteries of faith through it.

The medieval couplet summarizes the fourfold senses of scripture: *Littera gesta docet, quid credas allegoria, Moralis quid agas, quo tendas anagogia;* "The letter teaches what took place, the allegory what to believe, the moral what to do, the anagogy what goal to strive for." Jerusalem illustrates this: understood literally, Jerusalem refers to the ancient city of the Judeans in the land of Palestine; understood allegorically, Jerusalem refers to Christ's church; morally, it refers to the

Christian soul; and anagogically, heaven, the church triumphant. Therefore, when Isaiah 66 speaks of the laboring city Jerusalem who offers warm milk and consolation to "you," it could be read as referring to (1) the restoration of the sixth-century BCE city on the other side of Babylonian exile, (2) the church as spouse of the Lord and mother of all the faithful, (3) the individual soul who is drawn into the church's life, and (4) the final joy of those gathered into the city of God. The literal is the foundational sense of all the others; no spiritual senses can be had or understood without first engagement with the literal.

Reflection on scripture's literal and spiritual senses leads back toward points (A) and (B) of premodern interpretation: a reading that traces biblical figures, through and/or beyond the intention of human authors, moves through diverse passages of scripture as a unity, providentially ordered by its divine author and ultimately leading toward Christ, the central mystery of the Christian faith. In this way, a reading according to the fourfold senses moves from the diversity of passages in their literal sense to their unity within the Christian faith ("what we believe").

Conclusion

So far, I have highlighted three characteristic features of theological interpretation: attention to (1) scripture within the divine economy, (2) the ecclesial location of scripture, and (3) premodern interpretation. I have also suggested that the first two of these features are weakened by failure of attention to the historic Christian traditions and specific communities in which theological interpreters find themselves. Appreciation and use of premodern interpretation also look different across lines of denomination, confession, and/or communion, but it may also offer a partial antidote to this weakness. In particular, a robust understanding of the rule of faith requires a thick account of interrelationships between scripture, reading, and the church's proclamation of faith, and thus the space to inquire anew into how doctrinal claims follow from scripture and lead back to it. Extended reading within a particular time frame or corpus of a premodern Christian writer may form the theological interpreter's imagination to perceive interpretive possibilities present in the church's reading but sidelined by modern biblical criticisms.

HISTORY AND HISTORICAL CRITICISM

Theological interpretation of scripture has coalesced around a shared critique of historical criticism, owed in part to the debts of narrative biblical criticism to new criticism and of theological interpretation to both, even while divergent understandings of the necessary degree and kind of critique have persisted. Yet, on the whole, the movement seems to have shifted toward greater recognition of the – albeit limited – value of historical critical methods. The contrast between the Brazos Theological Commentary on the Bible, with its first published volume in 2005, and the T&T Clark International Theological Commentary (2016–) illustrates this shift. While volumes in both series are diverse, Reno, in the series preface of the former, makes clear that authors were not chosen on the basis of their historical and philological knowledge but as those who could best address the ways that Christian doctrine clarifies the biblical text. By contrast, Allen and Swain suggest that authors of the latter are chosen for "their capabilities as both exegetical and dogmatic theologians, demonstrated in linguistic and literary facil-ity, creedal and confessional clarity, and an ability to relate the two analytic exercises of dogmatic reasoning and exegetical reasoning."[24] In what follows, I describe how historical methods offer discrete tools and aims that can aid theological interpretation. This can enable theological interpreters to critique any totalizing or naturalizing claims of historical criticism while recognizing the value of some of its strategies and goals.

Theological interpretation, I have argued, is reading scripture with the aim of receiving the Word of God, through whom God draws readers into knowledge and love of himself. However, this aim is distinct from the ends toward which historical critics work, for example, knowledge of life in Persian-period Judah or in the Johannine community, under-standing how priestly editing has influenced the literary shape of the Pentateuch, identifying the semantic range and/or etymology of a word in its ancient setting, dating texts and locating their origins geographic-ally, and so on. Each of these tasks may be performed with theological sensitivity and, further, one might argue that any of these tasks supports the wider aim of theological interpretation. At the same time, some theological interpreters prioritize literary methods over historical ones. These too can serve some discrete aims within theological interpret-ation more broadly. Theological interpretation as a task, therefore, refers to the aim or goal of interpretation rather than a particular method, and theological interpreters may draw on a range of different historical- and literary-critical methods depending on many factors

---

[24] R. M. Allen and S. R. Swain, "Series Preface," *T&T Clark International Theological Commentary* (London: T&T Clark, 2016–).

including which are most appropriate to diverse biblical texts and the occasion and audience of diverse interpretive acts.

Still, not all pursuits of historical aims are theologically open. This can be seen in a distinction sometimes made between historical criticism proper and historical-critical methods. Historical criticism proper has been considered a distinct aim used in relation to texts that purport to be history-writing; the critic offers an alternative account of that history viewed more authoritative and uses this account to judge the biblical text. In contrast to this, historical-critical methods offer a range of tools for understanding the ancient biblical text in its historical setting, according to the intentions of its authors and editors. Textual, philological, literary, archaeological, and other types of analyses may be employed for this purpose. Toward the ends of theological interpretation, or indeed any aims of reading the Bible, historical criticism proper must be suspect, but historical-critical methods and their discrete aims are beneficial, if not also necessary, for theological interpretation. "Historical critical reconstructions can illumine the biblical text but cannot, if interpretation is to succeed, become a norm that displaces the biblical text."[25]

Often in response to this, theological interpreters focus on the narrative and/or textual mediation of history and an approach to biblical interpretation that stresses the biblical text's world-absorbing character. This insight may be associated with the work of Hans Frei, who, in *The Eclipse of Biblical Narrative*, argues that in the eighteenth and nineteenth centuries, biblical scholars and people generally lost the ability to read the Bible as realistic narrative as they became increasingly concerned about the reference of the text to something other than itself. In contrast to this trend, Frei sought to restore the integrity and realism of biblical narrative within biblical interpretation. The text does not neatly describe the facts of the world or history as they were but rather includes the evaluation of the speaker, writer, or hearer. Through the text, the reader perceives the world truthfully. In this broad category, I would place, for example, the different approaches of Richard Briggs, who explicitly draws on Frei's distinction between descriptive and ascriptive realism to read Daniel in light of the insight that the author was not trying to be historically accurate but to offer an alternative to the empire's account of reality, and of Joel Green, who draws broadly on

---

[25] H. Boersma and M. Levering, "Introduction," in *Heaven on Earth? Theological Interpretation in Ecumenical Dialogue* (Oxford: Wiley-Blackwell), 5, summarizing the perspective of Francis Martin.

insight into the perspectival nature of historiography, to suggest "a narrative representation of historical events that by definition must focus on the narrative of Acts itself, not on the events to which this narrative is able only partially to bear witness."[26]

One question that can be raised in response to such a narrative understanding of history is whether it is sufficiently realistic. The subject matter of the text may have a tendency to slip into the narrative itself.[27] At least one disciple of Frei argues for some qualification of a thoroughly perspectival reconsideration of historical narrative: Rae argues that Luke the Evangelist makes clear that, while knowledge of the resurrection of Christ spreads because of the testimony of those who believe it, the resurrection of Christ precedes the belief of the apostles and is not contingent on the latter. Whether the apostles come to faith on the road to Emmaus or not, Jesus Christ is risen. They do come to faith, however, through an encounter with Christ that changes their interpretation of what was accessible to their senses already: the empty tomb.[28]

Another way to state this insight is through the language of the Second Vatican Council's document on divine revelation, *Dei Verbum*: "This plan of revelation is realized by deeds and words having an inner unity: the deeds wrought by God in the history of salvation manifest and confirm the teaching and realities signified by the words, while the words proclaim the deeds and clarify the mystery contained in them."[29] Here, the interrelation of words and deeds preserves the integrity of deed as distinct from word. The unity of deeds and words is divine providence, which orders history toward its *telos*. Therefore, properly understood, history is not "one damned thing after another" but has an intelligibility. This intelligibility is one not only of chains of natural causes but in the openness of temporality to its Creator. Such providence does not override creaturely freedom but enables the possibility of true freedom: creaturely participation in the divine life.

---

[26] R. Briggs, "A Test Case in Ascriptive Realism: The Quest of the Historical Daniel and Its Complex Relationship to the Practices of Scriptural Interpretation," *JTI* 14, no. 1 (2020), 41–59; Green, *Practicing*, 51.

[27] See Healy's critique of P. Ricoeur in M. Healy, "Behind, in Front of ... or Through the Text? The Christological Analogy and the Lost World of Biblical Truth," in *"Behind" the Text: History and Biblical Interpretation* (Grand Rapids: Zondervan, 2003), 185–186.

[28] Rae, *History and Hermeneutics*, 83.

[29] www.vatican.va/archive/hist_councils/ii_vatican_council/documents/vat-ii-const_19651118_dei-verbum_en.html.

In sum, historical criticism challenges theological interpretation less with the tools it offers, which may serve the theological aim of receiving and responding to the Word of God, and more in the (anti-) theological and philosophical commitments that ground some pursuits of its incremental aims. Regarding historical criticism, Joseph Ratzinger/Pope Benedict XVI defends it as "an indispensable tool,"[30] appropriate to our historical moment. "Modern criticism remains a starting point for those who are modern," reflects Legaspi on Ratzinger's approach. "This need not be celebrated, but neither should it be ignored."[31]

As Cardinal, in his 1988 Erasmus lecture, Ratzinger suggested that the work of finding a way forward that does "justice to the irrevocable insights of the historical method, while at the same time overcoming its limitations and opening it up to an appropriate hermeneutics ... still requires the work of at least another whole generation."[32] The same could be said today. "What we need," stated Ratzinger, "is a criticism of the criticism ... a self-critique of historical exegesis that can be expanded into a critique of historical reason that both carries on and modifies Kant's critiques of reason."[33] Legaspi argues that Ratzinger's approach is distinctive in its "metacriticism," in his desire to see the history of biblical criticism as "spiritual history," in which scholarship "participates in the human condition and reflects the life orientation of individuals, societies, and cultures, either toward or away from God."[34] Greater attention to the limitations of our presuppositions given our historical situation is necessary in an ongoing way to prevent the overreach of certain types of interpretive acts, to give both historical and theological aims their due place in biblical interpretation.

Several theological interpreters have taken up this metacritical task.[35] It is beyond the scope of this essay to offer a historical study on

---

[30] J. Ratzinger [Pope Benedict XVI], *Jesus of Nazareth: From the Baptism in the Jordan to the Transfiguration* (trans. Adrian J. Walker; New York: Doubleday, 2007), xiv, xvi.

[31] M. C. Legaspi, "Scripture: Three Modes of Retrieval," in *Theologies of Retrieval: An Exploration and Appraisal* (ed. D. Sarisky; London: Bloomsbury T&T Clark, 2017), 171.

[32] J. Ratzinger, "Biblical Interpretation in Conflict," in *Opening up the Scriptures: Joseph Ratzinger and the Foundations of Biblical Interpretation* (ed. J. Granados, C. Granados, and L. Sánchez-Navarro; Grand Rapids: Eerdmans, 2008), 7–8.

[33] Ratzinger, "Biblical Interpretation in Conflict," 8.

[34] Legaspi, "Scripture," 169.

[35] E.g., Bowald, *Rendering the Word*; M. C. Legaspi, *The Death of Scripture and the Rise of Biblical Studies* (Oxford: Oxford University Press, 2010); M. Levering, *Participatory Biblical Exegesis: A Theology of Biblical Interpretation* (Notre Dame, IN: University

par with these or even to weigh their relative merits. Instead, I will simply make two observations. First, the need for metacriticism is ongoing because historical criticism is itself a moving target. Contemporary historical criticism may be less indebted to a naturalistic pursuit of historical facts over against the perceived contamination of traditions and their texts and more concerned with the presence and use of power and authority behind, in, and through the biblical text, which carries its own philosophical presumptions. Arguably, theological interpreters can and should concern themselves with the political character of texts and their interpretation as aspects of neighborly love and so ordered toward the goals of theological interpretation. Yet remarkably little has been written on theological interpretation and postcolonial criticism given the prominence of the latter in academic study of the humanities today.[36]

Second, any "criticism of the criticism" will need to be clear about its own location. For all of the gains and inspiration theological interpretation has received from Barth, this theological heritage also has its limitations. Following Frei, one interpreter states that, in direct contrast to what arose in modern hermeneutics, "Christ is not to be understood in the light of all else we think that we know about history. All else, rather, is to be understood in the light of Christ."[37] Christians absolutely should understand everything in light of Christ. But in the context of considering academic historical study, such a tendency to think theologically "all the way down" – perhaps a correlate of a Barthian allergy to philosophical thinking as such – may make it difficult to see how historical arguments included within theological interpretation stand as truly historical arguments, having integrity in their own right. This is not to say that historical methods are comprehensive in their own right; they are partial, and good use of them will acknowledge their limits and openness to revelation.

In sum, I have suggested that a range of historical critical tasks are not antithetical to the final aim of theological interpretation. Yet historical work leading to theological interpretation needs to avoid two pitfalls. On the one hand, it must avoid all kinds of naturalism. On the other hand, it must avoid so thoroughgoing a theological approach that

---

of Notre Dame Press, 2008), 17–62; Rae, *History and Hermeneutics*; D. Sarisky, *Reading the Bible Theologically* (Cambridge: Cambridge University Press, 2019), 151–187.

[36] Two exceptions to this are Briggs, "A Test Case"; and Treier, *Introducing*, 157–186.
[37] Rae, *History and Hermeneutics*, 153.

historical arguments do not have integrity in their own right, as historical arguments. Historical approaches must be theologically open but not so overtaken by theological aims that they cease to exist. One way theological interpreters can guard against the former is through "criticism of criticism," by which historical reason can be purified and rendered more appropriate to theological aims. As historical criticism changes, the need for this criticism of the criticism continues. One way theological interpreters can guard against the latter is by continuing to read widely in historical disciplines. Historical aims of biblical scholarship relate to theological interpretation both in their own right – by demonstrating the ways in which history is itself intelligible – and by providing background for understanding the mystery of God's action in history.

CONCLUSIONS, REBUTTALS, AND QUALIFICATIONS

The movement of theological interpretation of scripture lacks sufficient attention to its own theological and philosophical grounds, which results in superficiality regarding what is "theological" about it and how to incorporate historical aims within it. Close attention to the complex relationships between the unity of scripture, the church's proclamation of faith, and reading strategies that inhere in premodern interpretation could sharpen theological interpretation theologically. I have also advocated for ongoing criticism of historical criticism, with particular attention to power and authority, together with wider use of a range of historical- and literary-critical methods. Finally, for all of the ink spilled trying to define theological interpretation, there is a marked lack of discussion of its origins.[38] Further exploration of the origins of the movement of theological interpretation of scripture could enable the movement to grow through self-criticism and recognition of affinities between theological interpretation and movements in related fields.

By way of conclusion and in order to qualify these recommendations for theological interpretation, I offer two potential rebuttals to the arguments I have made above. The first observes the lack of biblical interpretation in this essay: "You are asking for a lot of prolegomena. Shouldn't theological interpretation just get on with the task of actually reading the Bible, and work out its internal disagreements along the

---

[38] One exception to this is Daniel J. Treier. See especially Treier, "Ecclesiological Reduction."

way? Why didn't you give us any extended readings of passages?" Now, I do think theological interpreters should "get on with it"; the movement of theological interpretation of scripture is nothing at all if we do not actually read the Bible. This is why I began with theological interpretation as a perennial task of the church. I mean only to observe that this kind of "just get on with it" argument may mask a biblicism that – while laudable for attending faithfully to the biblical text – does not get to the root of interpretive disagreements. However, the above recommendations regarding attention to premodern interpretation, perhaps through close discipleship of one Christian writer or time period, and to substantial and sustained use of a range of historical- and literary-critical methods will be best conducted with close attention to particular biblical texts and their interpretations. The rubber always meets the road in the act of reading.

A second rebuttal against my account of theological interpretation might suggest that it is rather too confessional. "Is not ecumenical renewal a main *benefit* of theological interpretation of scripture?" one might argue. "Why rehash well-worn debates?" In a recent essay, Hill references C. S. Lewis's analogy in *Mere Christianity*:

> I hope no reader will suppose that "mere" Christianity is here put forward as an alternative to the creeds of the existing communions – as if a man could adopt it in preference to Congregationalism or Greek Orthodoxy or anything else. It is more like a hall out of which doors open into several rooms. If I can bring anyone into that hall I shall have done what I attempted. But it is in the rooms, not in the hall, that there are fires and chairs and meals. The hall is a place to wait in, a place from which to try the various doors, not a place to live in.[39]

Drawing on this metaphor, Hill observes in the case of theological interpretation, "a thriving hermeneutical and methodological conversation taking place in the hallway; there is rather less noise coming from the particular rooms of the house."[40]

I have aimed to show in this essay why I think Hill's observation is correct. But the observation can be overstated. Both the hallway and the rooms have their purposes. If one only ever talks to those who have their home in the same room, one may be tempted to think that that which is common among various rooms is the sole property of one of them.

---

[39] C. S. Lewis, *Mere Christianity* (New York: Macmillan, 1943), xi.
[40] Hill, "In Defense," 22.

Theological humility is one gain of ecumenical engagement. Many – perhaps especially those of us who have lingered awkwardly in this doorway, then that one, for some time – have found hallway conversations crucial to our development as theological interpreters in any tradition. To speak only in the hallway is to gloss over important interpretive questions and to lose the depth and richness of traditions built to live in, but this does not lessen the importance of the hallway in its own right.

Further Reading

Allen, M., and S. R. Swain, eds. (2016–), *T&T Clark International Theological Commentary* (London: T & T Clark).

Boersma, H., and M. Levering, eds. (2013), *Heaven on Earth? Theological Interpretation in Ecumenical Dialogue* (Oxford: Wiley-Blackwell).

Fowl, S. E. (2009), *Theological Interpretation of Scripture* (Eugene, OR: Cascade Books).

Journal of Theological Interpretation 14, no 1 (2020).

Rae, M. (2005), *History and Hermeneutics* (London: T&T Clark).

Reno, R. R., ed. (2005–2020), *Brazos Theological Commentary on the Bible* (Grand Rapids: Brazos).

Treier, D. J. (2010), "What Is Theological Interpretation? An Ecclesiological Reduction," *IJST* 12, 144–61.

Vanhoozer, K. J., C. G. Bartholomew, D. J. Treier, and N. T. Wright, eds. (2005), *Dictionary for Theological Interpretation of the Bible* (Grand Rapids: Baker Academic).

13 Radical Orthodoxy

CATHERINE PICKSTOCK

The theological movement known as Radical Orthodoxy arose in the late 1990s as a small group of University lecturers and research students who met for seminars, to discuss papers responding to various cultural and philosophico-theological circumstances. What began as a small discussion group gradually expanded into a variegated network of scholars whose views were not always aligned with one another but who shared a commitment to exploring the value of pre-modern metaphysics in problematising contemporary philosophical and theological questions. The movement is not a singular edifice comprising individuals of the same opinion in all matters but has been described as a theological idiolect or style of approach, constructive and critical at once. In what follows, I will outline the cultural and theological context in which the movement arose and then enumerate the central characteristics of a 'radically orthodox' approach, insofar as that may be singularly identified, before suggesting areas for future development.

HORIZONTAL PARTICIPATION

What was the cultural context that led to the critical theological movement known as Radical Orthodoxy? It arose in response to the sense that one is today encouraged to imagine oneself as an isolated observer of objective reality, from within one's subjective watchtower. Each one of us, although isolated, surveys the same *extensio*. We check our observations against those of more expert observers who aggregate and test them. Otherwise, we are creatures of need and obscure promptings. Our requirements for shelter and food can be to an extent aggregated and regarded objectively. Systems grow for the efficient management of these requirements: a tangle of roads and cables crossing the tundra and adding a second layer of objectivity that can be expertly discussed by economists and other social scientists.

What remains of one's own self are quirks of character and vicissitudes of choice. All these need to be managed and coordinated by the protection of private spaces and the coordination of desires and profit-seeking through the 'free market'. Hovering between the external, objective world and the internal, subjective world lies the mysterious realm of 'fashion' that dictates everything from clothes to acceptable political opinion. Fashion, one might say, is the tribute that alienation from nature is forced to pay to our participation within natural forces that we do not command and do not understand.

The accepted standard for science is 'what works'. And the 'working' that is sought concerns the greater ease and satisfaction of needs and desires, aggregated and averaged by the dictates of fashion. A marginal area for public debate nonetheless remains: a contestation of value concerning the boundaries of freedom of choice and the priorities and efficiency of economic distribution. Democracy, itself limited to infrequent mass consultation of the people, manages this surplus to the rule of science: a surplus, however, whose extent increasingly diminishes in the face of the state and the market and their fusion.

Those who are suspicious of this, rightly raise the question of power. Who tends to benefit from the current outlook and the current system? The answer is the small number who combine the fortune of birth with the fortune of receiving a sophisticated education in the requisite set of experimental and informational skills. Objectivity and detachment give people a subjective advantage in the course of their lives. And the meaning of these lives would seem to be the thrill of power, of increased self-determination and the determination of others, along with the increased means to satisfy one's appetites and indulge one's whims. It is noted that the monopolisation of power tends to ravage nature through the unlimited range now granted to greed and seizure.

But the protests against the hoarding of power by a few do not seem to question power as an ultimate value. These protests desire its equitable distribution: a greater democracy of isolated subjects, all able to agree on what is objectively true but reserving to themselves citadels of autocracy over their own lives.

In short, not merely our philosophy but also our lives and social order are dominated by epistemology. It is assumed that there is a uniform flattening of things into the terms of the same measure. Everything exists equally, and how it exists is an accidental outcome of inexorable but meaningless natural forces. We know little of this existence, other than how it appears to us and how we frame it. In this way, knowledge has displaced being. And yet one assumes a reserve from all that one claims to know. What one knows is the natural, insofar as it can be known. But we ourselves as knowers do not really belong to irrational nature but exist purely beyond it, for otherwise our knowledge of nature would not itself be pristine. Exactly how one's mental understandings are correlated with the natural world remains obscure. The issue can be handled by implausible philosophies that try variously to reduce the mind to random natural processes, thereby abolishing it and cutting the ground of scientific objectivity from beneath our feet. Or else by idealisms that apportion everything to our subjectivity, which might be illusion, or else to a kind of lifeless computing, which fails to explain the manifestations of matter, or embodiment and life.

This question of correlation is often sidestepped and avoided. The social rule of epistemology assumes that reality is univocal, can be literally 'represented', is governed by merely efficient causality, and enacts pre-given logical possibilities. Everything outside these frameworks is less than real and subject to reduction, even though one supposes that one's feelings have real weight – that consciousness, love, beauty, and affinity are not merely fantasies.

The epistemological attitude, however, is not really a natural one. It is rather one of a strange kind of narcissism. One does not see one's own passions reflected in the waters, but nonetheless one sees one's docketing of reality mirrored on screens, and one ignores the way in which this assumption favours one's exercise of control over nature and the control of a few human beings over most others.

These structures do not reflect the way the world spontaneously is. Since we are embodied, we are inside our surroundings; each of us is part of its panoply. One thinks and acts with one's whole body, and yet one's feet are as distanced from oneself as the rocks upon which they tread. Indeed, one learns more about oneself and about reality also from the rocks that one traverses, breaks up, re-lays, hurls about, or sets up as symbolic monuments. There is nothing, including the most distant stars viewable through a radio telescope, that one can see unless it is thereby rendered in some sense part of one. I see the stars because they also see me; I think the stars by thinking something star-like.

The phenomenon of embodiment also points in an opposite direction. If we think the world by being in the world and thinking with the world, then we are in the world because we can sense, feel, and think it. Later, by a strenuous effort normally lasting centuries, we come to suppose that there is a cold meaningless world lying before us indifferent to our human concerns. But this takes an effort of reflection, as well as arbitrary bracketing, engendering the narcissism already spoken of. Why would one suppose that one's quantification of reality is a better clue to its inner character than one's feelings about the real? For a geometric measure is indifferently felt: its exact repeatability causes one to invest this measuring with unique objectivity. More instinctively, one does not detach one's feelings of appreciation or fearfulness, one's registering of beauty and terror from the things themselves about which one feels. For they are never manifest outside one's reactions to them. Naturally, one sees a mountain as a threat or as a promise, a tree as a riddle or a warning, flowers as particular kinds of announcement of joy or as yielding important medicines or dangerous poisons. In short, one participates in one's surroundings.

The 'critical' response to this supposedly primitive attitude is that it is fallacious – a projection upon nature of our human sensations, just as we are falsely deluded in supposing that nature has oracular concern for human beings. But the meta-critical counter-response would be to ask about the status of human sensations in the first place. In what way are one's sensations and feelings merely one's own? Is it not rather the case that one's continued self-awareness is composed of the skein of these feelings and sensations that are always qualitatively textured in a particular if inexpressible way? One's most basic responses to things are neither detached empirical observations, nor things welling up from within, much less deliberate choices or selections. We have no warrant to suppose that the manifestness of reality is not an original and indefeasible aspect of that reality.

When one has reached this point of counter-reflection, one might see that one's access to nature does not lie outside oneself, in other creatures such as plants and lizards and weasels, whose inner character one can but analogously guess at. Rather, one's access to nature lies within oneself as a living, breathing, and feeling being. Why would one imagine that the way in which one experiences oneself affords no clue to the reality of the real? If nature can issue in human beings, and thereby 'humanise', this reveals nature's deepest capability. And it is more adequate to explain the lesser in terms of its tendency towards the higher, than the other way round. For every reductionism abolishes what it is trying to explain, denying appearances.

This is not to deny that one experiences reality from without as well as within. Indeed, there is no pure interiority, even as one cannot exercise human superiority without a kenotic attention to the lesser capacities of earth, sky, and animal instinct that one does not possess to the same degree of perfection. Life, as the Radical Orthodoxy thinker Conor Cunningham has argued, is mixture; it lies in the middle, in the same way that one's thoughts and feelings are an interplay between what lies outside one and one's own modifying responses. There is, by contrast, no pure foundation, either without or within, just as the depths do not ground the heights, and yet the heights cannot dispense with the depths.

Reality constantly comes upon one. One's thoughts arise without one's prompting and yet one's existing habits allow one further to probe one's thoughts, through a searching desire further to shape and perfect them. This is free will: one's being led by a desire for truth and beauty that can be fulfilled in multiple, variegated ways. It is not pure choice or imposition or something of which one is in control. Indeed, if there were no controlling providence, no directing fate, then paradoxically there would be no free will either.

The mystery of manifestation is as old as the mystery of being – together with the mystery of one's awareness and self-awareness before this mystery and one's ability to intervene like a magus within it. Given that manifestation, awareness, and self-awareness are primordially inseparable, one has reason to suppose that the living and the psychic may be a property of everything, in such a way that human spiritual intelligence is the acme of finite being as such.

VERTICAL PARTICIPATION

It is this non-alienated stance towards reality that lies at the core of a radically orthodox perspective. Reality is something that one shares in and that is perpetually exchanged. It presents itself in complex analogical degrees of varying intensity. If certain things did not stand out more than others, one would see nothing at all. And reality cannot be mimetically copied in order to ensure its truth. Rather, human beings are in the truth when they further develop the beauty of what has already been given to them. Efficiency is not the whole of causality: things exist because they possess a 'shape' or form that holds them in place and includes a natural tendency in a certain direction and a natural set of habitual relations and responses to all other things. When something is acted upon, it appropriates that influence according to its own guise: although somewhat determined from without, it also renders its own mode of spontaneous response. This means that reality is not exhaustively governed by pre-existing possibility. The actual has a certain priority because it arrives ever-again unpredictably as the new, as the unforeseeable and ungovernable event. Yet at the same time, the actual has no priority in turn over the moving and the dynamic. It includes a potential for the emergence of future new actualities. What is basic is neither the potential nor the actual but creativity – the force of life at the core of being and its proto-reflexivity, which is itself a kind of intelligence.

However, to embrace (in some sense) a vitalist and panpsychic philosophy of horizontal participation in this way is not to embrace immanence. For one cannot legitimately absolutise either formed substance or a creative process prior to that substance, nor either logical potential or replete actuality, any more than one can favour the outer over the inner or vice versa or the low over the high or vice versa. Participatory gift-exchange means that one is always *in medias res*. If one does not assume this exchange to be pointless and illusory, if one naturally assumes that this is a symbolic exchange of meanings, which gives sacramental point to life, then, inevitably, one must embrace a Platonic vertical participation alongside a horizontal one. All that exists is a recall of the eternal and a call to seek to re-ascend to the vertical. But this is not a call to abandon the horizontal or the natural and human community. Rather, it is a call to raise the heart heavenwards that is also an expansion of the heart in charity outwards. There is a source of the shape of everything in the unity of the One that is identical with the Good, but there is also a source of the existence of all these particular finite shapes and of their aligning in unity – a form of the One, a form of Difference and of their interweaving. For the Gospel, the difference and the interweaving are equal with the One, and the One is such that it coincides with an infinite expressive elaboration, which is life, and an infinite reflective unification of life with its fountain source, which is the full achievement of artistic cognition in the life of the Spirit. In the finite world, this Trinitarian process weaves in and out of the emergence of individual consciousness through time and of social interaction in space. Our human spiritual understanding and feeling are as collective as they are individual, and this is why culture has more fright than fashion and is its inner character.

Radical Orthodoxy has affirmed vertical as well as horizontal participation, seeing both vertices as obtaining a Trinitarian ground. The arrival of this in time was the event of the Incarnation, which reveals how true philosophy is more than a matter of words, but of life and death, and an inter-human drama. It reveals that it is more than a matter of individual searching but also of a community and a new sort of academy involving all people of all ages, consummating reflection and everyday life as a liturgical offering of peaceful expression, anticipating eternity.

This is seen as central for a realist metaphysics to be articulated and expressed. This is considered to be necessary to an adequation to our sensibilities of the real, and to bring that sensibility to poetic expression. This work recedes for as long as we remain within time.

THE MAIN CHARACTERISTICS OF
RADICAL ORTHODOXY

The central concern of Radical Orthodoxy, therefore, is with this twofold sense of participation. Many of its other characteristics stem from this.

A Return to Christian Platonism

We have already touched on the important place of Christian Platonism, in terms of the assumed centrality for Christianity of the Platonic framework of *methexis*, or participation, recognised by St Paul when he proclaims the God 'in whom we live and move and have our being', of whom, he says, the Greek poets had already spoken (Acts 17:28).

When Radical Orthodoxy first emerged in Cambridge in the early 1990s amongst a group of mainly Anglican but also Roman Catholic academics and students (with Orthodox and Protestant adherents arriving later), a lingering suspicion of the supposed 'Hellenisation' of Christianity and its supposed distortion by metaphysical categories still held sway in academic discussions, sometimes coupled with a desire to confine theology to 'grammatical' regulation of Christian speech or, alternatively, the phenomenological articulation of Christian experience. Without denying the validity of these approaches, which they have usually sought to integrate, Radical Orthodoxy thinkers asked whether such confinements did not betray the claim of Christianity to offer an account of reality that effects all our knowledge and experience, and tends to qualify it, albeit in unpredictable ways.

In this context, the refusal of the Greek dimension looked somewhat like an attempted apologetic resignation to the Kantian denial of the possibility of theoretical knowledge stretching beyond the infinite. Was not early Christianity, beginning with the New Testament, in fact imbued in such claims? And does not claiming otherwise look rather convenient, if one seeks to palliate the claims of the Kantian confinement?

Since that period, such suspicions have been confirmed by the demonstration by scholars of the impact of a Hellenistic milieu upon New Testament authors, including certain currents that can be described as 'Platonic'. This confirms the later predilection of the Church Fathers for Platonic philosophy and for their understanding of the Creation as a theophanic manifestation of the eternal, which they saw as in keeping with a wide range of biblical writings. For this reason, Radical Orthodoxy's turn 'back to Plato' now looks arguably less eccentric.

The Overcoming of the Duality of Grace and Nature

The foregrounding of participation, and of a Platonic model of the *exitus/reditus* from and towards God, were linked with the rejection of a sharp separation of grace from nature. Radical Orthodoxy sustained and intensified the critique by the *nouvelle théologie* of the Neoscholastic notion of a 'purely natural end' for human beings, along-side a further, supernatural one as a misreading of Aquinas.[1] For a radically orthodox perspective, all creatures emanate expressively from God; and this emanation is inseparable from a 'gracious' lure of crea-tures back to unity with God, which is the mark of their beauty. Such a cosmic destiny for all things is heightened in the case of spiritual creatures, human beings and angels, to become a conscious apprehen-sion. Nevertheless, the creation of everything, as for the Greek Fathers, is mediated through this apprehension, just as the cosmos returns to God and is restored through spiritual mediation. As for Henri de Lubac, spiritual, mental existence is engraced existence, in the same way that to think is to be aware of God, to thank God for the gift of one's existence, and to seek to be ever-further united with God.

The Critique of Secular Reason

John Milbank's *Theology and Social Theory* and Catherine Pickstock's *After Writing* can be regarded as two of the foundational texts of Radical Orthodoxy, written respectively at the beginning and end of the 1990s. In both works, it is assumed that, since there is no pure nature, it follows that there is no area of discourse that is autonomous from theological questioning. *Theology and Social Theory* demonstrated the grounding of modern social scientific outlooks in presuppositions that were theologically heterodox or anti-theological in a way that was not rationally justified. Pickstock's *After Writing* took a somewhat similar approach to discussions of language and human understanding. The common ground was perceived at the time to be a sharp rejection of

---

[1] Aquinas, *In Boethiam de Trinitate*, q. 5, a 4; Jean-Luc Marion, *D'Ailleurs, La Révélation* (Paris: Grasset, 2020), 65–84; Andreas Speer, 'The Division of Metaphysical Discourses: Boethius, Thomas Aquinas and Meister Eckhart', in Philosophy and Theology in the Long Middle *Ages* (ed. Kent Emery Jr (Leiden: Brill, 2011), 91–115.

the notion that theology needed to accommodate itself to supposed secular cognitive advances or that it needed to enter into a merely respectful dialogue with secular expertises whose conclusions it was not competent to judge on its own grounds.

This attitude was at times taken to suggest that Radical Orthodoxy considered that theology was all-sufficient and could exercise a kind of preposterous intellectual theocracy. However, the radically orthodox perspective emphasised that theology has no proper subject matter of its own that is not always already mediated by finite discourses. This followed from its Christian Platonic view that one obtains knowledge of the divine through participation and the analogical language that both reflects that participation and sustains it.

The need to interact with other disciplines was therefore insisted upon. The matter being questioned was the notion that there are readily discernible boundaries between discourses and especially between those confined to this world and those claiming to speak of transcendence. The rejected perspectives were those that claimed, in a post-Kantian manner, to be paradoxically grounded in false theological doctrines of pure nature, that secular perspectives were absolute, rationally self-enclosed and self-sufficient. It was suggested by Radical Orthodoxy that if theologians accept this outlook, the discipline will make no headway or impact.

The importance of analogy for Radical Orthodoxy distanced it from Protestant Neo-orthodoxy. Where the latter had rejected 'natural theology', Radical Orthodoxy theologians increasingly questioned the idea of a difference between natural and revealed theology, which argu-ably did not arise before Aquinas, for whom the distinction remained more muted than for later scholastics. It was noted that Karl Barth's insistence that human beings know of God through the revealed word was grounded in a Kantian philosophical assumption of finite closure.[2] This being the case, it was not clear that for Barth the Word of God could make a decisive difference to finite experience, knowledge, and politics. By contrast, for a radically orthodoxy perspective, God impinges at the points where such differences are made and in unpredictable ways.

The Relationship of Radical Orthodoxy to Postmodernism
Both its Platonism and its refusal of an autonomous nature are relevant to the attitude of Radical Orthodoxy to postmodernism. This relation-ship is decisive both in the case of Milbank and Pickstock and perhaps

---

[2] *Cambridge University Reporter*, Volume 122, Number 22 (Wednesday 18 March 1992), 509; and Volume 122, Number 23 (Wednesday 25 March 1992), 514.

still more in that of the third 'founder', Graham Ward, whose work has been inspired by his literary engagements, commencing with his *Barth, Derrida and the Language of Theology*.[3] Characteristically, these three thinkers and those influenced by them problematised the critique of the postmodern in the name of reason, certainty, humanism, and essentialism that was characteristic of theology at the time. Divisions in Cambridge came to a head when different members of the Divinity Faculty found themselves on opposite sides of the Senate Chamber in the 1992 debate about whether or not to award Jacques Derrida an Honorary Doctorate of Letters.

The Radical Orthodoxy theologians found themselves siding with those, such as George Steiner, who, though by no means in full agreement with Derrida, acknowledged the critical value of his writings. More generally, they considered that postmodernism opened new apologetic avenues. For theological defenders of humanism and rationalism, it was hoped that a secular recognition of human dignity would prove a natural prelude to seeing how it is grounded in God. But the radically orthodox argument was that Foucault's 'death of man' following the death of God negatively proved that there could be no secure humanism outside religion. If one does not construe the human mind as mystery, as the mark of God within one, then one will naturally come to conclude that it possesses no coherence and that human beings are at the passive mercy of anarchic natural forces and the play of linguistic signs that can reach no non-arbitrary conclusions. Inherent uncertainty and indeterminism might be regarded as witnesses to nihilism, but Radical Orthodoxy's Neo-Romantic Platonism sought to regard them as witnesses to the truth of eternity. In order to make this case, they argued that the postmodernists were covertly (or indeed overtly, as brought out during an encounter between Derrida and Milbank at Villanova University in 1999) still committed to a new mode of Kantian closure, in such a way that uncertainty was absolutised as proof of final meaninglessness.[4] Rather, in a reworking of the attitudes of S. T. Coleridge and Friedrich Schlegel, the Radical Orthodoxy thinkers argued that within an unending semiosis, fragmentary glimmers of eternal truth could be apprehended – shining through as musical beauty that both advertises itself as form and points away from itself as the

---

[3] Graham Ward, *Barth, Derrida and the Language of Theology* (Cambridge: Cambridge University Press, 1995).

[4] Caputo, John D., Mark Dooley, and Michael J. Scanlon, eds., *Questioning God* (Bloomington IN: Indiana University Press, 2001).

promise of a hidden depth. This is not the concealed finite depth of interiority excoriated by the postmodernists but the depths of the eternal that is intimated by unfolding events within time.

The Return to a Realist Metaphysics

By questioning the continued Kantian closure of the postmodern, Radical Orthodoxy anticipated later developments within secular and atheistic thought. Subsequent generations of philosophers have begun to argue that the postmodern focus upon language and discourse remained a mode of disguised humanism, and, in an ecologically focussed era, they have begun to look for a philosophy that would embrace the whole of nature and break radically with anthropocentricity.

These developments have been accompanied by a questioning of the hitherto unquestionable: the Kantian notion that all one can know is one's own understanding of reality and not reality in itself. Was this 'Copernican' turn tantamount to a refusal of the Copernican displacement of human centrality within the cosmos? And how can it be supposed that one cannot transcend one's own categories of knowledge if one's mind is the result of natural historical evolution?

Radical Orthodoxy shared such reservations about Kant, to which it added the arguments of H. G. Hamann that language renders it impossible for human beings to distinguish the empirical from the rational, and consequently to conclude that the one is destined for the other, rather than its being the case that one's linguistic expression is one and the same with one's unfolding attempt to be more symbolically adequate to eternity. It has become increasingly interested in the ideas of Maine de Biran regarding the mediation of experience by the body, as rendering it impossible to sift the a priori from the a posteriori, and thereby to establish a realm of mutually mirroring but inexplicable correlation. If all that one can experience are the habits of one's body in attunement with the settled habits of nature, then must one not suppose that this is a kind of engraced striving towards the ultimate under the impulse of vital forces?

Radically orthodox thinkers have argued that these 'alternatively modern' thinkers, who have emphasised the primacy of language, such as Antonio Rosmini, Sergii Bulgakov, and Margaret Masterman, or the primacy of habit and embodied process, such as Félix Ravaisson, Henri Bergson, Maurice Blondel, and A. N. Whitehead, also rejected the Kantian critique of metaphysics, while not falling back upon a static essentialism. They rejected the priority of givenness, in favour of creativity as primary, which is not to say that they refused patterns of constancy or saw them as arbitrary. Radical Orthodoxy has come to argue that such thinking can be used further to articulate a Trinitarian ontology in the way outlined in the second section above. In doing so, an attempt is made to establish a realist metaphysics, which, while sympathising with new secular critiques of Kant, does not accept its attendant cult of the pure object or its proposal to start with objects rather than subjects. For radically orthodox approaches, this is simply a reversal of epistemological illusion, which does not sufficiently problematise the latter's juxtaposition of subjectivity and objectivity, however far this reversal appears to do so. Such an unsuspected conservatism is betrayed by the continuing assumption that the mark of realism is that things would be as they are known to be if the knower were absent. For this is to continue to model 'reality' on the basis of the objectively construed epistemological gaze. An alternative approach to realism, anticipated by Bergson and Whitehead, would seek to comprehend the natural integral reality that one experiences and that one can never escape. This is a reality that includes the objectivity of our subjective responses and the subjective colouring of everything that is naturally manifest, and which naturally provokes and inspires one's emotional reactions.

It is an irony that for over two hundred years, much of theology has sought to find a voice for itself within a post-Kantian space, assumed to be inviolable. And it is now secular thinkers who are questioning this inviolability.

Radical Orthodoxy and Genealogy

In Milbank's *Theology and Social Theory* and then Pickstock's *After Writing*, Radical Orthodoxy sought to accompany its contemporary conclusions with a genealogy of modern thought. Indeed, insofar as the movement seeks to suggest that secular discourses are not theologically innocent, this genealogical work is a crucial aspect of its endeavours, though by no means the entirety of them.

Central to this genealogy is the attempt to explain how the participatory vision of Christian theology up to approximately 1300 was lost. In broad terms, this meant the substitution of analogy by univocity; of knowledge by identity of form (within things and within our minds) with knowledge as corresponding representation; of complex causality at different, incommensurable levels with the idea of univocal efficiency operating in the same way at all levels, in such a way that false problems of how to reconcile divine causation with immanent worldly action now ensue, including with respect to issues of grace and free will;

of the primacy of logical possibility over eventful actuality, in such a way that divine action is now thought to be an admixture of God's instantiation of pre-defined rational packages attended by a set of arbitrary decisions. In the latter respect, a traditional integration of thinking with willing is abandoned. For as long as thinking was seen in terms of desire and willing, a discernment of hidden reasons, one perforce considered mind as non-autonomous and as participating in a thought always beyond itself. But according to the new model, reason as possibility and will as self-grounded election are both finitely foreclosed, initiating a consequent competition projected onto God.

The univocal tendency generated other shifts of perspective: a flattened reality is a known one, whose causal operations are surveyable and comprehensible, while being that is there or not there is no different in its essentiality from a possible being, as Kant concluded. Yet the decision for univocity was made, by John Duns Scotus and others, for theological reasons: under the assumption that one requires apophantic proofs for God with a stable middle term of the syllogism; that one requires the same for any certain knowledge of divine properties such as 'goodness'; and the obscure view that it is in the fallen world that one primarily knows realities through corporeal exemplifications, rather than literally and directly, as for God. But all of these specifically theological assumptions seem theologically dubious. They tend to confuse God as ontological with merely ontic realities, Being as such with beings, however great in magnitude.

And yet much of the philosophy that followed assumed this problematic theology. It forgot Being and the radical otherness of God (which is, for that reason, as Nicholas of Cusa argued, equally a not-otherness) in the same gesture. A knowledge confined to the unambiguous appearance of things mutated into epistemology and tended to encourage the sense of an independent nature that can be known apart from God, if all one knows of God is the infinitised projection of properties that one already knows about anyway. Such a God is not mysterious, or else one might say that such a God is radically and inaccessibly (even positivistically) unknown; and in either case, he is not a God who can make a worldly difference.

The bending of metaphysics towards a primacy of theory of knowledge and of semantics was present in Scotus: if Being as the merely there is 'formally distinct' from essence, then the character of real being becomes indistinguishable from its meaning for us. It is in this way that a Scotist-influenced early modern scholasticism turned ontology into epistemology, having already sundered the study of being from the study of God (once combined as 'metaphysics'), which came to be located within the ontic spirit that a univocal ontology reserved for it. Within this perspective, the Kantian turn looks somewhat like an ultimate development, rather than a critical reversal. It was not the rejection of the analogical metaphysics of Aquinas, which did not fall within Kant's purview.

Nothing about this genealogy is, however, original to Radical Orthodoxy, as many have mistakenly supposed. The road leading from Scotus to Kant via Ockham has been traced by many intellectual historians. Yet this story is often regarded as one of progressive advance. What is perhaps more distinctive about the radically orthodox stance, in the wake of Catholic thinkers such as Etienne Gilson, is the questioning as to whether this counts as progress and not arguably a lapse on the basis of dubious theological shifts in opinion.

Such a verdict may suggest the possibility that secular philosophy operates within a space opened up by such shifts. A theological critique of modern philosophy becomes a viable possibility, alongside the immanent critiques of the Kantian trajectory that secular thought has now carried out. Theology may be able to add to the diagnosis of a failed realism the incapacity of secular thought to deliver a convincing realism, for reasons already outlined.

Intensified Orthodoxy

More recently, Radical Orthodoxy has started to re-understand itself as being a programme of what one might describe as intensified orthodoxy. To begin with, it perpetuated the efforts of the *ressourcement* theologians to recover the riches of the Patristic and early to high medieval tradition, including a new account of Aquinas. But more recently, it has become conscious of possible deficiencies even in Aquinas himself, despite the crucial and inspiring creativity of his synthesis. The question of Aquinas's break with the Boethian unity of natural and revealed theology has been mentioned in the foregoing. If one can no longer by nature rise to an intellectual intuition of God, as he seems to suggest, then how can a revealed theology unsettle and deepen the conclusions of unaided human reason, though Aquinas declares that one take the principles of revealed science from the mind of God? Without the raising of natural reason into intuitive insight, how can one prevent 'revelation' from deteriorating into the communication of mere items of information, as after Aquinas tended to become increasingly the case.

Equally, one finds in Aquinas, as John Hughes argued after Bulgakov, the distinction between God's absolute and his ordained power.[5] But if God is simple, as Aquinas insists, how can there be something that is 'God' that God has not performed? It is this question of divine unity that requires a radicalising of orthodoxy, an insistence that Christian doctrine be strictly monotheistic in a biblical line, though this insistence is often carried through by Christian exponents of Neoplatonic henology, such as John Scotus Eriugena. Increasingly, Eriugena is seen as the thinker who fuses Augustine with the harvest of Eastern Patristic theology achieved by Maximus the Confessor.

Key to this refocussing is Eriugena's more consistent monotheism, with his foregrounding of creativity, to such a degree that he may now be put into conversation with Bergson and Whitehead, with the fourteenth-century theologian Nicholas of Cusa providing a mediating link. The God of unity is the God whom reason itself can understand to be unified as identically repeated: as equal to himself, and in turn equal to this repetition of the original, as the English theologian Achard of St Victor concluded in the twelfth century, bringing to completion a Boethian trajectory. God as Trinitarian because unified and simple is the God whose self-utterance and self-realisation must be at one with his utterance of the Creation and his bringing of the Creation back into unity with himself. This ecstatic God is within himself as outside himself and never outside himself. At the same time, the Creation is other from God and yet not other to him whatsoever.

The Incarnation, which must eternally have taken place from the simple divine perspective, exacerbates and yet resolves this paradox. Ultimate 'nature' is God-Manhood in which all creatures participate. If God, beyond pure act and pure potency, and beyond rest and motion (in a Neoplatonic qualification of Aquinas) is an eternal self-making and self-interpretation, then the life of creatures is this by participation, supremely and consciously so in spiritual creatures.

There can be no possible bridge between the infinite and the finite, and yet this incommensurability allows a paradoxical coincidence of the two without overlap or partiality of division. This paradox supports all of reality that one sees manifest in Christ. And it is because of the realisation of this paradox that lesser degrees of paradox in analogy are possible, because an analogy involves an unthinkable likeness of the unlike that is not reducible to explicable degrees of divisible likeness and unlikeness.

---

[5] John Hughes, "*Creatio ex nihilo* and the Divine Ideas in Aquinas: How Fair Is Bulgakov's critique?', *Modern Theology* 29, no. 2 (March 2013), 124–137.

Christological analogy takes us beyond the Law of Non-Contradiction, just as for Graham Priest and others, reality is riddled with or perforated by tiny violations, because a totality that coheres both exceeds and yet does not exceed all that it contains. Such an insight can be saved by theology from nihilistic implosion if one realises that the ineffable contained non-containment of each and every thing echoes both the unthinkable substantive relations of the Trinity and the unthinkable holding together of the finite and the infinite by the singular and yet universal 'character' of Christ, which is also the character of his body the Church.

The unity of God, which is all of reality, though this reality is ecstatically other from God, is also incompatible with a doctrine of eternal damnation. This is in agreement with Ilaria Ramelli's arguments that *apokatastasis* is more than a pious hope.[6] Rather, it is a certainty if God is God. To think of God as the eternally good and omnipotent alongside eternal suffering of hell is to think of God as operating alongside a rival power and of his infinite peace as existing adjacent to a metaphysical country endlessly torn by civil war.

The Politics of Radical Orthodoxy

I began by invoking epistemology as a politics and a lived experience, which some radically orthodox thinkers seek to question, both in practice as well as in theory. In what does such an alternative practice consist? In horizontal participation, liturgically grounded in the continuous enactment and further openness to vertical participation.

Sebastian Milbank has recently argued that the Platonic philosophy of *methexis* provides a foundation for an understanding of politics as the sharing of rule: a citizen politics of involvement, rather than a politics in submission to an alien state or an amoral market.[7] Such a politics can be realised, he argues, when it is no longer a refined rhetorical game for an elite, separate from familial, social, and economic concerns but when these matters are politicised. An involved sharing and exchange permeates human affairs, while politics must respect and work along with natural exigencies, the unavoidable animal aspect of human life.

More generally, Radical Orthodoxy, as a theology of paradox that insists that loyalty to tradition engenders the deepest transformations,

---

[6] Ilaria Ramelli, The Christian Doctrine of *Apokatastasis* (Leiden: Brill, 2013).

[7] Sebastian Milbank, 'Sacral Citizenship: Philosophies of the City from Plato to Augustine', Doctoral dissertation submitted 30 April 2021, University of Cambridge.

has engendered a politics of paradox alongside other contemporary so-called 'postliberals'. Phillip Blond's *Red Tory* led to the formation, in partial reaction, of Blue Labour under the leadership of the Jewish academic Maurice Glasman, a movement of 'traditionalist socialism' representative of some but by no means all followers of Radical Orthodoxy. Its outlook was expressed at length in *The Politics of Virtue* by John Milbank and Adrian Pabst.

At the centre of this Platonic vision of the political stands the view that a citizen-based politics is inherently a politics of education into virtue and that only a virtuous citizenship can govern itself justly and without corruption. For those radically orthodox thinkers who have developed a political critique, this view stands in contrast to the liberal notion that politics is about the pragmatic organisation of necessities between essentially distanced people who are not citizens but 'subjects' granted certain rights of protection under the law, together with the right to choose whichever substantive goods they prefer. For Milbank, Pabst, Blond, and others, this is the political correlate of epistemology, where human relations are reduced to objects surveyed from without, and one's individual surplus over the machinery of control to which one is 'subjected' is the lonely sphere under the blandishments of fashion for which one constantly pays and pays dearly.

The politics of participation is the mutual search for the objectively good and for the possibility of human flourishing in relationship, which ensures the achievement of individual personhood and freedom. It unites the transmission of tradition through time and the 'aristocratic' guidance of the wise few with the democratic modifying assent of the many and the 'monarchic' integration of the one, in keeping with the Platonic ideal of the Philosopher King. It espouses the duty of an equal contribution by all, as well as the equal rights of all to be the beneficiaries of such duties. It pits family, community, locality, and local ecology against the dominance of the market and demands that a genuinely free market not be biased towards capital but enact inherently just and sympathetic social exchanges. It is associated with a genuinely corporatist re-integration of the political with the economic to such a degree that agriculture, industry, and business are part of basic community while demanding that these areas also be subject to political debate and political organisation and a subsidiarist federalism within and across borders, which it argues should always be fluid. In this fashion, several radically orthodox have contributed, alongside many non-radically orthodox thinkers, to the attempt to find a just alternative to prevailing liberalism or to insurgent nationalist populism.

CONCLUSION: THE FUTURE OF RADICAL ORTHODOXY

The further integration of the theological with the philosophical remains to be achieved; as well as the explication of a Trinitarian and Christology ontology and the recently developing crafting of a Christian politics of 'free integralism', loyal to the unity of grace and nature that legitimates the political insofar as it promotes the uncoerced supernatural community of charity which is *ecclesia*. But this work is not that of a sect or a single movement: it must be undertaken in collaboration with many other interlocutors and fellow travellers who may share some aspects of the new ethos that Radical Orthodoxy has sought for the past thirty years to nurture.

Further Reading

Collections

Cunningham, Conor, and Peter Candler, eds. (2010), *The Grandeur of Reason* (London: SCM).
Davison, Andrew, ed. (2012), *Imaginative Apologetics* (London: SCM).
Milbank, Alison, ed. (2017), *Preaching Radical and Orthodox* (London: SCM).
Milbank, John, Catherine Pickstock and Graham Ward, eds. (1998), *Radical Orthodoxy: A New Theology* (London: Routledge).
Milbank, John and Simon Oliver, eds. (2009), *The Radical Orthodoxy Reader* (London: Routledge).
Smith, James K. A. (2004), *Introducing Radical Orthodoxy* (Grand Rapids: Baker Academic).

Founding Texts

Milbank, John (2003), *Being Reconciled* (London: Routledge).
(2014), *Beyond Secular Order* (Oxford: Wiley-Blackwell).
Milbank, John, with Adrian Pabst (2016), *The Politics of Virtue* (London: Rowman and Littlefeld).
(2006), *Theology and Social Theory*, 2nd ed. (Oxford: Wiley-Blackwell).
Milbank, John, with Catherine Pickstock (2002), *Truth in Aquinas* (London: Routledge).
(1997), *The Word Made Strange* (Oxford: Blackwell).
Pickstock, Catherine (1997), *After Writing: On the Liturgical Consummation of Philosophy* (Oxford: Blackwell).
(2020), *Aspects of Truth* (Cambridge: Cambridge University Press).
(2014), *Repetition and Identity* (Oxford: Oxford University Press).
Ward, Graham (1995), *Barth, Derrida and the Language of Theology* (Cambridge: Cambridge University Press).
(1996), *Theology and Contemporary Critical Theory* (London: Palgrave-MacMillan).

(2000), *Cities of God* (London: Routledge).

(2005), *Christ and Culture* (Oxford: Wiley-Blackwell).

(2014), *Unbelievable: Why we Believe and Why We Don't* (London: I.B. Tauris).

(2019), *Theology and Religion* (Cambridge: Polity).

14 Public Theology
KRISTEN DEEDE JOHNSON

In an essay exploring how Christian ethics became distinct from Christian doctrine, Stanley Hauerwas writes: "Once there was no Christian ethics simply because Christians could not distinguish between their beliefs and their behaviour. They assumed that their lives exemplified (or at least should exemplify) their doctrines in a manner that made a division between life and doctrine impossible."[1] We could write similarly of public theology: "Once there was no public theology simply because Christians could not distinguish between their beliefs and the public implications of those beliefs. It took particular social, historical, and intellectual circumstances for a division between 'theology' and 'public theology' to seem possible." In other words, historically contingent reasons led to the emergence of "public theology" as a theological discourse beginning in the 1970s.

Questions related to the relationship between Christianity and the social and political realities of the day are in some ways timeless. And yet the specific language of public theology has to do with questions that arise in modern societies in which religion is thought to more appropriately belong in the private sphere, raising questions about the public role and voice of religious traditions. Public theology is also connected to the recognition of pluralism within a political society; when people with a range of different convictions, beliefs, and ways of life reside together within a single society, the role of any singular belief system within that society has to be conceptualized. The question of the role of Christianity in the public realm and the recognition of pluralism were presenting and interrelated issues that led to the emergence of the term and concept of public theology.

---

[1] Stanley Hauerwas, "On Doctrine and Ethics," in *The Cambridge Companion to Christian Doctrine* (ed. Colin E. Gunton; Cambridge: Cambridge University Press, 1997), 22.

In the decades since the term was first articulated, many US scholars have wrestled with what the term means, offering different perspectives on public theology. Along the way, the term began to have resonance in other countries and continents, leading to the creation of a number of centers and institutes in public theology, the launch of the Global Network for Public Theology in 2005 (which includes membership from initiatives in Africa, Oceania, Latin America, North America, Europe, and Asia), the publication of the *International Journal of Public Theology*, and a number of works of scholarship.

Within these different writings and initiatives, we will not find neat consensus on what public theology is. Exploring the emergence of public theology and then the development of the concept will help provide a sense of its range of meanings and applications. We will then turn directly to public theologians to see how they have defined public theology in the years since its inception. We will also explore some parallel theological discourses, such as liberation theology and political theology, and how they overlap with and differ from public theology.

THE EMERGENCE OF PUBLIC THEOLOGY

The term "public theology" that spawned the contemporary discourse in this area was first used in an intentional way by US Protestant theologian Martin Marty. Marty was engaging with the work of Robert Bellah and his pioneering work on civil religion in the United States. Drawing on a concept from Jean-Jacques Rousseau, Bellah described American civil religion as the idea that the United States has a shared set of beliefs, symbols, myths, and rituals that the majority of its citizens share and in which they participate, regardless of their specific religious background. Civil religion plays a public and binding role within a society, bringing adherents of different religions together through a shared religious orientation or sensibility, reinforced by such rituals as the singing of national anthems and the celebrating of national holidays. Bellah introduced this term in an article published in 1967, which spawned much follow-up scholarly discussion. In Marty's contribution to this discussion, he argued that we need to acknowledge two different kinds of civil religion, one of which he called public theology. Although Marty originally conceptualized public theology as one form of civil religion, Bellah and other scholars believed that Marty had identified an important additional concept that was distinct from civil religion. One key difference is that public theology is rooted in particular religious traditions as adherents of those religions seek to engage wider public issues and concerns, whereas civil religion is about a shared societal religious sensibility.

For Marty, one important contribution that public theologians can offer is taking a critical, prophetic stance toward what is happening within a nation. In his aforementioned piece on civil religion, he offered Reinhold Niebuhr as one exemplar of a critical public theologian, while in another contemporaneous piece, "Reinhold Niebuhr: Public Theology and the American Experience," he explores in more detail his conception of public theology vis-à-vis Niebuhr. He identifies two strands of American public theology that he believes come together in Niebuhr. Jonathan Edwards, Horace Bushnell, and Walter Rauschenbusch are representatives of one strand, that which draws on its roots in a particular religious community as a basis for public action. Benjamin Franklin, Abraham Lincoln, and Woodrow Wilson are examples of the second strand, made up of public political figures who understood national life to have an ecclesial dimension. In Niebuhr, we find, according to Marty, one person combining these two strands. Niebuhr wanted, for example, churches to see that the gospel found in Christ has national as well as personal implications; he wanted Americans more generally to hear that they often acted idolatrously and succumbed to the temptations of power and pride. While not being uncritical of Niebuhr, Marty nevertheless believed that he served as a "paradigm for a public theology" and "a model which his successors have only begun to develop and realize."[2]

Within this work, Marty does not offer a definition of public theology, choosing instead to explore the concept through the legacy of Niebuhr. In the wake of his introduction of this term, many others began to use and consider the term, offering exploratory and constructive accounts. Figures such as David Hollenbach, David Tracy, Max Stackhouse, Ronald F. Thiemann, and Linnell Cady are considered pivotal in the early public theology conversation, articulating through articles and book projects their conceptions of public theology and its significance.

Marty himself turns his focus to "the public church," publishing a book by that name in which he considers ways churches in the United States could provide a Christian contribution to American public theology. He understands this contribution to be about "ordering faith" rather than "saving faith." By this he means ways that churches in the

---

[2] Martin E. Marty, "Reinhold Niebuhr: Public Theology and the American Experience," *The Journal of Religion* 54 (1974), 359.

United States could come together as a "communion of communions" with Jesus Christ at the center and with a common vocation to attend to the *res publica*, the wider public order. He focuses especially on churches from older Protestant mainline traditions, newer evangelicalism, and Roman Catholicism. He calls these churches to remain committed to the particularities of their faith and to civility, avoiding the pitfalls of the three predominant models of religion that he outlines: totalist (affiliated with theocracies), tribalist (focused on boundaries and self-protection), and privatist (religion as a private matter of individual choice and practice). In the face of pressures flowing from these models, Marty longs to see the public church play a significant role in shifting human sensibilities, that "people would learn to combine religious commitment with civility, spiritual passion with a public sense."[3]

Marty is clear that one reason he needs to issue this call to the church to be public is related to the rise of modernity and its impact on religious traditions. Marty narrates modernity as a story of choice that leads to the "chopping up" of existence, including the chopping up of religion into private faith that is separated from public life. Religion is divorced from its implications for politics, economics, and most of the rest of the institutions and realities of modern life. Life is compartmentalized, so that if God is in a box marked sacred, then most of the rest of life is in a box marked secular, Marty notes, and even the sacred box now contains not only God but compartments for psychiatrists, therapists, and others not historically considered part of religion. This leads to a number of challenges for churches, as it is made up of people who no longer consider themselves part of a shared communion but are "private strivers."

In other words, the need to emphasize the public nature of faith and its institutions arises within societies that have been shaped by modernity. In pre-modern societies, the collective is emphasized over the individual, while life is not compartmentalized between public and private. Marty briefly outlines societal shifts over time, noting that the rise of the Enlightenment led to the separation of private faith from public order, with religion moving into the category of choice, even for religious traditions into which adherents had historically been born. Ultimately, the existence of a plurality of religious traditions within one political society combined with this emphasis on choice, and the privatization of religion shifted the nature of the religious traditions

---

[3] Martin E. Marty, *Public Church: Mainline-Evangelical-Catholic* (New York: Crossroad, 1981), 8; see also 3–16, 167–170.

themselves, leading those strands that emphasized the private benefit of religion over its public obligation to have a competitive advantage and ultimately to win the day. Marty is not arguing for the elimination of pluralism or of choice, but he does want religious traditions to acknowledge that pluralism is here to stay while also finding ways to contribute to the public order.

Linell Cady is another significant voice within the origins of public theology. Looking at her work will further illuminate the extent to which the discourse of public theology, in all its variations today, is shaped by the larger context of pluralism as well as modern conceptions of public and private. Cady invites us to step back and reflect on the reality that configurations of public and private shift over time, thereby opening the door for us to question the contours of public and private that we have inherited. The Greeks, she notes, placed a much higher value on the public sphere than the private sphere, viewing the private sphere as a privation, in keeping with the origins of the term. (Privation refers to a lack of things considered essential for human well-being or a state of deprivation.). They associated freedom with the public world and viewed wealth as a means to escape the confines of the private sphere so that one might be able to exercise freedom in the public sphere. Cady notes that in the US context, the "privative sense of the private sphere has eroded," we now prioritize the private sphere over the public, and we understand freedom to be most actualized in the private sphere as we are freed from constraints in the wider, public world to pursue our own private ends.[4]

How did those particular conceptions of public and private become predominant? Cady traces this history in terms of the Enlightenment and the effort of Enlightenment thinkers to conceptualize a way forward in societies that were marked by religious wars. Accepting the narrative that European Enlightenment thinkers wanted to establish a secular sphere in order to free the public realm from intractable and violent religious conflict, Cady notes that, "religion was increasingly relegated to the sphere of the private, and a secular discourse was developed to articulate the nature of political and social life."[5] While scholars in the years since Cady wrote this work have problematized that particular narrative, very few dispute the upshot to which she points – Enlightenment thinkers and the political and moral philosophy of

---

[4] Linell E. Cady, *Religion, Theology, and American Public Life* (Albany: State University of New York Press, 1993), 7.
[5] Ibid., 10.

modern liberalism they conceptualized reimagined the spheres of public and private in ways that continue to shape Western societies.

As Cady describes it, liberal thinkers, operating with a conception of humans as radically autonomous individuals driven by the pursuit of their own self-interest, imagined political societies bound together not by public, common goods but as places where individuals choose to enter into social contracts so they can be freed to pursue their own private interests. This pursuit of private interests paired well with the rise of modern capitalism. Both economic and political thinkers of the time hoped that as individuals pursued private interests, the result would be public gain and an optimal society. Further, the freedom to pursue private ends was concomitant with the idea that individuals ought to be free to use their own reason, rather than relying on the traditions or Christian wisdom that had been handed down to them or the authorities associated with those traditions. That is to say, in addition to the public sphere being conceptualized as free from religion, even within the private realm the authority and role of religion was being questioned. Public reason, rather than religion, was to play a universal and unifying role.

Although overall the private realm took on more space and importance as a result of these intellectual, political, and economic developments, Cady makes sure to emphasize that in important ways the reconceptualization of public that took place during the Enlightenment led to a far more expansive notion of public than that held by Greeks. In Greek society, only wealthy, property-owning men could participate in the public realm, while all others were relegated to the private realm. In modern liberal societies, at least eventually, the public realm was opened to all persons. And yet, Cady points out, no space exists within this conception of public for those persons to enter the public realm with distinctive histories, stories, attachments, or faith traditions. "Public" is associated with "common," while anything particular, distinctive, or potentially divisive is relegated to the private realm.

While grateful for some of the gains brought by the Enlightenment, including the enhanced rights of individuals, Cady is concerned that the individualism at the core of its vision of public life is at risk of eroding what is needed to sustain collective life. The public virtue that was widely remarked upon by the Founding Fathers of the United States, which Alexis de Tocqueville viewed as essential to the maintenance of the American republic and understood to be cultivated through Christianity, appears to have been lost. This is certainly one contributing factor in the rise of the discourse in public religion, as many began to wonder if we needed religion to combat the radical individualism and narcissism that seemed to be on the rise.

According to Cady, this background is essential for understanding the task of public theology in our contemporary context. One cannot simply issue a call for theology to reengage the public realm without understanding that we need to wrestle with the assumptions upon which contemporary conceptions of the public realm are built and reimagine "public" itself. What if we are not, for example, primarily autonomous, atomized individuals but are rather embedded, relational, and interdependent? Do we want to assume it's possible or even ideal to enter the public realm as people without beliefs, backgrounds, and histories? For Cady, "a public theology seeks to elicit a recognition of and loyalty to a common public life that is more than a collection of autonomous individuals. By focusing upon the intricate and extensive interdependencies that mark human and cosmic life, it seeks to temper the radical individualism of the liberal ethos through identification with a wider common life."[6]

Another significant figure in the emergence of public theology is David Tracy, who explores the public nature of theology in relation to pluralistic cultures. Does the reality of a culture of pluralism mean that religious traditions need to either lose their particularities or become marginalized, private options, with no public impact? Tracy does not believe that any of the major religious traditions could accept either of these options. Theology, he argues, is public by its very nature. To speak about God, given God's nature, is to speak publicly, and so theology has to be a public discourse with public criteria. While affirming in no uncertain terms the public nature of theology and rejecting the privatization of religion, Tracy challenges theology to recognize that it is related to three publics, those of society, academy, and church. Tracy recognizes that these publics are distinct and argues that theologians need to attend to each one, exploring methodologically what that entails.

Central to Tracy's argument is an exploration of "the classic." As classic works of art achieve public status not despite but through their particularity, so Tracy calls religions to retain their particularity in our pluralistic context. "Each of us," he argues, "contributes more to the common good when we dare to undertake a journey into our own particularity (this family, this community, this people, this culture, this

---

[6] Ibid., 71.

religion) than when we attempt to homogenize all differences in favor of some lowest common denominator."[7] Tracy's methodological exploration of public theology is shaped by his embracing of pluralism, his commitment to particularity, and his conviction that all theology is public.

These three early voices within the development of public theology help us see some of the contours that led public theology to arise as a discourse when it did, where it did. We could legitimately say that in one sense public theology predates the term's existence. The Israelites, for example, certainly understood Yahweh and the way of life to which Yahweh called them to be public in nature. According to the Hebrew Scriptures, the God of Israel provided laws that covered politics, economics, the family, and (public) worship. And yet in another very real sense, the issues with which public theologians have wrestled in the late twentieth and early twenty-first centuries are historically contingent and mark the discourse in particular ways. Questions of the relationship between the public and private realms, as well as the role and place of religion and theology in a pluralistic society, have been profoundly shaped by the post-Enlightenment context of the West.

Marty, Cady, and Tracy wrestle with these questions, each in their own way. Indeed, one can view them as exemplars of different threads within the tapestry of public theology. The discourse of public theology being relatively new, it is still emerging as an academic discipline and defies easy categorization and definition. Some scholars in the area of public theology attempt to place the voices of public theologians into different types. Benjamin Valentin, for example, names three distinct projects being undertaken by public theologians. The first, of which Marty can be considered an exemplar, consists of articulating the role and character of the institutional church in the public sphere. The second, illustrated by Tracy, is dedicated to expounding the public nature of theology and theological discourse. The third, exemplified by Cady, is the effort to offer a theological mode of address that responds to issues facing a nation, transcends boundaries between religions as well as between the religious and the secular, and promotes the importance of our common life.[8]

[7] David Tracy, "Defending the Public Character of Theology," *The Christian Century* (April 1, 1981), 353. See also David Tracy, *The Analogical Imagination: Christian Theology and the Culture of Pluralism* (New York: Crossroad, 1981).
[8] See Benjamin Valentin, *Mapping Public Theology: Beyond Culture, Identity, and Difference* (Harrisburg, PA: Trinity Press International, 2002), 85.

DEVELOPMENTS WITHIN PUBLIC THEOLOGY

Valentin himself represents an important development within public theology, as he attempts to build on the work of early public theologians in the United States but expand the scope of discourse. His work is in an extended call to Latino/a theology to become a public discourse, as he argues that Hispanic/Latino theology has assumed the public relevance of its theological reflection but has not yet attended to its need to become a public discourse, which our fractious age and the demands of justice of this time need. In casting this vision for Latino/a theology, he builds on the third thread of public theology (that modeled by Cady) while noting the need to attend to the impact of racism, corporate capitalism, and identity politics on our ability to cultivate public dispositions in contemporary societies. In offering his constructive account of a public theology, he argues that public theology is a theological mode of discourse that needs to, first, engage broad national sociopolitical circumstances; second, nurture a sense of common life and concern for the social whole; third, offer an overarching emancipatory project that accounts for processes that produce social injustices and motivates citizens to take public action in the pursuit of justice; and, fourth, capture the attention of a broad audience, facilitating alliances across religious, racial, cultural, class, and gender lines.[9] Located in the US context, Valentin engages the American voices that developed public theology, recognizes additional issues that need to be addressed within the contemporary US context, and casts a vision for public theology that can shape the discourse of Latino/a theology as well as the growing field of public theology.

Max Stackhouse is another figure who represents a significant trajectory in the field of public theology. Arising in the 1980s as one of the early and influential voices in the United States calling for a public theology, Stackhouse's original work in this area argued that modern society had succumbed to the false conviction that the study of God is a private opinion or bias without public import, while the United States was in a malaise that is connected to its lack of a shared "metaphysical-moral" vision. While embracing the realities of contemporary pluralism, Stackhouse believed it both possible and necessary for theology to provide resources to guide public discourse or else "the mighty mechanisms of modernity will increasingly operate without cohesion, direction, or

---

[9] Ibid., 87; see also 81–116.

governing principle, subject to fad, fetishism, and fanaticism."[10] Twenty-
five years later, Stackhouse brought the resources of public theology to
bear within the context of globalization. Convinced that public theology
"is the most important theological development today in terms of its
potential capacity to address the issues posed by globalization,"
Stackhouse believes that the challenges posed by globalization and its
recognition of a wider public needs the resources of public theology.[11]
This is rooted in his conviction that "it is the duty of theology to provide a
reasonable proposal with regard to the moral and spiritual architecture
and the inner guidance systems of civilizations."[12] With similar underlying convictions about the nature and responsibility of theology in relation to the wider world around it, Stackhouse was attentive to changing
societal realities and believed public theology could rise to the task of
providing much-needed resources to a globalizing world.

Meanwhile, elsewhere in that globalizing world, public theology had
been taking root in all sorts of locations. In South Africa, for example,
while the term public theology was not in use, scholars and practitioners
had been doing public theology on the ground in the struggle against
apartheid. Nico Koopman points to the practice of public theology
through publications, conferences, public declarations, the creation of
the Belhar Confession, and opposition activities such as hunger strikes
and marches. Koopman became one of the theological voices in South
Africa connecting the South African context to the emerging discourse of
public theology. With post-apartheid South Africa established as a secular state, questions related to the role and contribution of religions in
public life arose anew. While wrestling with such questions, Koopman
engages with the wider scholarship in the area of public theology and
offers constructive christological and trinitarian contributions to the
discourse. Public theology, as Koopman understands it, is shaped by a
twofold focus: "on the one hand, the loving God, and on the other hand,
the world, the kosmos that is object of this Trinitarian love .... Public
theology faithfully endeavors to reflect upon the exciting implications
that this Trinitarian love has for South Africa, the rest of Africa, and the
rest of the world with all its joys and sorrows."[13]

[10] Max Stackhouse, "An Ecumenist's Plea for a Public Theology," *This World* (Spring/
     Summer 1984, no. 8), 57.
[11] Max Stackhouse, *God and Globalization*, Volume 4 (New York: Continuum, 2007),
     77.
[12] Ibid., 84.
[13] Nico Koopman, "Some Contours for Public Theology in South Africa," *International
     Journal of Public Theology* 14 (2010), 138.

In his work on public theology, Sebastian C. H. Kim observes a significant rise in contributions from Europe, South Africa, and Australia beginning in the 2000s and notes that in these contexts, the conversations related to public theology tend to be led by centres for public theology in universities and denominations rather than by individual academics. The University of Edinburgh was the site of the first center dedicated to public theology with the establishment of the Centre for Theology and Public Issues by Duncan Forrester in 1984, while others arose in countries throughout the world. Many of these centers have come together as a part of the Global Network for Public Theology (GNPT), initiated by William Storrar when he was director of the Centre for Theology and Public Issues. Launched in 2005 and formally established in 2007, GNPT consists of centers located in Africa, Oceania, Latin America, North America, Europe, and Asia. Its aim is to enable scholarly exchange about the contribution of Christianity to public discourse in a range of fields.

Toward that end, GNPT launched the *International Journal of Public Theology* (*IJPT*) in 2007. According to an editorial in the inaugural issue by Kim, the journal's founding editor, the journal was created to be a platform for original research in public theology, a field that emerged in response to the perceived need for theology to interact with the public issues facing contemporary society. As a field, it is committed to doing research in conversation with other academic disciplines, including politics, economics, cultural studies, and religious studies. While contributors to the international conversation on public theology are attentive to their local contexts and the particular issues arising in those settings, Kim highlights the themes of privatization and pluralism that were so clear in the early voices in public theology in the US context: "Public theology has emerged as theologians wrestle with the problem of privatization of Christian faith and seek to engage in dialogue with those outside church circles on various issues."[14]

Kim has made a significant contribution to the burgeoning field of public theology through his work with *IJPT*, by serving as coeditor with Katie Day of the first compendium of public theology, through his own constructive scholarship, and through faculty positions he has held in theology and public life in the United Kingdom and the United States. Kim's constructive work in public theology is concerned with the practical application of theology in the public realm. He weaves together

[14] Sebastian Kim, "Editorial," *International Journal of Public Theology* 1 (2007), 1.

242 KRISTEN DEEDE JOHNSON

examples of public theology from different contexts throughout the
world with methodological and theoretical considerations, with an
emphasis on public theology as Christian engagement with people
outside of the church on issues that are of common interest. He believes
public theology is deeply connected to public conversation and that
through this public conversation both individual and policy decisions
in economic, political, social, and religious matters can be impacted.

Kim agrees with other public theologians that theology is inherently
public, while emphasizing that "public" is not the opposite of "private"
but rather has to do with theology being open for all members of society
to debate and for all to access. Here he draws on the work of Jürgen
Habermas, who was the first to identify the "public sphere" as a space
between the state and society that emerged in modern societies. For this
realm to actually be "public," according to Habermas, it needed to
uphold the principle of universal access and be characterized by open
debate. Building on this concept of the public sphere, Kim identifies six
bodies or "players" in the public sphere of all modern societies: the state,
the market, the media, the academy, civil society, and religious communities. Each of these players contributes something to the public sphere.
Theology is rooted in both the academy and religious communities;
public theology, while maintaining these connections, "deliberately
expands its sources, audience and applications in the public sphere in
association with the other four players, depending on issues."[15] While
the methods of this engagement can vary, for Kim public theology is
intentional about engaging in public issues with these different players in
the public sphere. As Christian public theologians find common ground
with a range of conversation partners in the public sphere, Kim encourages them to preserve their Christian identity while simultaneously
being intentional about seeking shared solutions to public issues.

The relationship between faith-specific language and publicly
accessible language is a recurring theme within public theology.
Elaine Graham, a theologian in the United Kingdom, finds the idea of
being "bilingual" helpful for public theology. Public theologians ought
to be "fluent" in their own traditions, drawing on resources and concepts from their faith-specific traditions, while also fully conversant in
non-theological discourses. They need to listen well to those outside of
their traditions and they need to be able to contribute to the conversation in terms that are comprehensible to their conversation partners.

[15] Sebastian Kim, *Theology in the Public Sphere* (London: SCM Press, 2011), 14.

For this reason, Graham puts method right at the center of public theology. Public theology is not only about engaging public issues from a particular theological perspective but also involves "a commitment to a particular kind of theological method, which is prepared to submit to the procedural norms of public discourse."[16] Public theology, in other words, engages public issues in a public way, using modes of discourse that are widely accessible.

Graham's reflections on the bilingual nature of public theology are offered in the context of a larger project in which she explores the impact of post-secular contexts on public life and public theology. Theorists of secularization thought that religion would decline in authority and impact as societies became more secular, and at the least that religion would no longer have impact in the public realm. Both empirically and theoretically this secularization thesis has come under great scrutiny. Religion did not disappear in the way many scholars expected, while in recent years some forms of religion have experienced a resurgence and do seek to influence the public domain. And yet despite these indicators of the persistence of religion, the place and authority of religion after modernity are no longer the same. Religious beliefs and practices are largely privatized and de-institutionalized, even as they are seeking public influences. Secularity continues to shape our frameworks, our institutions, and the public sphere.

In this post-secular context, Graham points out that conceptions of public, private, religious, and secular are all being reimagined. The public square is simultaneously more open to religion and religious discourse and more suspicious of it. Indeed, more recognize that the public square is not a neutral place in which all reasonable people can equally participate and that it may be more accurate to recognize "publics," both local and global. With these recognitions, Graham argues that it becomes more important than ever for public theologians to be bilingual, rooted and conversant in their own traditions while entering into public discourse with language and concepts that can be understood by those outside of their traditions.

DEFINITIONS OF PUBLIC THEOLOGY

We have reached this point without venturing a definition of public theology. The young age of the field of public theology combined with

---

[16] Elaine Graham, *Between a Rock and a Hard Place: Public Theology in a Post-Secular Age* (London: SCM Press, 2013), 71; see also 99–103.

the variety of voices and perspectives in the field make it difficult to talk about, or define, a public theology. As South African theologian John de Gruchy writes: "Given the fact that there are many different currents, different contexts, different influences, different forms of discourse and different forms of reference, it seems self-evident that there will be and must be different approaches to public theology . . . . So it is necessary to talk now about public theolog*ies*, rather than *a* public theology."[17]

Rather than offering one definition, I've endeavored to demonstrate common animating questions related to the role of religion in pluralistic societies and the public nature of theology when religion has been largely privatized. Let's now, however, consider a few definitions of public theology offered by public theologians, listening first to early voices and then moving into more recent contributions.

For Max Stackhouse, "public theology . . . as the primary public task of ecumenical leadership, is concerned with the criteria, and their metaphysical-moral basis, for evaluating and guiding public discourse."[18]

Ronald Theimann describes public theology as "faith seeking to understand the relation between Christian convictions and the broader social and cultural context within which the Christian community lives . . . the goal is to identify the particular places where Christian convictions intersect with the practices that characterize contemporary public life."[19]

Linell Cady writes, "perhaps most basically, a public theology seeks to overcome the cultural marginalization so highly characteristic of contemporary theology. It seeks, furthermore, to contribute to the upbuilding and critical transformation of our public life. It refuses to remain confined to a private sphere, dealing with issues of personal spiritual, salvation, and ethics . . . . A public theology not only must address itself to the wider social and political issues, but it must appropriate a form of argumentation that is genuinely public."[20]

[17] John de Gruchy, "From Political to Public Theologies: The Role of Theology in Public Life in South Africa," in *Public Theology for the 21st Century: Essays in Honor of Duncan B. Forrester* (ed. William F. Storrar and Andrew R. Morton; London: T&T Clark, 2004), 56.
[18] Stackhouse, "An Ecumenist's Plea," 57.
[19] Ronald F. Thiemann, *Constructing a Public Theology: The Church in a Pluralistic Culture* (Louisville, KY: Westminster/John Knox Press, 1991), 21–22.
[20] Cady, *American Public Life*, 25–26.

Duncan Forrester describes public theology as "a theology, talk about God, which claims to point to publicly accessible truth, to contribute to public discussion by witnessing to a truth which is relevant to what is going on in the world and to the pressing issues facing people and societies today."[21]

For Benjamin Valentin, public theology "is a form of discourse that couples either the language, symbols, or the background concepts of a religious tradition with an overarching, integrative, emancipatory sociopolitical perspective in such a way that it movingly captures the attention and moral conscience of a broad audience and promotes the cultivation of those modes of love, care, concern, and courage required for both individual fulfillment and for broad-based social activism."[22]

E. Harold Breitenburg Jr. defines public theology as "theologically informed public discourse about public issues, addressed to the church, synagogue, mosque, temple, or other religious body, as well as the larger public or publics, argued in ways that can be evaluated and judged by publicly available warrants and criteria."[23]

In Nico Koopman's words, public theology attends to "the implications of God's love for the world" and "investigates the significance, meaning, and consequences of this Trinitarian love for a variety of specific contextual public challenges."[24]

According to Sebastian Kim, "public theology is Christians engaging in dialogue with those outside church circles on various issues of common interest. It involves urging Christians to take the opportunity to participate in the public domain in modern secular democracies and to converse with other citizens on issues wider than religious matters."[25]

For Elaine Graham, "public theology is the study of the public relevance of religious thought and practice .... It is both academic discipline and ecclesial discourse, in that it seeks to comment and critically reflect from a theological perspective on aspects of public life such as economics, politics, culture, and media ... public theology is not simply concerned *about* the public, but

[21] Duncan B. Forrester, *Truthful Action* (Edinburgh: T&T Clark, 2000), 127.
[22] Valentin, *Mapping Public Theology*, 87.
[23] E. Harold Breitenberg Jr., "To Tell the Truth: Will the Real Public Theology Please Stand Up?," *Society of Christian Ethics* 23, no. 2 (2003), 66.
[24] Koopman, "Some Contours," 134.
[25] Kim, *Theology in the Public Sphere*, 3.

concerns itself with a particular kind of theological method *in relation to* the public. It cannot simply be comprehensible to those who share its Christian reference-point, but offered into the pluralist public domain in the interests of a common good that transcends the sectional interest of any given religious creed or tradition."[26]

Despite the varieties and development over time, one can see some common themes: concern about areas of society beyond religion, engagement in the public realm, attention to concrete social and public issues, and, increasingly, commitment to speak in publicly accessible language, so that both the content and the method of engagement are public.

PREDECESSORS AND PARALLELS

As a relatively recent development within theology, the field of public theology raises some interesting questions about how to relate to figures who precede it as well as to parallel developments within theology in the twentieth and twenty-first centuries. Focusing first on predecessors, Marty certainly believes public theologians existed before he coined the term. He notes, as we saw above, figures like Jonathan Edwards, Abraham Lincoln, Walter Rauschenbusch, and Reinhold Niebuhr. He later points to black churches as a tradition that encapsulates his vision of public church, pointing to Martin Luther King Jr., in particular, as an exemplar. Rauschenbush, Niebuhr, and King are frequently cited as twentieth-century examples of public theologians, along with John Courtney Murray whose work on Roman Catholicism and American constitutionalism opened the way for Catholic participation in American public life. From the German context, Dietrich Bonhoeffer, Dorothee Soelle, and Jürgen Multmann are sometimes pointed to. In South Africa, as noted above, church-based resistance to apartheid beginning in the mid-twentieth century could be considered examples of public theological engagement.

The criteria for determining who "counts" as a predecessor are dependent upon one's definition of public theology. If it refers, broadly speaking, to how a faith community or religious tradition relates to the wider public world, then we can find innumerable antecedents. If public theology arises more specifically within the context of modern liberal

---

[26] Graham, 71, 97.

democracies and the accompanying privatization of religion, emergence of the public sphere, and the realities of pluralism, then we will be looking at a much smaller pool.

When it comes to parallel movements, public theology is ordinarily distinguished from political theology and liberation theologies. Although all three of these areas arose in the latter half of the twentieth century and are concerned with the intersection of theology and public realities, the approaches have some key differences. The emergence of political theology as an academic discipline traces its origins to thinkers such as Johann Baptist Metz, Jürgen Moltmann, and Dorothee Sölle and their post–World War II German location. Aware of the church's failures in Germany, Metz and Moltmann became convinced that the church is not supposed to remain in the private sphere but is to be publicly engaged with social, political, and economic structures and realities. Within political theology, classic theological themes are often probed for how they can support engagement with contemporary realities (so in Moltmann, eschatology provides a theological basis for Christian critique of current social structures).

Within liberation theology, Latin American liberation theology and black theology are considered the two most prominent threads. Latin American liberation theology first emerged in the 1960s through the pioneering work of Gustavo Gutierrez and tends to focus on poverty, injustice, and political and economic oppression of the poor. The initial development of black liberation theology is attributed to James Cone's *A Black Theology of Liberation* (1970) and black theology continues to explore injustices resulting from slavery, apartheid, and racial discrimination. Deeply attentive to social context, the method used by liberation theologians tends to be one of wedding theology with praxis. This means that theology itself is shaped by what is discovered in concrete historical and practical contexts.

Methodologically, the approaches of political theology and liberation theology differ from the approaches found in public theology, particularly when it comes to the mode of the theological discourse. For most public theologians, finding ways of engaging with public issues using language and concepts that are publicly accessible is considered essential. For the pure public theologian, this methodological approach separates public theology from other forms of theology, even if they have similar interests. Reflecting on these other theologies, Cady writes, "their methods of argumentation are, for the most part, not public. They generally remain confessional theologies, appealing to theological authorities to defend their positions." By contrast, "a public theology not only must address itself to the wider social and political issues, but it must appropriate a form of argumentation that is genuinely public."[27]

CONCLUSION

In the years since the term was first used by Martin Marty, "public theology" has become relatively common place. It may be hard to imagine that a time existed when there was no "public theology." In the broadest sense, the biblical narrative suggests that Christians are part of a great cloud of witnesses for whom being the people of God automatically had public implications. In a more specific sense, the rise of public theology as a discourse happens within post-Enlightenment contexts that bring questions related to the relationship between public and private realms and the role of religion within pluralistic societies to the fore.

These questions defy simple answers, which has led to a range of approaches to and articulations of public theology in recent decades. On the ground, people of Christian faith are enacting their answers to these questions through varieties of political activity and engagement. At the same time, scholars and centers dedicated to public theology endeavor to provide resources to help Christians, rooted in the particularly of their faith tradition, attend to social and public issues and engage in the public realm. The need for such resources shows no signs of abating as political societies and the faith communities that reside within them continue to wrestle with the role and place of religion in the public realm.

Further Reading

Cady, Linell E. (1993), *Religion, Theology, and American Public Life* (Albany: State University of New York Press).
Kim, Sebastian (2011), *Theology in the Public Sphere* (London: SCM Press).
Kim, Sebastian, and Katie Day, eds. (2017), *A Companion to Public Theology* (Leiden: Brill).
Marty, Martin E. (1981), *Public Church: Mainline-Evangelical-Catholic* (New York: Crossroad).
Tracy, David (1981), *The Analogical Imagination: Christian Theology and the Culture of Pluralism* (New York: Crossroad).
Valentin, Benjamin (2002), *Mapping Public Theology: Beyond Culture, Identity, and Difference* (Harrisburg, PA: Trinity Press International).

---

[27] Cady, *American Public Life*, 25–26.

15 Disability Theology

JOHN SWINTON

The field of disability theology is an emerging area of theological enquiry that seeks to explore the relationship between our understandings of God and human beings in the light of the experience of human disability. When it comes to disability, the tendency within the pastoral and ethical literature has been to concentrate on issues around pastoral care and ethics. Here disability is seen as a pastoral or ethical issue with little or no concentrated attention paid to the theological implications. The focus is on ethical dilemmas, such as whether or not prenatal testing for disability is appropriate, or pastoral matters around how to make sure that churches are accessible to people in wheelchairs. There is of course nothing wrong with such approaches. We all need pastoral care and all of us need the tools to deal with complex ethical challenges. Disability theology acknowledges the importance of such things but seeks to push further into a broader range of theological issues, which includes but is not defined by the pastoral and the ethical.

Disability theology is a theological discipline that seeks to explore the ways in which the Bible and Christian traditions interact with the experience of human disability, with a view to deepening, thickening, and challenging understandings of God and the human. It is an analytical and constructive theological enterprise, grounded in human bodily experience, which takes seriously the importance of historical, systematic, and philosophical theology for faithful theological construction. The penultimate intention of disability theology is to enable the voice of people living with disability to be heard and to allow that voice to be viewed as significant in the process of theological formation and Christian practice. By listening carefully to the questions that disability raises for doctrine and tradition, fresh insights and new possibilities emerge for both theology and practice. The ultimate intention of disability theology is to help all people to love God more fully and to realise that they are loved irrespective of the challenges they may face.

Disability theology, like all branches of theology, is rich and diverse, incorporating a variety of different perspectives, possibilities, and alternatives. Disability theologians have written from a diversity of theological perspectives including Feminist,[1] Narrative,[2] Liberation,[3] Pentecostal,[4] Practical,[5] Roman Catholic,[6] Systematic,[7] Philosophical,[8] Process,[9] Theological Ethics,[10] and Missiology.[11] There has also been important work done on specifically doctrinal issues such as Providence,[12] Theological anthropology,[13] Atonement,[14] Time,[15] the Theology of the Cross,[16] and Theodicy.[17] Most of the theological reflection has come from within the Christian tradition, but there is also some important interfaith work.[18] Disability theology is thus seen

---

[1]   D. Freeman, 'A Feminist Theology of Disability', *Feminist Theology*, 10 (2002), 71–85.
[2]   R. Stewart, 'Loop, Hook, Pull: Disabled by Design – Creating a Narrative Theology of Disability', *Theology Today*, 77 (2020), 179–185.
[3]   S. Danforth, 'Liberation Theology of Disability and the Option for the Poor', *Disability Studies Quarterly*, 25, no. 3 (2005), http://dsq-sds.org/article/view/572/749.
[4]   S. Clifton, *Crippled Grace: Disability, Virtue Ethics, and the Good Life* (Waco: Baylor University Press, 2018).
[5]   J. Swinton, *Becoming Friends of Time: Disability, Timefullness, and Gentle Discipleship* (Waco: Baylor University Press, 2016).
[6]   P. Matthews, *Pope John Paul II and the Apparently 'Non-acting' Person* (Leominster: Gracewing, 2013).
[7]   A. Yong, *Theology and Down Syndrome: Reimagining Disability in Late Modernity*, (Waco: Baylor University Press).
[8]   K. Timpe, 'Defiant Afterlife: Disability and Uniting Ourselves to God Disability and Uniting Ourselves to God', in *Voices from the Edge: Centring Marginalized Perspectives in Analytic Theology* (ed. Michelle Panchuk and Michael Rea; Oxford Scholarship Online: August 2020): https://oxford.universitypressscholarship.com/view/10.1093/oso/9780198848844.001.0001/oso-9780198848844-chapter-10.
[9]   H. Reinders, *Disability, Providence, and Ethics: Bridging Gaps, Transforming Lives* (Waco: Baylor University Press, 2014).
[10] B. Brock, *Wondrously Wounded: Theology, Disability and the Body of Christ* (Waco: Baylor University Press, 2020).
[11] B. T. Conner, *Disabling Mission, Enabling Witness: Exploring Missiology Through the Lens of Disability Studies* (Downers Grove, IL: IVP Academic, 2018).
[12] H. Reinders, *Receiving the Gift of Friendship: Profound Disability, Theological Anthropology, and Ethics* (Grand Rapids: Eerdmans, 2013).
[13] Reinders, *Receiving the Gift of Friendship*.
[14] McLachlan, David (2021) *Accessible Atonement: Disability, Theology and the Cross of Christ* (Waco: Baylor University Press).
[15] Swinton, *Becoming Friends of Time*.
[16] M. S. Fast, *God, Suffering, and Disability: A Trinitarian Theodicy of the Cross* (Minneapolis: Fortress Press, 2011).
[17] J. Swinton, *Raging with Compassion: Pastoral Responses to the Problem of Evil* (Grand Rapids: Eerdmans, 2011).
[18] D. Schumm, ed., *Disability and World Religion: An Introduction*. (Waco: Baylor University Press, 2016).

to be a rich, diverse, and lively field of enquiry within which there is no single approach.

That is not to suggest that the field is incoherent. There are key issues around which all these theologies coalesce. Most if not all theologies of disability push into the area of theological anthropology implicitly or explicitly asking the question: what does it mean to have a disability, to be made in God's image and to be fully human just as you are? This question raises crucial issues around justice, fairness, personhood, the purpose of healing, the nature of the resurrection body, the meaning of beauty, and so forth. Most disability theologies focus on one or more of these issues. Tied in with this, a central question for all theologies of disability is: "what is normal?" This applies to bodily shapes and forms, but it also applies to theology. What is a normal body? What is a normal mind? What is a normal theology? Who gets to define what such things are, and what are the theological and practical implications of our formulations and articulations of social, physical, psychological, and theological norms? Questions such as these sit at the heart of the task of disability theology.

AN EXPERIENTIAL THEOLOGICAL ANTHROPOLOGY: MANY BODIES, MANY WORLDS

It is worth pursuing disability theologies' perspectives on theological anthropology a little further. A brief focus on the work of the British practical theologian John Hull will provide a useful foundational perspective that gives a sense of the way in which theological anthropology works itself out within a disability theology framework. In his autobiographical book *Touching The Rock: An Experience of Blindness*[19] and a series on papers on theology and disability,[20] one of the earlier disability theologians John Hull relates his experiences of going blind late in life. Drawing on the phenomenology of Maurice Merleau-Ponty, Hull reflects on the ways human beings gather information and create knowledge. He notes that for sighted people, what is considered real is that which is looked at. 'Reality' is something that is 'out there' waiting to be seen. Using our sight, we gather knowledge from outside and draw it inside of us in order that we can make sense of it. The general assumption is that the dynamic of knowledge gathering is a movement from the

[19] J. Hull, *Touching the Rock: An Experience of Blindness* (London: SPCK, 2011).
[20] All of John Hull's papers can be accessed via this link: www.johnmhull.co.uk/blindness-disability.

outside to the inside, with the human body assumed to be a passive processor of external facts and conditions. This of course is a standard empiricist perspective: 'that which is true is that which falls upon the retina of the eye'. For something to be considered knowledge, we must see it and be able to measure it. When someone loses their sight, the immediate and apparently 'normal' response is to try to make them into as close an approximation of the norm as possible – glasses, contact lenses, eye operations, and so forth, in order that they can see the world again. Within this frame, blindness is inevitably perceived as a deficit, something to be overcome. All of this appears 'obvious' and 'normal'.

The sighted world is the world that Hull inhabited for the first fifty years of his life. But when he began to lose his sight, his knowledge of the world started to change. As his sight faded, he was forced to move inwards. He could no longer look out on the world and see it as he could before. He felt trapped within himself. How could he live in a world that he could not see? But then he had a revelation. The world that we can see when we look out on it is only one of many worlds. As his sight declined, he began to realise that he was moving into a different world, the world of blindness. The world began to reveal itself to him in new ways. He had to learn what colours meant when they are described and not seen. When a sound comes to us, we tend to look towards its source. What do sounds mean when you cannot see the source of the sound? His hands, which were previously used to write, to pick up, to push things around, now became primary modes of sensory perception. He would never again see his children. But he could feel them, and when he did, he discovered things about them that had been hidden when he was sighted. In the intimacy of that act of knowing through feeling, he encountered the feel of their skin, the bumps on their heads, the way their faces move when they smiled, the sound of their crying when tears could not be seen. Rather than being a deficit or a disability, Hull, eventually, discovered that being blind opened a whole new world that had not been accessible to him previously. He concludes that our bodies are a primary source of knowledge of the world. Because our bodies can differ in fundamental ways, we do not all encounter the world in the same way. When we recognise this, the idea of normality comes under serious pressure. All of us view and experience the world from different perspectives. None of these perspectives is definitive. We require all of them in order truly to come to know and understand the world. All of us, through our bodies, construct and abide in phenomenal worlds that may be quite different from one another but that nonetheless reveal something of the richness and diversity of human experience. The key point here is that being human is not a single thing, but a multitude of possibilities and perspectives held together by the shared image of God, but not defined by the presence or absence of any attribute or experience. Our task is not to attempt to colonise ways of being human and to enthrone them as normal. What is required is hospitable conversation and dialogue that aims not to convert one way of being human into another but rather to listen and learn in order that we can live and love together. Disability theology in all its forms attempts to give voice to these different ways of being human and to show the difference that these distinctive perspectives on humanity make to both theology and practice.

THEORETICAL ROOTS: DISABILITY, DISABILITY STUDIES, AND THE FOUNDATIONS OF DISABILITY THEOLOGY

Having laid out some basic perspectives on disability theology, we must now begin to look more closely at its roots, where it came from, what its intentions are, and what it contributes to the theological enterprise. An obvious place to begin this task is by thinking about what we mean when we use the term 'disability'. The World Health Organisation informs us that around 15 per cent (over a billion) of the world's population lives with some form of disability. 'This global estimate for disability is on the rise due to population ageing and the rapid spread of chronic diseases, as well as improvements in the methodologies used to measure disability.'[21] Experiencing a disability is not exceptional. All of us will eventually end up disabled. Disability is a normal aspect of human development. This is why disability theologians tends to talk about people being 'temporarily able bodied'. The term disability' does not refer exclusively to a particular group of people but is a shared destiny of all human beings. The question then is why is it that some forms of disability draw negative attention?

DISABILITY AS DIFFERENCE

At heart, disability is a particular form of human difference. Sometimes this difference arises naturally through birth or life processes, at other times it is thrust upon people through accident and circumstance. All of

[21] World Health Organisation (2011), 'World Report on Disability Summary', www.who .int/publications/i/item/WHO-NMH-VIP-11.01.

us are different, but not all forms of difference are perceived and treated in the same way. If I am an intellectual genius, I am considered different, but that difference will be respected and valued within society. If I have an intellectual disability, I will be considered different, but that difference will not be valued, indeed it may be actively devalued within a society that prioritises intellect as a desirable social good. Both forms of difference are either valued or devalued using the same criteria. The key is what kind of difference any given culture chooses to value. The value of differences is thus seen to be socially constructed. The difference that is named disability is not only a physical or psychological state, it is also a social process.

The World Health Organisation lays out its definition of disability in the International Classification of Functioning, Disability and Health (ICF). This report defines disability as follows:

> an umbrella term for impairments, activity limitations, and participation restrictions. Disability refers to the negative aspects of the interaction between individuals with health condition (such as cerebral palsy, Down syndrome, depression) and personal and environmental factors (such as negative attitudes, inaccessible transportation and public buildings, and limited social supports).[22]

There are two things that we need to learn from this definition that are helpful for current purposes. Firstly, it draws a conceptual distinction between impairments and disabilities. Impairments are the physical or psychological differences that reside within individuals. Some people may require medical intervention to relieve pain and improve quality of life if an impairment (e.g., swollen joints, remediable poor vision, broken bones) unnecessarily restricts a person's life. Impairments are not in and of themselves considered negative.

Becoming disabled emerges from a negative, interactive social process that occurs when a particular impairment rubs up against social and environmental factors. For example, if intellectual ability was not considered a source of value, it would make little difference whether you had a high intellect or a lower one. A negative sense of difference is therefore not inherent to the condition. The problem for those with intellectual disabilities is not internal, it is external, relating to the

---

[22] World Health Organization International Classification of Functioning, Disability and Health, www.who.int/standards/classifications/international-classification-of-functioning-disability-and-health.

priorities of their social context. Disability is thus seen to emerge from the interaction between personal and environmental factors.

DISABILITY STUDIES

This way of thinking about social implications of difference has its roots in Disability Studies, a discipline that has had a profound influence on the conceptual and theoretical roots of disability theology. Disability studies is

> an interdisciplinary area of study based in the humanities and social sciences that views disability in the context of culture, society, and politics rather than through the lens of medicine or psychology. In the latter disciplines, 'disability' is typically viewed as a distance from the 'norm' in order to bring the disabled closer to the established norm. This area of study questions that view and presents a variety of perspectives on disability, from contemporary society as well as from a range of cultures and histories. Seeking to broaden the understanding of disability, to better understand the experience of disability in society, and to contribute to social change for people with disabilities, the discipline challenges the idea of the normal-abnormal binary and suggests that a range of human variations are 'normal'.[23]

There are two strands of disability studies thinking that it will be useful to highlight here. In the United Kingdom, disability studies emerged from within sociology wherein a group of physically disabled sociologists began to comment on the role that the built environment played in turning impairments into disabilities.[24] These theorists noted that if the built environment was made accessible to wheelchair users, they would no longer be disabled. It was the built environment that caused their disablement. From observations such as this, they developed what has become known as the social model of disability. This model runs along the dynamic of impairment and disability that we have explored thus far and underpins key policy documents such as the World Health Organisation definition we looked at previously and the UK legislative document, The Disability Discrimination Act (DDA), designed to

---

[23] N. E. Rice (2018), 'Disability Studies', *Encyclopaedia Britannica*, www.britannica.com/topic/disability-studies.
[24] M. Oliver, *The Politics of Disablement* (Basingstoke: Macmillan, 1990).

protect the rights of people with disabilities in the United Kingdom and
Northern Ireland.[25]

In the United States, the conversation developed in a slightly different direction. The underpinning philosophical approach of the social
model remained important but was combined with thinking that
emerged from reflection on the successes of the civil rights movement
in the 1960s. The question here is: what is it that holds together diverse
experiences such as Down's syndrome, cerebral palsy, and spina bifida?
The answer is: a shared experience of injustice and oppression. People
with disabilities are best conceived as an oppressed minority group.
This approach has come to be known as the minority group model. It
seeks to apply the principles, ideas, and political methods that brought
liberation to people of colour, to those living with disabilities. The focus
is on justice, fairness, autonomy, freedom of choice, and political
change. A highlight for this movement was the implementation of the
Americans with Disabilities act (ADA) in 1990, which put into law anti-
discriminatory policies.[26] A significant problem with this legislation
was that the churches fought to be exempted, arguing inter alia that it
would be too expensive to modify ancient buildings to make them
accessible. This led to the anomalous situation wherein the rights of
people living with disabilities were protected by society but not by
the church.

IS GOD DISABLED?

It was into this complex political situation that Nancy Eiesland wrote
what is probably one of the most influential books for disability theology: *The Disabled God: Toward a Liberatory Theology of Disability*.
Eiesland was a sociologist who wrote this text as her master's dissertation in theology at Emory University in Atlanta. She was familiar with
the complexities of social change around issues of disability and deeply
disappointed by the church's apparent abandonment of people with
disabilities. She was, however, not surprised. As a person with a disability, she was painfully familiar with the injustice and oppression that
people experienced inside the church. The church's refusal to sign up to
the ADA was symptomatic of a deeper problem in relation to disability.

[25] 'Disability Rights', www.gov.uk/rights-disabled-person.
[26] ADA National Network, 'What Is the Americans with Disabilities Act', https://adata
.org/learn-about-ada.

Eiesland lived with a congenital bone problem, which meant that she experienced considerable amounts of pain and lived her life in a wheelchair. She had had a series of negative interactions with the church. She had felt a call to ordination but was turned down on the basis that she was disabled. She had also had numerous experiences of people responding to her situation by trying to heal her and insinuating that her condition remained because of a lack of faith. She points to these kinds of experience as examples of ableist theology, which is not only damaging for people with disabilities but is also based on theological ideas that are open to challenge. Eiesland sets out to uncover the theological roots of this problem and to offer a different theology that is open to the experience of disability. In order to do this, she draws upon a mode of liberation theology that finds its focus within the minority model of disability. This combination allows her to develop what she describes as a liberatory theology of disability.

AN ABLEIST IMAGE OF GOD

Central to Eiesland's theological concerns is the need to re-symbolise God. Because the perspective of people living with disabilities has not been a part of the hermeneutic that has underpinned our efforts to understand God, our images of God have been lacking. Eiesland identifies the basic theological problem that underpins the injustice experienced by people with disabilities in the church as relating to the creation of an ableist image of God. By this she means an understanding of God that only takes into consideration the experiences of able-bodied people. God is invisible and unknowable other than through revelation (Col. 1:15). Nevertheless, whatever revelation we receive needs to be deciphered and communicated through language and concepts that human beings can understand, otherwise nothing is revealed. And, of course, this is where the problems begin. Even with the help of the Spirit, humans remain fallen and fallible. Because God is invisible, we have no direct knowledge of what God might look like and only limited knowledge of how God thinks and functions, if indeed such terms are applicable to God. Scripture tells us that God is powerful, strong, beautiful, intelligent, perfect. The problem is that whilst these things may be true, our understanding of such concepts is inevitably bound to and shaped by what we assume them to mean. When we encounter these descriptors of God, we therefore have a limited range of ways in which we can understand them. From where do we get our images of beauty or cleverness? We are taught them by our society.

Disability is a highly stigmatised form of difference within Western cultures. If we begin our theological construction with the assumption that disability is to be considered negatively or primarily in terms of sin and fallenness then we will either take no cognisance of it when we are constructing our images of God, or if we do, we will assume its negativity. Eiesland points towards the tendency to project human ideals onto God. When we do so, we implicitly or explicitly assume that certain forms of human bodily and psychological experience are more representative of God's image than others. She argues that we need to re-symbolise God, that is, to develop an image of God that includes disability as an aspect of our theological and, as we shall see, our eschatological imagination.

RE-SYMBOLISING GOD

Eiesland finds the source of that re-symbolisation in two interlocking ways, one drawn from human experience and the other from a reimagining of Scripture. Her perspective on God changed when she encountered an African American man who lived with quadriplegia:

> My epiphany bore little resemblance to the God I was expecting or the God of my dreams. I saw God in a sip-puff wheelchair, that is, the chair used mostly by quadriplegics enabling them to maneuver by blowing and sucking on a straw-like device. Not an omnipotent self sufficient God, but neither a pitiable, suffering servant. In this moment, I beheld God as a survivor, unpitying and forthright. I recognized the incarnate Christ in the image of those judged 'not feasible', 'unemployable', with 'questionable quality of life'. Here was God for me.[27]

Here Eiesland uses a very different image to inform her imagination as to what the invisible God looks like. God is re-symbolised in a way that fully recognises the experience of people with physical impairments. In doing this, she raises important theological questions around the meaning of God's omnipotence, the nature of vulnerability in understanding God and humans, and the dangers of projecting human ideas about power and agency onto God.

The Scriptural dimension of her re-symbolisation comes when she begins to reflect on Jesus's resurrection appearances in Luke 24, she argues that God is in fact disabled:

---

[27] N. Eiesland, *The Disabled God: Towards a liberatory theology of disability*, (Nashville: Abingdon Press, 1990)

> While they were still talking about this, Jesus himself stood among them and said to them, 'Peace be with you.' They were startled and frightened, thinking they saw a ghost. He said to them, 'Why are you troubled, and why do doubts rise in your minds? Look at my hands and my feet. It is I myself! Touch me and see; a ghost does not have flesh and bones, as you see I have'. (Lk. 24:36–30)

The resurrected Christ carries the wounds of his crucifixion:

> The foundation of Christian theology is the resurrection of Jesus Christ. Yet seldom is the resurrected Christ recognized as a deity whose hands, feet, and side bear marks of profound physical impairment. In presenting his impaired body to his startled friends, the resurrected Jesus is revealed as the disabled God. Jesus, the resurrected Savior, calls for his frightened companions to recognize in the marks of impairment their own connection with God, their salvation.[28]

For Eiesland, God is disabled and carries the scars of that disability on into the afterlife. By re-symbolising God and pointing out that, in her opinion, Jesus was disabled after the resurrection, Eiesland intends to challenge traditional thinking around beauty, normality, and the image of God and in so doing allow for the development of a different theology and a different image of God that can guide the church more faithfully. If the resurrected God is disabled, then disablement in the present can no longer be seen as merely the product of evil, the fall, or any other negative theological interpretation. If Jesus is disabled, then disability is a part of the resurrection life.

There are of course problems with Eiesland's liberatory theology. The image that she develops seems detached from mainstream doctrinal development, which leaves it open to accusations that it is overly contextual and purely pragmatic. Similarly, when the bulk of the book argues for the social model and the minority group status of people with disabilities, it is difficult to see how the physical scars of Jesus can now be classified as marks of disability. It is perhaps better to think of the wounds of Jesus as reminders of the source of our redemption than marks of disability. Nevertheless, Eiesland's method and approach clearly illustrate a highly influential way in which theology has been and continues to be constructed within disability theology.

---

[28] Eiesland, *The Disabled God*, 11.

CONTEMPORARY DEVELOPMENTS IN DISABILITY
THEOLOGY: FROM LIBERATION TO TRADITION

Eiesland's liberatory approach has been highly influential and her constructive contextual theological approach runs through a good deal of
the early and contemporary literature on disability theology. It is, however, not the only way in which disability theologians have approached
the issue of doctrine and doctrinal construction. Whilst Eiesland sits
rather loosely to doctrine and tradition, recent thinkers have focused
more on the implications of engaging critically with Scripture, doctrine,
and tradition in the light of the experience of human disability. In their
book *Disability in the Christian Tradition*,[29] Brian Brock and John
Swinton explore the ways in which, despite common perception, disability has in fact been an aspect of the work of several key theologians
throughout the history of the church. They trace the ways in which
Augustine, Aquinas, Julian of Norwich, Luther, Calvin, Hegel,
Kierkegaard, van den Bergh, Bonhoeffer, Barth, and Hauerwas have all
made attempts to explore aspects of human disability in ways that have
been formative within the tradition. Whilst most contemporary disability theology like Eiesland's is done with the presumptions of modernity
in mind, listening carefully to pre-modern voices reveals crucial aspects
relevant to theology and practice and helps us to see that disability may
not be as absent from historical theological conversations as some
modern disability theologians may assume.

Within systematic theology, there have also been some useful contributions. Primary among them is the important work of the
Pentecostal theologian Amos Yong. In his book *Theology and Down
Syndrome: Reimagining Disability in Late Modernity*, Yong brings
systematic theology to bear on the issue of disability, making significant contributions to the doctrines of creation, providence, and the
imago dei, alongside of some important thinking around disability
and theodicy.

Deborah Creamer, in her book *Disability and Christian Theology:
Embodied Limits and Constructive Possibilities*,[30] engages with Sally
McFague to develop a model of disability and humanness that focuses
on the importance of limits. All human beings are limited and

---

[29] B. Brock and J. Swinton, *Disability in the Christian Tradition: A Reader* (Grand
     Rapids: Eerdmans, 2012).
[30] D. Creamer, *Disability and Christian Theology: Embodied Limits and Constructive
     Possibilities* (New York: Oxford University Press, 2012).

dependent, at least to a degree. This limitation is holistic: intellectual, spiritual, physical, and emotional. Limits should not be looked at as exceptional or as things that only people with disabilities encounter. They are an integral aspect of the human condition. Creamer develops an integrated model that brings together disability studies, systematic theology, feminist theology, and Scripture and makes three claims that she insists theology should take seriously in relation to disability: firstly, that limits are a shared human characteristic; secondly, that human experience is intricately tied in with limits; and thirdly, that limits are not inevitably bad. Sometimes they can be good. In doing this she challenges traditional theodicy and explanations of disability that begin with the assumption that the limits people encounter are inherently bad. She also challenges those dimensions of the social model that assume that everything about disability is a social construction. Suffering is real and is a genuine limit. But that limit need not be viewed as bad or evil. It is simply a focused aspect of the general human experience. It is not only the shared experience of oppression that binds people with disabilities together. It is also the sharing of limits.

Finally, excellent work has also been done by Hans Reinders on providence[31] and theological anthropology. His thinking on the development of our relationships with God as a gift coming from outside of ourselves opens up space for people with profound intellectual disabilities to relate to God without the need to respond at an intellectual level. Reinders develops a theological anthropology that is inclusive and centred on gift and grace. Taken together, all these approaches offer a significant contribution to our understanding of doctrine and the ways in which it is constructed, reconstructed, tested, and acted upon when we take into consideration disability issues.

RAISING DIFFICULT QUESTIONS: ARE THERE DISABILITIES IN HEAVEN?

In moving towards a conclusion to this chapter, it will be helpful to illustrate something of the basic method and approach that lies behind many strands of disability theology. The underlying dynamic is to juxtapose the experience of disability with traditional ideas and understandings about who God is and how God functions in order to reveal fresh understandings of God and human beings. We can see this process

[31] Reinders, *Disability, Providence, and Ethics.*

at work if we turn to the ongoing conversation around whether or not there will be disabilities in heaven. The discussion we have had in the earlier parts of the chapter already begins to problematise simplistic assumptions that we will look the way we imagine in heaven. Images of heaven tend to assume that that which we consider to be broken will be fixed and completed in heaven. The general assumption is that disabilities will be done away with when we get to heaven. We have already seen that this may be problematic if our theological constructions tend to be projections of our own ideas and if disability is not inherently or always a bad thing.

DISABILITY AND IDENTITY

In *Theology and Down Syndrome*, Amos Yong presents an argument that his brother Mark who lives with Down's Syndrome has no need for healing. He is whole and complete, just the way he is. Yong expects Mark to be the same person in heaven as he is in earth today. This sameness includes his Down's Syndrome. In this respect, Yong's position is similar to that found in Eiesland's work. Eiesland grew up being taught that she would no longer have her disability in heaven. We might assume that this thought is comforting and for some it is. But for Eiesland it was horrifying:

> having been disabled from birth, I came to believe that in heaven I would be absolutely unknown to myself and perhaps to God. My disability has taught me who I am and who God is. What would it mean to be without this knowledge?

For Eiesland as for Yong, disability is deeply tied in with identity. If you take away the person's disability, you take away something of their identity. Without their disability, a person would become a stranger to themselves.

In teasing out the implications of the suggestion that there may be disabilities in heaven, we need to begin by noting the difference between congenital and acquired disabilities. A congenital disability is one that has been with someone since before or immediately after birth. Something like Down's Syndrome, spina bifida, or brain damage due to birth trauma would be examples of congenital disability. An acquired disability is one that a person encounters during their life journey through trauma, illness, and so forth. Both congenital and acquired disabilities are identity forming but in different ways. Those disability theologians who live with or encounter congenital disabilities tend to assume that change in the eschaton is an incompatible change in identity. Those with acquired disabilities do not necessarily see the disability as a crucial aspect of their identity and may develop a theology that includes the eradication of disability in heaven. Like all theology, context matters. Here we will focus on the kinds of viewpoint put forward by Yong and Eiesland, which comes from the perspective of congenital disability.

ELIMINATING THE DISABILITY IS TO ELIMINATE THE PERSON?

In an interesting exchange between Amos Yong and the analytical philosopher Ryan Mullins,[32] this issue of identity in the eschaton is brought to the fore in a way that will help us to see the issues and tensions. Yong had indicated that there would be disabilities in heaven and mentioned Stanley Hauerwas's dictum that 'to eliminate the disability means to eliminate the subject'.[33] This was a rather unusual statement for Hauerwas to make and one that Mullins notes he simply states but does not argue. If Hauerwas is correct, it is necessary for disabilities to be present in heaven as they are central to the identity of the individual. Mullins thinks that Hauerwas mistakes metaphysical identity with a sense of self, a statement, which if correct, would also apply to Eiesland's proposal and Yong's assessment of his brother's eschatological future. According to Mullins, disability is a contingent state that is not an essential property. Hauerwas's dictum in this perspective is clearly flawed. As Kevin Timpe points out:

> It [Hauerwas's dictum] can't be true if there is any person such that they have a disability at one time and lack a disability at another ... there are such people, namely those with acquired or temporary disabilities.[34]

To tie the fullness of the person in with the presence of their disability makes no sense if one can at one moment have an identity that does not include disability and potentially seconds later to have an identity that is totally defined by the acquisition of a disability.

---

[32] R. T. Mullins, 'Some Difficulties for Amos Yong's Disability Theology of the Resurrection', *Ars Disputandi* 11 (2011), 24–32, www.ArsDisputandi.org.

[33] S. Hauerwas, 'Marginalizing the "Retarded"', in *The Deprived, the Disabled, and the Fullness of Life* (ed. F. Dougherty; Wilmington: Michael Glazier, 1984), 67–105.

[34] Timpe, 'Defiant Afterlife', 220.

However, Timpe continues:

rejecting Hauerwas's dictum doesn't entail that there won't be any
disabilities in heaven. If having a particular disability is an
accidental rather than an essential property of the person who has
that disability, then it is possible that the person could be
resurrected without having that property and yet not have their
personal identity endangered. Mullins is right about this
conditional. But note that not all accidental properties must be
lost in the resurrection. For instance, consider the following
properties: *the property of being Jameson's, Emmaline's, and
Magdalen's father* ... [Timpe currently has this property] .... But
nothing in the resurrection requires that I cease to be my children's
parent ... simply because those properties aren't essential to my
personal identity. We strongly identify with lots of our non-
essential properties; but our resurrection doesn't require that
they're not present in the eschaton.[35]

New Zealand practical theologian Maja Whitaker offers a helpful perspective that throws further light on the issues that Yong, Tempe, and
Mullins are wrestling with.[36] She contemplates the question of how
much change a body can undergo before it ceases to carry the same
identity. If a transformation is too drastic, the person will be put out of
existence and replaced by another new person. She asks: 'how different
can a person's post-resurrection body be from their pre-resurrection
body while still maintaining continuity of personal identity and so
fulfilling the Christian hope for a fully personal afterlife?'[37] Noting that
scripture points towards resurrection as a bodily process, not just the
survival of the soul, she points out that:

At times after his resurrection Jesus appears to function in a
relatively normal physical human body – eating and being touched
to prove his materiality – while at other points his body has otherworldly characteristics – walking through walls and disappearing
from sight. There is both continuity and discontinuity between
Jesus's pre-resurrection and post-resurrection body, and we can
expect the same for ours. Our bodies will not be abolished, but

---

[35] Timpe, 'Defiant Afterlife', 220.
[36] M. Whitaker, 'Perfected Yet Still Disabled? Continuity of Embodied Identity in
      Resurrection Life', *Stimulus: The New Zealand Journal of Christian Thought and
      Practice* 26, no. 2 (2019), 18–25.
[37] Whitaker, 'Perfected Yet Still Disabled', 8.

they will be transformed, as indeed will all creation, which waits in eager expectation for its redemption from decay (Rom. 8:21).[38]

Whitaker concludes with a tentative proposal:

And so perhaps the 'problem' with a disabled body is not the body itself, but the world which it inhabits. We look forward to God setting right everything that is wrong, but what is wrong is not the disabled body; instead it is everything that disables the experience of that body – both the physical and social environment of the old creation. The body of a person with a disability here and now does not need to be 'corrected' for resurrection life, because it does not fundamentally contradict the imago Dei in each of us. As Eiesland wrote, 'full personhood is fully compatible with the experience of disability.' Seeing the resurrected Christ with wounds intact, illustrates this most fully. Furthermore, if Christ's resurrection is the model for ours, then perhaps our resurrection bodies will still retain the injuries and defects of earthly life, whether they be an amputated leg, an intellectual disability, a hemiplegia, or a speech delay.[39]

And so, we find ourselves circling back into the social model but this time with a profoundly theological dimension. At a minimum, heaven will be a place where there are no more stigmatic interpretations of human bodies and no rejection on the basis of differences that are considered by some to be negative. All talk about heaven is speculative, but if we take disability into consideration, the speculation has implications for the present. If heaven is a place where disability is destigmatised but not necessarily eradicated, and if Jesus is correct that heaven is with us now and in the future ('Thy will be done on heaven as it is on earth', Matt. 6:10), recognising these facts has important implications for the way in which we live into heaven in the present, and respond to disability as we encounter it in our daily lives.

Of course, such a theological position will not be satisfactory for all people. Like all theology, the end point of theological conversations such as this is not to come to neat conclusions but to raise questions and challenges that enable us to think about doctrinal constructions in fresh, imaginative, and transformative ways. Disability theology does not claim to have all of the answers, but it does have a legitimate claim to be at the table.

---

[38] Whitaker, 'Perfected Yet Still Disabled', 3.
[39] Ibid.

CONCLUSION

In this chapter, we have delved into some key aspects of disability theology, exploring something of its history, its relationship to other forms of theological reflection, and its method and intentions. Whilst its roots lie within liberation theology, recent developments have moved it into mainstream theological and philosophical conversations that offer important possibilities for fresh conversations and important new discoveries. Nevertheless, it is important that as the field develops, it doesn't lose sight of its liberatory roots. The primary purpose of all theology is to participate with God in God's loving task of redeeming the world. A significant aspect of that task relates to issues around ensuring justice and fairness for those who are experiencing oppression. Indeed, the prophet Jeremiah tells us that social action in the defence of oppressed people is part of what it means to know God. He defended the cause of the poor and needy and so all went well. 'Is that not what it means to know *me?'*[40] declares the Lord (Jer. 22:16). Disability theology provides an opportunity to hold together the intellectual dimensions of theology with the embodied aspects of knowing God in a way that brings insight and liberation to all of us.

Further Reading

Brock, B. (2020), *Wondrously Wounded: Theology, Disability and the Body of Christ* (Waco: Baylor University Press).

Brock, B., and Swinton, J. (2012), *Disability in the Christian Tradition: A Reader* (Grand Rapids: Eerdmans).

Clifton, S. (2018), *Crippled Grace: Disability, Virtue Ethics, and the Good Life* (Waco: Baylor University Press).

Conner, B. T. (2018), *Disabling Mission, Enabling Witness: Exploring Missiology Through the Lens of Disability Studies* (Downers Grove, IL: IVP Academic).

Matthews, P. (2013), *Pope John Paul II and the Apparently 'Non-acting' Person* (Leominster: Gracewing).

Reinders, H. (2013), *Receiving the Gift of Friendship: Profound Disability, Theological Anthropology, and Ethics* (Grand Rapids: Eerdmans).

Swinton, J. (2016), *Becoming Friends of Time: Disability, Timefullness, and Gentle Discipleship*, (Waco: Baylor University Press).

Timpe, K. (2020), 'Defiant Afterlife: Disability and Uniting Ourselves to God Disability and Uniting Ourselves to God', in *Voices from the Edge: Centring Marginalized Perspectives in Analytic Theology* (ed. M. Panchuk and M. Rea; Oxford Scholarship Online).

Yong, A. (2007), *Theology and Down Syndrome: Reimagining Disability in Late Modernity* (Waco: Baylor University Press).

---

[40] Italics added.

16 Black Theology

WILLIE JAMES JENNINGS

Black Theology questions. It questions the way both the formal and informal enterprise of Christian theological reflection has come to exist in the modern world. Black theology questions modern theology because the modern theological enterprise is permeated with whiteness. This means that modern theology, theology from the fifteenth century forward, formed inside and helped form modern racial consciousness. This also means that modern theology directly and indirectly helped foster white supremacy and white hegemony. Black theology formed to give witness to Christianity submerged in the death-dealing realities of racial existence. Yet to be submerged in racial existence has brought the painfully difficult task of attempting to get people, especially Christians, to see the very thing they are inside of – this has been the burden of black theology.

When did black theology first form? It has two beginnings. Black theology began to form when the peoples of what we now call Africa began being enslaved by the peoples of what we now call Europe for the central purpose of profit. Slavery was not the new thing, nor was it new for the peoples of what we now call Africa to enslave one another as the result of war, territorial conquest, or various forms of patronage constituted by familial or clan obligations. The new thing was a form of slavery that was rooted in profit and justified by perceived differences in bodies, differences that were to be eventually organized hierarchically. Early Europeans created a scale of existence with white at the highest end of maturity and development and black at the lowest end. That scale was not just about Europeans and Africans. It was a scale used to gauge all peoples. All people could be plotted between white and black and then told implicitly and explicitly that the goal of human existence was to move, if possible, toward white, toward the European, in order to achieve one's humanity, that is to show the maturity and development necessary to be deemed fully human.

Modern slavery, slavery rooted in profit and racial difference, formed in and with Christianity. European Christians justified slavery through the use of two crucial doctrinal ideas, providence and salvation. Providence applied to modern slavery and colonialism meant that European Christians saw themselves as central to the unfolding plan of God for the world, especially the new worlds they were entering in power. Salvation applied to modern slavery and colonialism meant that they saw themselves as tasked by God to bring the nonwhite world into salvation, which included being brought into the maturity of European life, especially religious life. Just as peoples could be plotted racially in terms of their human maturity and development, so too could their ways of showing devotion and veneration be gauged in relation to the European. The concept Europeans used to capture these different ways of devotion and veneration was religion. They could gauge the religions of peoples along a racial scale of existence. At the highest end of spiritual maturity and mental development was Christianity followed by Judaism and Islam (all designated as monotheistic religions), then somewhere in the middle were the non-monotheistic and polytheistic religions, and at the lowest end were so-called nature religions.[1]

This scale of existence was also calibrated along the lines of gender and sexuality. Masculinity was aligned with mastery and femininity meant docile submission and applied to religion this meant that one could be evaluated through their rational mastery over religion. At the highest end was a masculinity articulated through the reasoned articulation of one's religion, while at the lowest end was a femininity articulated through the irrational adherence to one's religion. A reasonable religion was not only a masculinist religion in its articulation but a patriarchal and heterosexual one in its execution at the highest end of its maturity and its development. At its lowest end were religions that were matriarchal and sexuality that was non-heterosexual and therefore seen as antinomian.[2] Modern slavery was understood by Christian slavers and Christian slaveholding society as a tool for tutelage for bringing nonwhite peoples to Christian maturity. That maturity in effect patterned life according to the imagined world of a white heterosexual man who could offer a rational explication for his Christian belief and lived in a patriarchally structured home and society.

[1] David Chidester, *Empire of Religion: Imperialism and Comparative Religion* (Chicago: University of Chicago Press, 2014).
[2] Richard C. Trexler, *Sex And Conquest: Gendered Violence, Political Order, and the European Conquest of the Americas* (Ithaca: Cornell University Press, 1995).

Black theology formed first as a response to and negotiation with a colonial Christianity that created a brutal slavery-constituted form of Christian life. That form of faith executed a relentless evaluative logic that not only interpreted black life as permanently inferior but also put in place an obsessive desire to control the black body. This will to organize focused heavily on ordering the bodies and behaviors of black peoples, especially women. It would focus Christian discipline and practice through surveillance and the constant suspicion of the efficacy of black confession and morality in ways that would for white Christianity make leadership coming from black people always doubtful and black religious participation in white ecclesial spaces always undesirable.

There were three responses to this white Christianity by indigenous peoples in general and black peoples specifically that formed the basis of black theology. Even as we consider these responses, it is important to note that early Europeans did not introduce Christianity to Africans in toto. There were vibrant Christian communities already present on the continent, but modern slaveholding Christianity in its aggressive colonialist reality introduced these new struggles to existing African Christian communities that produced these responses.[3] All of these responses were constitutive elements of black theology.

A first response to hearing colonial Christianity and seeing it in operation was to reject it as nothing but nonsense. For many peoples, the ideas of Christian theology were abhorrent. Not only did they not believe it, but they understood Christian faith to be toxic to their people. They may have been very polite with the Christians in their midst. They may have even attended church, bowed their heads in prayer, and sung the songs of Zion, but all of it was nonsense for them. This trajectory of thinking summarized Christian reflection on life and on God as nothing more than the religion of the colonialists and was therefore nothing more than an object, an obscene object to take note of and maybe to seek to understand in the way a doctor would seek to understand a disease. This trajectory of thinking, if it engaged theological reflection and doctrine, did so in order to gauge the level of pathology at work in those who took it seriously. This first response formed as a kind of theology itself, a form of theological reflection that took theology and doctrine seriously as signatures of sickness. Doctrines and those who adhere to doctrines show the signs of

---

[3] Lamin Sanneh, *West African Christianity: The Religious Impact* (Maryknoll, NY: Orbis Books, 1983).

colonized minds, collaborators with the white colonial legacies of control and all that has followed from those legacies.

A second response to Christianity was to use it to reconstruct native religion. There are those who saw Christianity as simply a violent and oppressive system that had to be negotiated and, if possible, used to affirm and articulate their own native life and vision. For many peoples, Christianity was a religion and a system of thought that shattered their own indigenous religions and ways of knowing. The goal for these peoples became to gather the fragments that remained and sometimes use Christian rituals, symbols, ideas, and concepts and sometimes gut those same symbols, ideas, and concepts to form or reform their native or indigenous religions and ways of knowing. Two kinds of fragments were woven together, the fragments of their peoples and Christian fragments. For example, indigenous peoples in general and African peoples specifically took parts of the birth and death rituals of the various forms of Christianity they were introduced to and wove them with parts of the birth and death rituals of their peoples to create something that sustained their religious vision albeit now altered by interaction with Christian thought and practice. These folks may have known and understood Christian theology and Christian doctrines, but they had no interest in orthodoxy or adhering to a precise doctrinal articulation or understanding. Theological reflection for them was trying to weave together the fragments toward a way of living and a way of healing that moved beyond the confines of Christian faith and thought. This trajectory of thinking engaged in theological reflection in order to build religious vision that it believed would be more helpful than orthodox Christianity.

With either response one or two, the categories of atheist or agnostic would not really fit well because we are talking about trajectories of thinking that are what I call patterns of adaptation oriented to colonialism and modern slavery or, more precisely, colonial modernity. These first two responses show forms of theological reflection caught in the aftermath of colonial modernity that was yet oriented to that condition. But there was a third response that was also caught in the aftermath of colonial modernity, but its patterns of adaptation are oriented toward the gospel, that is, that there is something new, unique, and unprecedented in Christianity that should be life altering because it is life giving.

This third trajectory of thinking was rooted in those who accepted Christianity. In a way, this is the miracle that took place inside colonial Christianity and modern slavery – that some peoples believed and yet believe. These are folks who became serious Christians, and by serious I simply mean they believed the specifics of the faith and sought to think out of those specifics. But here we have to have an A and B.

In trajectory 3A were those who accepted the colonial configuration of Christianity. They accepted the scale of racial existence. They calibrated their lives toward white masculinist life and Christian theological articulation that would show its mastery. They fully assimilated to a Christianity aiming toward governmentality, that is, an imperial Christianity that aimed to control bodies, behaviors, and desires. They took into themselves the derogatory vision of their peoples as deficient, demonically possessed, or demonically influenced and dangerous without proper Christian tutelage. So, their Christian orthodoxy was articulated from within the logics of racial and cultural assimilation. No assimilation is ever perfect and so with this response, indigenous ways of thinking and envisioning life seeped through, but they were often held at bay or heavily policed so as to not affect or infect the shape of their Christian theological reflection. This meant that the emphases on interpreting texts, the places of doctrinal focus, the vision of the Christian life mirrored as tightly as possible the colonial masters. This was Christianity as a vehicle of assimilation and the theology formed in this response was a tool to transform people into white men by an abiding approximation of white masculinist intellectual dispositions.

In trajectory 3B were those who accepted Christianity but did not accept its colonial configuration. But this was a struggle, because to separate their Christianity from its colonial configuration was an unprecedented work. They had no model for doing this. They did however rely on three fundamental intellectual gestures that shaped the thinking that moved in this direction. First, they established Jesus himself, his life, his words, his death, his resurrection as the hermeneutic (interpretive) center of Christianity. They thought their faith from Jesus as the site of God's love for them and he became the fundamental point of reorientation against colonial logics and the racial vision of the world born of white colonial settlers. Secondly, they entered and enacted the biblical story as the way through which to read their lives and society. The biblical story understood here as the collective reality of the stories of scripture was much more than textual warrant for belief. The biblical story was the way one entered God's world and life with God that was not a world controlled by white Christianity and certainly not slaveholding society or colonial operations. Nor was it a world that centered white people as the first interlocutor for Africans or any other peoples. God was at the center of this world, its present and future.

Third, those in this 3B trajectory also became fragment workers. They too worked with the fragments of their peoples shattered into pieces by colonialist operations, but this fragment work moved inside a gospel logic, that is, it sought to articulate thriving life as a Christian in the specific realities of their peoples. This meant that they also engaged in weaving Christian fragments with indigenous fragments similar to those concerned with reconstructing their native religions on strange soil or in a transformed home world. Yet this fragment work sought to articulate Christian thought and practice both free of colonial forms and aimed at thinking through the conceptual problems of theology shaped to support colonialism and slavery – for example, how to articulate a doctrine of providence that did not support the idea that God wanted colonialism and European conquest or how to present a doctrine of salvation that did not make slavery acceptable as part of the Christian life or how to offer an account of the sacraments in ways that did not support the sustaining of slaveholding society.

These three responses to Christianity, (1) as obscene nonsense, (2) as resource for reconstructing indigenous religion, (3) as a genuinely commendable way of life and thought were not chronological, nor were they isolated from one another. Some or all of these responses existed in a variety of configurations in the same community, sometimes in the same churches, sometimes in the same family, and sometimes in the same individuals. These responses continue to exist in black diaspora communities (as well as other indigenous communities), and they reflect the same conceptual dynamics as existed under the conditions of slavery and colonialism. This means that black theology formed inhabiting and therefore exhibiting these three responses. Black theology formed as both an argument among black peoples over the value and truth of Christian faith and a set of strategies to be liberated from it or to find liberation through it. The word liberation brings us to the second beginning of black theology and that beginning is tied to the name of one particular theologian, James Hal Cone.

James Hal Cone (1938–2018) was an African American theologian who taught for many years at Union Theological Seminary in New York City. He was not the first person of African descent to gain theological training, nor was he the first African American to be formally trained in theology. He was not the first person of African descent to speak or write about the problems of race, modern slavery, white supremacy, and Christianity, but he was one of the first to articulate these problems as internal to Christian theology and at the same time to suggest a new form of formal academic theology that would build directly from the experiences and realities of black diaspora people. This theology, which he named a black theology of liberation, would inaugurate a new way of interrogating the articulation and dissemination of Christian doctrines by asking its relationship with the health, well-being, and struggle for justice for black diaspora peoples, especially African Americans.

Cone felt the urgency of black suffering like few other formerly trained American theologians had up to that point in the history of the Western world. And he allowed that urgency to fully capture his theological imagination. He thought black suffering and black life as a theologian and he thought theologically through black life and black suffering. In this regard, he was one of the most systematically consistent theologians ever produced in the United States. James Cone was born in the segregated south of the United States in the middle of the last century and was shaped by what W. E. B. DuBois famously called the color line, that is, the realities of the modern racial world, especially in the United States. Cone marked the late sixties (1967–1968 to be exact) as the moment of his emergence as a black theologian. Cone's first book, *Black Theology, Black Power*, was written in the aftermath of the race riots in Detroit and the assassination of Martin Luther King Jr. That first book announced the theological trajectory that would mark his entire career and the struggle at the center of all his work – the overcoming of white supremacy especially lodged in white Christianity for the sake of black flourishing life, that is, for the sake of liberation.

Cone was at the beginning of what would come to be called liberation theology and later contextual theology. His first two books were published in 1969 (*Black Theology and Black Power*) and 1970 (*A Black Theology of Liberation*). Around the same time, 1969, a Peruvian priest theologian by the name of Gustavo Gutierrez published his important work, *Theologia de la Liberacion*, translated in 1973, a *Theology of Liberation*. Around that time, 1973, a young catholic sister/theologian named Mary Daly published a crucial book, entitled *Beyond God the Father: Toward a Philosophy of Women's Liberation*. One year earlier in 1972, another soon to be called "feminist" theologian, by the name of Rosemary Radford Ruether, published an important book entitled, *Liberation Theology: Human Hope Confronts Christian History and American Power*. During this time, a very important Native American scholar by the name of Vine Deloria Jr. published two groundbreaking books; first, in 1969, he published *Custer Died for Your Sins* and then, in 1973, he published his epic book, *God is Red*. One year later in 1974, the Asian theologian Kosuke Koyama published his groundbreaking book,

Water Buffalo Theology. All these writings, though different, were trying to identify a cluster of problems deeply embedded in Western Christianity centered around white male power and white male intellectual form.

Cone's theological project aimed to re-center Christian theology inside the struggles of black flesh in order to do theological work from that crucial starting point, that is, to think the Christian from the reality of blackness and what is required for flourishing life not only for black people but for everyone. Cone's project became the template through which formal black theology, theology nestled in the academy, would form and form the lines of doctrinal inquiry and articulation that continue to this moment. These lines of thinking align with the historic responses to white Christianity that we noted earlier and that consti- tuted informal black theology, the theological reflection done by all those struggling with the Christianity presented within the conditions of colonialism and slavery. Three lines of doctrinal inquiry grew around the black theology of liberation project initiated by James Cone.

First was the importance of the black experience for doing theology. Cone wanted Christian theology in the Western world (that is contem- porary theology done by white theologians) to take seriously the lives of black people. To say that they had not is a massive understatement. Black people and their condition were not simply ignored, that ignor- ance, Cone argued, was a fundamental condition of doing theology in the Western world and a fundamental aspect of black oppression. Cone wanted to start theology with the black experience. But what he meant by the black experience was complex, more complex than people tended to understand. From 1970 onward, with the rise of liberation theology, a new basic but contested axiom or principle for Christian theology emerged: all theology is contextual, that is, all theology begins from a particular perspective on the world and on God. All theology begins with particular experiences. This axiom was aimed at white male theologians who wrote their theologies as though they existed above space and time and spoke to the universal, that is, to everyone and for everyone.

While Cone accepted this axiom, he was more concerned with articulating the specificity of the black experience along three dense lines of thought: first, the experience of black folks with white Christianity and white Christians and the absurd contradictions of that Christianity, a Christianity at home, at rest in white supremacy both in thought and practice. The second line of thought was the experience of black folks with the God of Israel and the bodily and psychic responses to that God's sustaining presence in their lives. The third line of thought was the experience of black folks drawing on their own cultural genius to help them fight for their freedom and form spaces of hope and joy in the midst of sorrow, spaces that could also be an invitation to white people and others to help them also enter freedom from white supremacy. When Cone articulated the black experience, he had all of this working in his thinking.

There were many scholars who took issue with this starting point for theology in experience, misinterpreting Cone to be downplaying the importance of revelation and promoting a theological ethnic chauvinism that would foment division. This critique was quickly shown to be less about the importance of revelation and more about the importance of who is allowed to articulate a doctrine of revelation. This meant for Cone that starting theology with experience was not starting theology over against something called revelation, nor did he need to distinguish between a God who reveals Godself to black people and a God who reveals Godself through black people. Cone would throughout his career draw on both the theological sensibilities of the theologian Karl Barth concerning revelation and the theological sensibilities of Paul Tillich concerning experience, which was not a pairing that other theologians imagined as possible. The central point Cone was pressing was the idea that God is with us, that is, God is with black people (and the historical, ethical, and theological position of blackness as a site of revelation and salvation), and modern theology must take that seriously. Yet the idea of a black experience of God opened a conversation about the character of that experience.

There were many scholars who saw the black religious experience as much wider than Christianity could account for and in fact Christian theology presented a harmful narrowing in understanding that experience. One particular scholar, Charles Long, argued against Cone that the kind of liberation that Cone wanted for black people could not happen as long as theologians like Cone failed to reckon with two realities of black life. First, that Black or African religious consciousness is wider and deeper than Christianity – that African religious consciousness is part of basic human religious consciousness of which Christianity is just one expression and understanding that wider African religious consciousness should be the central task of black theology. Second, black liberation and black flourishing life cannot begin until black folks are freed from the confinement of Christianity and its narrowed vision of the religious consciousness. Our freedom begins with freedom from the confines of Christianity. Even if we remain Christian, to Long's way of thinking, we do so in full awareness that what we are expressing in our faith is an African religious consciousness that binds all of us together and through that consciousness to all humanity.

This line of inquiry concerning the black (African diaspora) religious experience sustains a lively conversation about the nature of theological reflection for black people. Cone for his part was a Christian theologian, gladly of African descent, and happy to see connections with others of African descent who were not Christian, but the freedom he saw in the black experience was a freedom rooted inextricably in the experience of Christian faith from the prayers, the liturgical practices, and the faith confessions of black folks. Others lodged the energy of freedom and for freedom beyond the Christian faith, arising from an African spirituality itself already content-laden and belief-specific, rooted in the religious practices of black people. The status of Christian doctrine in this line of inquiry remains fluid, moving along a continuum. At one position, we find doctrinal articulation forming the grammar or language that materializes black religious experience and in turns creates both an archive and repertoire through which to understand that experience. At the other end of the continuum, doctrinal articulation is a transparency through which to interpret African diaspora religious experience. Yet all along this continuum, black religious experience is taken seriously as a site for theological reflection. This continuum is also present in the second line of inquiry formed of formal black theology.

The second line of inquiry flowed around the importance of scripture for doing theology. Cone's theology was embedded in the gospel story, which meant he drew on a bedrock sensibility of African American Christianity – we are a storied people. We live in the biblical story. As we noted earlier in terms of the African responses to white Christianity, the whole world is in God's story. The Christianity that African slaves were given sought to read them into the story of scripture as slaves. The problem for slaveholding Christianity and for colonial Christianity more generally is that the slaves brought their whole world into the story as well. So that they were not only slaves, but they were Israel in slavery, and the slave masters were in the story too, and slave society was in the story as well, and so too was their deliverance from that society, and also their justification and sanctification and freedom and victory. Most importantly, God was in the story, guiding, helping, saving, redeeming. African diaspora scriptural reading practice underscored the significance of the axiom of black theology – that we do our theology as well as read scripture from a particular place, a particular context.

Situated readings, that is, contextual readings of scripture informed by black liberation theology emerged as biblical scholars began to see the hermeneutical implications of contextuality for the work of exegesis and interpretation. Contextuality as an intellectual starting point affected both how biblical scholars understood and articulated the various cultural, political, social, economic, gendered setting of texts and how they surfaced their own situatedness in the world as fundamental to the ways they and we read biblical texts. Approaching the Bible with a view toward the liberation of black people meant for Cone that he read history inside the story of God's liberation of God's people. God was on the side of the poor and oppressed and thusly the theological task was to illumine the connection between the biblical story and the story of black people in their ongoing struggle for freedom.

Claiming that God was on the side of the poor and oppressed and interpreting God as a liberator, however, surfaced once again the contradictions of Christianity formed under the conditions of colonialism and slavery and the responses to that Christianity that saw it as nonsense. In 1973, then Professor of Religion and Philosophy at Florida State University, William R. Jones wrote what was to become a very important book in black theology. His book entitled *Is God a White Racist?* challenged the idea that God is a God of liberation, more precisely that God wanted the liberation of black people. Jones, who was a self-avowed humanist, challenged several black scholars and theologians in that book, but he took particular aim at James Cone. His central thesis was straightforward – if you, Cone, say that God is a God of liberation and, when I look at the plight of black people not only in the United States but around the world and see the continued power of white supremacy globally, then the only conclusion I can come to is that either God does not exist, and all God-talk must therefore be grounded in the real world as human projections of what we hope a god would do and be, or if God exists, then God is a white racist.

According to Jones, a God who has liberated Israel in scripture, and who therefore has the power to liberate but has not liberated Black folks is a serious problem for theology. For black people to be liberated and have flourishing life two things must happen. First, we must abandon all God-talk, if by it, we wish to speak realistically about God's actions in the world of black suffering, because according to Jones, there are no actions – we are not saved.

Second, we need to form a philosophy of life that may acknowledge God as the one who empowers us to fight for our freedom, what Jones called a human-centric Theism. Jones's point was that flourishing black life begins by recognizing what we must do rather than what God has done or will do.

Jones's argument aligned with the historical responses of many Africans to the Christianity espoused by Europeans and other Africans, but Jones's argument in the context of the academy functioned inside the problem of theodicy, that is, the problem of a powerful God who allows suffering. While the problem of theodicy is wider than matters of biblical interpretation, how one interprets the biblical text in light of the plight of black people was exactly where Jones formed his critique of black theology. Cone appreciated Jones for forcing black theologians and biblical scholars to clarify what they meant by theology and what function their God-talk served. Cone saw Jones's work much like Karl Barth saw Ludwig Feuerbach's work, in that both Jones and Feuerbach pressed on theologians to come clean on the status of their theological speech – where did it come from and where was it going?

Cone, however, saw in Jones's critique a failure to understand the nature of black Christian faith. For Cone, black life has come to him and us in story, the story of God's involvement, and of God's sustaining help in a world disordered and distorted by white supremacy. It is from the place of life inside the story of God that Cone reads history. Jones, on the other hand, imagined that he should read history outside of story, that is, Jones does not know whose story he was inside of as he critiqued black Christian faith. For Cone, Jones's world is a world where God is yet to be seen and known and probably will never be seen and known. It is a world where we struggle alone against white supremacy or under the watchful eye of a distant god, forming our vision of life based on immanent possibilities. Cone's world, on the other hand, is a world where God's struggle against injustice is seen and known and whose victory over this world's injustice is yet to be fully realized; in short, Cone's world is already God's world and history should be read from this starting point. It is precisely this starting point that is necessary for flourishing life, because without it, life can only be calibrated by setbacks and the absurdity of a racial world. What energizes this starting point brings us to the third line of inquiry, Jesus Christ.

The third line of inquiry was the place of Jesus Christ for understanding God's solidarity with black people. It all hangs on Jesus Christ. Jesus is certainly the God-human for Cone in full agreement with the doctrine of the incarnation, but equally important is what Jesus Christ means for solidarity with black suffering. From early in his career, Cone sought to distance himself from the accusation that he was overly Christocentric in his theology and still too indebted to Karl Barth, but this accusation always missed the central point of Cone's theology, which was an extended meditation on Christ's identification with black flesh, that is, with blackness as both the site of the despised, the exploited, and those on whom were projected the fears and horrors of the white world, as well as a site of hope and creativity where we struggle against injustice.

All of Christian existence flows for Cone out of the life of Jesus Christ because he is one who collapses white supremacy, breaking its power over the lives of everyone. From his life, we live and move and have our being. For Cone, whiteness and blackness do not map onto oppressor and oppressed as permanent conditions of existence. Blackness in this regard becomes a state of grace whereby people can come to identify with those who have been oppressed. This flexible way of thinking about whiteness and blackness grew for Cone out of his reading of the writers of the Harlem renaissance. Blackness in this regard can become a shared subject-position and whiteness can be renounced as a failed or sinful subject position. As a shared subject-position, blackness can be lived into as a social, political, economic, and theological form of life.

Cone was unrelenting in his searing critique of white people and their propensity to identify with white supremacy, explicitly or implicitly. He wanted everyone who saw themselves as white to be wholly uncomfortable in their whiteness. This meant that his readers often failed to see the pedagogical and theological importance of his anger, his righteous indignation – it was a form of exorcism, trying to pull the whiteness out of the Christian and drawn them into the blackness of their faith. Jesus Christ was key to this exorcism because to identify his body with the black body was to issue an invitation to join the black struggle for liberation. There was, however, a set of conversation partners that pressed Cone to clarify his commitment to Jesus Christ as the basis for liberation. In 1984, James Cone published a book called *For My People: Black Theology and the Black Church*. In this book, Cone acknowledge two critiques of his work, the first coming primarily from his own brother Cecil Cone, in his book, *The Identity Crisis in Black Theology* (1975). Cecil Cone, a pastor-theologian in his own right, argued that black theology, especially that of his brother, was aimed at the white academy and spent little time talking to or with the black church and about African American Christian life, its specific needs and struggles. Cone agreed with this critique and, beginning with this 1984 book, sought to correct this problem.

The second critique that he acknowledged in that book came from black feminists, soon to be called womanists, who found Cone's work lacking in recognition of and reflection on and with black woman. Cone admitted that he had not given appropriate focus on the particular interlocking character of the challenges of sexism, racism, and patriarchy for black theology and the black church. The 1980s saw the rise of womanist thought beginning with Katie Geneva Cannon's important book, *Black Womanist Ethics* (1988), Jacquelyn Grant's book, *White Women's Christ, Black Women's Jesus: Feminist Christology and Womanist Responses* (1989), and Delores S. Williams's, *Sisters in the Wilderness: The Challenge of Womanist GodTalk* (1993).

Delores Williams's groundbreaking text summarized both these critiques and the clarification that Cone needed to make in his Christology. Williams argued in her book, *Sisters in the Wilderness*, that black women had been and continue to be harmed by the emphasis on Christ's sacrificial death and the surrogacy it represents as being paradigmatic for the lives of black women. That is, what Black women learn from the sacrifice of Jesus is the righteousness and the appropriateness of their ongoing sacrifice of their bodies and health for the sake of the flourishing of the black community. While not aimed directly at Cone, Williams's critique demanded theologians like Cone clarify what it means for us to identify with Jesus Christ's life and death.

For Williams, for us to promote black flourishing life requires we focus not on Christ's death as in any way salvific but on his ministerial life and the ways he fostered life for oppressed people, especially women. Cone appreciated Williams's critique of various substitutionary theories of the atonement with its obsessive focus on divine punishment for sin. Yet Cone understood Christ's death on the cross as less a substitution for and more of an identification with those suffering under the realities of a fallen world. In one of his final books, *The Cross and the Lynching Tree*, Cone aligned Christ's crucifixion and the historic lynching of black flesh, each enfolding the other in true meaning of divine solidarity with the oppressed and God's judgment on those who commit violence. For Cone, black flourishing in this regard is rooted in the invitation to solidarity with Christ and black flesh, where people are joined together in common purpose aiming at the liberation of black people and through them the liberation of other oppressed peoples.

The conversations in black theology catalyzed by James Hal Cone were, as we have shown, not invented by him, nor were they ever limited to him. Black scholars and others interested in theologies of liberation in the fields of theology, historical theology, African American religious historical studies, ethics, biblical studies, practical and pastoral theology, and homiletics have all been profoundly influenced by the conversations in black theology. Those conversations continue with matters of sexuality. The turn to sexuality was already anticipated by the work of womanist theologians and ethicists who pressed the importance of gender analysis in understanding the formation and continued operations of misogyny and patriarchy in the theological academy, the black church, and the black community. In relation to Christianity and Christian theological reflection, black life and queer life have always been profoundly intertwined in terms of the multiple forms of oppression that have and continue to crisscross oppressed bodies. In this regard, the historical responses to a Christianity formed under colonialism and slavery also have resonances with the ways queer black Christians have negotiated a life of faith and engaged in theological reflection. The other way black life and queer life within Christianity have been intertwined is in the ongoing project of articulating a theology of liberation that addresses what pastor and US senator Raphael G. Warnock calls the divided mind of the black church. That divided mind reveals the continuing power of the responses black diaspora peoples and all indigenous peoples made and continue to make to a Christianity and Christian theology shaped under the conditions of colonialism and modern slavery.

Further Reading

Bowens, Lisa M. (2020), *African American Readings of Paul: Reception, Resistance and Transformation* (Grand Rapids: Eerdmans).

Cone, James H. (1975), *God of the Oppressed* (Maryknoll: NY: Orbis Books).

(2011), *The Cross and the Lynching Tree* (Maryknoll, NY: Orbis).

Cannon, Katie Geneva(2006), *Black Womanist Ethics* (Atlanta: Scholars Press; reprinted, Wipf and Stock).

Cannon, Katie G., and Anthony Pinn (2014), *The Oxford Handbook on African American Theology* (New York: Oxford University Press).

Daly, Mary (1973), *Beyond God the Father: Toward a Philosophy of Women's Liberation* (Boston: Beacon Press).

Deloria, Vine Jr. (1973), *God Is Red*. (Golden, CO: Fulcrum).

Douglas, Kelly Brown (1999), *Sexuality and the Black Church: A Womanist Perspective* (Maryknoll, NY: Orbis Books).

Gutierrez, Gustavo (1973), *A Theology of Liberation: History, Politics, Salvation* (Maryknoll, NY: Orbis).

Jones, William R. (1973), *Is God a White Racist: A Preamble to Black Theology* (Boston: Beacon Press).

Ruether, Rosemary Radford (1972), *Liberation Theology: Human Hope Confronts Christian History and American Power* (New York: Paulist Press).

Williams, Delores S. (1993), *Sisters in the Wilderness: The Challenge of Womanist GodTalk* (Maryknoll, NY: Orbis Books).

17 Pentecostal Theology

HARVEY KWIYANI

This chapter explores the subject of Pentecostal theology. It makes a quick cursory look at the story of the development of Pentecostal theology in the past 120 years since the birth of the Pentecostal movement in the early years of the twentieth century. The purpose of the endeavour is to try to understand the emergence of a distinct Pentecostal theology that today caters to the theological needs of more than a quarter of the world's Christians. It will attempt to map the evolution of Pentecostal theological discourse over the closing decades of the twentieth century when the Pentecostal movement has spread to all parts of the world and has, in the process, developed its identity and claimed its place in the global Christian landscape. Before exploring some of the key contemporary themes in Pentecostal theology, the chapter offers a short discussion of what Pentecostal theology is and what it is not. To do this well, it is necessary to also discuss, even in cursory manner, the history of Pentecostal Christianity. The essay intentionally takes a world Christianity perspective in telling both the history of the movement and the narrative of its theological development. This is to situate this discussion of Pentecostal theology in the wider and growing discourse of global theologies, which then will allow us to see the growing influence of Pentecostal thought on world Christianity and vice versa. The global nature of Pentecostal theology itself informs the second half of the chapter in which it engages some of the key Pentecostal voices in Africa, Asia, and Latin America, in addition to those in Europe and North America, to help us understand the current theological concerns of Pentecostal Christians in the world. In the end, I explore some pressing themes in Pentecostal theology, hoping to build bridges between Pentecostal theologians and those of mainline traditions.

PENTECOSTALISM: A SHORT INTRODUCTION

Before we can discuss Pentecostal theology, it is necessary to have a short introduction to Pentecostalism itself. The word 'Pentecost' is Greek, *pentekosté* (Πεντηκοστή), which is translated 'fiftieth'. It is an Old Testament word that was commonly used in relation to the Feast of Pentecost – also known as the Festival of Weeks – that took place in Jerusalem fifty days after the Feast of First Fruits (which, for Christians, is Resurrection Sunday or Easter). Pentecost was one of the major festivals that took place in Jerusalem and naturally required Jewish men from around the nation and the diaspora to come to Jerusalem to celebrate, giving thanks to God, especially for the blessing of harvest. Some Jews also believe that the Ten Commandments were given on Pentecost on Mount Sinai, calling it Matin Torah for the 'giving of the Law'. In the New Testament and for the Early Church, Pentecost became an immensely important event because, for some reason, it was on the Pentecost Day after the crucifixion of Jesus that the Holy Spirit was given. If, indeed, the Law had been given on a similar day hundreds of years earlier, this giving of the Spirit on the Day of Pentecost signifies a significant shift in the nature of God's covenant with God's people. The Spirit would take over and write the Law inside the hearts of God's people (Jer. 31:33; Heb. 8:10; 10:16).

The term 'Pentecostal' is a somewhat limited and yet all-encompassing term that includes not only self-identified Pentecostals but also Charismatics, renewalists, revivalists, and many other spirit-empowered (or spirit-oriented) Christians in the world. According to Wolfgang Vondey, a Pentecostal scholar in England, 'Pentecostalism refers in a broad sense to the complex diversity of classical Pentecostals, the Charismatic Movement, and Pentecostal or "Pentecostal-like" independent churches'.[1] Indeed, the *New International Dictionary of Pentecostal and Charismatic Movements* identifies as 'Pentecostal' the so-called classical Pentecostals connected with the revival at the Azusa Street Mission in Los Angeles (1906–1909); the members of the so-called charismatic movements in the established Roman Catholic, Protestant, and Orthodox churches that surfaced in North America during the 1960s; and so-called neo-charismatic groups, 'a catch-all category that comprises 18,810 independent, indigenous, post-denominational denominations and groups that cannot be classified as either Pentecostal or charismatic

---

[1] Wolfgang Vondey, *Pentecostal Theology: Living the Full Gospel* (London: Bloomsbury, 2017), p. 3.

but share a common emphasis on the Holy Spirit, spiritual gifts, Pentecostal-like experiences (not Pentecostal terminology), signs and wonders and power encounters'.[2] In fewer words, the *Dictionary of Pentecostal and Charismatic Movements* suggests that the global Pentecostal movement is 'one worldwide trans-denominational outpouring of the Spirit of God'.[3] Pentecostals, understood loosely to include all enthusiastic Christians in the world, have grown from zero in 1900 to more than 600 million adherents today,[4] with another 300 million affiliates scattered across the continents.[5] The largest numbers of Pentecostals are in Africa, Latin America, and parts of Asia; and because of this, it does seem as if Pentecostalism is world Christianity. It is Christianity breaking free from the yoke of the European Enlightenment (which explains why the movement is exploding outside the West). Indeed, it appears that Pentecostalism is what happens when Christianity meets those non-Western cultures that, having been minimally affected by the European Enlightenment, still understand the world to be filled with powerful spirits (or spirit beings) that influence the material world. For many of those cultures, for instance, those of sub-Saharan Africa, religion is then about the relationship between humans and spirits (and without such connection, there is no religion).[6] As will be argued in the course of this chapter, Pentecostalism offers such cultures a way for a continuity with their religious practices within the context of Christianity.

PENTECOST AND PENTECOSTALISM

When the Spirit was given in Acts 2, it was nothing short of a miracle. As a matter of fact, it was a day filled with miracles: a violent rushing wind came down from heaven and filled the entire house in which the disciples lived, tongues of fire settled on each of them, and then they spoke in tongues. The people outside understood the tongues to be

---

[2] Stanley M. Burgess and Eduard M. Van der Maas, eds., *The New International Dictionary of Pentecostal and Charismatic Movements*, rev. and exp. ed. (Grand Rapids: Zondervan, 2002), xx.

[3] Stanley M. Burgess, Gary McGee, and Patrick Alexander, eds., *Dictionary of Pentecostal and Charismatic Movements* (Grand Rapids: Zondervan, 1988), 159.

[4] Todd Johnson and Gina Zurlo, *Introducing Spirit-Empowered Christianity: The Global Pentecostal and Charismatic Movement in the 21st Century* (Tulsa, OK: Oral Roberts University Press, 2020), 6.

[5] Pulitzer Centre, 'The Atlas of Pentecostalism: Pentecostal Growth', (Washington, DC, 2021), www.atlasofpentecostalism.net.

[6] Harvey Kwiyani, 'Can the West Really Be Converted?', *Missio Africanus Journal of African Missiology* 4 (2019), 77–96.

languages spoken wherever they had come from – and Luke is clear, there were Jews from every nation on earth in Jerusalem on that day (Acts 2:5). The disciples were understood to be speaking great things about God. Thus, the first miracle of speaking in tongues was followed by a second, that of the hearing of tongues, which leads to a third: Peter's bold sermon and the piercing of the hearers' hearts. He explained the strange behaviour as the influence of the Holy Spirit – 'these people are not drunk, it is only 9am anyway', and made a direct connection with an Old Testament prophecy by Joel: 'And it shall come to pass afterward that I will pour out My Spirit on all flesh; your sons and your daughters shall prophesy, your old men shall dream dreams, your young men shall see visions.[7] Pentecost could not stand alone as an event. It had to be connected to the prophets (Joel) and to the Law (Mount Sinai). In addition, Pentecost was not just a Jewish event. It had implications beyond the nation of Israel that had been, until this time, God's only chosen nation in the world. The Spirit is given for the whole world – it would be poured out upon all flesh – Middle Eastern, European, American, African, Asian, and everyone else. Furthermore, the promise goes beyond the generation that received the Spirit at Pentecost. Peter said, 'this promise is for you and for your children, and for all who are far off, as many as the Lord our God will call' (Acts 2:39). In response to the piercing of the spirit in their hearts, 3,000 people joined the fellowship of disciples on that day and the church was born. This Pentecost event of Acts 2 grounds the work of the Spirit at the centre of the church. There is no *ecclesia* without the Spirit. Vondey is correct to suggest that 'Pentecostalism is a form of living fundamentally concerned with the renewing work of God as it emerges from the outpouring of the Holy Spirit on the day of Pentecost'.[8]

The shifting of the covenant from the Law to the Spirit – a theme that is the foundation of Paul's work in the Epistles of the New Testament – opens up the possibilities of Christian discipleship to the rest of the world, even for those who had no knowledge of the Law because the Spirit writes the Law upon their heart. The Spirit presents to us a new way of being religious that is made possible for nations around the world and, therefore, the mission of Jesus to have followers in every nation, tribe, and tongue can be fulfilled. Therefore, the pneumatology of the Gospels makes sense. The ministry of Jesus was

---

[7] Luke's report in Acts suggests that Peter substituted the word 'Afterwards' and used 'In the last days' in its place.

[8] Vondey, *Pentecostal Theology*, 12.

built upon his ability to discern the will of the Father (which, in other words, is about his hearing the voice of the Father) and the anointing of the Spirit to enable him to do whatever the Father wills. Both the hearing and the anointing are to be best understood as the work of the Spirit. It is the anointing that enabled Jesus to perform all the miracles of the Gospels. The healings, the exorcisms, even the teachings can only be explained in the context of a Spirit-anointed ministry. Jesus did not start his ministry until he had declared, 'the Spirit of the Lord is upon me for he has anointed me'. Christ is not Jesus's last name. It is a descriptor of who he is, the Spirit-Anointed One.

Jesus would also make sure that his disciples do not start off in their ministries, bearing witness to him in the world, without being endued with the power from on high that would be received through the baptism of the Spirit (Acts 1:8). Thus, the same Spirit that anointed Jesus would be upon the disciples, allowing them to perform many more miracles recorded in the Book of Acts and beyond. A spirit-centred understanding of the faith emerged as central to the Christian faith and the identity of the church, which, as seen in the Gospels, was born with a worldview where it was normal for spirits to impact the material world (like many non-Western cultures of the world today). The message of the kingdom of God has to do with the inbreaking of the Spirit of God into our world to destroy the stronghold of evil and show God's power and glory. When a name was sought for a new community of followers of Christ in Antioch (Acts 11:26), they were called Christians, which, of course, means not only followers of the Anointed One but themselves as 'anointed ones' as well. Christianity, as a whole, is the faith of the Spirit-anointed ones.

Pentecostalism, as a movement, came into existence in the early years of the twentieth century. Popular narratives locate its start at a revival that broke out in 1906 on Azusa Street in Los Angeles, led by a black man named William Seymour. Some place its beginning at Charles Parham's Bible school in Topeka, Kansas, in 1900, where they prayed for a new Pentecost and were filled with the Spirit as evidenced in the speaking in tongues. However, it has become more accepted to speak of Azusa Street as one of the many places that experienced a revival in the late 1800s and early 1900s. Indeed, there were many revival movements that eventually prepared the way for Pentecostalism. For instance, there was a revival in south India from at least the 1860s, where it is believed that people spoke in tongues. In Europe, there was a huge revival in Wales from 1904 to 1906 – one whose impact is still seen today every time Welsh sports supporters sing hymns in their stadiums. There was another revival in northeast India in 1905. In the same year, another revival took place at Pandita Ramabai's Mukti Mission near Bombay. Another revival called the 'Korean Pentecost' happened in 1907 to 1908 in Pyongyang. In West Africa, where Western missionary work really took off in the decades leading to 1900, African Independent Churches (AICs) were also gaining ground at the same time and harnessing a series of small revivals led by local prophets like William Wade Harris (largely due to the pneumato-logical question of the missing work of the Spirit on the missionaries' Christianity). By the turn of the century, some AICs had already gained popularity and would flourish well into the 1920s, when ties with Western Pentecostals were established.

Over the decades since 1906, the Pentecostal movement has grown from a handful of followers to more than 600 million self-identifying Pentecostals around the world in 2020. Indeed, one in four Christians in the world is a Pentecostal. This has happened because Pentecostalism was and has always been a doing movement, active and busy, evangel-ising the world to 'plunder hell and populate heaven'.[9] With a quarter of the Christians in the world identifying as Pentecostals – and that per-centage is rising each year – the Pentecostal movement has transformed Christianity's character in the world, especially in Africa, Asia, and Latin America. For Africa, all mainline denominations have had to 'pentecostalise' to various extents to cope with the threat of losing their members to Pentecostal churches. Indeed, it is quite hard today to find an African Christian who has not been influenced, even remotely, by the Pentecostal and Charismatic revivals that have been going on in parts of the continent for decades.

WHAT IS PENTECOSTAL THEOLOGY?

Let us start with the understanding that it would be more correct to talk about Pentecostal theologies here, as there is no one theology that encompasses all the theological thought among Pentecostals and Charismatics in the world. However, there exist some foundational theological pillars that make Pentecostal theological thought distinct, and that are expounded upon contextually, to create different theological expressions among Pentecostals, whether they are in North America,

---

[9] The phrase, 'to plunder hell and populate heaven' was used a motto of Reinhardt Bonnke's ministry, Christ for All Nations (CfAN), across Africa during his evangelistic campaign that lasted from 1974 to 2017 and catalysed the explosion of Pentecostal Christianity in the continent.

Latin America, Africa, or Asia. We will come back to these theologies later, but for now, let us explore these foundational pillars that actually make it possible for us to talk about a Pentecostal theology.

Pentecostal theology is a general term used to describe the theological thought that undergirds Pentecostal expressions of Christianity around the world. Pentecostal theology is, thus, a collective term for the theological tradition that seeks to make sense of the issues that are dear to Pentecostal and Charismatic Christians around the world, especially that of the person and the work of the Holy Spirit. In a nutshell, Pentecostal theology tries to understand and articulate a spirit-centred basis for the Christian life. This pneumatological basis for Christianity is, generally speaking, derived from the Bible – the New Testament in particular (with the understanding that what happens in the New Testament is a fulfilment of that which was spoken of in the Old Testament). The powerful presence of the Spirit in the Gospels (in the baptism and miraculous ministry of Jesus), Acts (the birth and growth of the church), and the Epistles (the Christian salvific calling to walk in the Spirit by grace through faith) reflects the centrality of spirit-empowered life, both as a fulfilment of the promises of the Old Testament and an invitation to a victorious life for the New Testament believer. The language of a powerful Spirit of God in the Bible, of the Holy Spirit anointing people and enabling them to accomplish superhuman feats, is relatable to many Pentecostals around the world. It forms the foundation upon which a Pentecostal understanding of God, Christianity, and the world is built. The miracles that Jesus and the apostles performed (be it the exorcism of the Gadarene demoniac [Mk. 8:28–34], or the healing of the multitudes through Peter's shadow [Acts 5:15–16], or Paul's handkerchief [Acts 19:11–12]), reflect the power of God expressed through God's Spirit touching the material world of human life. They do not need to be demythologised because they actually explain and justify the presence and work of the Spirit. Where God's Spirit is in action, humanly impossible challenges are expected to become possible, and when they happen, we call them miracles.

However, this power is not limited to the Spirit of God alone. Spirit beings, whatever they are, are infinitely more powerful than human beings and can affect the human world at will. They do this often, on a constant basis. We do not need Christianity to understand the spirit world. Many indigenous religions, whether in Africa, America, or Asia, are based on the existence of a spiritual world. The spirit medium of indigenous religions, be it in Amazonia, the Congo, or the Philippines, is accessing only a small, limited and often corrupted portion of the spiritual power accessible to Christians (because, of course, Jesus has all the power and authority). The Bible assumes a world in which spirits affect human life on a constant basis. Paul's invitation for Christ's disciples to walk in the Spirit (Gal. 5:16) is to help them negotiate a spiritual life in a world full of spirits, created and ordered by a God who is Spirit and who, by the Spirit, dwells within them.

The term 'Pentecostal Theology' is, thus, used to differentiate the kinds of theology that emerge out of these spirit-oriented Christian communities from those of other theological traditions, such as, for instance, Reformed theology, Lutheran theology, and Catholic theology. Since Pentecostalism is only around 120 years old, Pentecostal theological discourse is relatively new compared to other theological traditions that have been around for much longer. The subject of Pentecostal theology, as an academic discipline, is an even more recent phenomenon, having emerged in the past five decades. Because the Pentecostal movement is somewhat new, and is still establishing itself as a theological movement, Pentecostal Christians are often the denominational other, confined to the theological margins of the Christian community, especially in the Western world. Pentecostal theology is also, generally speaking, the other theology that most Departments of Theology at many Western universities and seminaries are still unable to engage with properly. For example, in some circles of the European academy, Pentecostal theology is wrongly spoken of as if it is synonymous with prosperity theology.

In the crowded world of theology, Pentecostal theology is the 'new kid on the block' that is often defined and understood in terms of what it is not. It is not mainline theology. It is not confessional theology (in the traditional sense of confessionalism). It is not connected to any confessional statements, be it Westminster or Augustana, or any other confession. Of course, it does not have a Martin Luther, a John Calvin, or even Karl Barth. As a result, it does not align itself to the doctrinal standards and systems of the more established traditions. As a matter of fact, it rejects and dismisses any cessationist claims to theology. Essentially, both the Pentecostal movement and its theology are built upon the belief that the miraculous and powerful gifts of the Spirit are operational in the world today just as much as they were in the Early Church. The movement's original leaders were doers and practitioners who placed an emphasis on the wondrous workings of the Holy Spirit in the church.[10]

---

[10] Essentially though, both the need for experience itself and the commitment to doing greater things by the power of the Spirit reflect a theology that believes that God can be experienced and is active in the world today. Often though, once people have the

Its theologians came later, attempting to articulate the narrative of the
work of the Spirit in theological terms. This has been the story of the
development of Pentecostal theology – it follows experience. It is a
theological thought that reflects on experience (often, for the sake of
further experience). Thus, its primary concerns focus on issues that
would be of little interest to mainline theology, issues to do with the
day-to-day life happenings of common people, such as miraculous healings and provision, charismatic gifts and anointed ministry, and, of
course, spiritual warfare and protection from evil forces. Indeed, while
a great number of Pentecostal scholars are located in Europe and North
America, Pentecostal theology, at the popular level, is the fuel driving
most of the Christian communities in Latin America, Africa, and Asia.

Pentecostal Christianity has at the centre of its self-understanding
the experience of the presence and work of the Holy Spirit among God's
people. Without this experience – the sense of hearing God's voice, or of
Jesus's healing power, or of the Spirit's calming presence – Pentecostalism
loses its 'pentecostalness'. God, for Pentecostals, is a living Spiritual
Being that is active in the world, especially in their lives, and can be
experienced making things happen for, through, and around them by
the power of God's Spirit.[11] Here, Pentecostals are in agreement with
the spiritualist followers of indigenous religions around the world –
spirits exist and affect the human world and that when the spirits break
through into the human world, they are usually experienced. Often,
whenever there is an intensification of spiritual activity in a community,
it will be experienced. Spirits have a way of touching and moving human
bodies, and this is easily noticeable in cultures and contexts that are open
to the presence of spirits in the human and material world. The spirits
break through to the human world to communicate with humans information that cannot be passed otherwise, to protect their communities
from contrary spirits, and, ultimately, to bless them with good life. (Yes,
contrary spirits, generally harnessed and sent by enemies and ill-wishers,
will also break through into the human world to frustrate and
harm people, to diminish the goodness of their life.) When a spiritual

experience, they see no need for further theological reflection, and this has led to
criticisms of anti-intellectualism within the Pentecostal movement.

[11] I would argue here that most religions of the world exist for the sole reason of
mediating the gap between the human and the spiritual worlds. Thus, many
religions are driven by spiritual activity – they are shaped as human response to the
activity of the spiritual world. Most Pentecostals will agree that the Holy Spirit does
shape their world even though in that world there are also myriads of contrary spirits
(that are no match to the Holy Spirit).

in-breaking takes place, extraordinary phenomena like speaking in tongues, (be it *glossolalia* or *xenolalia*),[12] trances, healings, prophecy, and others similar to the ones we see in the book of Acts become commonplace. Indeed, *glossolalia* is not exclusive to Christians. Many spirit-possessed followers of traditional religions also speak in tongues. In Pentecostal theology, however, it is the Spirit of God that is active in a community, and these same phenomena are expected, if not encouraged. Indeed, the Spirit of Jesus is, among Pentecostals, the spirit that both distributes the charismatic gifts and sets captives free, liberating them from bondages placed upon them by the contrary spirits.

Consequently, the Pentecostal Christians' God is neither distant nor idle but is very close and deeply involved in all issues of their life. The Pentecostal God is active in the 'here and now' of life, open and keen to be experienced, to show forth God's glory and power. Therefore, experience is often the starting point of Pentecostal theologising. Generally speaking, God acts, Pentecostals experience God's action, and then go on to theologise about the God behind the experience and, sometimes, about the experience itself, intending to understand theologically what it is that God has done. This reflection often leads to appreciation – praise and worship – which leads to further experiences. Again, this is normal for all spiritualist religions of the world. West African Pentecostalism makes the connection between praise and worship, experience, and African religion more visible. Praise language and titles reserved for deities and conquering kings (whose victories were always attributed to the intervention of their deities) in pre-Christian times now form the bedrock of worship music. Both the poetic works of Afua Kuma and the lyrical adulations of Tope Alabi, Sinach, or Ada Ehi testify of a warrior God who wages war on behalf of God's human subjects.[13] The Supreme Being of old, whose deities blessed people with abundance and rained fire on their enemies, has now been replaced by the Pentecostal God who often blesses people but also fights on their behalf. In a sense, then, for such Pentecostals, the spirit medium who mediated between humans and the spirits has lost his place to the prophet, and the community chief has been replaced by the apostle. The key players in societal life have changed, but the foundations of the

---

[12] Glossolalia is used to describe speaking in tongues that are unknown to human beings while Xenolalia is speaking in tongues that are actually a language that is spoken in another part of the world but is unknown to the speaker.

[13] See, for instance, Harvey C. Kwiyani and Joseph Ola, 'God in Oral African Theology: Exploring the Spoken Theologies of Afua Kuma and Tope Alabi', *Conspectus* 31 (2021), 54–66.

worldview and the culture have remained the same. Throughout Africa, Pentecostal theology tries to break away from indigenous religion, but this is a futile exercise – the two share too much in common, to the extent that we can argue that there is a direct line connecting the two.[14] African Pentecostals demonise African religion and yet their own growth cannot be explained without acknowledging the many ways in which African religion prepared the way for Pentecostalism.

Most Pentecostals, however, are happy to live within the realms of experience. Their theological reflection is geared towards helping them understand God for the sake of their day-to-day living. It is to help them process their experience of God. Thus, the experience of God through the Spirit has often been the most important form of currency among Pentecostals. Pentecostal theologians teaching at universities often find that their denominations are not necessarily interested in academic theology. As an experiential expression of Christianity that has become very popular among the less affluent and less educated (but experientially rich) cultures of the Latin America, Africa, and Asia, it has often downplayed the need for theological education – but this does not mean, however, that it has not formulated its own theological thoughts. Wolfgang Vondey suggests that, from its beginning, 'Pentecostalism was marked by an ad hoc doxology rather than a systematic and dogmatic theology'.[15] Indeed, there are only a handful of works of Pentecostal systematic theology, and almost all of them are written and published in Europe and North America where Pentecostalism is a minority faith, wrestling with – or using as a starting point – Western, Enlightenment-shaped theologies that do not translate well for the non-Western world. In addition, Western Pentecostal theology has spent a great deal of its academic history justifying the validity of its claim that experience is a good resource for theological thought, and, therefore, it is a trustworthy epistemological foundation for doing theology.

Pentecostal hermeneutics of the Bible, those that highlight the spirit-centred experientially based narrative that we see in the Book of Acts, for instance, make strong sense among Christians living in cultures whose understanding of the cosmos includes spirit beings (living in the unseen world of the spiritual realm) that have direct interaction

[14] I have made a longer argument about this in Harvey C. Kwiyani, 'Independent, Enthusiastic, and Africa: Reframing the Story of African Christianity', in *African Pentecostalism and World Christianity: Essays in Honor of J. Kwabena Asamoah-Gyadu* (ed. Nimi Wariboko and Adeshina Afolayan; Eugene, OR: Wipf and Stock, 2020), 30–44.
[15] Vondey, *Pentecostal Theology*, 3.

with humans living in the material world. Consequently, Pentecostal theological thought exists in different expressions around the world as it is shaped by the cultural context in which the theologising is done. For example, there exists a North American Pentecostal theology that, for various reasons, will have nuances that make it somewhat different from the Pentecostal theology coming out of Africa, Asia, or Latin America, even though they are all fundamentally concerned with the express manifestation of the presence and work of the Holy Spirit. In addition, as Pentecostal Christianity has grown around the world, its influence on other theological traditions has also become more pronounced, expanding the Charismatic Movement of Pentecostal-leaning Christians in mainline denominations theologising in the grey zones between Pentecostal theology and what can be called mainline theologies.

SOME PENTECOSTAL THEOLOGIANS

As we have seen, the Pentecostal movement is only around 120 years old. Its representation in the academy began a few decades into its existence, in the second half of the twentieth century and, therefore, its academic theological thought is still very young. The list of its theologians is quite short even though it is currently growing exponentially (largely because of the increasing numbers of Pentecostal Christians from the non-Western world engaging in theological education).[16] Many scholars have emerged in the past few decades who are bringing their Pentecostal hermeneutics to various aspects of the theological discourse including in study of mission, systematic theology, the Old and New Testaments, and others. The first generation of Pentecostal theologians include such scholars as Vinson Synan (1934–2020), William Menzies (1931–2011), and Walter Hollenweger (1927–2016). Other scholars of that generation include Russell Spittler (b. 1931), Gordon Fee (b. 1934), and Stanley Horton (1916–2014). They published a majority of their works beginning in the 1960s, focusing on two key areas. First, they sought to make an

---

[16] Many Pentecostal denominations especially in sub-Saharan Africa have established their own institutions of higher learning to train leaders both for the sustaining of their church movements but also to try and transform their nations through other means beyond mission and evangelism. Good examples of such universities in Africa include Pentecost University (belonging to the Church of Pentecost in Ghana), the Malawi Assemblies of God University in Lilongwe, Malawi (owned by the Malawi Assemblies of God), and Covenant University in Nigeria (belonging to Bishop David Oyedepo of the Living Faith Church, also known as the Winners' Chapel).

apology for the Pentecostal movement to a wondering, suspicious, and often dismissive world that did not know or understand Pentecostalism. A key theme in their works is the Holy Spirit, what he is and what it does. Second, they began to formulate, articulate, and explain a distinct Pentecostal theology, answering the question: what does theology actually look like when imagined from a Pentecostalist reading of God's story in the Bible? While Pentecostal Christianity was taking root in Africa, Asia, and Latin America between the 1960s and 1970s, it was not until the 1980s and the 1990s that Pentecostal scholars began to emerge in the non-Western world. To a great extent, this explains why Pentecostal studies bibliographies are dominated by Westerners, especially from the United States, when most Pentecostal Christians live in Africa, Latin America, and parts of Asia. This is slowly changing as many Pentecostal leaders from around the world begin to make their theological contribution heard.

The current generation of Pentecostal theologians writing from the 1990s is noticeably diverse as it includes, among many others, Veli-Matti Kärkkäinen, Roger Stronstad, Chris Thomas, Wonsuk Ma, Julie Ma, Lee Roy Martin, Alan Johnson, Frank Macchia, Simon Chan, Allan Anderson, Amos Yong, Craig Keener, and Cecil M. Robeck. From Africa, prominent Pentecostal theologians include Kwabena Asamoah-Gyadu, Jörg Haustein, Opoku Onyinah, Nimi Wariboko, Ogbu Kalu, Matthews Ojo, Wanjiru Gitau, Babatunde Adedibu, Israel Olofinjana, Bosco Bangura, Clifton Clarke, and many others. From Asia, we have Lora Timenia, Aaron Zhuang, Joshua Iap, Timothy Yeung, Robert Yeung, Tin Kwan Lei, Gani Wiyono, and Dong Soo Kim. From Latin America, key scholars of Pentecostalism include Gastón Espinosa, Eldin Villafañe, Samuel Solivan, Arlene Sanchez-Walsh, Sammy Alfaro, Elizabeth Ríos, Darío Lopez, Raymond Rivera, plus many others.

KEY THEMES IN PENTECOSTAL THEOLOGY

Just like the body of Pentecostal scholars (and scholars of global Pentecostalism) has grown to include voices from all parts of the world over the past few decades, theological interests of the movement have also evolved. The early days of classic Pentecostalism were shaped by a theological discourse that was dominated by the revivalist themes of baptism in/with the Holy Spirit (with the evidence of speaking in tongues) and mission and evangelism. The gift of speaking in tongues was always controversial, with some denominations, such as the Assemblies of God, insisting it was the initial evidence that followed the second blessing after conversion while other denominations maintained a nuanced stance, allowing prominence to other gifts of the Spirit. The rise of the Charismatic movement in the 1960s helped open the windows of the mainline churches to Pentecostal influences and highlighted further the work of the Spirit beyond *glossolalia*. By the end of the twentieth century, even the Assemblies of God was losing its confidence in the tongues-as-initial-evidence theology.

Mission

It was believed that the Spirit would empower Pentecostal Christians for mission as well as enable them to communicate in other languages through the gift of tongues. The Spirit was believed to have been given for the sake of mission, to endue them with power to be Christ's witnesses to the very ends of the earth. Within two years of the revival at Azusa Street, Pentecostal missionaries had travelled to many countries in the world, famously including South Africa (which, by 1910, had more Pentecostal Christians than the United States). Thus, Pentecostal theology has always had a propensity towards mission even though this has not always been a sound theology of mission – it can be colonial and militaristic – and has not always been properly articulated. Nevertheless, this Pentecostal zeal for mission continues today with an even greater sense of urgency, as many of them believe that the last days started at Pentecost (courtesy of Peter's misquoting of Joel at Acts 2:17) and, therefore, the return of Jesus is long overdue, (which means that Pentecostal Christians must evangelise as much as possible to save people from eternal hell fire, to plunder hell and populate heaven). It is this sense of urgency embedded in Pentecostal mission theology that makes Pentecostalism a very mission-minded movement, evidenced by evangelists like Reinhard Bonnke whose ministry claims to have converted 61 million Nigerians in the twenty years between 1998 and 2017.[17] The same mission theology now energises thousands of Brazilian, Nigerian, Ghanaian, and many other non-Western Pentecostals to send missionaries to other parts of the world as well, including Europe. Black Pentecostals, for instance, accounted for 60 per cent of church attendance in London in 2021.

Health and Wealth

Later on, in the 1920s and 1930s, the ministries of healing evangelists, such as Aimee Semple McPherson, brought to the fore the subject of

[17] Christ for All Nations, 'About Us', www.cfan.org.uk/articles/story-of-cfan.

miracles and divine health. By this time, in the aftermath of the
1918 Influenza Epidemic, healing movements of praying people, the
Aladura,[18] had emerged in Nigeria with the theological belief that
God alone is the healer and that Pentecostal Christians ought not take
medicine or make use of hospitals. Beginning in the 1920s, the *Aladura*
movement not only spread wider in West Africa, it also fostered
Pentecostal connections with North America and Europe, led to the
formation of several Pentecostal denominations in West Africa, and
established channels of theological cross-pollination. Healing ministries
became the hallmark of Pentecostal ministry and a central locus of
Pentecostal theological dialogue for the decades to come. A healing
theology emerged among Pentecostals that has continued to shape the
movement until today. This theology of a healing God who does not
want God's people to be sick would later lead on to the health and
wealth gospel (known in some circles as Prosperity Gospel), which
argues that God wants faithful followers to live healthy lives with
material blessings often received in exchange for a seed given to God
through the preacher's ministry. Prosperity preaching was popularised
largely by American preachers including Kenneth Copeland, Morris
Cerullo, and T. D. Jakes. Prosperity preaching has also permeated the
Pentecostal landscapes of other continents. Latin America has the
Universal Church of the Kingdom of God, first established in Brazil
but now present in more than 100 countries in the world. Asia has
had its own prosperity preachers such as David Yonngi Cho (South
Korea) and Joseph Prince (Singapore). Nigeria is home to many African
prosperity preachers including David Oyedepo (of the Winner's Chapel)
and Chris Oyakhilome (of the Christ Embassy Church) both of whom
have led their denominations since the 1970s and 1980s.

In the years following 2000, a new generation of younger prosperity
preachers has emerged in Africa, calling themselves prophets. Most
popular among these are Shepherd Bushiri (Malawi), Emmanuel
Makandiwa (Zimbabwe), T. B. Joshua (Nigeria), Paseka Motsoeneng
Mboro (South Africa), and Alph Lukau (South Africa/Democratic
Republic of Congo). Through their miracle-making ministries, these
prophets have contributed quite significantly to the explosion of both
Christianity in general and Pentecostalism in particular in Africa and in

---

[18] The *Aladura* was an African independent prayer movement sparked in Nigeria
starting in 1915 and reaching a tipping point in 1918 during the Influenza epidemic.
For more on this subject, see Allan Anderson, *African Reformation: African Initiated
Christianity in the 20th century* (Trenton, NJ: Africa World Press, 2001).

the African diaspora. They promise their followers God's riches, usually in the form of miracle money that gets deposited in people's wallets and bank accounts. In the context of abject poverty in parts of Africa, this is a very attractive message. Critics of the prosperity gospel focus on the lavish lifestyles of these preachers. However, for most Pentecostals in Africa, this is not an issue of concern. If anything, the preachers' riches have a motivational effect on the followers, saying, 'If God can do this for the pastor, God can do this for me as well.' Followers of African indigenous religion also believe the same; any god has to meet the needs of its followers if it is indeed a god (at least, in exchange of a sacrifice – that is why people must bring an animal, generally speaking, to move the spiritual world of the gods). As such, most African Pentecostals do not find it strange to give sacrificially to the prophets.

Social Justice

Pentecostal theology has often been criticised for being too heavenly minded to be of any use in this world, that it produces Christians who are not interested in engaging in the struggle against injustices in the world. To a great extent, this is improving. Issues of social justice, such as gender imbalances, economic inequalities, racism, militarism, and others, have begun to draw the attention of Pentecostal scholars and preachers. For instance, many Pentecostal denominations publicly reckoned with the social ill of racism in the wake of the murder of George Floyd and the rise of the Black Lives Matter movement. Many public apologies were said, and black and brown leaders were promoted. However, committing to fight for social justice is a challenge not only for Pentecostals. Most theological thought that has come out of Europe over the past 500 years has condoned or justified Europe's violent domination of the world. As an African, I am painfully aware of the centuries of European exploitation of Africa, first in the enslaving of Africans for free labour in the Americas and the Caribbean Islands and then followed by decades of European political colonisation of Africa (again followed by the ongoing economic – and psychological – colonisation of Africa by Europeans Christians). I am also aware of the close connection between white supremacy, the Western missionary movement of the past two hundred years, and the European colonisation of Latin America, Africa, and parts of Asia. Therefore, paying theological attention to social justice must go deeper than dealing with the symptoms and focus on the evil systems that form an unjust world. A theology that justified slavery or colonialism cannot faithfully engage in social justice. Pentecostal theology has some potential to do this if it follows the Spirit in its work of dismantling unjust systems of the world. However, shaped by Western thought as it is, it often struggles to even notice the injustices that God's people at the margins of society face on a daily basis.

CONCLUSION

In conclusion, it is quite likely that Pentecostal theology will increase in significance over the next century as it continues to grow in numbers, especially in Africa, Asia, and Latin America. Pretty soon, by 2050, anyone studying world Christianity will have to learn something about Pentecostalism and its theology. By their sheer numbers, Pentecostals will begin to dominate the landscape of Christianity around the world just as they have done in Africa and in parts of Latin America and Asia. In the African diaspora too, it is African Pentecostalism that has found its way to Europe, North America, Australia, and other places. In the United Kingdom, for example, Black Pentecostal Churches (of African and Afro-Caribbean origin) represent the growing section of Christianity. In London, Black Pentecostals will account for more half of church attendance on any Sunday throughout the year, with other cities lagging not too far behind. Because of this, their voice will need to be heard. It was Andrew Walls who said that if anyone wants to learn about Christianity in the twenty-first century, they will need to learn something about Africa.[19] I agree that this is true, but I add that they will need to learn something about Pentecostalism too. Pentecostal theological thought will matter, not only in Pentecostal circles, but in world Christianity.

Further Reading

Asamoah-Gyadu, J. Kwabena (2005), *African Charismatics: Current Developments within Independent Indigenous Pentecostalism in Ghana* (Boston: Brill).
(2013), *Contemporary Pentecostal Christianity: Interpretations from an African Context* (Eugene, OR: Wipf and Stock).
Burgess, Richard (2020), *Nigerian Pentecostalism and Development: Spirit, Power, and Transformation*, 1st ed. (London: Routledge).
Cartledge, Mark J. (2010), *Testimony in the Spirit: Rescripting Ordinary Pentecostal Theology* (Farnham: Ashgate).

---

[19] Andrew F. Walls, 'Of Ivory Towers and Ashrams: Some Reflections on Theological Scholarship in Africa', *Journal of African Christian Thought* 3, no. 1 (2000), 1.

Clarke, Clifton R. (2014), *Pentecostal Theology in Africa* (African Christian Studies Series 6; Eugene, OR: Wipf and Stock).

Johnson, Todd, and Gina Zurlo (2020), *Introducing Spirit-Empowered Christianity: The Global Pentecostal and Charismatic Movement in the 21st Century* (Tulsa, OK: Oral Roberts University Press).

Kalu, Ogbu (2008), *African Pentecostalism: An Introduction* (New York: Oxford University Press).

Miller, Donald E., and Tetsunao Yamamori (2007), *Global Pentecostalism: The New Face of Christian Social Engagement* (Berkeley: University of California Press).

Mugambi, Kyama M. (2020), *A Spirit of Revitalization: Urban Pentecostalism in Kenya* (Studies in World Christianity; Waco: Baylor University Press).

18 Analytic Theology

OLIVER D. CRISP*

Analytic theology is sometimes said to be a research programme in search of a definition. What is it? A complete answer to that question might helpfully give some account of how analytic theology came to be – before considering what it is – and we shall do that presently. However, it is in fact fairly easy to give a preliminary working definition of analytic theology: it is an approach to the theological task that utilises the tools and methods of analytic philosophy. This will need to be finessed as we progress. But it will serve as a place to begin.

First, then, let us consider some background concerning how analytic theology came to be. The term 'analytic theology' entered theological parlance in 2009, when the original edited volume that kick-started the current phase of analytic theology was published by Oxford University Press.[1] But really, analytic theology is continuous with something that had been happening since the early 1980s in the development of an interest in philosophical theology among Christian philosophers in the Anglo-American tradition. This was itself a 'theological turn' begun by philosophers who had cut their teeth, so to speak, on theological issues in the philosophy of religion, which had made an intellectual comeback in the 1950s in the heyday of the ordinary language philosophy that succeeded logical positivism. So, one way to characterise the development of analytic theology is as a research programme that had a first phase in the second half of the twentieth century in the renewal of philosophy of religion, a second phase in the 'theological turn' from the early 1980s to tradition-specific topics in philosophical theology such as the Trinity, Incarnation, and atonement practiced primarily by Anglo-American philosophers, and then a move

---

* Thanks to Michael Rea, Danielle Ross, Andrew Torrance, and Judith Wolfe for comments on a previous draft of this essay.
[1] O. D. Crisp and M. C. Rea, eds., *Analytic Theology: New Essays in the Philosophy of Theology* (Oxford: Oxford University Press, 2009).

into doing theology-as-such heralded by the 2009 volume. What changed in this third phase was that the work being done on theological topics by philosophers began to be taken up theologians as well. There were one or two precursors to this in the work of theologians such as Richard Sturch and Bruce Marshall. But at the time, their contributions tended to be notable exceptions to prevailing approaches in theology faculties, unlike the philosophical-theological work that was flourishing in philosophy departments of the same period (in the work of Marilyn Adams, Robert Adams, Thomas Morris, Alvin Plantinga, Eleonore Stump, Richard Swinburne, and Nicholas Wolterstorff, among others).

Since 2009, there has been a proliferation of analytic theology aided by major grant funding from the John Templeton Foundation, which has long had an interest in science-engaged theology and in work at the interface between philosophy and theology. Today there is a dedicated online open-access, peer-reviewed organ, the *Journal of Analytic Theology*. There are also several monograph series devoted to research in the area including *Oxford Studies in Analytic Theology*, *Routledge Studies in Analytic and Systematic Theology*, and *Analyzing Theology*, a short monograph series in analytic and systematic theology recently started with Wipf and Stock. In addition to this, there are also other recently founded journals that have a serious interest in analytic theology other than *Faith and Philosophy* or *Religious Studies*, which lead the field in philosophy of religion. These include *TheoLogica*, *Perichoresis*, and *Open Theology*. There are philosophers with interests in analytic theology in many philosophy departments in the United States, United Kingdom, and in mainland Europe. There are also theologians in divinity schools and theology departments in the United Kingdom, mainland Europe, North and South America, and Australia who work in this area, including a number of major research institutions. And there are graduate programmes that are devoted to analytic theology or that have analytic theology as a major focus, including centres in the Logos Institute in St Andrews, the University of York, Oxford, Helsinki, and Notre Dame, as well as institutions with faculty working in the area in Munich, Chicago, Trinity Evangelical Divinity School, and Cambridge, among others. There are conferences dedicated to analytic theology, such as the HEAT (Helskinki Analytic Theology) conference series in Helsinki, the (now concluded) Logos workshops series at Notre Dame, and the occasional Logos conferences at St Andrews. Analytic theology also flourishes in many other major theological forums as well, from regional meetings such as the Los Angeles

Theology Conference series to the American Academy of Religion. It is a truly international enterprise.

Thus, analytic theology is a thriving research programme that has practitioners among philosophers and theologians. But it is not a movement characterised by specific doctrines, though this is sometimes misunderstood. Not infrequently, one hears the claim that analytic theologians are theological realists, or that they are theologically conservative, or that they hold to particular doctrines such as penal substitution or the inerrancy of Scripture. None of this is accurate, because analytic theology commits its practitioners to no substantive doctrines; it is methodologically 'thin'. As a matter of sociological fact, many practitioners of analytic theology have been fairly traditional theists, are theological realists, and often have traditional views about theological authority. But that is a different matter.

We should distinguish between the conceptual content of analytic theology as a research programme and the research culture of analytic theology. As William Wood has pointed out,[2] analytic theology is both of these things, but its research culture could in principle change (some say is changing), whilst its rationale as a research programme remains substantively the same (a matter to which we shall return presently). This is in large measure because its conceptual commitments are so thin. Analytic theology is a research programme with a particular culture, which tolerates a plurality of approaches. In the Christian tradition, this is expressed by theologians that represent almost all of the major Christian denominations and communions. Thus, you can find Christian analytic theologians who are Roman Catholic, Orthodox, Lutheran, Anglican, Reformed, evangelical, and charismatic. But you can also find Christian analytic theologians who are conservative, traditionalist, progressive, theologically liberal, or revisionist. It is also true that analytic theology crosses theological divisions that are material and not merely formal in nature. So, there are Christian analytic theologians who are Thomist, Arminian, Molinist, Calvinist, Augustinian, and so on. This is one of its great strengths. The fact that analytic theology is a research programme means that within a kind of shared framework of understanding, different topics can be discussed from widely different points of view both ecclesially as well as doctrinally. It is a truly ecumenical enterprise.

---

[2] W. Wood, *Analytic Theology and the Academic Study of Religion* (Oxford Studies in Analytic Theology; Oxford: Oxford University Press, 2021).

This brings us back to the question of the nature of analytic theology. There are several different streams of analytic theology that are beginning to emerge as the movement grows and as its literature matures. There are those, mainly philosophers in the Anglo-American tradition, who regard it as in large measure a new name for philosophical theology – a kind of intellectual rebranding. In this context, 'philosophical theology' connotes the philosophical investigation of the claims of particular religious traditions, such as Christianity. In principle, philosophical theologians could be engaged in analysing the concepts and doctrines of any particular religious tradition, and there is currently a broadening of such work to encompass more research in religious traditions other than Christianity, from Wicca to Islam.

Whereas topics in philosophy of religion are usually not tradition-specific – such as arguments for or against the existence of a god, or the relationship between faith and reason, or the concept of God or gods – Christian philosophical theology might be characterised as a philosophical treatment of, say, the Trinity, incarnation, or atonement, among other doctrines specific to Christianity. The important thing to notice here is that on this way of characterising philosophical theology, it is concerned with the philosophical examination of these things. That is, it is carried out by those with an interest in the subject matter but without an explicit confessional commitment. Often such work is done in one of two ways, as Scott MacDonald has characterised it.[3] On the one hand, it could be focused on the justification of particular theological views, such as providing reasons for thinking that God is triune, say, or that Jesus is divine. On the other hand, the philosophical theologian might focus instead on the task of clarification. This is more to do with assessing the coherence of a particular doctrine and whether it fits within a broader theological context in a given tradition. Thus, one might ask whether, say, the two-natures doctrine of the incarnation can be expressed without generating significant intellectual problems as part of the fabric of the Christian doctrine of God and salvation. But notice that this task of clarification does not carry with it commitment to the view in question. One can, after all, defend the coherence of a particular view without endorsing it.

As I have indicated, some philosophers regard analytic theology as philosophical theology rebranded. (Eleonore Stump is a good example of this sort of approach, as was the late David Efird.) Others think of

---

[3] S. MacDonald, 'What Is Philosophical Theology?', in *Arguing about Religion* (ed. K. Timpe; London: Routledge, 2009), 17–29.

analytic theology as it is often practiced as a species of systematic theology. On this way of thinking, analytic theology provides a theological method. It is, in essence, the practice of theology engaging the tools and methods of analytic philosophy. Although systematic theologians have by and large been engaged with more hermeneutical and phenomenological streams of philosophy in pursuit of their theological goals, there is nothing in principle objectionable about the use of other philosophical interlocutors. In a similar way, theologians of the past have used Aristotelian philosophy, Neoplatonic thought, and German idealism, amongst other philosophical approaches to similar theological ends. The introduction to Christian analytic theology by Thomas McCall showcases this sort of analytic-theological approach,[4] as does the recent work by Crisp, Arcadi, and Wessling.[5] Some Christian theologians are suspicious of analytic theology as a theological research programme. But it is not clear why this should be the case given that there is already a plurality of approaches in systematic theology and nothing about the theological task that cannot be carried out by someone approaching the topics with the sensibilities of an analytic theologian.

These may not be the only ways of understanding analytic theology, but they do, I think, represent the two dominant genera in the field at present. We might call these analytic theology as philosophical theology, and analytic theology as systematic theology, respectively. Although as I have characterised them here, they are two distinct approaches, in practice the two are not always clearly differentiated, and analytic theologians who favour one sort of conception find no difficulty in engaging those who adopt the other conception because they share in common a method with which they can both pursue their respective projects.

The fact that there are different ways of construing analytic theology and different approaches is not regarded by those working in this area as an embarrassment but a strength. Similar things can be said of many different intellectual movements. As these movements develop, they diversify so that within their bounds different schools or approaches emerge such as the two I have elaborated upon here in

---

[4] T. H. McCall, *An Invitation to Analytic Christian Theology* (Downers Grove, IL: IVP Academic, 2015).

[5] O. D. Crist, J. M. Arcadi, and J. Wessling, *The Nature and Promise of Analytic Theology* (Brill Research Perspectives in Humanities and Social Sciences; Leiden: Brill, 2020).

contemporary analytic theology. Thus, for instance, one can find different sorts of theology in the nineteenth century that are influenced in one way or another by German idealism. But under that general description can be found theologians of very different theological persuasions and temperaments whose particular approach is quite different, though they share a kind of philosophical affinity. (Think of the differences between, say, Samuel Taylor Coleridge, John Williamson Nevin, Isaac Dorner, and Friedrich Schleiermacher.)

Having provided a brief overview of the development and breadth of analytic theology, we may now give a more summary statement of analytic theology as such. I began by offering a working definition of analytic theology as an approach to the theological task that utilises the tools and methods of analytic philosophy. Let us call this the generic view. For, having considered some issues in the development of analytic theology, as well as some of the ways in which it is currently understood by its practitioners, it should be clear that the working definition with which this chapter began represents a kind of generic account of analytic theology. It is an overarching characterisation of analytic theology that may be made more specific in particular ways by factoring in things like the religious tradition in question, whether it is understood to be philosophical theology or systematic theology, and so on. Thus, the generic view needs to be particularised when referring to more specific areas and clusters of research in the field. For instance, someone who practices analytic theology in the Christian tradition as a systematic theologian might say that their way of doing analytic theology does indeed involve an approach to the theological task that utilises the aims and methods of analytic philosophy (i.e., the generic view). But they would want to make this more specific by stating that this is analytic theology in the Christian tradition, practiced in a confessional manner by one who stands within that tradition as a systematic theologian. This is analytic theology done by an 'insider', that is, one who stands within a given tradition, seeking to give some account of it either in terms of justification or clarification (in MacDonald's sense) or even attempting to give some constructive account of a particular doctrine or doctrines as an aspect of the metaphysical worldbuilding that is part of the very raison d'être of the systematic theologian. In this way, we might speak of Christian analytic systematic theology – a classification that may delight theological lepidopterists, despite being rather unwieldy. But, as this example indicates, there are other ways in which the generic view could be parsed. Thus, the Jewish thinker who aligns her work with analytic theology might adopt the generic view as a Jew who is

interested in giving an account of the doctrinal claims of Judaism with
or without a specific confessional commitment – either construing
analytic theology as a constructive theological task or as a kind of
philosophical theology.[6]

Thus far, I have characterised analytic theology as a research programme without saying very much about what this means. Michael Rea
has written at length about research programmes.[7] He characterises
them as a set of dispositions that a scholar or group brings to bear on a
set of research questions. Such a programme may be pre-theoretical. It
may take the form of a kind of conceptual framework that helps organ-
ise and give shape to particular data and that can be revised in light of
evidence gathered and analysed. That seems to express something of
what analytic theology is about. Others have suggested that analytic
theology is something akin to a MacIntyrian tradition.[8] While that
may eventually be the case, it seems rather premature to characterise
analytic theology in this way.

Nevertheless, there is a research culture associated with analytic
theology, and analytic theologians tend to read the same works, interact
with the same authors and thinkers, consider a cluster of closely related
issues, and associate together in various formal and informal ways in
publication and peer-interaction in conferences and professional societies. (This is a common feature of academic life. Other recent theological research cultures include those associated with postliberalism,
contextual theologies of various stripes, Radical Orthodoxy, evangelicalism, so on.) As I have already intimated, analytic theologians also tend
to hold certain sorts of theological views or certain sorts of views that
have a theological bearing. For instance, most analytic theologians are
theological realists. That is, they hold that there is a God and that the
deity is a mind-independent thing that creates and sustains the world –
God is not a projection or an illusion or a superstitious hangover from
our evolutionary past. Moreover, most Christian analytic theologians
hold to a fairly traditional understanding of the Trinity or the
incarnation – most but not all. This sociological dimension to analytic
theology may change and is changing in some respects. Again, it is not
essential to analytic theology that its practitioners are theological

---

[6] For an example, see S. Lebens, *The Principles of Judaism* (Oxford Studies in Analytic
Theology; Oxford; Oxford University Press, 2020).
[7] See M. C. Rea, *World without Design: The Ontological Consequences of Naturalism*
(Oxford: Oxford University Press, 2002).
[8] See the discussion of this in Wood, *Analytic Theology and the Academic Study of
Religion*.

realists. But clarifying the difference between what analytic theology is as a method, how it is construed in particular contexts, the distinction between its status as a research programme, and the research culture or cultures of particular groups of analytic theologians is important. The failure to distinguish these things leads almost inevitably to confusion and misunderstanding, even caricature, which does no one any service.

Thus, to sum up, we can say analytic theology is an approach to the theological task that utilises the tools and methods of analytic philosophy (generic view). It is not confined to any particular religious tradition but can be (and has been) practiced within a variety of different traditions. It may be construed as philosophical theology or systematic theology (or the equivalent sort of constructive theological task in other traditions). It is a methodology that represents a particular research programme in contemporary theology, which has particular research cultures associated with it. And, as it is practiced in the Christian tradition, it is typically understood in theologically realist terms, alongside fairly traditional theological commitments about central doctrinal claims such as the Trinity, incarnation, and atonement, as these are represented by the particular ecclesial and denominational proclivities of the individual analytic theologian.

OBJECTIONS TO ANALYTIC THEOLOGY

Having given some account of the development and nature of analytic theology, we may now turn to consider some of the main objections to it. There are, in fact, relatively few published critical accounts of analytic theology. Nevertheless, several objections are often raised informally and are worth rehearsing here.

First, it is sometimes said that analytic theology is a new scholasticism or that it is philosophy disguised as theology. Analytic theology does share some affinity with scholastic theology, but it is not quite the same. Perhaps there is a family resemblance. Like scholasticism, analytic theology focuses on careful distinctions, argument, objections and counterexamples, and metaphysical worldbuilding. Much scholastic thought is indebted to Aristotelian metaphysics, however. The same is not true of analytic theology per se, much of which is indebted to more recent developments in analytic metaphysics. Nevertheless, there are important similarities between the two ways of doing theology. An affinity with scholasticism is not an objection, however. (Indeed, some might think it a recommendation.) It only becomes an objection when the interlocutor considers scholasticism to be a moribund method of theology and the supposed affinity with analytic theology a kind of guilt-by-association. But this hardly amounts to a serious objection and is easily turned back.

Let us set aside the scholasticism worry in favour of the concern about analytic theology being a kind of philosophical Trojan horse. For those who pursue analytic theology as philosophical theology, analytic theology is pursued from the perspective of philosophy. So, describing it as philosophy disguised as theology is not much of an objection: it is philosophical analysis of theological claims, plain and simple. However, for those who think of it as a method for pursuing systematic theology it is not – in fact, it is more like scholasticism, where philosophy plays the role of handmaiden to the theological content. So, the objection that analytic theology is philosophy (if that is an objection) depends on how analytic theology is conceived – whether as philosophical theology or systematic theology. Theologians may be more worried about this than philosophers because of the spectre of rationalism, that is, the fitting of theology to prefabricated philosophical patterns of thought, which distort theology in the process. But there is no good reason to think that this must be how analytic theology is pursued, even for those who think of it as a species of philosophical theology. Others may worry that the blurring of boundaries between philosophy and theology is accentuated by analytic theology. Most practitioners of analytic theology do not seem particularly troubled by such considerations, however. They reason that epistemological pluralism (i.e., the toleration of multiple competing ways of approaching matters of knowledge and the justification of belief) make such concerns otiose. For, if many approaches to a given discipline are tolerated, then why not think it possible to have an approach that effaces any clear boundary between philosophy and theology?

A second sort of worry is that analytic theology is ahistorical. Here the concern is something like this: (Christian) analytic theologians are not really interested in the history of theological positions but only in mining the literary remains of particular historical figures for arguments and concepts. But this is to emphasise one aspect of theology at the expense of others. For as Judith Wolfe, following Thomas Aquinas, has recently reminded us, Christian theology encompasses 'the study of God and all things in relation to God'.[9] Thus, this ahistorical worry as it bears on Christian analytic theology in particular is really as much a

[9] J. Wolfe, 'Theology', in *Saint Andrews Encyclopaedia of Theology*, www.saet.ac.uk/article/theology.

worry about the deformation of theology, or the abstraction and reification of aspects of theology to the detriment of other aspects, as it is about concerns that analytic theologians in particular do not really pay attention to the history of theology.

There is certainly something to be said for the fact that Christian theology is a rich and variegated tradition and that the argumentative spine of that tradition should not be abstracted and reified at the expense of other aspects of the tradition (e.g., its liturgy, its ecclesial praxis, its focus on confession or on worship or on religious experience). But to be fair to analytic theologians, this concern is being addressed in analytic theology in increasingly sophisticated ways. The 'liturgical turn' in recent analytic theology is evidence of this with work being done by Reformed thinkers such as Nicholas Wolterstorff, Roman Catholics such as Alex Pruss and Eleonore Stump, Eastern Orthodox philosophers such as Terence Cuneo, and Anglicans such James Arcadi, David Efird, and Joshua Cockayne. There is also a recognition in some analytic theological circles of the need to attend to different ways of approaching standard theological problems, including the history of such problems, from the perspective of the lived experience of certain marginalised voices – as has been true more broadly in much contextual theology.[10] So, even if there are some examples of analytic theology that are ahistorical in their treatment of the theological tradition, it is not something that is essential to analytic theology and is, in any case, not true of the best work in the field or of recent developments in analytic theology.

A third sort of worry is that analytic theology is a kind of idolatry. Sometimes this is construed in terms of 'ontotheology'. But since ontotheology is a controverted term, I shall refer to worries about idolatry instead.[11] Here the concern is something like this: analytic theologians work with a concept of God that is a kind of facsimile of the God of Christian theology and Scripture. It is a God made

---

[10] See, e.g., M. Panchuk and M. C. Rea, eds., *Voices from the Edge: Centering Marginalized Perspectives in Analytic Theology* (Oxford Studies in Analytic Theology; Oxford: Oxford University Press, 2020); B. Hereth and K. Timpe, eds., *The Lost Sheep in Philosophy of Religion: New Perspectives on Disability, Gender, Race, and Animals* (London: Routledge, 2020).

[11] For a discussion of ontotheology and analytic theology, see K. Hector, *Theology without Metaphysics: God, Language, and the Spirit of Recognition* (Current Issues in Theology Book 8; Cambridge: Cambridge University Press, 2011); M. M. Adams 'What's Wrong with the Ontotheological Error?', *Journal of Analytic Theology* 2 (2014), 1–12.

understandable and cut down to size in order to be a suitable subject for analysis. But such a God cannot be the ineffable, inconceivable, and incomprehensible deity of traditional Christianity. It is a kind of golem or idol created by analytic theologians for their own purposes.

There are several lines of response one could make to this objection. First, much analytic theology is done using conceptual models. Modelling a particular thing in the natural sciences usually involves providing a simplified description of more complex data. Such models are usually proxies that do not have a one-to-one correspondence with the target of the model. Consider the picture of an atom in a physics textbook as a good example of this. There is certainly value in such models, and theologians other than analytic theologians have acknowledged their importance in theology, for example, Sally McFague or Janet Martin Soskice. Often, in works of analytic theology, the analytic theologian provides a model of God in order to test certain theological claims that may have important theological implications even if it is understood at the outset that the conceptual picture of God being used is merely a proxy of the sort often used in the philosophy of science. Thus, one might provide a model of the Trinity such as the compositional account or the Latin account or a social account and not think that this corresponds to how God is in Godself but, rather, that it offers a conceptual model that addresses certain worries about the doctrine. This may be valuable if, for example, one thinks that providing a conceptual model may address issues of coherence or conceptual confusion that attend ways of thinking about this particular Christian dogma. But, of course, if one pursues theology in this fashion then clearly one is not guilty of idolatry just by virtue of adopting the methods of analytic theology that include the use of such models. It might still be the case that the analytic theologian in using a model of God ends up with mistaken views about the divine nature, but that is another matter and not one that is necessarily due to the adoption of a given method.

A second line of response to the idolatry worry is to push back against the claim that analytic theologians as a group have a given account of God that is idolatrous. Sometimes it is said that (Christian) analytic theologians have a penchant for an Anselmian perfect being theology, which is a philosophical conception of God that trades on a univocal account of the divine nature that is problematic. On this way of thinking, God is said to have all those great-making qualities requisite for divinity – qualities that are like those possessed by creatures, just perfected and enlarged (hence, univocal). Now, although there are many analytic theologians who find perfect being theology attractive (including the present author), this does not necessarily commit the theologian to a univocal account of predication when it comes to ascribing attributes to God, any more than it did in the case of the historic Anselm from whom perfect being theology derives. Nor does it entail idolatry any more than it did in the case of Anselm. But the more important point is this: there is no single account of the divine nature to which analytic theologians as such are committed, for – to repeat – analytic theology does not commit its practitioners to any substantive doctrines. There are analytic Christian theologians who have a very high tolerance of apophatic theology, who are sympathetic to Eastern Orthodoxy or to traditional Roman Catholic theology or to historic Protestant ways of thinking about the divine nature that are anything but idolatrous in the sense intended here. And not all analytic theologians adopt perfect being theology either. So, this objection is also wide of the mark.

The fact that there are many examples of analytic theologians who do adopt a univocal account of religious language predicated of God, or who do think of God in theistic personalist terms, is no evidence against the point being made here. For this is to be expected of a theological method that does not commit its practitioners to any particular theological doctrines. In other words, analytic theologians are free qua analytic theologians to adopt all sorts of views about the divine nature. The fact that some may end up with idolatrous views about God is no argument against analytic theology as such. At most, it is an argument against certain sorts of substantive theological commitments in addition to the commitment to analytic theology as a method.

A third, related, sort of response to the worry about idolatry: the analytic theologian may push back against the idea that there is such a thing as the Christian doctrine of God, if by this is meant a particular way of construing certain theological claims about God in the Christian tradition. For there are multiple ways of understanding the divine nature in Christianity and not all of these are compatible with one another. So, the very idea that there is a concept of God that is shared in the Christian tradition is itself an assumption that may be questioned and for good reason. Return to the dogma of the Trinity once more. If anything is a central and defining Christian doctrine, this is – although there are groups that claim to be Christian and deny this, such as Oneness Pentecostals. But leaving such limit cases aside, there are multiple accounts of the Trinity in the Christian tradition. Often, theologians begin with the classical understanding of the Trinity in the catholic creeds. But this does not yield a complete account of the

Trinity, only the bare bones of a doctrine – its skeleton, if you will, to which theological flesh must be attached. Thus, we have versions of a Latin account of the Trinity, according to which (in its Thomist version at any rate) the divine persons are subsistent relations within the Godhead. Then there are social accounts of the Trinity according to many of which the divine persons of the Godhead are particular centres of will and consciousness that all share a common trope, which is the divine nature. And, in recent analytic theology there are relative identity and constitution accounts of the Trinity where the divine persons are like Aristotelian forms, which 'compose' the stuff of divinity in three distinct ways. But clearly these are very different accounts of triunity, which are incommensurate with one another in important respects. Now, there are analytic theologians who defend each of these models of the Godhead and other models besides these as well. So, the idea that analytic theologians as a group are committed to a particular idolatrous conception of God is predicated on a caricature. There are as many ways of construing the doctrine of God in Christian analytic theology as there are in any other way of approaching divinity in Christian theology.

The worry about idolatry has been broadened in some recent literature to a concern about whether analytic theologians are engaged with idealised, abstracted concepts that do not correspond to the complexity and difficulty of actual theological notions. But in response to this sort of worry we can say two things. First, this is surely a concern for all modes of theological inquiry. We must attend to the conceptual content of our arguments to make sure that we are not abstracting or reifying notions in ways that will damage the theological content of our reasoning, as well as skewing the conclusions we reach. So, in one respect, this is not a problem peculiar to analytic theology, though I suppose it might be thought a particular besetting sin of analytic theology. But second, it is not at all clear to me that analytic theologians do attempt to idealise and abstract messy and complex religious ideas to make them more manageable and malleable. Here as before the usual caveats apply. That is, it is perfectly possible to point to egregious examples in a field where someone does indeed cross a particular line or instantiate the sort of concern envisaged by the critic. But that is not the same as claiming that there is something about the warp and weft of analytic theology that requires or implies this sort of mistake. There are very good examples of analytic theologians acknowledging the complexity and difficulty of articulating theological claims – the literature is large and examples abound. Here as before it must be stressed that analytic theology is already a research programme that tolerates a range of research cultures, which include very different theological commitments. Thus, it is very difficult to pin claims about conceptual reification on analytic theology as such, though particular whipping boys may, I suppose, be found, as they can be found in, say, Thomism, postliberalism, or contextual theologies.

NEW DEVELOPMENTS

In the course of explicating analytic theology and its development, I have already mentioned in passing some of the new developments in the field as it moves into its next phase (the initial phase being about its establishment as a viable mode of theological inquiry). But it is worth pausing to consider some of the most promising lines of current research as a way of considering possible future trajectories in analytic theology in the next phase of development. These include recent interest in marginalised voices such as those of women, persons of colour, and the disabled. The liturgical turn in recent analytic theology is also worth highlighting, as it has brought into focus issues that are not only new topics for analytic theologians but also has begun to generate a sophisticated literature on issues to do with the nature of the Church, worship and liturgical action, sacramental theology, religious affections, and the indwelling of the Holy Spirit, as well as matters pertaining to the nature of faith that are the subject of some attention in philosophy of religion as well. With the development of analytic theological approaches in the other Abrahamic faiths, there is also scope for a kind of analytic comparative theology. And finally, and perhaps most tantalising, is the prospect of a rapprochement between analytic and continental approaches to theology. It might well be a significant step forward for (Christian) theology as such, as well as work on specific Christian doctrines, if analytic and continental theologians were able to find common ground in order to forge a new constructive way of thinking about old theological problems.

Further Reading

Adams, M. M. (2014), 'What's Wrong with the Ontotheological Error?', *Journal of Analytic Theology* 2, 1–12.

Crisp, O. D., J. M. Arcadi, J. and Wessling (2020), *The Nature and Promise of Analytic Theology* (Brill Research Perspectives in Humanities and Social Sciences; Leiden: Brill).

Crisp, O. D., and M. C. Rea, eds. (2009), *Analytic Theology: New Essays in the Philosophy of Theology* (Oxford: Oxford University Press).

Hector, K. (2011), *Theology without Metaphysics: God, Language, and the Spirit of Recognition* (Current Issues in Theology Book 8; Cambridge: Cambridge University Press).

Hereth, B., and K. Timpe, eds. (2020), *The Lost Sheep in Philosophy of Religion: New Perspectives on Disability, Gender, Race, and Animals* (London: Routledge).

Lebens, S. (2020), *The Principles of Judaism* (Oxford Studies in Analytic Theology; Oxford: Oxford University Press).

MacDonald, S. (2009), 'What Is Philosophical Theology?', in *Arguing about Religion* (ed. K. Timpe; London: Routledge), 17–29.

McCall, T. H. (2015), *An Invitation to Analytic Christian Theology* (Downers Grove, IL: IVP Academic).

M. C. Rea, (2002), *World without Design: The Ontological Consequences of Naturalism* (Oxford: Oxford University Press).

Panchuk, M., and M. C. Rea, eds. (2020), *Voices from The Edge: Centering Marginalized Perspectives in Analytic Theology* (Oxford Studies in Analytic Theology; Oxford: Oxford University Press).

Wolfe, J. (forthcoming), 'Theology', in *Saint Andrews Encyclopaedia of Theology*.

Wood, W. (2021), *Analytic Theology and the Academic Study of Religion* (Oxford Studies in Analytic Theology; Oxford: Oxford University Press).

19 Apocalyptic Theology

WESLEY HILL

No contemporary New Testament exegete can supply a firsthand recollection of what it was like to read Karl Barth's commentary on Paul's letter to the Romans, best known by its original German title *Der Römerbrief*, when it first appeared.[1] Its impact was dramatic and game-changing – it is now routinely identified as representing an exciting and unsettling new era of "apocalyptic" theology – but eyewitness reports of that impact are now several generations removed.[2] In more recent times, perhaps no New Testament commentary has had an impact more resembling Barth's than the commentary on Paul's earlier letter to the Galatians by J. Louis Martyn (1925–2015). First published in 1997 in the Anchor Bible Commentary series, Martyn's commentary was quickly feted as a watershed in New Testament exegesis as well as in theology more broadly conceived. Pauline scholar John Barclay described Martyn's *Galatians* in epochal terms: "Rarely since Luther has the radical, polarising, indeed shocking force of Paul's letter been so well appreciated by a reader with a visceral antipathy towards the multiple domestications of Paul."[3] And Richard Hays, another celebrated Pauline scholar, made the connection with Barth explicit: "Martyn has written what I take to be the most profound and powerful biblical commentary since Karl Barth's *Römerbrief*."[4]

---

[1] Karl Barth, *Der Römerbrief* (Münich: Chr. Kaiser, 1929). English translation: *The Epistle to the Romans*, 6th ed. (trans. Edwyn C. Hoskyns; London: Oxford University Press, 1933). The first, greatly different edition was published in 1919, though the second edition is now the most well-known.

[2] In a presumably unintentionally grisly metaphor, Karl Adam spoke of the commentary falling "like a bombshell on the playground of the theologians" (Karl Adam, "Die Theologie der Krisis," in *Hochland: Monatsschrift für alle Gebiete des Wissens der Literatur und Kunst* 23 [1926–1927], 271–286).

[3] John Barclay, "Review of Galatians by J. Louis Martyn," *Review of Biblical Literature* (2001), www.sblcentral.org/API/Reviews/2064_1356.pdf.

[4] Richard B. Hays, "Review of Galatians by J. Louis Martyn," *Review of Biblical Literature* (2001), www.sblcentral.org/API/Reviews/2064_1359.pdf.

Like Barth's *Römerbrief* but in its own distinctive idiom, Martyn's *Galatians* portrays Paul as the herald of a divine interruption of the normal course of human religiosity. Far from urging his hearers to make a choice between two alternative ways to live, Paul proclaims a vertical intervention from beyond "the present evil age" (Gal. 1:4) in the death and resurrection of Jesus Christ to rescue a humanity unable to extricate itself from enslavement to the anti-God powers of sin and death. This intervention is so discontinuous with what has gone before that it could not have been predicted and cannot be plotted (as much New Testament scholarship has argued that it can) on a linearly unfolding timeline of "salvation history." Rather, for Martyn's Paul, God has acted in Jesus in such a way that all that came before in the history of Israel must be understood in a new light: not as the faltering but faithful history of human religious questing and piety but as God's electing and justifying of the ungodly.[5]

Martyn's *Galatians* has been so influential that many observers would trace much of the current interest in apocalyptic theology back to its publication and reception by biblical scholars, systematic theologians, and Christian preachers alike.[6] What follows takes its cues from Martyn, first summarizing what Martyn's commentary presents as Paul's version of an apocalyptic theology. Next comes a discussion of the roots of Martyn's work in post-war German Protestant theology, especially that of Ernst Käsemann, to whom Martyn's *Galatians* is dedicated. Finally, some of the problems and unfinished tasks of apocalyptic theology will be discussed.

---

[5] As Fleming Rutledge has written: "I do not believe it is possible to read the Old Testament through the lens of radical, unconditional grace unless one has had one's fortifications stormed by the gospel. Hence I resist the language of *continuity* [between the Old Testament and the Pauline gospel] in the way it is usually understood." See Fleming Rutledge, "How Apocalyptic Theology Changed Me," *Ruminations* (2013), https://generousorthodoxy.org/rumination/how-apocalyptic-theology-changed-me. According to Susan Grove Eastman, such a perspective need not "mean abandoning the past, let alone denying or erasing Israel's history," but "God does a genuinely new thing in Jesus, and that genuinely new thing breaks into history and becomes the vantage point for understanding everything that preceded it …. God, whom Paul identifies as the Father of our Lord Jesus Christ, has indeed been acting in the events leading up to the present, but one sees that rightly only through the lens of Jesus Christ. It is as if the cross and resurrection shine spotlights on certain parts of Israel's scriptures and leave others in shadow.' See Susan Grove Eastman, "N. T. Wright's Creative Reconstruction of Paul and His World," *The Christian Century* (2018), www.christiancentury.org/review/books/n-t-wright-s-creative-reconstruction-paul-and-his-world.

[6] Joshua B. Davis and Douglas Harink, eds., *Apocalyptic and the Future of Theology: With and Beyond J. Louis Martyn* (Eugene, OR: Cascade, 2012).

J. LOUIS MARTYN'S APOCALYPTIC THEOLOGY OF PAUL

The chief emphases of Martyn's commentary are best summarized by Martyn himself in a subsequently published essay.[7] There he lists three themes that, he argues, mark Paul out as a theologian of God's "apocalypse."

First, Martyn notes that although Paul in Galatians does not employ the standard array of apocalyptic images and motifs (more on this below), he appears to transform the standard Jewish Christian emphasis on Jesus the Messiah having made possible the forgiveness of sins into a more radical emphasis on Jesus as God's means of contestation of the anti-God powers that hold humanity in thrall. In line with much early Christian tradition, Paul does speak of Jesus as the one "who gave himself for our sins" (Gal. 1:4), but he immediately goes on to point toward a more comprehensive soteriological scheme whereby believers are "set ... free from the present evil age." The human plight, as Paul constructs it in Galatians, is not merely one in which believers need to be forgiven for past wrongs but, more fundamentally, liberated from a cosmic oppression. For Martyn, Paul's reference to the "revelation" – ἀποκάλυψις (apokalypsis) in Greek – "of Jesus Christ" (1:12; cf. 1:16; 3:23) that he received points toward a divine interruption or incursion from beyond the realm of human religious possibility:

> God would not have to carry out an invasion in order merely to forgive erring human beings. The root trouble lies deeper than human guilt, and it is more sinister. The whole of humanity – indeed, the whole of creation (3:22) – is, in fact, trapped, enslaved under the power of the present evil age. That is the background of God's invasive action in his sending of Christ, in his declaration of war, and in his striking the decisive and liberating blow against the power of the present evil age.[8]

The divine remission of individual transgressions is not the key soteriological moment in Pauline theology; rather, the conquest of the forces of sin and death, which are understood as exerting "downward causality" on humanity (not merely by humanity), is the center of Paul's account

---

[7] J. Louis Martyn, "The Apocalyptic Gospel in Galatians," *Interpretation* 54 (2000), 246–266.

[8] J. Louis Martyn, *Galatians: A New Translation with Introduction and Commentary* (Anchor Bible 33A; New York: Doubleday, 1997), 105.

of redemption.[9] As Fleming Rutledge, an Episcopal priest and preacher whose writing has done much to move the concerns of apocalyptic from academic settings into ecclesial spaces, has said (albeit in an accent owing more to the Synoptic Gospels): "There are *three* parties in the apocalyptic drama, not two: God, enslaved humanity, and the Powers of Sin and Death. The incarnate Son did not arrive in neutral territory. His entrance called out the demonic forces."[10]

This leads to the second theme of God's "invasion" of the enslaved cosmos and what Martyn calls "the consequent line of redemptive movement" from God to humanity rather than the reverse.[11] Part of the rhetorical force of Martyn's commentary lies in its extensive reconstruction of the identity, message, and agenda of Paul's opponents in Galatia, whom Martyn calls "the Teachers" (older scholarship referred to these figures as 'the Judaizers', following the verb in Gal. 2:14).[12] According to Martyn, these Teachers were Christian evangelists. Like Paul, they came to the churches of Galatia bearing "good news." Their message, as Martyn's commentary portrays it, is a development of the Mosaic law's 'two ways' (Deut. 30:11–20).[13] However, whereas in the law the choice of life or death is presented to Israel only on the basis of a prior divine act of unconditioned election (7:6–11; cf. Exod. 20:2), the Teachers have turned the law's offer of two alternative ways to live into a means of circular exchange. The Galatian Christians must commit themselves to observe the law, starting with the command for the males in the community to be circumcised, and may thereby be assured of God's commitment to make them full-fledged members of the covenant community of Abraham's family in response to their obedience. Thus, as Martyn says, the "good news" the Teachers bring to the Galatians is, first, an announcement of "bad news": the Galatian Christians are in a state of theological limbo, a kind of religious halfway house. They have (rightly) hailed Jesus as God's anointed eschatological savior, but they have (wrongly and fatefully) stopped short of becoming observers of the Torah and are thus dangerously exposed to the evil impulse of the flesh (5:16). In order to remedy this situation, the Teachers recommend that the Galatians avail themselves of the law and move from their present

---

[9] Matthew Croasmun, *The Emergence of Sin: The Cosmic Tyrant in Romans* (New York: Oxford University Press, 2017).

[10] Fleming Rutledge, "A Modest Proposal: Apocalyptic Theology," *Ruminations* (2009), https://generousorthodoxy.org/rumination/a-modest-proposal-apocalyptic-theology.

[11] Martyn, "The Apocalyptic Gospel in Galatians," 254.

[12] Martyn, *Galatians*, 18.

[13] For a hypothetical sermon from the Teachers, see Martyn, *Galatians*, 302–306.

state of precarity into a firm confidence that, on the basis of their own fidelity, God will not abandon them to corruption.

While this message may resemble much current Christian evangelism, for Martyn it is nearly the polar opposite of Paul's gospel.[14] For Martyn's Paul, the "line of redemptive movement" does not proceed vertically from below, from the sphere of human decision and habit, but from above, from the fount of divine initiative and merciful power:

> It is not as though, provided with a good religious foundation for a good religious ladder, one could ascend from the wrong to the right. Things are the other way around. God has elected to invade the realm of the wrong – "the present evil age" (1:4) – by sending God's Son and the Spirit of the Son into it from outside it (4:4–6). And it is in this apocalyptic invasion that God has liberated us from the powers of the present evil age …. Galatians is a particularly clear witness to one of Paul's basic convictions: the gospel is not about human movement into blessedness (religion); it is about God's liberating invasion of the cosmos (theology).[15]

This leads Martyn, finally, to his third summarizing theme: the crucified cosmos and the new creation. The key text from Paul is Gal. 6:14–15, here given in Martyn's translation: "For me boasting is excluded, except in the cross of our Lord Jesus Christ, by which the cosmos has been crucified to me and I to the cosmos. For neither is circumcision anything nor is uncircumcision anything. What is something is the new creation."[16] What interests Martyn about this passage is that it features no imperatives: everything is cast is the indicative ("boasting is" – not "should be" – "excluded"; "the cosmos has been" – not "should be" – "crucified ..."; "What is" – not "should be" – "something is the new creation"). Paul announces the existence of a new world; he does not urge his hearers to go out and create one by their obedience.[17] Furthermore, the text indicates the dissolution of the importance of the structuring elements of the "old cosmos," the means whereby the contours of the world before Christ were maintained. No doubt the chief of these structuring elements for Paul during his

---

[14] Cf. Douglas A. Campbell, *The Deliverance of God: An Apocalyptic Rereading of Justification in Paul* (Grand Rapids: Eerdmans, 2009), chs. 2–3.

[15] Martyn, "The Apocalyptic Gospel in Galatians," 255.

[16] Ibid., 255.

[17] Here echoes of Barth's celebrated Romans commentary are present: the kingdom of God is not something to be built, advanced, or ushered in by human projects of self- or world-improvement but simply attested and received in gratitude, faith, and witness.

upbringing as a Jew in the Diaspora was the distinction between circumcision and uncircumcision, the practice marking Israel out as a
distinct community from the surrounding nations. Now, because of
what God has done in Jesus, that primal marker of human difference
is rendered of no soteriological significance (cf. Gal. 3:28; 5:6; 1
Cor. 7:19; Col. 3:11).

Martyn is quick to underscore that "what God has done in Jesus" is
not chiefly, in Galatians, raising Jesus from the dead, although Paul
certainly affirms that reality, as do his opponents (1:1). At least in the
climactic theological slogan of 6:14–15, it is specifically Jesus's cross
that represents the shattering of the old cosmos and the incursion of
God's new creation. For Martyn, this is what the much-contested phrase
πίστις Χριστοῦ in 2:16 (cf. 2:20; Rom. 3:21–22; Phil. 3:9) refers to: Jesus's
faithful death ("the faithfulness of Christ") in fulfillment of God's determination to powerfully step on the scene for the world's rescue. And so
this apocalyptic inbreaking is, paradoxically, best understood and displayed in Paul's faithful participation in Christ's cross through suffering
love (6:17) as well as in the community's cruciform mutual concern and
care (6:2).

In every way and at every turn, Martyn's reading of Galatians is
bracing – even caustic in its opposition to domesticated readings of
Paul – and galvanizing. It has been dismissed by some critics as "historical fiction," insofar as Martyn's attempt to reconstruct the historical situation "behind" the text relies on far more than only
supposedly "assured results" of historical study. But far more often,
it has been received with appreciation by a widely diverse readership
and deepened and extended in further directions by a large number of
colleagues and former students.[18] At root, Martyn presents Paul as a
theologian of God's cosmic revelation of Jesus Christ; he eschews
individualistic and demythologized versions of Paul's gospel, emphasizing the militaristic and corporate dimensions of Paul's understanding of "rectification" (Martyn's memorable rendering of what most
English translations call "justification" [δικαιοσύνη, δικαίωσις, etc.]);
and, most significantly, he insists that, for Paul, what has taken place
in Jesus does not create merely a new possibility for human religion
but rather actually constitutes the arrival of God's new creation
in power.

---

[18]   See especially Davis and Harink, *Apocalyptic and the Future of Theology.*

THE BACKGROUND OF MARTYN'S INTERPRETATION
OF GALATIANS

Aside from theological concerns, the value of Martyn's work as descriptive history has been significantly disputed, even as its theological utility has continued to be fleshed out and put to work in many adjacent theological conversations. Grasping the wider project of (Pauline and other) apocalyptic theology will be easier if the reasons for this twofold reaction to Martyn's work are sketched.

The history of the study of New Testament – and specifically Pauline – apocalyptic theology is usually traced back to two New Testament scholars: Johannes Weiss (1863–1914) and Albert Schweitzer (1875–1965). In 1892, Weiss published the first edition of *Jesus' Proclamation of the Kingdom of God*, a book focused not on Paul but on the historical Jesus, whom Weiss portrayed as an apocalyptic-eschatological prophet who predicted the end of the space-time world. Citing 1 Cor. 7:31 ("For the present form of this world is passing away"), Weiss argued furthermore that the early Christianity stemming from the Jesus movement was banking on the imminent *parousia* of the risen Lord. The problem, for Weiss, was simply that "our modern Protestant world-view" cannot share this primitive conviction, since with 2,000-plus years of hindsight, we see the obvious falsity of belief in the imminent parousia.[19]

Within the realm of the Protestant theology of his time, Weiss's treatment was polemical. Against those who sought to reimagine and retain for contemporary faith Jesus's teaching on the kingdom, shorn of its eschatological urgency and translated into the category of the human project of moral self-improvement, Weiss insisted that, while contemporary translation was necessary, interpreters should always bear in mind that it is translation and not a repetition of what the historical Jesus believed and proclaimed. For Jesus, "the actualization of the Kingdom of God is *not* a matter for human initiative, but entirely a matter for God's initiative."[20] If modern believers find it necessary to speak of human initiative as bringing in or extending the kingdom, they should admit that such was not Jesus's outlook.

Albert Schweitzer, especially in *The Mysticism of Paul the Apostle* (1931), made a powerful and influential case that the deepest roots of

---

[19] Johannes Weiss, *Jesus' Proclamation of the Kingdom of God* (ed. Richard H. Hiers and D. Larrimore Holland; Philadelphia: Fortress, 1971), 135.

[20] Ibid., 132.

Paul's thought were to be found in Jewish apocalyptic-eschatological expectation, rather than in Hellenisitic thought, as so much German historical criticism of Paul had said. In this Schweitzer thought that Paul was in complete agreement with the historical Jesus. Schweitzer bequeathed to later interpreters a focus on three primary emphases in Paul's apocalyptic theology: first, the place of cosmic angelic powers who resist God's reign; second, the imminent end of the space-time world and the coming of the next; and third, an understanding of redemption in Christ being participatory or "mystical" rather than legal and juridical. According to Schweitzer's Paul, believers come to share in the struggle against the cosmic forces of which death is the ultimate, expecting to participate in Christ's triumph over them and ushering in of the new age "so that God may be all in all" (1 Cor. 15:28).

More recent studies, building on rather than fully repudiating the work of Weiss and Schweitzer, have focused more on apocalyptic as a literary genre. The title of the last book of the New Testament canon, the Revelation (or Apocalypse), has come in post-Weiss and -Schweitzer scholarship to serve as the designation of a type of Jewish and early Christian texts that share similar distinguishing features, even if such a use of the term is novel from the standpoint of pre-first-century Jewish texts. In 1979, the Society of Biblical Literature Genres Project published a proposed definition of "apocalyptic" understood this way: "[Apocalyptic is] a genre of revelatory literature with a narrative framework, in which a revelation is mediated by an otherworldly being to a human recipient, disclosing a transcendent reality which is both temporal, insofar as it envisages eschatological salvation, and spatial, insofar as it involves another, supernatural world."[21] Examples of this genre would include, in the Old Testament, Daniel 7–12, as well as the non-canonical 1 Enoch, 4 Ezra and the *Apocalypse of Abraham*. Although the social conditions giving rise to apocalyptic literature continue to be studied and debated, it seems that apocalypses are usually written to audiences suffering persecution or undergoing some difficult ordeal, assuring them that they belong to the final chapter before God acts to vindicate his people and overthrow his enemies.

However, while helpfully noting lines of literary development and cross-fertilization, that disciplinary focus on apocalyptic as a genre of texts has mostly stayed at the descriptive level, leaving the theological challenges posed by Weiss and Schweitzer for contemporary Christian

[21] John J. Collins, *The Apocalyptic Imagination: An Introduction to Jewish Apocalyptic Literature* (Grand Rapids: Eerdmans, 1998), 5.

belief largely untouched. But in order to understand the work of Martyn, it is essential to see him engaged in a conversation about the meaning of apocalyptic for contemporary speech about God, reasserting the enduring importance of apocalyptic in the face of attempts to relegate it to a past stage of faith and proclamation.

Martyn stands downwind of Ernst Käsemann (1906–1998), to whom his Galatians commentary is dedicated, as noted above. Käsemann, in turn, stands downwind of his teacher Rudolf Bultmann (1884–1976). Bultmann, responding to Weiss and Schweitzer, had largely agreed with them about the character of the New Testament writings: "[The NT's] language of mythology, and the origin of the various themes can be easily traced in the contemporary mythology of Jewish Apocalyptic and in the redemption myths of Gnosticism."[22] Where Bultmann pressed their points was in underscoring the impossibility of retaining the apocalyptic perspective in a secular, scientific age: "We are therefore bound to ask whether, when we preach the Gospel to-day, we expect our converts to accept not only the Gospel message, but also the mythical view of the world in which it is set. If not, does the New Testament embody a truth which is quite independent of its mythical setting?" Bultmann's answer was a resounding and memorable yes, and his project of seeking to rescue the kernel of the New Testament's proclamation from the husk of its outdated apocalyptic framework is known as "demythologization."[23] In reaction to this perspective, Bultmann's student Käsemann sounded once again the Schweitzerian note: "Apocalyptic was the mother of all Christian theology."

Käsemann initially meant this remark as a historical claim – one that Bultmann did not straightforwardly deny. But as Käsemann further developed his response to his teacher, he came to think that it was impossible fully to remove the husk from the theological kernel in the way that Bultmann had attempted. Käsemann pointed out that although Paul laid the groundwork for Bultmann's program by bringing the future apocalyptic hope of resurrection into present perspective by focusing on Jesus's resurrection in the midst of history, Paul nonetheless retained a future apocalyptic hope. That future could not simply be collapsed without remainder into the present experience of salvation without distorting Paul's theology at a fundamental level. Käsemann also pointed out that the translation Bultmann effected – from Paul's

[22] Rudolf Bultmann, *Kerygma and Myth* (ed. Hans Werner Bartsch; New York: Harper, 1961), 3.
[23] Ibid.

mythic, cosmological portrayal of salvation to an individual, existential demand for decision – neglected the embeddedness of individuals in a cosmic situation subject to the rule of powers above and beyond themselves (a perspective that more recent understandings of racism as a structure that exerts pressure independently of individual human actors may find more compelling than Bultmann did). If Paul is seen merely as a preacher asking for individual acts of conversion, his profound understanding of the solidarity of all humanity under sin and death is blunted and his equally sweeping understanding of redemption as cosmic in scope (Romans 8) is truncated.

Martyn's work on Galatians should be read as a contribution to this ongoing conversation not only about the historical composition of the New Testament and one of its particular genre backgrounds in early Jewish literature but also about the meaning of Pauline theology for today. Clearly, Martyn shares the perspective of all the above-named figures in his insistence that Paul speaks the language of visionary prophecy when he describes the human plight. But he parts ways with Bultmann and sides with Käsemann when he insists on the ultimate futility of extricating a Pauline *kerygma* from a discardable apocalyptic shell.

QUESTIONS AND DEVELOPMENTS

All of the above indicates how stimulating and generative apocalyptic theology in the vein of Martyn's Paul has been and may be for Christian theology. As Martyn's work (and that of others in similar veins) continues to be deepened and refined, it prompts significant critical questions even as it provokes positive doctrinal development in salutary ways. Three of these questions are mentioned below.

First, as several others have noted, Martyn's penchant for speaking of God as "invading" the cosmos does not sit easily with traditional Christian theological claims about creation and providence.[24] Robert Jenson puts it bluntly: "God has no call to invade the world, since he already rules in it."[25] If God is the cause of all creaturely being, then there is an obvious and profound sense in which God does not – cannot –

---

[24] Michael Allen, "Review Article, Philip Ziegler's *Militant Grace: The Apocalyptic Turn and the Future of Christian Theology*," *International Journal of Systematic Theology* 22, no. 3 (2020), 287–299; repr. in *The Fear of the Lord: Essays in Theological Method* (London: T & T Clark, 2022), 103–116; and Grant Macaskill, "History, Providence and the Apocalyptic Paul," *Scottish Journal of Theology* 70, no. 4 (2017), 409–426.

[25] Davis and Harink, *Apocalyptic and the Future of Theology*, 159.

"invade" the world from outside. Here Martyn's work would benefit from closer attention to accounts of the non-competition between God and the world that have underscored that God is not a "being" among other beings, jostling with other creatures for space in the world of finite agents and causes, but rather the "radically transcendent" source and sustainer of the world.[26] Many recent theological and exegetical accounts of divine transcendence and causality neglect to discuss how God's infinite causal agency relates to human sinfulness (older theology asked: "Is God the 'author' of evil?"), and insofar as Martyn's work raises the question of God's redemptive overcoming of human rebellion in an especially acute and dramatic form, it remains a useful stimulant for dogmatic theology. But insofar as it offers no reflection on what an appropriately "demythologized" version of talk about divine "invasion" might mean, it may hamper reflection on God's "ceaseless activity" of providential governance that cannot "invade" because it has never been inactive.[27]

While the language of divine invasion may appeal to biblical texts for support ("O that you would tear open the heavens and come down" [Isa. 64:1]), furthermore, it is also the case that other biblical material suggests a more qualified, less univocally literal approach to such language (e.g., Isa. 40:25; 46:5, 9b). Also, arguably, when the Bible does use language reminiscent of invasion, it is more about God's accession to the throne, God's "becoming king," rather than, as Martyn has it in a less determined idiom, "God's stepping powerfully on the scene from beyond."[28]

Second, and relatedly, Martyn's construal of Galatians is one in which the agency of God in "rectifying" the ruined human situation is contrasted with the agency of believers in a zero-sum fashion: less of one means more of the other. "It is not by means of something the human being does – observe the Law – that God has elected to carry out his rectification., his making that human being right. God's means of rectification is solely the divine act of Christ's faith."[29] Some interpreters have noted that all of Martyn's emphasis falls on the movement of

---

[26] Kathryn Tanner, *God and Creation in Christian Theology: Tyranny or Empowerment?* (Minneapolis: Augsburg Fortress, 1988).

[27] Macaskill, "History, Providence, and the Apocalyptic Paul," 423, 425.

[28] Martyn, *Galatians*, 158.

[29] Ibid., 252. Since the publication of the commentary, Martyn has qualified and nuanced his views considerably. See his "Epilogue: An Essay in Pauline Meta-Ethics," in *Divine and Human Agency in Paul and His Cultural Environment* (ed. John M. G. Barclay and Simon J. Gathercole; London: T&T Clark,. 2006), 173–183.

initiative in his portrayal of divine or human agency – is God or the human being the temporal origin of the making right of the cosmos? Yet certain Pauline texts fit awkwardly in this way of framing matters. Martyn's prioritizing of a subjective-genitive interpretation of the πίστις Χριστοῦ phrase in 2:16 seems to render human agency threatening to God's rectifying activity, which seems incongruent with, for instance, Paul's lack of embarrassment about issuing imperatives for human behavior (cf. 1 Cor. 15:10; Phil. 2:12–13). As Barclay observes, for Paul, "the prior grace of God was not in the least compromised by saying that its purchase on human lives takes effect through human faith in God's Christ-embodied saving power."[30] Paul shows little anxiety in speaking of human participation in God's apocalyptic invasion.[31] Is there a way to tease out a more robust ethics and politics from Martyn's work, without watering down his insight about the fundamental priority and efficacy of divine action?

Third and finally, although Martyn represents Paul as a Scripture-reading theologian, he emphasizes that Paul does not read Scripture objectively, as modern historical critics attempt to do. Rather,

> a major factor separating Paul from [his] opponents is the identity of the determinative point of interpretive departure. For while ... he continues to learn things from scripture, his exegesis thoroughly reflects the fact that he did not come to Christ because, being the interpretive point of departure, scripture led him there, but rather because of God's act in the *apokalypsis Iēsou Christou* (Gal 1:11–16; 2:19). Thus, in his inner-church debates he now comes to scripture from Christ, and it is that interpretive point of departure and the resulting line of movement that undergird [his Scriptural exegesis].[32]

This way of putting things makes it sound as though Christ is a kind of hermeneutical filter or rubric that predetermines what Paul finds in the Scriptural texts he interprets. He comes to Scripture from Christ, but he does not derive insight into Christ from Scripture.

Francis Watson's work has convinced many interpreters that this framing does not do justice to the to-and-fro character of Paul's Scriptural interpretation. Watson poses the question: Does Paul replace

---

[30] Barclay, "Review of *Galatians*."
[31] See Campbell, *The Deliverance of God*.
[32] J. Louis Martyn, "Article Review, Francis Watson, *Paul and the Hermeneutics of Faith*," *Scottish Journal of Theology* 59, no. 4 (2006), 437.

Scripture with Christ, thus ensuring that, even when he cites Scripture, it is not the Scriptural voice itself but rather Paul's theological ventriloquism that is speaking? Or does he understand Scripture to have been reconfigured in the light of Christ, so that it retains agency, so to speak, in shaping the way Paul understands and proclaims the gospel?[33] Watson opts firmly for the latter, citing Martyn's own image of a ring with a jewel as a metaphor for the hermeneutical circle or spiral that Paul inhabits: the effort to proclaim the gospel leads Paul back to Scripture, and reading Scripture leads Paul back to proclamation, but the jewel – which is the raison d'etre of the ring – is the gospel of Christ that thus retains a sort of priority or centrality, even as it does not simply replace the need for the ring (i.e., the movement from the gospel to Scripture and from Scripture to gospel and so on).

This finely calibrated correction from Watson also opens the door for a rehabilitation of "salvation history," which Martyn relegates to the teaching of Paul's opponents. Martyn and other apocalyptic interpreters are so committed to the singularity and radical newness of the gospel that they typically prefer not to speak of a linear progression of redemption through history (in which the Exodus leads smoothly to the covenant with Israel, which in turns leads on to the monarchy and covenant with David and so on, in which each new covenant extends and deepens the former). But, contrary to certain crude criticisms from N. T. Wright, Martyn does not in any way present Paul as a proto-Marcionite.[34] Although he claims that Paul invites the Galatians to contemplate the upsetting possibility of "a godless Law," Martyn equally insists that the Torah witnesses to Jesus.[35] It speaks, as Watson argues it does, in a twofold fashion: of judgment and death but also of life and rectification – it "pre-preaches" the gospel (Gal. 3:8). Furthermore, as Jenson notes, the gospel proclaims a God who, by making promises, commits himself to a people whose identity perdures in time.[36] There are ways to understand linear continuity that fail to appreciate the radical caesura of the Christ-event, but, equally, there are ways to speak about what has happened with Jesus that in effect cut off or diminish the Old Testament from functioning as Christian Scripture.

---

[33] Francis Watson, *Paul and the Hermeneutics of Faith*, 2nd ed. (London: T&T Clark, 2015), xxv.

[34] N. T. Wright, *Paul and His Recent Interpreters* (Minneapolis: Fortress, 2015), 167–186.

[35] Martyn, *Galatians*, 358.

[36] David and Harink, *Apocalyptic and the Future of Theology*, 161.

Richard Hays, who has been much more sympathetic to Martyn's concerns about "salvation history" than Wright has, has contended that "Paul's understanding of the new age in Christ leads him not to a rejection of Israel's sacred history but to a retrospective hermeneutical transformation of Israel's story in the light of the story of God's startling redemptive actions .... [T]his requires a dramatic rereading of Israel's story, but what is required is precisely a rereading, not a repudiation."[37] How far apocalyptic theology in the vein of Martyn can avoid such repudiation and augment such rereading will be one of the tests of its viability going forward.

CONCLUSION

As in the early twentieth century European context, much contemporary Christian theology finds itself contending with social and cultural powers that seem to exceed the capacities of individual persons and institutions to grapple with them. By heralding a God whose action in Jesus demonstrates the limits of even these powers and guarantees their destruction, apocalyptic theology in the key of J. Louis Martyn – and, if Martyn is right, of Paul himself – is a vital resource for the ongoing mission of the gospel.

> Apocalyptic theology disturbs settled opinion, resists fixities of all sorts, demands existential response. It is an enemy of accommodation, a friend to radical critique. It attacks dogma, often seen as an illegitimate attempt to tame a God who is too lively to be confined in categories, a God who bursts free from every conceptualization. God breaks in to shatter every pathetic little intellectual and cultural structure we feebly erect.[38]

Insofar as apocalyptic theology insists on the radical transcendence, freedom, and creativity of the God of the gospel, it will continue to have a role to play in the life of Christian doctrine.

---

[37] Richard Hays, "Apocalyptic Poesis in Galatians: Paternity, Passion, and Participation," in *Galatians and Christian Theology: Justification, the Gospel and Ethics in Paul's Letters* (ed. Mark W. Elliott, et al.; Grand Rapids: Baker Academic, 2004), 204.

[38] Peter Leithart, *Revelation 1–11* (T&T Clark International Theological Commentary; London: T&T Clark, 2018), 59.

Further Reading

Collins, John J. (1998), *The Apocalyptic Imagination: An Introduction to Jewish Apocalyptic Literature* (Grand Rapids: Eerdmans).

Käsemann, Ernst (1969), *New Testament Questions of Today* (trans. W. J. Montague; London: SCM Press).

Kerr, Nathan R. (1998), *Christ, History and Apocalyptic: The Politics of Christian Mission* (Eugene, OR: Cascade).

Louis Martyn, J. (1997), *Galatians: A New Translation with Introduction and Commentary* (Anchor Bible 33A; New York: Doubleday).

Rutledge, Fleming (2009), "A Modest Proposal: Apocalyptic Theology," *Ruminations*, https://generousorthodoxy.org/rumination/a-modest-proposal-apocalyptic-theology.

(2013), "How Apocalyptic Theology Changed Me," *Ruminations*, https://generousorthodoxy.org/rumination/how-apocalyptic-theology-changed-me.

Ziegler, Philip G. (2018), *Militant Grace: The Apocalyptic Turn and the Future of Christian Theology* (Grand Rapids: Baker Academic).

20 Reformed Catholicity

J. TODD BILLINGS

In its most basic sense, "Reformed catholicity" involves approaching Reformed theology, in its historic and contemporary forms, as one who belongs to the larger Christian tradition, the "holy, catholic church" confessed by the Apostles' Creed. While this approach operates from within the Reformed theological tradition, it does so with an attentive ear to the catholic Christian voices from all eras; for those who embrace Reformed catholicity do not approach the Reformed tradition as an end in itself but rather as a way to fruitfully inhabit the larger catholic tradition. In its recent instantiation as a contemporary "sensibility," "Reformed catholicity" generally means combining a theocentric focus upon theology as knowledge of the Triune God and creation in relation to God. It also involves a commitment to recovering the core catholic trinitarian and christological convictions that provide a framework for a theological journey of faith seeking understanding. Within this context, the task of biblical exegesis is embraced as fundamental to the renewal of a modern theological imagination. These catholic and Reformed convictions can help frame a way for the reception of the Word by the Spirit that moves God's people away from self-serving and truncated ends and toward the fullness of maturity in Christ in life, worship, and witness.

WHAT IS CATHOLIC ABOUT REFORMED CATHOLICITY?

For this contemporary theological task, in what sense is the word "catholic" or "catholicity" used? While this term refers to doing theology in an intentional way from within the catholic tradition, further specification can help clarify what is at stake. The word "catholicity" combines two Greek words, *kath* and *holou*, which in their basic sense mean "on the whole," or "broad," as opposed to narrow or limited. Beginning in the second century, its use emerged in the midst of challenges posed by gnostic and docetic sects. In response to these sects, the notion of the "whole" or "catholic" church became connected with early anti-gnostic baptismal creeds and a basic trinitarian "rule of faith" for rightly reading scripture. On the term "catholic," scholars have noted two interrelated senses of use in these early centuries of the Christian faith: ecclesial catholicity and qualitative catholicity.[1]

On an ecclesial level, the term "catholic" referred to the oneness of the church, as opposed to schismatic and heretical groups. The "catholic" church was seen as united as the body of Christ, though dispersed in congregations. Catholicity was characterized by a set of ecclesial offices exercising sacramental authorization and clarification of what faith and practice belongs to the "whole" of Christ's worldwide church.

Second, the use of "catholic" pointed beyond the idea of a universal church to the specific character of catholic teaching: unity and oneness that led to growth in fullness. Thus, catholicity was a quality of the church – not simply determined by having properly ordained offices and a proper baptismal formula and creed but also by growing in wholeness and fullness in Christ. As developed by Cyril of Jerusalem in his *Catechetical Lectures* and reflected in various ways in other patristic writings, "catholic" was utilized as a term for fullness and richness, such that all of God's people in the church are growing up in virtue through all of its doctrines.[2]

Historically, Reformed theologians have often turned to the book of Ephesians as a biblical source for the extra-biblical term, "catholic," as the book addresses both senses of the term described above, framed within a theocentric context. In the context of the church as those chosen, adopted, and lavished with grace in Christ, Paul describes how God has, in fact, created "one new humanity" in Christ (2:15) such that "through the gospel the Gentiles are heirs together with Israel, members together of one body" (3:6). God's action in making "one" people in Christ corresponds with "one hope when you were called; one Lord, one faith, one baptism; one God and Father of all, who is over all and through all and in all" (Eph. 4:4–6, NIV). In light of the indicative of God's accomplished work in Christ, Paul adds the imperative: "live a life worthy of the calling you have received. Be completely humble and

---

[1] While drawing upon Cornelis van der Kooi and Gijsbert van den Brink in utilizing this distinction, Willem Van Vlastuin gives the most extensive articulation to date of how this distinction can illuminate various early Christian uses of the term "catholic." See Willem Van Vlastuin, *Catholic Today: A Reformed Conversation about Catholicity*, (Göttingen: Vandenhoeck & Ruprecht, 2020), 15–77.

[2] Van Vlastuin, *Catholic Today*, 36–44, 66–68.

gentle; be patient, bearing with one another in love. Make every effort to keep the unity of the Spirit through the bond of peace." This exhortation to seek "the unity of the Spirit" in a way that displays Christlike virtues (humility, patience, love) is grounded in the Triune God's own work. God makes those divided by a "dividing wall of hostility" into "one body" for "through him [Christ] we both have access to the Father by one Spirit" (2:14, 16, 18). Thus, this ecclesial calling to catholicity seeks to live into God-given oneness in Christ, by the Spirit.

Yet, in Ephesians, this pursuit of ecclesial unity is intertwined with what we have labeled as "qualitative" images of catholicity as well. After speaking about the offices of the church in Eph. 4:11, Paul describes their purpose in terms of edification and equipping for service until "we all reach unity in the faith and in the knowledge of the Son of God and become mature, attaining to the whole measure of the fullness of Christ" (Eph. 4:13), This pursuit of fullness, *pleroma*, involves a process of "grow[ing] to become in every respect the mature body of him who is the head, that is, Christ" (Eph. 4:15). Paul's language alludes back to the "fullness" possessed by the Ascended Christ alone (1:23) and to the process of growth into the "one new humanity" in chapter 2, for "you too are being built together to become a dwelling in which God lives by his Spirit" (2:22).

Thus, the sense of growing into fullness and maturity in Christ, by the Spirit, is a dynamic quality of the one body of Christ, the church. Indeed, Michael Allen helpfully suggests "fullness" may be a permanent quality of the people of God:

> In his *Life of Moses*, Gregory of Nyssa defines perfection as endless progress. He does so because perfection is defined by conformity to and participation in an endlessly full God. Given that God is without bounds, surely the calling to be holy as he is holy is itself unbounded and thus unending. Reading this portion of the epistle jolts attention to such questions …. Maturity involves growth; wholeness contains the notion of being built up within it.[3]

If this is the case, then catholicity as a process is also a type of *telos* for Christian teaching: from the first to the twenty-first century, no congregation, not even the global church, has attained catholicity in this sense. Rather, it is a quality of the Christian life that extends to Christian teaching, the process of growth into fullness, into maturity in Christ.

---

[3] Michael Allen, *Ephesians* (Brazos Theological Commentary on the Bible; Grand Rapids: Brazos, 2020), 102.

No culture or theologian has "captured" or "mastered" this sense of catholicity. It is possessed by Christ alone, and the church, as the Creature of the Word, belonging to Christ by the Spirit, is on the path of growth into this fullness.

These two dimensions of what we might call "catholicity," involving oneness and growth in fullness in Christ, are inseparable for Paul. Yet the two aspects are distinguishable, particularly as points of emphasis. Some Reformed scholars have focused their efforts upon removing barriers to ecclesial unity in our sharply divided world, addressing the complex issues separating various Protestant, Roman Catholic, and Orthodox communions. In recent decades, George Hunsinger, in *Eucharist and Ecumenism*, and other Reformed theologians involved in formal ecumenical dialogues about baptism, the Lord's Supper, and the church, have sought to contribute to the effort to pursue ecclesial oneness. This is important work that, one hopes, may contribute to a growth in fullness in Christ, even as overcoming visible division is the primary focus. Many of these theologians would identify their goal as occupying Reformed theology in a catholic way.

As a broader theological sensibility for Reformed catholicity, however, most of the recent constructive contributions accent the qualitative sense of catholicity: doing theology with the one, historic people of God in a way that focuses upon growth in fullness and maturity in Christ by the Spirit. This need not be seen as an attempt to minimize the ongoing wound of visible ecclesial division, in which the Reformed tradition has certainly been complicit. Rather, as a Reformed sensibility coming from a variety of ecclesial standpoints (from Baptist to Presbyterian to Anglican to nondenominational), there are a variety of ways to pursue ecclesial unity, and a deepening Protestant catholicity (in a qualitative sense) may open fresh opportunities for "grassroots ecumenism."[4] In any case, while not disconnected from the specific questions of ecclesiology, the primary emphasis of recent Reformed catholicity conversations has been qualitative in *telos*, while recovering the core trinitarian and christological convictions of early catholic Christianity, from within a Reformed framework.

---

[4] See J. Todd Billings, *Remembrance, Communion, and Hope: Rediscovering the Gospel at the Lord's Table* (Grand Rapids: Eerdmans, 2018) 63–68.

THE THEOLOGICAL PROGRAM OF
REFORMED CATHOLICITY

Theologians displaying a Reformed and catholic sensibility are far from uniform; but in recent decades, the works of numerous scholars have come to share overlapping priorities that fit into a broadly shared theological program. Any collective summary will be schematic, but in general terms, the contemporary Reformed and catholic theological sensibility is characterized by four features:

(1) A theocentric focus, such that, by faith, theology seeks understanding of and communion with the Triune God and all things in relation to God. The Triune God is the object of theology, both *in se* (in himself) and in his external works in creation. As a part of this theocentric focus, many in the Reformed-catholicity discussion are particularly attentive in framing how the doctrines of God, Trinity, and Divine Perfections hold together.

(2) Embrace of a dynamic theology of the Triune God's action through the written Word by the Spirit, not simply in prolegomena but in the ongoing task of biblical exegesis, which is undertaken alongside pre-modern as well as modern commentators.

(3) Approach of pre-modern catholic and Reformed theologians as sites for deep listening and retrieval, seeking to reframe particular problems, polarities, and impoverishment found in late modern theological discourse.

(4) Exploration of the vast and multifaceted ways in which knowledge of the Triune God and his relation to creation has profound significance for all areas of Christian doctrine and life.

With this framework, the purpose of this theological work is both bold and modest. Reformed and catholic theologians boldly seek understanding of the incomprehensible God. Yet they do so as pilgrims on a journey of "faith seeking understanding" who enter into a space of mystery, knowledge, and doxology bound up together. While these priorities characterize numerous recent scholarly works, particularly influential examples include works by John Webster, Katherine Sonderegger, and Kevin Vanhoozer. In his groundbreaking work, *Holy Scripture*, Webster sets a theology of scripture within the context of the Triune God's action and work. In *God without Measure*, he refines a theocentric focus that entails retrievals from the church fathers, Calvin, Aquinas, Ursinus, Owen, and Barth in his account of the object and purpose of theology. Sonderegger, while always respectful to Barth, moves quite boldly against the metaphysics of his doctrine of God and the Trinity, claiming that theology needs to recover an exploration of "what God is" not just "who God is." Drawing deeply upon patristic writings, as well as Aquinas and Bonaventure, her two-volume *Systematic Theology* retrieves these voices in steady dialogue with Calvin, Schleiermacher, and Barth, as she engages in extended biblical-exegetical reflection to champion a recovery of a theology of divine aseity and glory in a theocentric, doxological fashion. In *The Drama of Doctrine* and *Remythologizing Theology*, Kevin Vanhoozer brings together a dynamic theology of the Triune God's action through scripture as setting forth a drama wherein disciples are participants in Christ by the Spirit. Employing and exploring the doctrines of God, Christ, and the Trinity, he engages in catholic retrieval from Augustine and Aquinas in a Reformed key, reframing the categories of classical theism in theodramatic terms, thereby giving a nuanced restatement of divine impassibility.

A PROTESTANT ENTRYWAY TO CATHOLICITY?

Why would the Reformed tradition, in particular, be an attractive Protestant entryway for theologians interested in embracing catholicity? To some extent, it may be the way in which the Reformed tradition can provide a coherent frame for ongoing catholic retrieval. As Michael Allen and Scott Swain point out, "many Protestant programs of retrieval to date cannot seem to get beyond practicing a kind of 'theological bricolage.'"[5] For example, while Robert Webber's "Ancient-Future" Christianity and similar movements have generated interest in early Christian retrieval, they can easily conform to the late-modern tendency to treat "catholicity" as a smorgasbord for dabbling, to meet our own needs, rather than fitting within a more coherent theological and ecclesial approach. In light of that deficit, not only Reformed catholicity but the development of other distinctive Protestant appropriations of catholicity (e.g., Lutheran, Wesleyan) would be a gift to the church and academy as well.

For many in the Reformed tradition, the initial objection to embracing a catholic theological program is that it appears to undermine a doctrine of *sola scriptura*. Indeed, it does contradict modern reductions of *sola scriptura* to hermeneutical individualism or framing earlier Christian traditions as idolatrous distractions when reading scripture.

[5] Michael Allen and Scott Swain, *Reformed Catholicity: The Promise of Retrieval for Theology and Biblical Interpretation* (Grand Rapids: Baker Academic, 2015), 12.

But neither of these are accurate framings of a Reformation or post-Reformation doctrine of scripture.

Instead, as Allen and Swain explain, a distinction between magisterial and ministerial authority can show how the sufficiency and finality of scripture goes hand in hand with a catholic and Reformed place for tradition. On the one hand, "Jesus Christ is the only magisterial authority in the church; the term magister, or lord, speaks to his final sovereignty in the church."[6] Yet, ministers (servants) of the Word carry an authority as well in their God-given role to steward God's Word for edification in Christ. Thus, although this may seem counterintuitive from our late-modern standpoint, "to be more biblical, one must also be engaged in the process of traditioning," receiving and stewarding the Word by the Spirit and simultaneously listening attentively to the "communion of the saints" in this act of service.[7]

Certainly, ministerial authority in service to the Word is not final or absolute, for Allen and Swain. But insofar as it bears witness to the Lord of the church through scripture, it should be embraced as a gift from the Spirit. Christians need guidance in interpreting Holy Scripture. For example, while early creeds and patristic and medieval writings are not framed by the Reformed as authoritative in themselves, they exercise a form of secondary authority behind scripture precisely because of their usefulness in service to the Word, helping us embrace biblical teaching in a more fulsome and faithful manner.

In order to see various ways in which this role of tradition in "service to the Word" has been enacted in practice, as well as to understand why many Protestant theologians look today to the Reformed tradition for models and resources in retrieving catholicity, a brief historical account is instructive. The quest to hear scripture with the church of all ages, with special attention to the interpretive wisdom of ancient Christian voices, was part of a Reformed program from the opening generations of the Reformation.

THE "CATHOLICITY" OF REFORMED THEOLOGY IN THE SIXTEENTH AND SEVENTEENTH CENTURIES

Within a decade of Luther's excommunication in 1521, Melanchthon and Zwingli both fully embraced Nicene trinitarian confessions and the Chalcedonian christological formulation in the Augsburg Confession

---

[6] Ibid., 90.
[7] Ibid., 84–85.

(Lutheran) and *Fidei Ratio* (Reformed) of 1530. These public confessions articulated patristic orthodoxy on the Triune God and Christ as biblical truths to be embraced, a point that set Lutherans and Reformed apart from certain groups of more radical evangelicals at the time.

Early Reformers claimed a lineage within the ancient, historic church. "We retain the Christian, sound, and catholic faith, whole and inviolable," Bullinger wrote in the Second Helvetic Confession. Since there is "one mediator" between God and human beings, "one shepherd of the whole flock, one head of this body," there is "one church: which we, therefore, call catholic because it is universal," spread "abroad" through the world, and it "reaches unto all times." In contrast, "Roman clergy," presumptuously "vaunt that the Church of Rome alone is in a manner catholic," thus seeking to limit and contain the catholicity of the "whole flock" under Christ the shepherd.[8]

Thus, while committed to the supremacy of the scriptures, in 1536 the Swiss Reformed would declare that the "ancient fathers" of the church could provide needed insight and guidance, such that "not only do we receive them as interpreters of the Scripture, but we honor them as chosen instruments of God."[9] In the same year, John Calvin presented a kind of wager to King Francis that "if the contest were to be decided by patristic authority, the tide of victory would turn to our side."[10]

Of course, these sixteenth and seventeenth century claims to "catholicity" had a strongly polemical edge. Amidst the fierce social, political, and ecclesial tumult of the early modern era, a theological argument against Rome's exclusive claim to "catholicity" was a valuable arrow in the quiver. The polemics would continue at the turn of the seventeenth century as English Puritan William Perkins famously published *A Reformed Catholicke* (1598) arguing that the Reformed faith was authentically catholic, shorn from the errors of Rome. Basel professor Amandus Polanus in *Symphonia catholica* (1607) argued for a "catholic symphony, or catholic and orthodox consensus," drawing upon his extensive work with patristic writings to display continuity between early Christian and Reformed teaching. But this Reformed tradition, from Zwingli and Calvin to Perkins, Polanus, and many others, not only

---

[8] "Second Helvetic Confession," in *Reformed Confessions*, Volume 2 (ed. James T. Dennison; Grand Rapids: Reformation Heritage Books, 2010), 831, 845.

[9] "First Helvetic Confession," in *Reformed Confessions*, Volume 1 (ed. James T. Dennison; Grand Rapids: Reformation Heritage Books, 2008), 344.

[10] John Calvin, *Institutes, 1536 edition* (trans. Ford Lewis Battles; Grand Rapids: Eerdmans, 1986, 5–6.

shared polemical barbs but received many exegetical and doctrinal gifts
from the ancient Christian teachers as well.

In this way, while clear about the sufficiency and finality of scripture, this stream of Reformed theologians left no doubt that they
intended to read scripture with the pre-Reformation church, as
members of the same elect people of God in Christ, sharers in the same
Spirit. Calvin, in the decades following his bold declarations to King
Francis, grew extensively in his knowledge and expertise in the patristic
writing, a quest that led to engaging voices from far beyond the bounds
of western Europe. He drew deeply upon north African theologian
Augustine of Hippo, with around 1,700 direct references, plus an esti-
mated 2,400 additional quotations or paraphrases drawn from
Augustine without direct references.[11] Calvin loved the sermons of
John Chrysostom, who served in Antioch and Constantinople (in
modern day Turkey), and he attempted to have these sermons translated
into vernacular French, a groundbreaking idea for his day. Not content
to leave behind later medieval voices, Calvin drew deeply upon the
medieval abbot Bernard of Clairvaux, developing his theology of union
with Christ in substantial engagement with the French abbot.

In these endeavors, Calvin reflected a voracious appetite for patristic and medieval learning that was characteristic of other Reformed
peers. Like him, numerous reformers were trained in the methods of
Renaissance Humanism, seeking to "return to the sources" (ad fontes),
utilizing humanist methods of textual and linguistic study. They did so
for the biblical texts, in Hebrew and Greek, but also for the Latin and
Greek church fathers and later theologians of the medieval church. At
times, this was limited because patristic texts were difficult to access
and contained errors in attribution. But the Reformed tradition
embraced this as an opportunity. Indeed, as Irena Backus has shown,
the Reformed tradition was at the forefront of Protestant efforts to
publish, translate, and comment upon numerous patristic editions, as
well as disambiguate wrongly attributed patristic works into the seventeenth century.[12] Utilizing humanistic skills in giving close readings of
texts and a desire to embrace and display the catholicity of their faith,
the Reformed tradition set forth a theological program that involved
continuous learning from earlier Christian voices.

[11] Luchesius Smits, *Saint Augustin dans l'oeuvre de Jean Calvin* (Assen: Van Gorcum,
      1958), 6.
[12] See Irena Backus, *Historical Method and Confessional Identity in the Era of the
      Reformation (1378–1615)* (Leiden: Brill, 2003), 1–5, 196–252.

As the Reformed faith spread to various locations in the late sixteenth and seventeenth century, theologians continued to articulate and develop Reformed theology within the context of regional confessions of faith, continuing the priorities of biblical exegesis and reception from patristic and medieval voices. As Reformed faculty came to occupy universities with more extensive medieval collections, and Reformed theologians in various contexts responded to new challenges and developments, Reformed theology expanded its appropriation of medieval sources in both academic and practical theology. While sometimes this is framed as a process of "rationalization" that distanced theology from its biblical-exegetical sources, recent scholarship has shown how it is more accurately framed as a deepening catholic reception that became manifested in various genres and theological contexts. For example, *Theoretical-Practical Theology* of Petrus van Mastricht (1630–1706), newly translated into English, clearly displays the four major genres of Reformed orthodox discourse side by side on each locus of theology: exegetical theology (biblical exegesis), dogmatic theology, elenctic theology (theology addressing controversies and objections), and practical theology. Questions of biblical exegesis, reception, piety, and concrete practice were all addressed by "Reformed scholastics," but the focus upon works of just one genre, such as *The Institutes of Elenctic Theology* by Francis Turretin (1623–1687) has often given recent theologians a quite misleading account of Reformed Orthodoxy.

Moreover, Reformed movements that are often labeled "Pietistic" displayed the Reformed-catholic program in a variety of powerful ways. For example, seventeenth-century Puritans occupied a strongly Augustinian version of the Reformed tradition that drew deeply upon scripture and medieval doctrinal and mystical theology to bring together scriptural exegesis, doctrine, and devotional piety. Whether Congregationalist, Presbyterian, or Episcopal in polity, Puritans sought to hold together Word and Spirit, in head and heart, generating a vast body of devotional and doctrinal works. Of particular interest to recent scholars of Reformed catholicity has been the voluminous work of John Owen (1616–1683). Owen combined a sophisticated Protestant appropriation of Aquinas with a rich pneumatology and trinitarian theology, giving a theology that is deeply traditional in its catholic theology, embraced in a distinctly Reformed way. Owen does this with a doxological and devotional tone that retains close connections between cultivating growth in piety and maturity in Christ with the broader work of theology. Reformed pietistic theologians in other contexts likewise display a deep desire to hold together scripture and the

Reformed tradition with ongoing catholic retrieval. For example, in the same era, the Dutch *Nadere Reformatie*, or "Further Reformation," displayed a deep and nuanced reception of Bernard of Clairvaux and Thomas à Kempis in figures such as Willem Teellinck (1579–1629), Theodorus à Brakel (1608–1669), and Guiljelmus Saldenus (1627–1694).

In sum, early Reformed claims to confess an "ancient" and "catholic" theology not only fulfilled a polemical function for the time but helped generate a vision with far-reaching methodological and material implications for doing theology. While far from uniform, a wide range of sixteenth- and seventeenth-century Reformed theologians modeled different forms of a shared Reformed catholic framework: that early creeds on God and Christ should be confessed in light of ongoing scriptural exegesis, and patristic and medieval voices should be attentively received and retrieved in the course of hearing the Word of God in its scriptural fullness.

RETRIEVAL AND THE MODERN THEOLOGICAL IMAGINATION

The retrieval of pre-modern biblical exegesis and theology has particular urgency today because of the ways in which the late modern theological imagination has been impoverished. In the analysis of Charles Taylor, a default backdrop of the late modern imagination is an "immanent frame," assuming "our lives as taking place within a self-sufficient immanent order."[13] While we may seek to confess that God is central to the order we inhabit, late modern Christians frequently become preoccupied with spheres we perceive as under our own control. To enliven theological reflection, the late modern project assumes that theology's object should be where the real drama is: in human beings, in their faith, their action, their differences and commonalities. If addressing a topic such as the Triune God, theology should frame the Trinity as a model social program that could be useful for our own [immanent] human purposes.

Modern and late modern theologians have often exemplified this trend through the displacement of the material content of the Baptismal Creed (such as the Apostles' or Nicene Creeds) to have a marginal role in theological reflection. Some have sought to "demythologize" the Baptismal Creed into a still usable ethical or mystical substratum.

---

[13] Charles Taylor, *A Secular Age* (Cambridge, MA: Belknap Press, 2009), 543.

Others put the Creed on the shelf while focusing upon a defense of the "authority" of scripture through various apologetic strategies. Either way, the primary object of theology becomes something other than the mystery of the Triune God in the theandric person, Jesus Christ.

This deep and pervasive pressure to pursue theology within an "immanent frame" is compounded by cultures of consumerism and scientism; "the customer is always right" and "new is always better" shape the church and its theological reflection to prioritize present human preference over what is divinely given. Rather than inhabiting the spacious territory of the church's broad exploration of the trinitarian, baptismal faith seeking understanding, our pressing cultural questions become the north star, the point of orientation to "correlate" with responses from the Bible and theology. Theology in the church as well as the academy displays both "conservative" and "progressive" forms of this correlational approach, which, in light of the "immanent frame," fits the demands of the "market" for theological ideas.

In this context, Reformed catholic theologians seek to renew the contemporary theological imagination through a quite intentional immersive encounter: deep, attentive listening to pre-modern voices who do not share our modern and late modern imagination. This is a difficult, counterintuitive task. But in a way that echoes the Roman Catholic movements of "ressourcement" in the twentieth century, as well as the Renaissance and Reformational cry of *ad fontes*, Reformed-catholic theologians seek to return to the fundamental sources of theology afresh. Scripture, early Christian theology, and other pre-modern theology may illuminate possibilities that the immanent frame of modernity conceals.

Moreover, a theology of retrieval hinges upon a commitment to the particularity of theological discourse that resists typical forms of modern reductionism. In the words of John Webster, modern theology tends to ground theology in appeals to "common human experience" or "a general theory (hermeneutical, symbolic, anthropological) which can ground theological construction." Yet "theologies of retrieval, by contrast, do not consider Christianity as a version of anything: it is irreducible." This conviction that theology is "irreducible" is shared with postliberal theologians such as George Lindbeck. Yet holding this idea together with "retrieval" signals a quite distinct theological, ecclesial, and methodological assumption: "the presupposition that resolutions to the questions which they address may well be found already somewhere in the inheritance of the Christian past." Webster is quick to differentiate this definition of retrieval from "formulaic repetition, still less in endorsing everything the tradition has ever said."[14] Instead, it is a deep and attentive listening, an "immersion in the texts and habits of thought of earlier (especially premodern) theology" that enables "a certain liberty" in making theological judgments that is "unharassed by current anxieties." Webster is not assuming that an earlier era offered a "golden age" to which the theological thinker should retreat. Rather, his imagery is one of an anthropologist, willing to allow late modern ethnocentric assumptions to be challenged: immersion into an alien world and culture of earlier texts, opening our own questions to being reframed, our own agenda being altered. This immersion in pre-modern sources enables both a "liberty" from being harassed by present concerns and a means of discovering the riches of Christian doctrine in greater depth and breadth. Thus, when combined with a strong theology of Holy Scripture, retrieval can offer gifts through the Spirit in our hearing of the divine address through scripture.

POSSIBLE MODERN MODELS FOR REFORMED CATHOLICITY

There are numerous possible models of a Reformed catholic vision that seeks growth into fullness in Christ in the modern and late modern age. Far from a comprehensive list, here are five examples that have garnered recent scholarly attention.

The Black Ecclesial Tradition in North America

Historians have done important initial work on theologians in the Black ecclesial tradition who embraced revivalistic Christianity over against modern movements of unitarianism, deism, and individual liberty, often in quite theocentric and Reformed forms. An early example is Lemuel Haynes (1753–1833), a gifted Congregationalist pastor-theologian in Rutland, Vermont, and the first Black person to be ordained in the United States. In over 5,500 sermons, along with published theological works, he countered deist and unitarian theologies in New England with a theocentric Reformed vision. He also presented a wide-ranging and powerful theological account of providence and sanctification that simultaneously undercut pro-slavery arguments and set forth a calling toward benevolence and affection across racial lines.

---

[14] John Webster, "Theologies of Retrieval," in *The Oxford Handbook of Systematic Theology* (ed. John Webster, Kathryn Tanner, and Iain R. Torrance; Oxford: Oxford University Press, 2007), 593.

As Esau McCaulley points out, this strand within the Black church in America, extending from "Black Puritan" pastor-theologians in the late eighteenth century to a variety of denominational and independent forms into the twentieth century, brings together a "call for individual and societal transformation within the context of the historic confessions of Christianity."[15] These African American leaders, whether "puritan" or more broadly "revivalist" or "evangelical," called sinners to salvation through the lavish love of Christ as they further developed a Reformed anti-slavery tradition in light of changing circumstances. In the Reformation era, John Calvin (erroneously) assumed that slavery no longer existed in his day. He declared that a return to this "horrible" institution would be unthinkably wicked. For black ecclesial theologians the stakes were significantly higher. Not only was slavery reinstituted, chattel slavery was racialized and defended with scripture by Christians (both Reformed and non-Reformed). Thus, drawing upon and yet transforming the Puritan and later revivalistic theologies of their day, black ecclesial theologians confronted prevailing forms of social sin as they preached a word of forgiveness and new life for sinners, calling forth a holistic response from their hearers.

This black ecclesial tradition deserves retrieval both to recover its neglected theological and pastoral insights, as well as its disclosure of the deformation resulting from modern Christianity's partnership with colonial, racial, and pro-slavery forces. This North American tradition has implications for a variety of global contexts today, giving a variety of theocentric responses to oppression: from debates about slavery before the civil war, through the devastation of reconstruction, to the wave of thousands of Black men lynched at the turn of the twentieth century. Indeed, ongoing retrieval from similar contexts around the world will continue to be significant, disclosing how modernity could deform the Reformed faith as an instrument of colonial purposes and yet how the Reformed faith could also provide sites of resistance, challenging idolatries used to obscure God's work in creating "one new humanity" in Christ (Eph. 2:15). Heard on their own terms, these voices of resistance often offer surprises. For example, as Malcomb Foley has noted, although recent theological reflection on the history of lynching tends to emphasize Christ's solidarity with the oppressed, key Black pastor-theologians at the time, such as Presbyterian Francis Grimké (1850–1937) proclaimed "the immediacy and inevitability of divine judgment" and that the good

---

[15] Esau McCaulley, *Reading While Black* (Downer Grove, IL: IVP, 2020), 171.

news "was not merely that Christ suffered with them, but also that He would ultimately end their suffering."[16]

Nevin's Retrieval of a Reformed Catholic Sacramental Vision

For scholars interested in the renewal of theology and worship in a way that gives an alternative to the memorialist and anti-sacramental tendencies of revivalistic Christianity, the theology of John Williamson Nevin (1803–1886) has emerged as a model for navigating modernity in a Reformed catholic way. Nevin and his colleague Philip Schaff are seen as providing a "model" for a Reformed catholicity in a context where it had become nearly unintelligible to some. Nevin chronicles a decline from earlier Puritans (i.e., John Owen) to what he calls "modern puritans," namely Puritans after the First Great Awakening whose evangelical heirs continued to his day. In contrast to some "modern" puritans who claimed the Apostles' Creed was outdated, Nevin champions the Creed with its core trinitarian and christological convictions, providing a frame and guidance for truly "evangelical" belief and theology. On the Lord's Supper, Nevin argues that unlike the early church and the Reformed confessions, modern Puritans reduce Christ's words of Institution into a "mere figure," denying communion with Christ apart from a rationalistic act of remembrance. Instead of embodied, external means of grace, which provide communion with the incarnate Christ by the Spirit, the modern Puritans sought an internal experience of "conversion" as a mark of grace. This not only obfuscates a God-given gift, distorting it in a rationalistic direction – it also obscures the centrality of the doctrines of the incarnation and union with Christ through the Triune God.

Nevin's book on the Lord's Supper, *The Mystical Presence*, received a lengthy, scathing review from Charles Hodge of Princeton Theological Seminary, Nevin's former professor. The ensuing Nevin-Hodge debate has fascinated historians and theologians ever since. On the one hand, Nevin showed himself to be an extremely capable "theologian of retrieval," having immersed himself in Calvin's work, in particular. Nevin sharply differentiates his view from Hodge's heavily Zwinglian account. On the other hand, Nevin also embraced categories and insights from the German idealism of his day, using them to conceptualize the connections between incarnation, union with Christ, and church; this gave him categories to oppose Hodge's appropriation of

---

[16] Malcolm Foley, "Ought We Kiss the Hand That Smites Us? Black Protestants in the Age of Lynching, 1890–1919," PhD thesis, Baylor University, October 5, 2021, 13.

"common sense realism" and the more biblicist cast to his theology. Nevin's theology continues to be instructive both on the grounds of his positive, theological claims in engagement with the broader catholic and Reformed tradition and for his diagnostic account of how the Enlightenment and revivalism can de-catholicize the Reformed faith through embracing "biblicism" and "conversionism." This analysis continues to be widely relevant today.

Bavinck's Expansive, Trinitarian Reformed-Catholicity

Another possible model for a theologian of retrieval gives a more comprehensive doctrinal approach to how catholic retrieval and Reformed theology can fit together in the modern era: Herman Bavinck (1854–1921). After a critical edition and translation of *Reformed Dogmatics* edited by John Bolt was released in English in four volumes (2003–2008), scholarship on Bavinck outside of the Dutch language moved from a trickle to a torrent, becoming the focus of numerous dissertations, conferences, an Institute, a scholarly society and a peer-reviewed journal.[17] In addition to lively discussions in English and Dutch, Bavinck's works have generated recent scholarship in Mandarin , Korean, and Portuguese.

Bavinck's theological formation took place in two different worlds: after being shaped by a strongly confessional Reformed church in his youth and young adult years, he pursued doctoral work at Leiden, a bastion of historical-critical biblical scholarship and liberal Protestant doctrine at the time. In *Reformed Dogmatics*, Bavinck brings together these worlds in a highly innovative way. For Bavinck, dogmatics is theocentric, with a singular focus upon "ponder[ing] and describ[ing] God and God alone, whose glory is in creation and re-creation, in nature and grace, in the world and in the church." This is set forth in a deeply catholic framing, as each volume of the dogmatics is part of an extended exposition of the Apostles' Creed. Throughout, Bavinck presents a trinitarian theology in which God's grace restores the goodness of God's creation, as grace redeems nature. "The creation of the Father, ruined by sin, is restored in the death of the Son of God and re-created by the grace of the Holy Spirit into a kingdom of God. Dogmatics shows us how God, who is all-sufficient in himself, nevertheless glorifies himself in his creation, which, even when it is torn apart by sin, is gathered up again in Christ."

---

[17]   https://bavinckinstitute.org/.

While Bavinck regards early Reformed theology and Reformed confessions with gravity, he engages in nuanced, eclectic, and at times groundbreaking Reformed retrieval from a variety of patristic and medieval theologians, especially Augustine and Thomas Aquinas. Yet as he does this, he does not leave behind distinctively modern gifts from his time at Leiden, such as historical-critical biblical scholarship and the work of modern thinkers such as Kant, Schleiermacher, and Hegel.

While Bavinck critically appropriates a wide variety of sources, central to the coherence of his vision is the way in which he ties together his trinitarian theology with the glories and diversity of creation. Often described as the "organic" aspect of Bavinck's theology, he is eager to draw insights from thinkers in deep tension with one another with a sense that "these tensions are not necessarily bad or undesirable," as James Eglinton has argued. Instead, "reality is non-uniform because it reflects its Creator" – part of God's glory in creation, reflected by the God who is unity-in-diversity in his Triune being.[18] While insisting that God's triune being is utterly unique, he presents a theology of the *vestigia trinitatis* (a vestige of the trinity in creation) in a nuanced appropriation of this notion in Augustine. While assessments of Bavinck are ongoing, many see his work as a compelling example of Reformed catholicity, holding a strong exegetical sensibility, a deep and expansive retrieval from catholic and Reformed thinkers with a theocentric, trinitarian approach to the whole of doctrine. In addition, his rich theology of creation and general revelation has promise for theologians today developing a theocentric theology of culture and for theologians in the global south seeking a more positive theological appraisal of pre-Christian religious heritages.

Barth, Torrance, and Reformed Catholic Possibilities

The immensely influential work of Karl Barth (1886–1968) has offered a model for modern Reformed catholicity for some. And even for scholars who look elsewhere for models, his work's impact on historical and contemporary theological discussions makes it significant for theologians today pursuing Reformed catholicity. In turning away from the Protestant liberalism of his teachers, Barth adopts a deeply trinitarian, theocentric, and yet highly original approach to theology. In *Anselm: Fides Quaerens Intellectum* (1931) Barth articulates a broad framework of the Creed as an exploration of faith seeking understanding, and the

---

[18] James Eglinton, *Trinity and Organism: Towards a New Reading of Herman Bavinck's Organic Motif* (London: Bloomsbury T&T Clark, 2014), 208.

next year he published the first volume of his massive *Church Dogmatics*. Through the course of that great work, his method gave a significant place to biblical exegesis, and he engaged in extended, detailed dialogue with Augustine, Luther, Calvin, and medieval and Protestant scholastics, as well as numerous philosophers and theologians in the modern era.

Both Barth's own corpus of writing and the secondary literature on his work are vast. For the purposes of the contemporary movement in constructive theology of Reformed-catholicity, two observations are in order. First, a valuable historical-contextual strain of Barth scholarship has made significant developments in the last two decades, which has provided valuable entry points for some theologians pursuing Reformed catholicity in a way that draws deeply upon Barth. Partly in response to a quite chaotic use of Barth in the late twentieth century, which justified a variety of theological programs with little in common with a contextual understanding of his work, this more recent historical-contextual strain offers dozens of dissertations, monographs, and articles that have sharpened the descriptive work on Barth's theology, exploring his significance in relation to the larger Christian tradition. Theologians such as George Hunsinger, Keith Johnson, Adam Neder, and John Webster have been able to combine close contextual readings of Barth with a concern for catholic breadth and ecumenical discussion. Second, others find an entryway to a Reformed-catholic appropriation of Barthian themes through Barth's student and exponent in the English-speaking world, Thomas F. Torrance (1913–2007). As co-supervisor of the English translation of *The Church Dogmatics* and a prolific scholar both on Barth and in his own constructive work, Torrance gives a distinctly "catholic" accent to his appropriation of Barthian themes and seeks to be more deeply "catholic" than Barth in patristic retrieval, theology of union with Christ, and the sacraments. Thus, the writings of both Barth and Torrance continue to be significant for many contemporary theologians pursuing Reformed catholicity.

Post-Barthian Historians of Reformation and Post-Reformation Theology

Ironically, precisely because of the widespread reception of Barth's energetic work engaging Luther, Calvin, and the Reformed scholastics, a significant stream of post-Barthian historical scholarship has developed to read such theologians and movements on their own terms. David Steinmetz provided a snapshot from his student days in the 1960s illustrating the presenting problem: scholarly interest in Calvin's

theology was booming, set in the context of "the possibility or impossibility of natural theology, the relation of reason and revelation, the
inspiration of scripture, the critique of theological liberalism, and
the recovery of Christology." Thus, Calvin's writings were read in the
context of Barth and his interlocutors, along with "a large company of
Barthian and erstwhile Barthian interpreters of Calvin, from Thomas
Torrance and Wilhelm Niesel to Ronald Wallace and Paul Van Buren,
theologians who often found it difficult to draw sharp lines of demar-
cation between Calvin's theology and the theology of Karl Barth."[19]

In his doctoral studies with Heiko Oberman at Harvard, however,
Steinmetz discovered a completely different context for interpreting
Calvin, one "in his own time and space."[20] Steinmetz found himself
researching Calvin's own instructors, his relationship with Bucer and
other Reformers, and his development over the course of multiple
editions of the *Institutes*. Steinmetz became convinced that, like an
anthropologist's immersion in an alien language and culture, an immersive, contextual approach to Reformation and post-reformation theologians can be instructive "in unexpected and boundary-breaking
ways."[21] In the decades to come, Oberman, Steinmetz, and many of
their doctoral students would remake the discipline of historical theology of the Reformation and post-Reformation eras, overall providing a
much more "catholic" portrait than what Barthian scholars gave. They
found that while Reformers like Calvin differed from later Reformed
scholastics in particular ways, these developments did not fit a "Calvin
against the Calvinists" decline narrative advocated by many Barthian
scholars. Early figures in the Reformation had far more "scholastic" and
"catholic" elements than Barthian scholars had recognized, and
Reformed scholastics continued to give biblical exegesis and its connection to piety a central place, even as discussions became more complex
and expanded into various subgenres. Dozens of scholars have contributed to this renaissance in scholarship that sought to give contextual
accounts or Reformation and post-Reformation theology on its own
terms, with Richard A. Muller's work being most decisive in overturn-
ing a Barthian historiography. In addition, this stream of contemporary
scholarship has revived interest not simply in doctrinal issues but the
variety of biblical-exegetical work done in noting how biblical

[19] David Steinmetz, *Taking the Long View: Christian Theology in Historical Perspective*
      (Oxford: Oxford University Press, 2011) 150.
[20] Steinmetz, *Taking the Long View*, 151.
[21] Ibid., 149.

commentary was essential for Reformation and post-Reformation theologians' self-understanding. Over forty scholars have joined together to edit and translate the Reformation Commentary on Scripture Series (RCSS), which includes a wide range of Reformation-era voices on each pericope in the Bible, including previously neglected voices such as Katharina Schutz Zell (1497/8–1562) and Anna Maria van Schurman (1607–1678).

As a result of this stream of historical scholarship in recent decades, the complex, eclectic, yet broadly catholic character of sixteenth- and seventeenth-century Reformed theology can be apprehended more clearly. Perhaps even more significantly, in moving beyond caricatures and discovering other significant authors and works of the era, these scholars have opened up a much wider canon for contemporary theologians to consider in catholic and Reformed retrieval.

VARIETIES OF SCHOLARSHIP, POSSIBILITIES FOR RETRIEVAL

A Reformed catholic sensibility among contemporary theologians pivots upon a remarkable convergence in various areas of scholarship: the results of recent historical scholarship on the sixteenth and seventeenth century reviewed above; ongoing work in patristics that clarifies how the doctrines of God, Trinity, and divine perfections fit together in ancient Christian discussions; lively discourse on reviving the theological dimensions of the task of biblical exegesis;[22] revived interest in key modern figures displaying Reformed and catholic possibilities; and significant works in doctrinal theology from leading theologians such as Katherine Sonderegger, Kevin Vanhoozer, and John Webster who have taken various approaches to a theocentric, Reformed catholic theology intended to cultivate growth into fullness and maturity in Christ.

Much recent scholarship has been in the form of dogmatics or systematic theology, whether in monographs in or series with a focus on catholic retrieval within a Protestant framework, such as New Studies in Dogmatics. Even when discussing the same doctrinal *loci*, the sensibility results in a variety of responses, with room for ongoing discussion, debate, and development. For example, Michael Horton's *Covenant and Salvation* makes a case for retrieving the post-Reformation categories of the covenants of redemption, works, and grace, all the while

---

[22] See Andrea Saner's chapter in this volume on "The Theological Interpretation of Scripture" (Chapter 12).

constructively engaging a wide range of biblical scholars and theologians, even giving a Reformed rendering of *theosis* in dialogue with Orthodoxy. Oliver Crisp embraces catholic christological and trinitarian assumptions as he explores the retrieval of "minority positions" within the Reformed tradition in *Deviant Calvinism*, such as the hypothetical universalism of John Davenant (1572–1641). Suzanne McDonald, in *Re-Imaging Election*, presents a substantial and appreciative retrieval of the (contrasting) voices of John Owen and Karl Barth on election, situating her account within the recent work of Jewish and Christian biblical scholars. The results vary, but each seeks a biblical, theocentric, trinitarian theology of retrieval that is both Reformed and catholic.

In other instances, a Reformed catholic sensibility has been generative to bring to other ongoing theological discussions or interdisciplinary discussions. In *Do This in Remembrance of Me*, Martha Moore-Keish retrieves from Nevin's Reformed catholicity to generate a fruitful conversation with ritual theory in liturgical studies. *A Visible Witness* by Jules A. Martinez-Olivieri unites a trinitarian and christological catholicity with the soteriological concern of the Reformation, creatively engaging them with Latin American theologies of salvation and liberation. Kyle Strobel and Tom Schwanda retrieve from the Puritans to develop an evangelical and Reformed approach to discussions of contemplative prayer. In *The Logic of the Body*, Matthew LaPine retrieves from Aquinas, Calvin, and recent Reformed thinkers in developing a theology of emotion within the landscape of recent models in psychology and neuroscience. These examples provide only a small sample from the larger, burgeoning body of work.

In various genres and across a range of doctrinal and ecclesiastical commitments, the programmatic vision of Reformed catholicity provides a shared frame for theological research intended to cultivate growth deeper into the fullness of Jesus Christ.

Further Reading

Allen, Michael, and Scott Swain (2015), *Reformed Catholicity: The Promise of Retrieval for Theology and Biblical Interpretation* (Grand Rapids: Baker Academic).
Bavinck, Herman (2008), *Reformed Dogmatics*, 4 Volumes, (ed. John Bolt; trans. John Vriend; Grand Rapids: Baker Academic).
Hunsinger, George, Keith L. Johnson, eds. (2020), *The Wiley Blackwell Companion to Karl Barth*, Volumes 1–2, (Hoboken, NJ: Wiley Blackwell).

Mercersburg Theology Study Series (including critical editions of John Williamson Nevin's works) (2013–), Lee C. Barrett and David W. Layman, eds. (Eugene, OR: Wipf and Stock).

Muller, Richard A. (2003), *Post-Reformation Reformed Dogmatics: The Rise and Development of Reformed Orthodoxy, Ca. 1520 to Ca. 1725*, Volumes 1–4 (2nd ed.; Grand Rapids: Baker Academic).

New Studies in Dogmatics (2015–), Michael Allen and Scott Swain, eds. (Grand Rapids: Zondervan Academic).

Reformation Commentary on Scripture Series (RCSS) (2012–), Timothy George, general ed.; Scott M. Manetsch, associate general ed. (Downers Grove, IL: InterVarsity).

Saillant, John (2003), *Black Puritan, Black Republican: The Life and Thought of Lemuel Haynes, 1753–1833* (New York: Oxford University Press).

Sonderegger, Katherine (2015–2020), *Systematic Theology*, Volumes 1 and 2 (Minneapolis: Fortress Press).

Van Vlastuin, Willem (2020), *Catholic Today: A Reformed Conversation about Catholicity* (Göttingen: Vandenhoeck & Ruprecht).

Vanhoozer, Kevin J. (2005), *The Drama of Doctrine: A Canonical Linguistic Approach to Christian Theology* (Louisville, KY: Westminster John Knox,).

(2010), *Remythologizing Theology: Divine Action, Passion, and Authorship* (Cambridge: Cambridge University Press);

John Webster (2003), *Holy Scripture: A Dogmatic Sketch*, (Cambridge: Cambridge University Press);

(2018) *God Without Measure: Working Papers in Christian Theology*, volumes 1 and 2 (London: T&T Clark).

21 Ressourcement Thomism

THOMAS JOSEPH WHITE, OP

Ressourcement Thomism refers to an emergent trend of theologians who seek to reassess the contribution of Thomas Aquinas both within his historical context and in a contemporary context. It is best explained genealogically in relation to other recent theological movements and has distinctive characteristics. In this chapter, I seek first to identify this historical context and characteristics of Ressourcement Thomism and then to illustrate its relevance by examining two typical theological claims found among those associated with the movement. The first of these is the claim that the modern focus on the "immanent and economic trinity" after Karl Rahner is conceptually problematic and that the Thomistic distinction between Trinitarian processions and Trinitarian missions serves as the more feasible one for a reasonable analysis of the way that the mystery of the Trinity is revealed in the economy of salvation. The latter model allows one to acknowledge more perfectly the New Testament revelation of the transcendence and unity of the Trinity and to avoid problematic historicizations of the divine life of God. The second claim is that key figures in modern kenotic theology such as Karl Barth and Hans Urs von Balthasar, despite their theological creativity, have failed to preserve a sufficient sense of the distinction of the divine and human natures in Christ. Aquinas's Chalcedonian and dyotheletist Christology provides one with ways of thinking about how the crucifixion of God reveals the mystery of the Trinity in and through the sufferings of Christ without the problematic projection of human characteristics of the Lord onto the inner life of the Trinity, as constitutive of the inner life of the Trinity. In both these respects, Ressourcement Thomism as a theological movement suggests ways that historical theology that is concerned with the contribution of patristic and medieval sources can lead to a renewal of and creative engagement in modern theology.

RESSOURCEMENT THOMISM IN CONTEXT

Ressourcement Thomism is perhaps best understood against the back-drop of three antecedent intellectual movements, which are positioned both chronologically and logically in reaction to one another. I am referring here first chronologically to Leonine Thomism; second, the Nouvelle théologie movement initiated by Henri de Lubac and Jean Daniélou in the 1940s; and third, the Thomasian movement of historical study of Aquinas in his medieval context, represented by figures such as Étienne Gilson, Marie Dominique Chenu, and Jean-Pierre Torrell.

The first of these movements, broadly understood, refers to the initiative undertaken by Pope Leo XIII in his 1879 encyclical letter Aeterni Patris, which called for the renewal of scholastic theological and philosophical studies in the Catholic Church in response to the onset of secularizing philosophies issued from influential Enlightenment authors and from the social revolutions of the nineteenth century. The movement this initiative gave rise to was widespread, creating new centers of medieval scholarship and Thomistic thought, in places such as Rome, Leuven, Toulouse, Fribourg, and eventually in a number of centers in North and South America, such as Toronto and Santiago. From the 1870s to the 1950s Catholic theology in Europe was characteristically scholastic in tone, as represented by thinkers such as Johann Baptist Franzelin, Matthias Joseph Scheeben, Réginald Garrigou-Lagrange, Michel Labourdette, Jacques Maritain, and Charles Journet. In response to Enlightenment criticisms of Christianity, this movement placed great emphasis on philosophical formation in metaphysics and epistemology, the reasonableness of belief in God, the logical possibility of divine revelation, the intelligibility of the mysteries of Christianity, and the Christian mystical life as one superior to that of purely natural reason.

The Nouvelle théologie movement was inaugurated by De Lubac and Daniélou and can be dated symbolically by their creation of a famous series of patristic translations, Sources Chrétiennes, in 1942. Critically speaking, they reacted against what they took to be the too narrow focus in modern Catholic theology on scholastic philosophy, definitions, and arguments. Modern scholasticism, as they saw it, often lacked sufficient historical consciousness, engagement with contemporary philosophy and literature, cultural urbanity, and existential and spiritual relevance to modern persons. Where Leonine theology relied heavily on classical philosophy and argumentative demonstrations, they sought to retrieve and reappropriate a patristic model of exegesis of scripture as a propaedeutic to theology, with emphasis on the spiritual senses of scripture. De Lubac's famous work *Surnaturel* (1946) was controversial not only because of its thesis (of a natural appetite in all persons for the supernatural) but also because it advanced a new way of studying Aquinas in historical context and suggested that were one to do so, central tenets of thinking about grace and nature in subsequent "Thomistic" theology should be revised or overturned. De Lubac's theology was more historical in method, associative in theme rather than argumentative, and culturally engaged within a modern secular context. It sought in its own way to establish Catholic theology as a normative thought-form within a modern European intellectual context. The movement was of major influence during the Second Vatican Council and in the papacies of John Paul II and Benedict XVI, both of whom were in diverse ways influenced by the movement.

The Thomasian movement of historical studies developed in great part from the example of mid-twentieth century medievalists such as Gilson and Chenu who sought to resituate Aquinas within his original context so as to apprehend his original insights and contribution to the patrimony of Christian thought. In differentiation from Leonine scholasticism, this vein of modern Thomism has tended to treat Aquinas primarily as a theologian rather than a philosopher and as an interpreter of scripture and patristic tradition, with a view toward the assimilation of the Aristotelian and classical philosophical heritage. In regard to its method of reading Aquinas, this movement has taken inspiration from the Nouvelle théologie movement in many respects. However, it has done so in order to maintain a privileged role for Aquinas's thought within Christian theological venues; and in this respect, it maintains some of the aims of the Leonine revival. In differentiation from that movement, however, theologians associated with the historical study of Aquinas in the post–Vatican II period tend to focus on Aquinas as a dogmatician, spiritual teacher, and exegete, rather than as a metaphysician. Where the Leonine authors tended to treat "the Thomistic tradition" as a theoretical set of principles maintained in continuity by Thomists down through the ages, Thomasian scholars are more likely to treat Aquinas's teaching historically with a view toward inspiring contemporary projects but not per se so as to extract a living form of teaching from Aquinas for promotion in the modern context. As a historical project this movement is more conservationist than innovational and its practitioners may eschew constructive proposals concerning the objective content of a "Thomistic tradition."

In many respects, Ressourcement Thomism has come out of the latter movement, making use of its resources of examining Aquinas in medieval context. Its typical practitioners do so, however, so as to reassert the idea of a viable and ongoing Thomistic intellectual tradition, and therefore they tend to treat the commentatorial tradition of Renaissance and baroque "Thomists" (like Thomas de Vio Cajetan and Domingo Báñez) as an additional historical resource and subject of study. By attempting to promote principles of Thomistic thought within a contemporary context, members of this movement resemble practitioners of the Leonine revival. However, in similitude to the Nouvelle théologie, this movement tends to place emphasis on the centrality of Aquinas's exegesis and patristic influences, as well as engagement with contemporary non-Thomistic and non-Christian intellectual thought forms. In this sense, Ressourcement Thomism could be said to result sociologically from a selective synthesis of influences of these past three movements. In a way, that is different from the other three movements, it has a consistent and wide ecumenical scope – engaging Protestant scripture scholars and theologians – and even theoretical questions of what authentic and reasonable ecumenicism consists in.

Initial sources of inspiration for this movement would include Servais Pinckaers, Alasdair MacIntyre, and Romanus Cessario, whose writings in ethics center on virtue theory.[1] They undertook a genealogical analysis of virtue theory, noted how it was largely neglected as a resource in modern ethics, and identified key elements of Aquinas's theory of personal agency, moral objects and ends, grace and freedom, virtue and vice. They undertook this analysis while placing Aquinas's normative claims in conversation with contemporary alternatives, typically arguing that his principles are more explanatory and intellectually compelling, compared with alternative theories. Following this methodological stance, historical *ressourcement* is aimed eventually at the retrieval and identification of principal truth claims that in turn need

---

[1] Servais Pinckaers, *The Sources of Christian Ethics*, 3rd ed. (trans. M. T. Noble (Washington, DC: The Catholic University of America Press, 1995); Alasdair MacIntyre, *First Principles, Final Ends, and Contemporary Philosophical Issues* (Milwaukee, WI: Marquette University Press, 1990); Alasdair MacIntyre, *After Virtue: A Study in Moral Theory*, 3rd ed. (South Bend, IN: Notre Dame University Press, 1997); Romanus Cessario, *Introduction to Moral Theology*, rev. ed. (Washington, DC: The Catholic University of America Press, 2013; Romanus Cessario, *The Moral Virtues and Theological Ethics*, 2nd ed. (South Bend, IN: Notre Dame University Press, 2008).

to be demonstrated to have superior explanatory power in comparison with contemporary alternatives. Only then are the principles both understood sufficiently from within their original historical context and deployed in a sufficiently intellectually compelling way within the horizon of contemporary culture.[2]

Based on this core idea, we can detail common proposals of the Ressourcement Thomistic movement by paying attention to themes found in the work of some of its key figures. First and foremost, Matthew Levering has sought to identify Aquinas's theological method by returning to his conception of *sacra doctrina*, or theology as a discipline of biblical explanation.[3] Read in this way, Aquinas is primarily a scriptural theologian, with patristic commitments, who makes use of metaphysical and philosophical reflection in subordination to his interpretation of scripture. Levering's Thomism seeks to narrow the divide between scholastic and historical-critical forms of modern theology by centering on the reading of sources, while insisting on the essential importance of metaphysics as a dimension of Christian doctrine.[4] He also seeks to employ Aquinas's dialectical method of scholastic comparison of opinions in a contemporary context by comparing Aquinas's own theological ideas with a host of modern alternatives, seeking to manifest their potential veracity by comparing Thomistic options with those represented by other schools. Levering founded the quintessential Ressourcement Thomism journal, the English edition of *Nova et Vetera*, and is coeditor of an influential series of monographs published under the title from which the movement is named.

Serge-Thomas Bonino, Gilles Emery, and Bruce Marshall are other emblematic figures whose respective works on the mystery of God and the Trinity are especially influential. Bonino has composed what is simultaneously a thorough historical study and theoretical defense of the classical "divine names" treatise in Aquinas, the *de Deo Uno*

---

[2] See MacIntyre's argument to this effect in *First Principles, Final Ends, and Contemporary Philosophical Issues* (Milwaukee, WI: Marquette University Press, 1990); *Three Rival Versions of Moral Inquiry* (London: Bloomsbury, 1990), 196–197.

[3] Matthew Levering, *Scripture and Metaphysics: Aquinas and the Renewal of Trinitarian Theology* (Oxford: Wiley-Blackwell, 2004; Matthew Levering, *Engaging the Doctrine of Revelation* (Ada, MI: Baker Academic, 2014).

[4] See the arguments to this effect in Levering, *Participatory Biblical Exegesis: A Theology of Biblical Interpretation* (South Bend, IN: Notre Dame University Press, 2008); *Engaging the Doctrine of Creation: Cosmos, Creatures and the Wise and Good Creator* (Ada, MI: Baker Academic, 2017).

treatment of the divine attributes.[5] In his analysis of divine simplicity, perfection, eternity, immutability, omnipresence, providence, and so on, Bonino challenges the normative character of trends in post-Hegelian kenotic theology (as found, for example, in Jürgen Moltmann or Sergius Bulgakov) as well as contemporary analytic revisionist theology that often places God in time as a mutable subject living in co-simultaneous duration with creatures (as found, for example, in Richard Swinburne or William Hasker). Emery, meanwhile, has had great influence in rehabilitating the historical study of medieval Trinitarian theology with a view toward its uses in a modern theological context. His study of the notions in Aquinas of processions, relations, persons, and modes of Trinitarian presence of God to the world, especially in divine missions, is of widespread influence. It offers contemporary theologians an idiom in which to consider the way God subsists in himself, and reveals himself to the world, as a counter alternative to the theologies of Barth, Rahner, and Balthasar (a point I will return to below).[6] Bruce Marshall has underscored similar themes, employing Aquinas's theology of God to critique formulations of divine suffering that are present in contemporary Trinitarian theology.[7] In light of the classical doctrine of divine unity, Marshall has also presented argumentation against those who would claim that the persons in God acquire their identity in virtue of their relations to creatures or to one another that obtain, supposedly, in light of the economy of salvation.[8]

Simon Gaine, Thomas Joseph White, and Dominic Legge have produced substantive christological treatises that stand largely in logical congruity with the work of Bonino, Emery, and Marshall.[9] They have in diverse ways sought to present Aquinas's christological claims anew

---

[5] Serge-Thomas Bonino, *"Celui Qui Est"– De Deo ut Uno* (Paris: Parole et Silence, 2016). (Translation forthcoming in English, Thomistic Ressourcement Series, The Catholic University of America Press.)

[6] Gilles Emery, *Trinity in Aquinas* (Naples, FL: Sapientia, 2006); *Trinity, Church, and the Human Person* (Naples, FL: Sapientia, 2007); *The Trinitarian Theology of St. Thomas Aquinas* (trans. F. Murphy; Oxford: Oxford University Press, 2010).

[7] Bruce D. Marshall, "The Dereliction of Christ and the Impassibility of God," in *Divine Impassibility and the Mystery of Human Suffering* (ed. J. Keating and T. J. White; Grand Rapids: Eerdmans, 2009), 246–298.

[8] Bruce D. Marshall, 'The Unity of the Triune God: Reviving and Ancient Question', *The Thomist* 74 (2010), 1–32; "The Absolute and the Trinity," *Pro Ecclesia* 23, no. 2 (2014), 147–64; "Personal Distinction in God and the Possibility of Kenosis," *Angelicum*, forthcoming.

[9] Simon Francis Gaine, *Did the Saviour See the Father? Christ, Salvation, and the Vision of God* (London: Bloomsbury and T&T Clark, 2015); Thomas Joseph White, ed., *The Incarnate Lord: A Thomistic Study in Christology* (Washington, DC: The

with a view toward their modern relevance. Gaine and White have defended, in different ways, the traditional teaching that Christ enjoyed the beatific vision, or the immediate knowledge of God, in the heights of his human intellect during the time of his earthly life and so knew clearly of his own identity as the Son of God in a fully human way, expressing this knowledge in the cultural and linguistic terms of his day. White has underscored the importance of Aquinas's single subject Christology in critical engagement with the Christology of Rahner, which he characterizes as leaning toward Nestorianism. Legge, meanwhile, has employed Aquinas's doctrine of Trinitarian missions to underscore how Jesus's human life reveals the Trinity, in critical dialogue with Rahner's theology of the economic Trinity.

Richard Schenk, Reinhard Hütter, Bernhard Blankenhorn, and Lawrence Feingold have each in various ways presented contemporary Thomistic proposals in theological anthropology.[10] Schenk's work centers on Aquinas's Aristotelian, hylomorphic conception of human persons, read in his original medieval context against the backdrop of Augustinian anthropology. He presents Aquinas in dialogue above all with Augustine, Luther, Heidegger, and Rahner, arguing that St. Thomas's realism regarding the tragedy of death and the reality of human finitude invites one to understand the gratuity of the grace of faith in a way that speaks to the concerns of modern thinkers, while presenting at the same time a superior anthropology of human embodiment and Christ-centered sacramental dependence. Hütter has produced a project of the study of teleology in theological anthropology, arguing that Aquinas's analysis of eschatological beatitude provides him with a key point of orientation for interpreting the meaning of human existence, one of increasing relevance in an era of metaphysical disorientation. In a way that parallels MacIntyre, Hütter argues that Thomistic metaphysics and anthropology can play a key role for modern theology when it is confronted with the twin challenges of

Catholic University of America Press, 2015); Dominic Legge, *The Trinitarian Christology of St. Thomas Aquinas* (Oxford: Oxford University Press, 2016).

[10] Richard Schenk, *Soundings in the History of a Hope: New Studies on Thomas Aquinas* (Naples, FL: Sapientia, 2016); Reinhard Hütter, *Dust Bound for Heaven: Explorations in the Theology of Thomas Aquinas* (Grand Rapids: Eerdmans, 2012); *Bound for Beatitude: A Thomistic Study in Eschatology and Ethics* (Washington, DC: The Catholic University of America Press, 2019); Bernhard Blankenhorn, *The Mystery of Union with God* (Washington, DC: The Catholic University of America, 2015); Lawrence Feingold, *The Natural Desire to See God according to St. Thomas Aquinas and His Interpreters*, 2nd ed. (Naples, FL: Sapientia Press, 2010).

postmodern philosophical skepticism and biological material reduction-ism.[11] Thomism has a superior explanatory power when one seeks to understand personal identity within this modern context. Blankenhorn has made use of extensive study of Aquinas's doctrine of the gifts of the Holy Spirit in its original historical context to argue for a profound harmony of the natural and supernatural orders and of the grace faith with natural intellectual insight, against the backdrop of what he argues is a tendency toward "grace-nature extrinsicism" in the theology of the gifts as interpreted by John of St. Thomas and Garrigou-Lagrange. Lawrence Feingold has produced what is no doubt one of the most controversial works of contemporary Catholic theology. Making use of the historical critical study of sources emblematic of the Nouvelle théologie, he revisits the theological sources employed by De Lubac in *Surnaturel* in order to argue for an alternative reading of Aquinas on the natural desire for God, one that is concordant with subsequent Thomistic commentators such as Sylvester of Ferrara. Feingold carries this commentatorial tradition forward to argue for its conceptual super-iority over both that of De Lubac in his theology of the absolute desire for the supernatural and Rahner in his supernatural-existential theology of grace, in which grace is always, already a co-compositional principle with human nature.

There are also characteristic Ressourcement Thomist treatments of topics in ecclesiology and sacramental theology. Benoit-Dominique de la Soujeole has produced a series of major studies of the mystery of the Church, which are of Thomistic inspiration and that make use of the thought of Journet.[12] De la Soujeole interprets the teaching of the Second Vatican Council that the Church is a "sign and instrument of salvation" in light of Aquinas's understanding of sacraments, distin-guishing the *sacramentum tantum* (sign or sacrament itself) of the Church, the *res et sacramentum* (reality and sacrament), and the *res tantum* (reality itself).[13] In this schema, the first term designates the visible ecclesial means of salvation instituted by Christ in view of the eschaton. The second designates the visible Church now living mysteri-ously the eschatological life to come, while the third designates the mystery of plenary salvation in the echaton, in which all those who are

[11]   Hütter, *Dust Bound for Heaven*, 387–422.
[12]   De la Soujeole, *Benoit-Dominique, Introduction to the Mystery of the Church* (trans. M. J. Miller; Washington, DC: The Catholic University of America Press, 2016); *Benoit-Dominique, Le sacrement de la communion: essai d'ecclésiologie fondamentale* (Paris: Cerf, 1998).
[13]   De la Soujeole, *Benoit-Dominique*, 438–496.

currently invisible members of Christ will be manifest as part of the visible life of the Church. Correspondingly, Emmanuel Perrier has produced reflection on human agency as a nexus-concept in Aquinas's theology that allows one to understand Christ's human agency and its role in our redemption in concord with the theology of human action under grace and our active participation in the sacraments, which function as a medium of grace.[14] Christ's human instrumental agency and the instrumentality of the sacraments are not opposed to genuine human freedom but rather are the condition for it. Reginald Lynch has studied Thomistic sacramental theology of the post-Reformation era to examine how Aquinas's notion of sacraments as instrumental causes of grace and his theology of the Mass as a sacrifice were taken up and developed in the early modern context.[15] Thomistic theories of sacramental causality in the baroque era offered answers to objections from alternative Catholic schools that anticipate the critical objections of "post-metaphysical" sacramental theologians in contemporary theology influenced by Martin Heidegger and modern phenomenology.

What becomes manifest in this tapestry of examples is the recent emergence of a thematic form of Thomism, one that seeks to advance principles and normative claims derived from the theology of Aquinas and his traditional interpreters. In differentiation from the earlier Leonine Thomism, this form of theology is more historical in method, more overtly theological and exegetical, with an eye toward the spiritual and existential horizon of Aquinas's thought. It is more committed to the enduring importance of the scholastic heritage of Christian theology than authors associated with the Nouvelle théologie but expresses that commitment against the backdrop of postmodern hermeneutics, geneological historicism, and methodological pluralism in modern theology. It is more robustly metaphysical in orientation than the Thomasian movement, and more critically engaged in making contemporary theological claims, but does so without characterizing the latter movement as inessential or problematic. On the contrary, in the thought form characteristic of the above-mentioned authors, the historical study of Aquinas typically plays a key role as an irreplaceable moment within a larger process of retrieval and rearticulation of Thomistic principles in a contemporary idiom.

---

[14] Emmanuel Perrier, *L'attrait divin: la doctrine de l'opération et le gouvernement des créatures chez saint Thomas d'Aquin* (Paris: Parole et Silence, 2019).
[15] Reginald Lynch, *The Cleansing of the Heart: The Sacraments as Instrumental Causes in the Thomastic Tradition* (Washington, DC: The Catholic University of America Press, 2017).

FROM THE ECONOMIC TRINITY TO PROCESSIONS
AND MISSIONS

As an illustration of typical notions of theologians associated with Ressourcement Thomism, it is helpful to consider two examples: the first, pertaining to the theology of Trinitarian processions and missions, and the second, pertaining to the theology of the two natures of Christ. In each case, analysis of what Aquinas argued in his original historical context can be seen to be of potential assistance to contemporary theological discernment.

Trinitarian theology in the twentiety century has no doubt been marked quintessentially by the exploration of Rahner's *Grundaxiom*, the idea that the immanent Trinity is the economic Trinity and vice versa.[16] The idea seemingly has its origins in Barth's *Church Dogmatics* I, 1, where Barth sought to place the Trinity at the center of his treatment of revelation and in doing so assigned reasons for the distinction of the persons in God to the diverse economic functions or activities of the persons.[17] The Father is characterized, for example, as the revealer, the Son as the one revealed in the human life of Christ, and the Spirit as the immanent source of the revealing in human history, the one who manifests Christ as the Son and, in doing so, manifests the original source of revelation who is the Father.[18] This idea could be defended by recourse to the classical theology of Trinitarian attribution, in which each of the persons always act together, but in such a way that each one is revealed more particularly by some of their common actions.[19] (The Father, Son, and Spirit can act co-simultaneously so as to reveal one person in particular, the crucified Jesus as Lord, for example.) Barth's formulation is more ambiguous, however, since his presentation raises the question of whether God the Trinity is characterized "always already," that is, eternally by relations of the Trinitarian persons to creatures in virtue of divine election, covenant, and redemptive incarnation. Barth's later theology of election (CD II, 2), the *analogia relationis* (CD III, 3), and Christ' filial dereliction (CD IV, 1) augments the tension in this perspective as it is possible to understand the identity of

---

[16] Karl Rahner, *The Trinity* (trans. J. Donceel; London: Continuum, 2001), esp. 22.

[17] Karl Barth, *Church Dogmatics* (trans. and ed. G. W. Bromiley and T. F. Torrance, 4 vols. (Edinburgh: T&T Clark, 1936–1975) [hereafter 'CD'] I, 1.

[18] Ibid., 306–334.

[19] See, for example, Aquinas, *Summa Theologiae* [hereafter ST] I, q. 38, aa. 7–8, who appeals to expressions and ideas taken from Paul, Augustine, Abelard, and Peter Lombard.

the Trinity in historical terms, as a mystery of three persons eternally self-determined by and in the decision for relationality to creation.[20]

Rahner offers his own creative appropriation and reinterpretation of Barth's somewhat open-ended idea. Rahner claims that the economic activity of the Trinity is characterized by real relations of the distinct persons to human beings to whom the revelation of God is addressed.[21] This implies that God self-determines in view of the economy and does so differently in each person. He also distances his account from any reliance upon the traditional theology of the divine attributes of divine nature (pertaining to the unity of God as such) or that of the psychological analogy (of the Son as Word and the Spirit as Love) to characterize the immanent Trinity.[22] What results is a theology in which one can only intelligibly understand the real distinction of the persons in God from their distinct activities in the economy of revelation in which they communicate divine life to humanity by grace. Rahner maintains that this economic life of God's three persons present in the world corresponds to what God is immanently and eternally, but the expression of this idea is inevitably ambiguous. Does Rahner mean that we know from revelation that the historical act of self-communication of God corresponds to what God is and would be as Trinity independently of creation, or does he mean that God is himself not only in virtue of this "pre-creation" identity but also only always because of his economic history as one present among us? Regardless of how one interprets Rahner on this score, his position inspired intellectual successors who sought to develop the later interpretation. Moltmann, for example, understands the history of Christ crucified to take place, in some real respect, within the very being of God, so that the suffering and death of the Son as human is historically constitutive of the relational identity of the persons in God.[23] Balthasar, meanwhile, argues like Barth that whatever happens in the economy must have its precondition in the eternal identity of the Trinity. However, he adds the idea of a Trinitarian potentiality for development that occurs actually in the economy. From all eternity, in the immanent Trinity, the Spirit proceeds from the Father and the Son. However, in the economy the order is inverted. In the life of Jesus, the Spirit precedes the Son and sends

[20] See, for example, Barth, CD II, 2, 94–194; CD III, 3, 94–107; CD IV, 1, 157–357.
[21] Rahner, The Trinity, 26–30.
[22] Ibid., 10–21, 46–48, 115–120.
[23] Jürgen Moltmann, The Crucified God: The Cross of Christ as the Foundation and Criticism of Christian Theology (trans. R. A. Wilson; San Francisco: Harper and Row, 1974), 200–278.

him, so that God adopts internally a distinct order of personal processions for the sake of the redemption. It is inverted once again when the
redemption is accomplished, but in the process, the immanent Trinity
undergoes ontological enrichment in virtue of its economic history.[24]

Without denying the remarkable creativity and modern intellectual
verve of these projects, authors associated with Ressourcement
Thomism typically seek to preserve key insights and elements of classical Trinitarian theology. This is notably the case with regard to the
theology of divine processions, relations and persons, the employment
of the psychological analogy, and the regulatory role in theology of the
divine attributes (divine simplicity, perfection, eternity, immutability,
and so forth). Aquinas, for example, argues in light of the doctrine of
divine simplicity that the persons of the Trinity are equally divine and
therefore must each possess the fullness of the divine life and essence.[25]
It follows that they are not distinguishable from one another personally
in virtue of properties they exert as God in the economy of creation and
salvation but only in virtue of their eternal immanent processions from
one another and the relations of opposition that arise therefrom.[26] The
Father is eternally characterized by his paternal generation of the Word
and spiration of the Spirit, just as the Word is characterized by his
reception of all he is from the Father and by his spiration of the Spirit
with the Father, while the Spirit is characterized by the eternal receptivity of all he is from the Father and Son as their mutually spirated
Love.[27] As Emery has noted, what results from this conception of the
immanent Trinity is a Thomistic notion of conceptual "redoubling"
when thinking of the persons in God.[28] Each is wholly relational in all
he his (toward the other two persons), and each is wholly God. Without
thinking of each of these aspects, one cannot think rightly of any of the
persons. What follows from this for one's theology of the economy is a
threefold idea. First, each person is constituted from all eternally by
relations of origin, in virtue of the processions of generation of the Word
and spiration of the Spirit, not by their historical relationships to creation. Second, in the economy of creation and redemption, each person
only ever acts with the other two in all they do, so that no person acts by

---

[24] Hans Urs von Balthasar, *Theo-Drama Theological Dramatic Theory III: The Dramatis
Personae: Persons in Christ* (trans. G. Harrison; San Francisco: Ignatius, 1993),
183–191 and 521–523.

[25] Aquinas, ST I, q. 42, aa. 1–4.

[26] Aquinas, ST I, q. 29, a. 4.

[27] Aquinas, ST I, q. 27 and 28.

[28] Emery, *Trinity in Aquinas*, 165–208.

a divine power lacking to the other two. Yet each person also only ever acts in a distinct personal mode, that is to say, in a way that is paternal, filial, or spirated, even when they act together. This means that the activity of God in the economy of grace does indeed reveal each person, as Rahner wishes to underscore, but it does so also by revealing the persons in their divine unity and perfection as well. When the persons act together by grace, for example, to reveal Jesus as Lord and eternal Son of God made man, they do so in such a way as to reveal the preexistent Father of the Son, and the Spirit of the Father and Son as well.[29] Third, Aquinas follows Augustine in arguing from scripture that the missions of the Trinitarian persons are distinct from their eternal processions but that they reveal the processions, manifesting to us in time the true eternal identity of God.[30] Aquinas defines a mission of a divine person as an eternal procession with the addition of a temporal effect.[31] In other words, when the Son of God is "sent by the Father" (Jn. 3:16) from all eternity into the world, his mission consists in the real ontological mystery of the Son in himself, as the eternally begotten Word, now rendered present to human beings in a new way, in virtue of his personal subsistence in a human nature, as one who is fully human. God therefore reveals himself in the "otherness" of human flesh, human activity and suffering, and even in human death and resurrection. The mission of God the Son among us is therefore truly revelatory of the eternal identity of God but his temporal mission is not constitutive of that identity.

It follows from this understanding of eternal processions and temporal missions that the relational order of the persons of God cannot evolve or change in virtue of the missions. The missions reveal who God truly is. It is precisely for this reason that they cannot give rise to new intra-Trinitarian relations that would "re-constitute" God anew in himself but rather they can only ever reflect who God truly is in himself antecedent to his redemption of the human race. Consequently, the Balthasarian notion of the Trinitarian inversion seems problematic, as it would suggest first that the identity of the persons that occurs in virtue of their mutual relations is malleable just in virtue of the modalities of divine action and suffering that occur in the economy. In this case, God seems to be constituted essentially as God by the economy.

[29] Emery, *Trinity, Church, and the Human Person*, 115–154.
[30] Aquinas, ST I, q. 43, which depends in part on the biblically based arguments of Augustine in *On the Trinity*, IV, chap. 20.
[31] Aquinas, ST I, q. 43, a. 2, ad 3.

Meanwhile in light of Aquinas's approach, Rahner's famous claim that the Son alone could become incarnate appears problematic. Rahner argues that God must self-communicate in his Word and can only self-communicate perfectly through incarnation, so if God does create, the Word must become human.[32] It is true that the Son's mission from the Father reveals his eternal identity as Word and expresses this "outwardly" in the divine self-communication that takes place in virtue of the Incarnation. However, God could in principle manifest himself otherwise than he has (even if, as Aquinas argues, he has done so most fittingly through the incarnation of the Word).[33] This freedom of God to save us in diverse ways must be the case if the processions "precede" the missions and are not determined in their ontological content by them but, on the contrary, determine the ontological content of them. God could have "sent" the Spirit in a form of manifestation that was analogous to that of the incarnation of the Son, even if he more fittingly sent the Son as his Word, in human nature. This possibility of an alternative economy is not a merely frivolous counterfactual thought experiment of scholastic theologians. The idea is bound up with the notion that the Trinity is eternally transcendent as creator, preceding and giving rise to all that has being from God. Consequently, the Trinity is free to self-unveil to humanity in a plurality of modes. If indeed God has chosen to do so in one distinct economic pattern (through incarnation of the Son, crucifixion, resurrection, and Pentecost of the Spirit), then the decision is not an arbitrary one but one that must be inwardly marked by the wisdom and goodness of God and thus intelligible to human thought.

Likewise, as Bruce Marshall as argued, if the Son's human suffering is genuinely indicative of the eternal love of the Trinity for the human race, and revelatory of that love, it is not for that reason constitutive of the Trinitarian relations (pace Moltmann) nor need it mirror precisely (by a supposed analogy) the inner life of God as Triune.[34] That is to say, we are not obliged to infer from the suffering of the Son what the Son is eternally in his procession from the Father. The three persons are one in virtue of their shared nature and not in virtue of their ethical cooperation in the economy of the crucifixion and resurrection. In fact, their capacity to save the human race in and through Jesus's human life,

---

[32] Rahner, The Trinity, 29, 33.
[33] Aquinas, III, q. 3, aa. 5 and 8. See the analysis of Legge, The Trinitarian Christology of St. Thomas Aquinas, 61–102.
[34] Marshall, "The Dereliction of Christ and the Impassibility of God."

suffering, and resurrection presupposes and depends upon their transcendent unity in wisdom, goodness, and free omnipotent love. It is
because they possess this unity of love antecedent to the mystery of
salvation, with its corresponding power, that they can be present and
active within the event of atonement as the primal creator, who is able
to redeem the human race even from within the dark night of extraordinary suffering. It is this salvific mystery of the transcendent Trinity
that is revealed to be immanently present and operative in the crucifixion, death, and resurrection of Christ.[35]

THE TWO NATURES OF CHRIST

Analogous themes emerge in Ressourcement Thomist authors who
engage in contemporary debates in Christology. Undoubtedly in
modern Christology of the past century, German-speaking Protestant
and Catholic theologians alike have underscored kenotic themes. The
famous dereliction theologies of Barth and Balthasar, for example, have
placed great emphasis on the Son's human obedience, suffering, and
godforsakenness in the crucifixion as a particular locus of revelation of
the divinity of the Son, in his relation to the Father.[36] By an appeal to
what he calls the *genus tapeinoticum* in the use of the communication
of idioms, Barth asks to what extent the human attributes of Christ may
be ascribed to his divine nature, to the Son in his mode of being as
God.[37] This inquiry leads to the idea that there exists a likeness of
similitude or analogy between the Son in his divine nature and the
Son in his human nature, such that the human activities of obedience,
suffering, and free acceptance of abandonment correspond to something
transcendent in the divine nature, making these human activities possible. The dereliction of Christ crucified reveals the inner capacity of
the divine nature for self-emptying and suffering as motivated by divine
love. Balthasar attempts to give thematic expression to this idea in the
form of an *analogia entis Christi*: the analogy of being discovered in
Christ, whereby the human freedom of love in Christ that leads him to
embrace the abandonment by God on Holy Saturday is indicative of a

---

[35] See the argument to this effect by White, *The Incarnate Lord*, 340–464.
[36] This amounts to a creative re-interpretation of Luther's *theologia crucis*. See Barth,
      CD IV, 1, section 59; and Hans Urs von Balthasar, *Theo-Drama Theological-Dramatic
      Theory IV: The Action* (trans. G. Harrison; San Francisco: Ignatius Press, 1994),
      319–328.
[37] Barth, CD IV, 1, 215, 239, 264, 306, 308, 458, 566, 590; CD IV, 2, 84–85, 108–115.

mutual surrender and free exchange of separation and reconciliation that exists in the Trinity and in the life of God from all eternity.[38]

When comparing these ideas with the christologies advanced by recent Thomists, points of convergence appear, as well as points of potential difference. Aquinas follows Maximus the Confessor and John Damascene in his interpretation of the Third Ecumenical Council of Constantinople, which affirmed that there are two natural wills and activities in Christ, as God and as human respectively. In interpreting this Council, Damascene underscored that the human nature of Jesus is the instrument of the divine person of the Son. This means that the activity of Christ's human mind and heart are distinct from and subordinate to his divine nature and activity. However, due to this same subordination, both his actions and sufferings, as one who is human, are truly entirely expressive of his divine personal identity.[39]

Thomists have noted a number of parallels to and points of contact with the modern kenotic tradition that emerge from this standpoint. First, it follows from Aquinas's understanding that all that Christ is conscious of, and knows and wills as a human being, is expressive of his filial identity as the Son of God and of his relation to the Father and the Spirit.[40] Likewise, all that he suffers as man is expressive of this same set of personal relationships. Jesus has a filial way of being human, because his human nature is the human nature of the Son subsisting as man. Consequently, just as the Son's divine nature is filial in its mode of being, as being eternally received from the Father, so too his human nature is filial in its mode of being and expresses in a human way who he is personally as the Son. Therefore, even when it is expressed in a distinctly human way rather than a divine way, Jesus's receptivity to the Father in obedience and suffering is indicative of his personal derivation of life from the Father.[41] On this reading, the human acts and sufferings of Christ in the crucifixion are indicative of the eternal identity of the Son in relation to the Father and the Spirit. However, obedience, suffering, and the experience of abandonment cannot be properly ascribed to the divine nature nor are they somehow constitutive of the Trinitarian persons in their eternal relations, even by a

---

[38] Hans Urs von Balthasar, *Theo-Logic Theological Logical Theory II, The Truth of God* (trans. A. Walker; San Francisco: Ignatius Press, 2004), 94–95, 128–134, 173–218, 273 n. 109.

[39] In ST III, q. 19, a. 1, Aquinas follows Damascene's interpretation of the Third Council of Chalcedon found in *On the Orthodox Faith*, III, c. 16.

[40] See White, *The Incarnate Lord*, 236–274.

[41] Ibid., 277–307.

kind of faint analogy (of inner divine suffering or eternal poverty). The
reason is that these features of being are rightly ascribed to the Son of
God only in virtue of his human nature and as attributes pertain to
created dimensions of reality. The Trinity is not capable of eternal
obedience, since the biblical concept of obedience implies created
dependency and a movement from imperfection to greater perfection
acquired by ontological subordination to a superior principle.[42] The
Father and the Son, however, are eternally one in divine perfection,
power, and authority. The notion of obedience also implies free consent
between two subjects with distinct wills. However, the Father, Son, and
Spirit are one in essence (*homoousios*) and therefore also one in will. In
fact, there can be no free consent between persons in the Trinity as a
constitutive feature of their self-differentiation (i.e., as the condition for
the generation and spiration of persons), since this would entail a free
decision of the persons to receive their identity. God would become
Trinity by way of a freely accepted engagement of his being.

Aquinas also underscores the importance of Jesus's perfection of
grace as man. Precisely because his human life is meant to reveal his
personal identity as Son, Jesus must have a sufficient human understanding of his own identity and must possess a plenitude of charity in
his human heart sufficient to surrender his own life freely to the Father
on behalf of the human race.[43] Thomists emphasize then the special
character of Jesus's human knowledge as evinced in the Gospels,
whereby he is clearly aware of who he is and seems to know of his
divine origin as well as the terminus of his temporal mission and its
salvific import. (Mk. 10:45; Matt. 11:27; Jn. 2:25; 3:11; 18:4) Instead of
taking these scriptural references as merely post-Paschal theologou-
mena projected back onto the historical Jesus, one may defend them
as ontologically significant indications of Jesus's true identity. This is
why authors such as Simon Gaine have defended the importance of the
traditional teaching that Jesus in his earthly life has the beatific vision,
that is to say, the immediate and intuitive understanding of who he is as
Lord, by a form of noninferential knowledge.[44] On this view, Jesus can
experience dereliction at the crucifixion, and take on effects of our
godforsakenness in solidarity with us, but in so doing he still retains a
human awareness of his hidden union with the Father and of the even-
tual triumph of God's designs that is unfolding even in the midst of his

[42] See the arguments of Aquinas, ST III, q. 20, aa. 1 and 2.
[43] Aquinas, ST III, q. 7, a. 1; q. 9, a. 2.
[44] See Gaine, *Did the Saviour See the Father?*, 4–14, 129–178.

human suffering. (Jn. 19:30; Lk. 23:34, 43) His perfection of charity, likewise, is an important facet of his free self-sacrifice in the passion. On Aquinas's view, it is precisely because Jesus gives his life in obedience to God by knowledge and by love that the crucifixion is meritorious as a human act and can be a source of grace for the whole human race.[45] Christ's human headship in the order of grace (Col. 1:18; Eph. 4:8; 5:23) is grounded in his meritorious self-offering, which in turn presupposes an action of free self-giving.[46] If the Son is subject to lowliness and abasement in the passion, then it is also essential to underscore his understanding of the meaning of the passion, and obedient consent to it, even as it unfolds.[47]

Aquinas's Christology presents us with a biblically informed reflection on the mysteries of the life of Christ, influenced by key patristic insights from both Latin and Greek sources. Aquinas is deeply concerned to maintain a Chalcedonian Christology that emphasizes the singular subject of the Son and the distinct two natures in which he personally subsists, while noting many ways the human nature is subordinate to the divine nature and thereby expressive of the divine person. When this approach is reappropriated in the modern context, one can see some motifs that converge with those of modern kenotic christological tradition. However, a clear difference emerges regarding the distinction of natures in Christ. On Aquinas's view, the divine nature remains in many respects transcendent of and dissimilar to the human nature of Christ, even within the hypostatic union. There is a soteriological importance to this point of emphasis. The divine identity of Christ is not altered or sundered by the passion but is dynamically active in the crucifixion, even in the midst of God's human suffering. His human abasement does not provide an analogy for the inner life of God as such but simply is the human suffering of God. The perfection of Christ's human understanding and love in his passion, meanwhile, are also important, since they indicate in a distinctly human way his deeper divine union with the Father.

CONCLUSION

Paradoxical though it may seem, the historical work of De Lubac and the dogmatic projects of Barth, Rahner, and Balthasar paved the way for

---

[45] Aquinas, ST III, q. 48, a. 2.
[46] Aquinas, ST III, q. 7, a. 9; q. 8, aa. 1 and 3.
[47] Aquinas, ST III, q. 22, a. 3, and White, *The Incarnate Lord*, 353–359, 367–372.

a new appropriation of Aquinas in a contemporary key. By their emphasis on the creative reappropriation of classical themes in theology within a modern landscape, they made space for new projects of this kind. Ressourcement Thomism functions as a sociological category for an emerging trend toward the recovery and inventive use of ideas derived from the work of Thomas Aquinas. That such a restatement of Thomistic themes can exist anew in novel theological circumstances, and with new resonances or points or inflection, is a sign of the living vitality of Thomism, as an intellectual tradition of enduring character. This tradition itself is a testament to the depth and perpetual pertinence of Aquinas's philosophical and theological insight. It is also a sign of the chronic vigor of traditional Christian theological ideas more generally, which reemerge in their perennial intellectual value and power of explanation, through a variety of intellectual idioms and forms of expression, from age to age.

Further Reading

Emery, Gilles (2010), *The Trinitarian Theology of St. Thomas Aquinas* (trans. F. Murphy; Oxford: Oxford University Press).

Feingold, Lawrence (2010), *The Natural Desire to See God according to St. Thomas Aquinas and His Interpreters*, 2nd ed. (Naples, FL: Sapientia Press).

Hütter, Reinhard, and Matthew Levering, eds. (2010), *Ressourcement Thomism: Sacred Doctrine, the Sacraments & the Moral Life* (Washington, DC: The Catholic University of America Press).

Levering, Matthew (1994), *Scripture and Metaphysics: Aquinas and the Renewal of Trinitarian Theology* (Oxford: Wiley-Blackwell).

MacIntyre, Alasdair (1997), *After Virtue: A Study in Moral Theory*, 3rd ed. (South Bend, IN: Notre Dame University Press).

Marshall, Bruce (2010), "The Unity of the Triune God: Reviving and Ancient Question," *The Thomist*, 74, 1–32.

White, Thomas Joseph, ed. (2015), *The Incarnate Lord: A Thomistic Study in Christology* (Washington, DC: The Catholic University of America Press).

White, Thomas Joseph (2022), *The Trinity: On the Nature and Mystery of the One God* (Washington, DC: The Catholic University of America Press).

Index

1 John
christological criterion, 114
1918 Influenza Epidemic, 296
1963 Faith and Order report, 134

a posteriori, 222
a priori, 222
Aaronic priesthood, 143
ableist theology, 257
adoptionism, 7
Aeterni Patris, 353
Aladura, 295–296
Allen, Michael, 204, 332, 335–336
analogical language, 13, 220, 223–226
analytic theology
  as ahistorical, 308–309
  caricature of, 307
  as clarification of views, 303
  on conceptual models, 310
  definition of, 306–307
  developments in, 313
  as diverse thought, 302–303
  on divine nature, 310–311
  generic view of, 305–306
  as idolatry, 309–313
  institutions of, 301–302
  as justification of views, 303
  liturgical turn, 309
  on lived experience, 309
  as MacIntyrian, 306
  objections to, 307–313
  as philosophical theology, 303
  as philosophy of religion, 300–301
  on a preliminary definition, 300
  as research programme, 302, 306–307
  as systematic theology, 303–306
  as too philosophical, 307–308
  on use of philosophy, 304
  on the Trinity, 311–312
  response to critiques, 312–313

theology on philosophy, 301
Ancient near Eastern
  creation account, 20–21
  study of, 4
annihilationism, 167
Anselm, 310
anthropogony, 45, 47, 51
anthropology
  as embodied, 214–216
  human development, 52
  on human limits, 261
  humanity as multiple perspectives, 253
  ideal human, 51
  image of God, 46–47
  on intellectual capacity, 261
  intellect, maturation of, 49–51
  man, nature of, 45
  two-fold nature, 47
antinomianism, 268
apartheid, 240
apocalyptic theology
  apocalypse as genre, 322
  on apocalyptic hope, 323
  on continuity of Scripture, 326–327
  on creation, 317
  on crucified cosmos, 319–320
  definition of, 316
  on divine initiative, 319, 321
  on Galatian opponents, 318–319
  on God's invasion of creation, 324–325
  on human initiative, 325–326
  on the incarnation, 318
  Jewish apocalyptic background, 321–323
  on new creation, 319–320, 322
  on Pauline theology, 317–321
  plight of man, 317
  on racism, 324
apokatastasis. *See* universalism
Apollinarius, 85

creation as fallen, 98
creator/creature distinction, 26–28, 111, 325
creatura Verbi. See Church, as creature of the Word
Crisp, Oliver, 350
crucifixion, 39
  purpose of, 91
Cunningham, Conor, 215–216
Cyprian, 143
Cyril of Alexandria, 74
  on the Son's impassibility, 80
Cyril of Jerusalem, 331

D'Costa, Gavin, 67
Dabney, Lyle, 106
Daley, Brian
  on Chalcedon, 83
Daly, Mary, 175, 273
  God as a Verb, 186
  on radical feminism, 182–183
Daniélou, Jean, 353–354
Darwin, Charles, 22, 33
de Biran, Maine, 222
de Gruchy, John, 244
de la Soujeole, Benoit-Dominique, 359
de Lubac, Henri, 197, 219, 353–354
de novissimis. See eschatology, as newest things
death, 159–161
Decalogue. *See* Ten Commandments
deification. *See* divinization
deism, 30, 107, 342
Deloria Jr., Vine, 273
demythologization, 323
Derrida, Jacques, 219–220
Deuteronomy, 5–6
diakonoi, 142
difference feminism, 180
disability model
  minority group model, 256
  social model, 255, 265
disability studies, 255–256
  on acquired disabilities, 262–263
  on congenital disabilities, 262–263
disability theology
  anthropological focus, 251
  blindness, 251–253
  on church tradition, 260
  definition of, 249
  definition of disability, 253–254
  as difference, 253–255
  on disabilities in heaven, 263–266

disability as identity, 262–266
  on diversity of approaches, 249–251
  as fate of all humanity, 253
  impairment vs disability, 254
  on normalcy, 253
discourse analysis, 124
divine economy, 10, 168, 202–203
divine incomprehensibility, 15, 334
divine ineffability, 15
divine singularity, 6
divinization, 41, 95, 158, 350
Doceticism, 331
Dorner, I. A.
  on kenosis of reason, 77
downward causality, 317
doxa. See splendor
Dulles, Avery, 153
Duns Scotus, 223–225
  on the incarnation, 79–80
dyotheletism, 352, 367–369

Eastern Orthodoxy
  on Scripture and tradition, 135–136
ecological crisis, 34
economic Trinity, 10, 73–74, 352, 358, 361–366
economy of salvation, 55, 64–66, 103, 201–202, 318, 357, 362–363
Ecowomanist theology, 190
Edet, Rosemary, 187
effective history, 198
Efird, David, 303
egalitarianism, 14–15
Eiesland, Nancy, 256–260, 262–265
ekklēsia, 140
election, 65
  of the Son, 79
Emery, Gilles, 356–357, 363
Enlightenment, 234–237, 248, 345, 353
  on anthropomorphic center, 107
Enuma Elish, 20
episkopoi, 142
epistemological pluralism, 308
epistemology, 213–218, 222–225, 251–253, 353
  on personal experience, 292
  as politics, 227–229
eschatology, 32
  on death, 159–161
  on four last things, 156, 160
  on glorification, 166–167
  on heaven, 164–167, 265
  on hell, 167–171

Taylor, Charles (cont.)
  on anthropology, 37
  on social imaginary, 107
Temple of God
  God's people as temple. *See* Jesus
    Christ, as Temple
Ten Commandments, 127, 283
  first commandment, 5
Tertullian, 115, 143, 201
  on crucifixion, 39–40
tetelestai, 38
Tetragrammaton. *See* YHWH
The Book of Common Prayer, 149
The Father
  as unbegotten, 363–364
The Son, 361–362
  divine essence of, 74
  divine nature, 8–9, 37–38, 366–369
  the flesh, perfecting of, 42
  form of God, 8
  form of incarnate Servant, 8, 74
  human nature, 8–9, 37–38, 364,
    366–369
  immutability of, 80–81
  impassibility of, 80–82, 85
  kenosis, 73, 76–78, 83
  as *logos asarkos*, 78–80
  as sent, 70–75
  as the suffering one, 366–367
The Spirit, 361–362
  as advocate, 113
  on atonement. *See* atonement on the
    Holy Spirit
  biblical patterns, 110–111
  breadth of meaning, 109
  as breath, 111
  central in dogmatics, 106
  on charismatic works, 112
  Christology, overshadowed by,
    114–116
  as comforter, 113
  on loss of control, 112–113
  as creator of church, 140–141
  as empowerment, 288
  foundation of Christian life, 103
  as illuminating guide, 336
  on illuminating Scripture, 130
  as Love, 187
  neglect of, 103–104
  as paraclete, 113
  participation of, 42
  personhood of, 115–116
  procession of, 9

  on subjective relations, 111–114
  taxonomic neglect, 105–106
  trinitarian foundations, 103–105
Theimann, Ronald, 244
theodicy, 260–261, 278
theological interpretation
  on adaptability, 208
  as ambiguous, 200
  on biblicism, 209–210
  on confessionalism, 210
  as ecclesial act, 198–199
  fourfold senses of Scripture,
    202–203
  history of, 195–197
  on legitimacy, 196
  on naturalism, 205–207
  as participation in church, 198
  rebuttals of, 209–211
  as retrieval, 341–342
  on Scripture, 197
  on shifts within the movement,
    203–205
  telos of, 194, 197
  on theological anthropology, 199
  on theological orthodoxy, 202
  on typology, 202–203
  on unity of Scritpure, 200
theological theology, 16–17
theology of creation, 19
Theophilus of Antioch
  on creation, 23
theos. *See* God
theosis. *See* divinization
theotokos, 83–84
Third Article Theology, 106–107
Thomas Aquinas, 7, 17, 219–220, 225,
    308, 335, 339, 346
  on Christ's two natures, 85, 352, 368
  on classical theism, 312
  on creator/creature distinction, 26–27
  on divine names, 356
  on eschatology, 359
  on *ex nihilo*, 24
  on God as wisdom, 186
  on grace and nature, 359
  on the Holy Spirit, 359
  on hylomorphic conception, 358
  on implicit faith, 67
  on incarnation, 80–81
  on inspiration, 128
  on invincible ignorance, 67
  on Jesus' obedience, 369
  on primary causes, 31

Printed by Printforce, United Kingdom